This auto/biographical business history
of one working man, Stan Dibben, who fashioned an entrepreneurial
mindset to contend with the industrial realities of the second half of
the 20th century. It is also in part a biography of that man's great
friend, Andrew Mustard.

A study of their lives and of the numerous businesses they were
associated with, worked for and established, shows that the shift in
industry from small to large, from entrepreneurial to corporate, is
not simply a shift in scale. It is a shift of mindset, outlook, attitude
to others – a shift not all choose to make and for good reason.

Stan Dibben and Andrew Mustard, and their families, are
united by a serendipitous yet multi-generational experience of,
and resistance to, corporatisation. Theirs were lives on the edge of
industry.

Rarely has it been possible to study multiple industries in
multiple countries and multiple generations over 100 years, to
uncover the challenge of business growth and the times when owners
decided against it – as well as the implications of their decisions
for them and their employees. This story is helped considerably also
by a biography of another of Stan's friends, and greatest business
associate, the Japanese business leader Noboru Torii.

Our purpose in this book is to apply the ideas of the Anglo-
German economist E.F. Schumacher in telling the otherwise
unobservable entrepreneurial business history that is embedded
within the personal life-stories. In so doing, we question the
economic nature of our lives in the twenty-first century.

In this book, ideas tumble out of every page. Ideas that show how it is impossible to see where you are going unless you appreciate where you are and from where you have come. It is a personal and emotional story of three generations with deep insights into life throughout the 20th century, as well as pointers for the 21st. No wonder that Schumacher's economic insights are used to explore this history and to provide a drive against 'giantism' with an appeal that, above all, people matter. The result is a perspective on real business, literally the nuts, bolts and chains businesses, intertwined with sport, that brings alive the need – even in business – to *genuinely* care about human beings and relationships.

Ian Roderick, Director of the Schumacher Institute, Bristol

This book is replete with unique insights into the development of eight industries through a century's life and work experiences of three generations. It offers great learning and flashes of essential qualities that are not easy to find in today's big business and global business mindsets. It does this by emphasizing the value of practicing smallness, entrepreneurial curiosity, a genuine positive attitude and acting with a focus on the wellbeing of others as secrets of success. It is not only about the past, but may actually help to shape the future in a sustainable way.

Dr Harald Dolles, Professor in Sport Management & International Business, Molde University College, Norway

ENTERPRISE
ON THE EDGE OF
INDUSTRY

Experiencing Corporatisation
and Its Impact 1914–2014

Stan Dibben & Mark Dibben

Stan Dibben

AUSTRALIAN SCHOLARLY

To Mark,
Thanks so much for
all your help & support
in that other time and that
other place.
Now I'm retired I can usefully
say this is another business
history — a pass time!
Cheers, Mark

First published 2018 by
Australian Scholarly Publishing Pty Ltd
7 Lt Lothian St Nth, North Melbourne, Vic 3051
Tel: 03 9329 6963 / Fax: 03 9329 5452
enquiry@scholarly.info / www.scholarly.info

ISBN 978-1-925801-48-4

Back Cover: Bluebird on Lake Eyre, South Australia, 1964; NGK Spark Plug Co. Ltd Headquarters in Nagoya, Japan. Source: Noboru Torii

Cover design: Wayne Saunders

This book is dedicated to all those who have served their country and who have suffered or died as a result of that very service.

The Courage to know the pain of knowing
The Strength to bear it and keep growing
The Wisdom to breathe – and let it be
The Faith to transcend it – and so
Knowing still, be free!

CONTENTS

History is still undervalued as a necessary contribution to social understanding. To a considerable extent, though far from entirely, we are the products of our history; a fact often forgotten or ignored by our masters.

Allan Fox, 1985: xii

Business history is made real through industrial archaeology.

Steve Vokins, Archive Director Emeritus
National Motor Museum, Beaulieu
22 January 2017

The light from a distant star falling on our retinas at night allows us to see that star as it was at the moment that light left that star. If we apply the same principle to all we see then, however momentarily but still yet in a very real sense, the past is all around us.

John B. Cobb Jr, in coversation

People call me a crank. A crank is a very elegant device. It's small, it's strong, it's lightweight, energy efficient, and it makes revolutions.

E.F. Schumacher, in lecture

FOREWORD TO
HOLD ON! (2008)

There's a near total and virtual blank in literature on the history of the working man, his life and times, for anyone born post World War One. A life spent at work in the twentieth century and which will certainly close in the 21st, is much neglected. Perhaps all humanity has been too busy building our life today?

Stan Dibben born over 90 years ago, was a mere lad during the poverty-stricken days of the Great Depression, and he was brought up and educated in a manner which those whose life began post 1985 would reject out of hand! It was not an easy time.

In this revealing and startling book Stan Dibben outlines a life that could have interested Charles Dickens in an earlier century still. Although small in stature and light in weight Stan seemingly has the heart of a lion. He served with distinction in World War Two for he was the perfect age for the armed services. Like so many brave men, his financial rewards from being a fighting man were negligible and he faced a post war life that could have ground him into abject poverty. Yet he can look back on a happier time over the post war years than may have been his lot had war not occurred, and involved him in the tale he tells so well in the following pages.

In a war-torn Europe without motorways or any of the other infrastructures that serve travellers, he took up motorcycle racing as a passenger in a sidecar driven beyond any sensible limits by the fearless but astute Eric Oliver. As a team, they became World Champions. This astonishing feat which today would result in financial security for life, left Stan at the same financial level that he had enjoyed when demobilised in 1946 with about three months' pay at the average working man's wage.

Chronicling the years as vividly as he does, shows us the World's capacity to rebuild itself and within the revitalisation of the industrial world – and in particular that of the British motorcycling industry – is an invaluable autobiographical account. All who have lived all or even part of a working lifetime with Stan Dibben will empathise with every line of this book. Those of us who have enjoyed knowing the man will enjoy even more revelations about him of which we were unaware.

This work will surely become a valuable document for researchers of industrial history. In an era where millions moved on from poverty, simple resources that were scarce, and life was largely without hope or comfort that many of us take for granted in the modern society we all live in today. That the winning of a World Championship made little difference to a worthwhile life was perhaps to that life's advantage. It is a pleasure to commend the book and to compliment the man.

Alan Robinson MBE

FOREWORD TO
ENTERPRISE ON THE
EDGE OF INDUSTRY

A psychiatrist once said to his patient, 'You drink and gamble in order to escape the reality of life.' The patient replied, 'That's why everyone does everything.'

This book is about a man, Stan Dibben, who never had to escape the realities of his life. He merely created new realities time and time again, each one more interesting than the last, and each one with lessons for us all.

Enterprise on the Edge of Industry, co-written by Stan and his son Mark, a brilliant academic, is a fascinating tome about Stan's life, times, business principles, experiences, influences, and wisdom. Stan, a post-World War Two era World Champion motorcycle sidecar racer, went on to build a versatile, decades-long business and sporting career, based on an ethos of trust and entrepreneurial passion. An ethos that can, even today, transform how one should look at one's own professional and personal life.

I met Stan at the Isle of Man TT motorcycle races a decade ago, where he still holds court each year as one of the most beloved figures in the paddock. At 93 years of age, Stan remains sprightly, engaging, with a glint in his eye and hearty sense of humor, and is easily one of the most interesting and inspiring men I've ever had the honor of knowing. This book captures his spirit, while providing incredibly valuable intelligence for the reader.

Now, that should be as effusive a description as needed for you to plunk down your hard- earned money on this opus, but I'll go a bit further. Somehow, Mark Dibben has artfully weaved a compendium of business theory, history and practices from the yarn of his father's warm and engaging biography. This book captures the ways, means, methods, and theories of how business can be ethically *and* successfully conducted by an entrepreneurially-spirited individual. And most importantly, Mark shows how Stan's principles and passions, the ones that have coursed through his life and career, can be utilized in the modern business world.

And the bonus? It is wrapped around a fantastic motorbike-centric epic, Stan's autobiography, originally published under the title of *Hold On!* which means you are getting two books for the price of one! *Hold On!* was a coming-of-age story about a young man's early adventures in life, through military service, a stint as a musician, a motorcycle racer and test rider, and then as a successful serial businessman who never lost sight of the wellbeing of customers and partners as a driver of success. I told you, he's an interesting bloke.

How do people like Stan rise above the quotidian lives of mere mortals like you and me? Well, American master comedian Jerry Seinfeld recently riffed on people who, in conversation, say things like 'You know, I'm thinking about doing ...' At which point Jerry interrupts with 'Stop. You're not going to do it. Whatever it is. You know why? Because you're thinking about it. It's too late.'

You can think your way out of doing. Stan Dibben, on the other hand, has lived a life based on his line from the lovely 2014 short film about him, *No Ordinary Passenger*. The line: 'Always say yes ... then sleep on it.' The slight, but important hedge notwithstanding, Stan has reached remarkable heights in business and sport, by saying yes to myriad and diverse opportunities, and following through with grit and passion.

As a business executive, and card-carrying member of the American media-industrial complex for nearly 40 years, I have seen some things. Multi-million-dollar deals done in smoky hotel parlors. Three martini breakfasts. Weapons-grade client entertainment boondoggles. There were also some bad things. But while my career has been satisfying, and at its zenith pretty high-powered, it has also been quite linear. Somewhat risk averse. Kind of safe. Not so Stan's.

As the esteemed playwright Neil Simon once said, 'If no one ever took risks, Michelangelo would have painted the Sistine floor.' *Enterprise on the Edge of Industry* shows us how the application of considered risk taking, entrepreneurial curiosity, strong values, positive attitudes and passion towards one's business, creates a magnetic quality that persuades and inspires others to want to work with you. And buy from you. It mixes in family and economic history, famous and obscure business figures, and the perspectives of times of depression, war, boom, and bust as the 20th century morphs into today.

Now, let's say a prospective reader of this destined-to-be-classic title is a member of the emerging millennial generation. One who rode the digital wave from childhood Nintendo straight into your adulthood, and now the business world. You entered your working age concurrent with the big-bang atomization of product distribution and consumer control brought on by the internet and globalization. You consider today's self-provisioning, screen-to-screen, disintermediated way of doing business as normal as prior generations considered face-to-face meetings, travelling salesmen, and long, lugubrious lunches with vendors. How can this book possibly be relevant to you? Isn't this, like, old school?

Stop rolling your eyes, young man! There is magic in these pages. Whether you are an up-and-coming data scientist, consultant, sales executive, operations manager or marketer, this book will help you avoid getting hit by the rubble of old business models collapsing. It will prove how entrepreneurial creativity, 'thinking small,' passion, and leaning in to say 'YES!' still matters in getting ahead, breaking down barriers, and creating trusted partnerships just as much as it did in Stan Dibben's day.

This book is about a passionate man, no ordinary passenger, who pursued his sporting, business and personal goals without betraying his values. The lessons within this book are forever relevant. The stories, priceless. The man at the book's center, timeless. Say yes to *Enterprise on the Edge of Industry*.

Andrew Capone
Managing Director
Bray Hill Media, New York
July 2018

INTRODUCTION

Ernst Friedrich Schumacher (19/8/ 1911–4/9/1977), whose economic principles shape the analysis contained herein. Source: The Schumacher Institute, Bristol

Corporatization – the process of reorganizing public institutions on a corporate or business basis.

Managerialism – an ideologically determined belief in the importance of tightly managed organisations, and the value of professional managers and the concepts and methods they use.

Wikipedia

The life of the village labourer had been changed irrevocably by the Enclosure Act of 1797, which led to the assimilation of what had been commonly owned land – commons – into large estates. The process of enclosure eventually removed from the English countryside what might be termed today the 'artisan farmer' (Tudge, 2016), who had been the mainstay of farming in England up until that point. As a result of a series of systemic failures these folk, who had previously been able to own their own small cottage, keep a cow, some pigs, and a strip of land in a field enough to grow vegetables self-sufficiently, were effectively driven into poverty. As the land was gathered up into estates owned by powerful landowners, lords of the land, the landed gentry, often presided over by ruthless farm managers, so the artisan farmer was no longer able to contribute meaningfully to the economy, other than by selling his labour to the landowner (Hammond and Hammond, [1911] 1995; also Howkins, 1992).

The Enclosures represent an early example of the shift from micro-firms and small firms to large corporate businesses. Immediately we note that *Corporatisation*, for the purposes of what follows, is not just the reorganisation of public institutions to run on large business corporate lines, but the reorganisation of small business, often as it grows, to run on large business corporate lines – and we have used the letter s instead of z as a sign of this throughout. As a result of this latter form of 'corporatisation' (in this case instituted by the state and as such strictly speaking an example too of corporatism, i.e. the reorganisation of society itself), the age of the artisan farmer was over. The age of industrial agriculture was beginning. With the industrial revolution and the growing demand for food in the cities, agriculture was now about efficiency of production (Howkins, 1992; O'Brien, 1977). The beginnings of scale in agriculture wrought through large farms run not for the benefit of the people who worked the land but for the benefit of the land owner through the onward sale of that produce, removed forever the economic independence of tens of thousands of previously self-sufficient country folk. This is because not only were such folk no longer allowed to be artisan farmers in their own right, the laws of the day prevented land owners from hiring people to work on the land unless they were in abject poverty; the ownership of assets removed the right to work. Only once all assets were sold, his pigs, his cow, his cottage, could the once-independent man be legally allowed to be hired for his labour. At best, it seemed, abject poverty and at worst the poor house were the only destination for him, through no fault of his own (Mingay, 1990; Horn, 1976).

One example of the effects of this change can be found in Martin, a small village and parish south of Salisbury in the United Kingdom. It is surrounded by farms even today. According to Kelly's Directory of Wiltshire 1867, the village dates to 1590 and in 1867 the principal landowner was the Reverend Edward Peacock with the Lord of the Manor being E. Cootes Esquire who at that time was a minor, a child; it is reasonable to surmise both these landowners would have had farm managers running the estates. Farming was the major source of the parish's economic wellbeing, its main products being wheat and barley from a total parish area of 4,501 acres and a population (in 1861) of 574. According to the 1859 Post Office Directory of Wiltshire, it had had a population of 601 in 1851 so it had already begun to experience in a small way the effects of outward migration. In both directories, a Mr John Dibben is listed alongside two dozen other people as 'Commercial'. These included eleven farmers, two farm bailiffs, two shoemakers, two wheelwrights, two shopkeepers, a publican and a blacksmith. John Dibben was the carrier and dealer of the village (1867: 453), the person who transported people and produce to Salisbury and the surrounding villages on a scheduled timetable; carters were the self-employed bus drivers and lorry drivers of their day, operating a regular service with a horse and cart (Horn, 1976: 63–4). He is also listed in the Directory under the more generic listing of 'Cattle Dealers, Graziers and Jobbers' (ibid.: 535).

In fact, from the censuses of the period, the Dibben family seem to be centred in and around Martin. In the nearby village of Bishopstone, Edwin and George Frederick Dibben are listed as farmers (ibid.: 221). George Dibben, who was born in 1796 in Martin and died in 1846 in nearby Fordingbridge, had eight children. Neither he nor his wife Sarah (1793–1878) could read or write; their marriage certificate contains not signatures of the couple but 'the mark of' them instead. All of the children seem to have lived in or near to Martin, and been either labourers or engaged in other work connected with the village and the farms. The eldest son Charles (1819–1847), for example, was a shepherd. Another son, Joseph (1834–1906) was a carpenter. The second-eldest son, Thomas (1821–1896), started his work life as a mason's labourer (1851 England Census). From the business standpoint, these examples at the time of and in the generation after the Enclosures, suggest a general tendency to attempt to become more skilled and stand beyond the poverty that overtook the artisan farmer.

Indeed, Thomas Dibben worked hard to improve his lot in life. By the time of the 1881 England Census, he is listed in Martin as being a 'grocer, baker and bricklayer'. By the 1891 census he is the head of the household living in Martin's grocers shop. He had gone from being a labourer to a mason to not only being a bricklayer himself, but had branched out to make the most of the opportunity afforded him in the village and was in business for himself as the village shopkeeper. He must also have learnt to read and write. According to the 1901 census, his son Herbert took over the grocery business after his death, while another son Charles (1848–1861) had continued the family tradition of his namesake Uncle and was a shepherd.

In two generations, an enterprising spirit had seen at least some of the Dibbens of Martin escape the poverty wrought by the Enclosures and become instead self-employed businessmen. Working on the edge of the first move towards industrial-scale agriculture in the UK, they fashioned livelihoods through skilled work and shopkeeping to meet the needs of the local farming and village community. At a time when village communities were still very much self-contained and fixed, they were also willing to leave Martin and seek their fortunes elsewhere. William (1868–1954) learnt his father's first trade and was resident in Martin as a bricklayer in the 1901 census, but would become a wealthy tenant farmer in Ropley in Hampshire, and then in Walderton in Sussex. In a time of no social services or welfare state, enterprise was the default category in the UK; you either found a way to make a living or ended up destitute. The Dibbens were evidently enterprising enough to see opportunity and grasp it. They were working class, yes, but they were not in poverty, dependent on casual farm labour to eke out a daily existence; they had largely found a way to fashion their own livelihoods.

This book is an auto/biographical business history based primarily on the life of one working man, the youngest grandson of William Dibben who, as we shall see, inherited much of that entrepreneurial mindset and fashioned it to the different industrial realities of the second half of the Twentieth Century. It is also in part a biography of that working man's great friend Andrew Mustard, and of both their families' relations. Separated by only 5 years on the one hand, but by a completely different family background on the other, Stan Dibben's and Andrew Mustard's experience of business and their views on it were nonetheless almost identical and these views were passed on to the next generation. Through a study of their lives and the lives of some of their relatives, and an examination of the businesses and the men they worked for *at the time they worked for them*, we hope to show the shift from small to large, from entrepreneurial to corporate, is not simply a shift in scale. It is a shift of mindset, of outlook, of attitude to one's fellow man – a shift that not all choose to make. As Michael G. Scott, one of the founders of entrepreneurial studies in the UK, made clear 'Small firms are not little big firms' (Scott, 1989).

Both Stan Dibben and Andrew Mustard in their own way, both families in their own way, are united by an entirely serendipitous multi-generational experience of – and resistance to – the shift to corporatisation. We shamelessly take advantage of that serendipity. Rarely has it been possible to study multiple industries in multiple countries and multiple generations, over 100 years, to uncover the challenge of business growth, and explore the times when owners decided against it – as well as the implications for employees when they decided to embrace it. Our purpose in this book, then, is to grasp that opportunity and tell the otherwise unobservable entrepreneurial business history enmeshed within the personal life-story of Stan Dibben, his friends and relatives.

Stan Dibben's *Hold On!* was an autobiography that, as published, was shaped by the publisher around the author's motorcycle racing, and particularly his life as a World Champion sidecar rider. While natural for a motoring publisher such as the now-extinct *Panther*, this rather hampered the telling of the larger tale. Stan Dibben is known by and large only as a racing motorcyclist, as one of the last links to the famous British motorcycle names of BSA and, primarily, Norton. We have written this book in the belief that it is time to see Stan Dibben and his friends more so in the round, to serve as a detailed exemplar of phenomena we suspect are more widely experienced but little written about. Exploring a life as rich and varied as Stan Dibben's through a different lens, the lens of enterprise, provides a different set of insights into that life, and into what was involved in building a post-war income and life on the edge of the motor industry's establishment. This book retraces the steps of the autobiography, by taking that different approach.

Here we tell the story always with an eye to the business history that the story unveils. In this sense, the story is one of a series of lucky happenstances, of work opportunities grasped, of multiple encounters with a vast array of quite different but always in their own way entrepreneurial characters and, as a result of these encounters, an approach to business that focuses on pioneering the new rather than cementing the old. It is a story of the development of an entrepreneurial mindset focused above all on being true to oneself and one's own beliefs, where honesty and long-term care of one's customers always trumps personal short-term profit. Whatever the cost. The story reveals a way of doing business almost lost in the modern-day era of oligopolies and multinationals, and provides a glimpse of what is involved in introducing new ideas and products under the noses of the establishment – and of making a living by so doing.

Our approach to the telling of the tale is to base it upon the autobiography's original draft and to allow it largely to stand, suitably updated, with the addition of biography and as determined by the business history requirements. In this respect, the historical account relies on a range of interviews not least but not only with the book's main subject, supplemented with archival research, to give a unique insight into the companies concerned. That is, an insight that comes from being able to adopt an otherwise unavailable 'inside-out' as opposed to the more usual 'outside-in' perspective (c.f. Munro, 2003: 7).

However, despite the emphasis on particular individuals, this book is not simply auto/biographical. The biography enables us to study these individuals' approaches to business and to see their life history in the setting of the business ventures with which they were associated, the circles within which they moved and often broke free from. To do this, it is better to think of entrepreneurship as far more than simply the making of money, far more significant than the focus on personal wealth. Entrepreneurship is the creation and integration of value in an environment, whatever that environment may be, and success in this way of being is dependent on always being open to opportunity.

We therefore turn not to entrepreneurship theorists such as Israel Kirzner or Joseph Schumpeter, who were mostly concerned with the acts of spotting opportunities and the creation of radically different substitute products to disrupt established industrial players respectively, but rather to E.F. Schumacher. This hugely popular economist of the 1960s and 1970s, two of the key decades for Stan Dibben as a self-employed businessman, is renowned for at least two mantras: 'small is beautiful'; and 'economics as if people mattered' ([1973] 2011). In this sense, Schumacher, a German who left his home country to escape Nazism and settled in the UK, becoming one of the architects of the economic revival that distanced the country from the Second World War, is concerned more than anything with the question of human value, the underpinning purpose of the human being in the context of meaningful work. Today, his thinking shapes the work of, amongst others, a Schumacher College in Devon, the Schumacher Institute in Bristol, the Soil Association, a Centre for Alternative Technology in North Wales (all in the UK), and the Schumacher Centre for A New Economics in Massachusetts.

He argued small firms were crucial to the modern economy because they allowed people to do 'good work' (Schumacher, 1980) that emphasised community and relationships, by maintaining the purpose of work at the human scale, rather than the remote multinational scale. He was clear too that (Schumacher, [1973] 2011: 49–50)

> When it comes to action, we need small units because action is a highly personal affair, and one cannot be in touch with more than a limited number of persons at any one time … Today we suffer from an almost universal idolatry of giantism. It is therefore necessary to insist on the virtues of smallness … For every activity there is a certain appropriate scale, and the more active and intimate the activity, the smaller the number of people that can take part, the greater the number of such relationship arrangements that need to be established.

That is to say, work that provides an economic return for oneself but, in contrast to a purely utilitarian view, whose real satisfaction was in the achievement of meaningful and mutually sustaining business relationships with and for other people. The focus of economic activity, for Schumacher, is the wellbeing of the people one works for, be it customers, fellow workers in a company, or the community at large ([1973] 2011: 57):

> The economic calculus, as applied by present day economics, forces the industrialist to eliminate the human factor because machines do not make mistakes which people do … This means that those who have nothing to sell but their labour remain in the weakest possible bargaining position. The conventional wisdom of what is now taught as economics by-passes the poor, the very people for whom development is really needed. The economics of giantism and automation is a left-over of nineteenth century conditions and nineteenth century thinking and it is totally incapable of solving any of the real problems of today. An entirely new system of thought is needed, a system based on attention to people, and not primarily attention to goods – (the goods will look after themselves!).

E.F. Schumacher's grasp of the consequences of a traditional economic view precisely explains the realities faced by George and Thomas Dibben in the

1800s and forecast the challenges faced by their heirs. In short, his economic principles and philosophy – which continue to resonate today (Schumacher, 2011) – are rather more likely to shed light on the day-to-day realities of life as a small business man, than those of writers focused on the economy or even the market in the more traditional sense.

Studying the entire working life of an ordinary small businessman, albeit one who did some extraordinary things, allows us to trace the origins of his approach and set his success and failures, as an example of one such individual, and his friends and relatives, in their proper context not as isolated incidents but as part of a greater whole. We are concerned with five distinct but related themes of general interest. First, the question of how Stan Dibben, as an example of an ordinary working-class man with no secondary education to speak of, went about crafting a life on the edges of the motor industry. What values, attitudes and beliefs enabled him to succeed in an industry where mentioning his World Championship success invariably did more harm than good – *bragging about nothing.*

It is perhaps only recently that we have begun to understand the connection between sport and business. Yet there has long been a close connection in motorsport at least, between the two; the racing successes of the 'Bentley boys' of the 1920s and 1930s was founded in private enterprise wealth. A second theme is therefore to explore the ways in which sport and business overlapped in post-war motorsport, a time when the privations of World War Two were still keenly felt, and funding was thus comparatively scarce; we can reasonably surmise entrepreneurial creativity would be a key business asset. We shall do this by examining how two of the key protagonists in Stan Dibben's motorcycle racing success, Eric Oliver and Cyril Smith, approached *the business* of being professional motorcycle racers. This will shed new light on their different motivations and popularity among their fellow racers. We will show that, in many respects, the way they each went about the business of sidecar racing in the 1950s was not only quite different but was a key factor in their comparative successes. We can address the question 'Is the entrepreneur-sportsman quite a different person to the small business-sportsman?'

Through the friendship between Stan Dibben and Andrew Mustard, and their work on the now-infamous Bluebird Land Speed Record project, we will also explore the enigma that was Donald Campbell. Much of the explanation for his successes, or lack of them, on Lake Eyre in 1964 stemmed just as much from the concerns of Campbell-the-businessman as ever they did from Campbell-the-record-breaker; the two were intertwined. We shall then briefly extend the study to another Australasian land speed record and its entrepreneur, Phil Garret, to further consider the role of the entrepreneur sportsman in enabling land speed record projects. In each of these sport-as-business settings, motorcycle racing and land speed record breaking, we will reveal the tough business realities inside motor and motorcycle sport (and the wider motor industry) in the 1950s, 1960s – and 2000s – and their consequences.

A third theme concerns the histories of the businesses Stan Dibben came into contact with during his fifty years of working life. To some extent, there is a serendipity in joining these businesses together. Some of them, such as BSA, Norton and Watsonian do bear valid comparison. For others, such as Perry Chains and NGK Spark Plugs, there is an objectively valid reason for inclusion given their presence in the wider motor industry. Including the story of a business such as Mid-Southern Utility Company (MSUCo) is rendered valid only in the context of the auto/biography, but we hope to show they are no less interesting and indeed revealing of the realities of business during and immediately after the Second World War, in terms of the question of growth and its impact on the firm. Further, as Brassley et al. (2016) note, the historiography of the rural electrification of England as told from the perspective not of policy but instead of the local small businesses that actually took on the commercial risk to carry it out, is virtually non-existent. It is apposite to explore it.

The opportunity to study their history is one to be grasped, particularly when the history of a company such as MSUCo is intimately bound up with not only the quasi-military camp that became the South of England immediately in the months leading up to the invasion of France, but also with the societal and economic changes that were made possible by general electrification. The business of electrifying Britain through the early years of the electricity supply industry when a multitude of small firms sprang up, were consolidated through merger and acquisition among a small number of 'power entrepreneurs' and their successors, who then benefited enormously from the Second World War before the entire industry was nationalised post-war. This was itself an attempt to regulate what had by then become very large private enterprise utility companies. The story of MSUCo is therefore worthy of study in the context of the 'Growth' challenge and its multitude of implications. It also allows us to shed light on the union response to such success, while Stan Dibben's own response to both nationalisation and unionisation is itself instructive in a study of small-scale versus large-scale, entrepreneurial versus corporate perspectives on life.

The same is true of NGK for, while much has been written about the foreign direct investment (FDI) of Japanese firms into the UK, Europe and the United States, rarely has it been possible to examine this story for such an important motor parts manufacturer, now world leader, from the inside-out. We will shed light on the impact of individuals and their personal perspectives on business that may underpin that FDI success, rendered again from the lens of small-to-large transition, i.e. of corporatisation. That is to say, as but one example of one of the indviduals discussed, Stan Dibben's approach to pioneering NGK over three decades in which he grew the business in his area of the UK from '10 sets 4 spark plugs to try' to a turnover of over one million pounds – from a considerably smaller area than that which he had at the start, and that at no time in the quarter of a century of his association with the company had a major city within it – reveals much by way of explanation of the differences between large and small. And yet, with the change from Japanese to English management, there came increasing tension, despite the success. With E.F. Schumacher's theories as an implicitly primary guide, we will pay some considerable attention to Stan Dibben's pioneer selling, for it is an approach to selling now almost forgotten.

In order to widen the scope and examine further whether its starting premise, that Scott's statement 'small firms are not little big firms' has a genuine universality to it, the book moves beyond the UK to consider the life of Stan's great friend Andrew Mustard. The touching off point for this is of course the 1964 Bluebird Land Speed Record Project, of which Mustard was project manager. Much has been written about this project, but largely from the perspective of Donald Campbell, be this through his own words or those of the most famous commentator, John Pearson (2002). More recent accounts, such as that of David Tremayne (2004), have painted a picture of Mustard that is at best one-sided and at worst plain inaccurate. We believe it is time to redress the balance, by painting a more complete picture of the man, his background, his namesake father's First World War and commercial achievements and subsequent experience of being interned in 1941 as a prisoner of the Japanese in Singapore 'on the edge' of the second industrial world war, his personality and subsequently his own achievements.

Why was it, for example, that Andrew Mustard declared to Ken Norris, the car's designer, that he would 'give his left ball to drive the car' (Tremayne, 2004: 297; also, pers. comm. 1998)? Was he, as Norris has suggested (Tremayne,

2004: 297), the 'one sod like that' in any team? What were his real motivations, and where did the mutual dislike of Campbell for Mustard and Mustard for Campbell originate? From the point of view of business history, what might the answer to this tell us about the nature of sport as business, and of attitudes to business in general among its post-war elite? Beyond the sport-as-business question, and in the context of a book examining enterprise 'on the edge' of industry, what impact did Andrew Mustard's experience of Campbell have on his future work life? What values were formed as a result and, importantly, how did these shape his dealings with others as a self-employed expatriate Englishmen – with a very strong upper-class English accent – making a living as a geologist and a garage owner in North Queensland? In short, does the Andrew Mustard example add to or detract from the thesis that there is a qualitative difference to be discerned in the approach to business between large and small?

A fifth theme looks to extend Scott's 'small is not little-big' thesis beyond private for-profit enterprise to the public and social enterprise sectors. The early encounters between British and German troops in Belgium in 1914 were fast-moving and led to many British soldiers being captured and transported to Germany to be interned in prisoner of war (PoW) camps for the duration (Atkinson, 1952; Lewis-Stempel, 2014). In an intriguing and instructive parallel to Andrew Mustard Sr's experience twenty-seven years later after the fall of Singapore, one of these soldiers was Corporal Reginald Dibben of the Hampshire Regiment, William's son – and Stan's father-to-be. These prisoners of war included people from many nations, Russians, French and Australians as well as British. It soon became evident that the German authorities increasingly did not have the means to care for these prisoners, many of whom were badly wounded. The result was that, almost spontaneously, so-called 'help committees' sprang up around the United Kingdom and Australia, as well as other countries, to provide food, clothing and medicine for the PoWs, the British and Australian parcels being sent from London via neutral Holland and Switzerland (Paterson, 2012). The prisoners of war and the help committees were a largely forgotten group of combatants and a vital part of the war effort respectively; in comparison with the rest of World War One, they have been comparatively under-studied.

From the perspective of social enterprise, therefore, we will consider the development of the help committees, and their evolution into a single organised entity, with representatives in the camps. Reginald Dibben's prisoner of war experience in Germany and reliance on them provides the biographical rationale. We are therefore able to consider the organisational and leadership aspects of growth both on the home front and, sometimes, *in extremis*, i.e. in the context of Reginald's experience in an environment quite unlike any other, where death was a constant companion. Do E.F. Schumacher's arguments regarding the efficiency of and reward for small groups of people working in collaboration hold true for the (mostly) women who took it upon themselves to establish the 'help committees', and even in the extremes of wartime imprisonment, on the edge of the very first war fought on an industrial scale? After Schumacher's 'small is beautiful' adage, can smallness conjure beauty in human action from even the most miserable of circumstances?

As a final discussion, the attention will turn to the – moral as well as 'business' – challenge of growth and transition in the not-for-profit sector, and an examination of a central theme of the book, namely the different values and perspectives of, as E.F Schumacher would put it, 'small-scale' thinking as opposed to 'large-scale' thinking ([1973] 2011: 22–3). Higher education, particularly in Australia, is increasingly being seen by both politicians and students as a private benefit, not a 'public good'. A study by Miles et al. (2017) surveying Australian university executives, suggests that universities are now best seen as social enterprises, in which the top 'strategic driver' is a 'focus on increasing revenue from international enrolments and teaching'. Faculties of Business and so-called Business Schools in English-speaking countries are feeling this pressure given the demand from – in particular – Chinese students for business education in the world's *lingua franca*; the international student fees help subsidise the sciences. The downturn in government funding witnessed since the early 2010s has forced universities to restructure their Faculties in order to find economies of scale. This has followed the trend witnessed in the commercial sector, i.e. an increase in the size of individual business units. With its unusual reliance on and exposure to international student markets, trends witnessed and experienced in recent history in Australia are worthy of study as predictors of the pressures to be faced in other English-speaking countries, as the trend towards commercialised higher education gathers pace.

Higher education is recognised as one of the most significant so-called 'export industries' in Australia, and increasingly around the English-speaking world (Miles et al., 2017). Mark Dibben's experience of leadership as a Head of School and, contemporaneously, as Deputy Chair of an Academic Senate (the ultimate decision making body in regards to academic matters in a university), as well as other roles in universities spanning twenty years of significant change in the higher education industry located 'on the geographical edge' of Australia and New Zealand, and also in the UK, provides a potentially valuable insight into some of the very real and immediate challenges faced in that industry. It will allow us to consider, for example, whether there are circumstances in which, despite the attempt to keep small-scale values and ways of being, the pressure to corporatize becomes simply overwhelming. Is this an example of Schumacher's observation that 'we suffer from an almost universal idolatry of giantism' ([1973] 2011: 49)? We examine the shifts in thinking that occurred and consider the impact on individuals and cultures. Are there parallels between Stan Dibben's experience of and resistance to large-scale thinking at NGK in the 1990s and Mark Dibben's experiences? Do E.F. Schumacher's arguments in relation to the de-humanisation of organisations as they grow (1980 and [1997] 2004) hold true even in higher education, and with what impact on the leader and the staff?

In following the five themes through the 100 years between Reginald Dibben's imprisonment at the hands of the Germans in 1914 to the conclusion of Mark Dibben's term as Head of the School of Management in the Faculty of Business & Economics at the University of Tasmania in 2014, we will be attempting to bridge eight major 'industries' – grocery, the military, public utilities, motorcycle, motorsport, motor parts, geological exploration, and higher education. We hope to demonstrate that, at the time in which we encounter them through the organisations we examine, the challenges of growth and personal perspective are usefully understood to be similar, if not indeed identical; they transcend eras, industries and even countries. The real substance and interest in what we have to say lies in the connection, and at times unfortunate disconnection, between peoples' business values, ownership, strategy, market development and attitudes to key stakeholders. Further, to focus on growth solely from the perspective of 'large-scale', excluding the possibility of the 'small-scale' alternative is to miss a vital window opening onto post-war work life. And yet, there are so many 'stories within stories' herein that, in truth, all we can hope to do is point the way to the reader rather more than tread the path. Nor will we expose each story or even necessarily each chapter to an *immediate* Schumacher-driven analysis; where more apposite we will 'bring the stories to the Schumacher' in the conclusion. Sometimes the plain losses (and more often than not they are losses) felt at a human level speak more powerfully than would an analytical interpretation. In seeking to reveal some of the universal realities that underpin the otherwise innocuous 'Growth' imperative, however, we hope at least to show there is a genuine difference between 'small business thinking' and 'large business thinking' – the implications of which stretch far beyond the immediate example of two families' business and social enterprise experiences.

Some notes for the reader seem apposite since we appreciate an auto/biographical business history is not the most widely seen approach to any of the – business, sports, local or war – history genres. The book intentionally proceeds chronologically and adds new autobiographical material that has been written in the intervening years, thus benefiting from much that was not known at the time of *Hold On!*. It also attempts the analytically reflective aspect, looking to provide an account that focuses on the entrepreneurship of the individuals and the strategic realities of the businesses and industries concerned. The autobiography therefore becomes in some ways 'data' for the biography that surrounds it, but it is data the reader may – of course – at one and the same time interpret for herself. To achieve this, each chapter begins with Stan Dibben's autobiography, reworked and revised on occasion from its original rendering in *Hold On!*, by way of introduction to the biographical business history that follows. For ease of reading, we have separated the two accounts in each chapter with asterisks (***), used Arabic numerals (1, 2, 3) to enumerate the subheadings of the autobiography section, and by contrast used Roman numerals (I, II, III) for the biography and business history section. The book is also extended via 'photo essays' arranged by chapter that are available via the publisher's website. Other audio visual material is to be found on the Facebook public group page that Stan Dibben set up in support of Hold On!: *Hold On!* by Stan Dibben. This can be viewed and listened to separately, so there are intentional overlaps in the stories as one might expect, but insofar as that is the case we hope the photographs, film and audio material adds a richness and colour that would not otherwise be possible. That said, there are stories in the book that are not in the photo essays and vice-versa.

The vast majority of the remarkable assistance we have received in putting this project together has been in regards to the photo essays in particular; we have been careful to acknowledge that support as fully as we can therein. The book itself could not have been so extensive or made the various contributions we hope it has perhaps, without the tremendous support of Colin Bulleid, Frank Burchill, Monika Dolles (for both her translations of German texts and for helping tremendously with final page-proofing), Claire Gray, Richenda Goldfinch, Ben Matthews, Morgan Miles, Harry Mustard, Sarah Patterson, Donald Stevens, Katie Thompson, Noboru and Kan Torii, Nick Walker and his staff at Australia Scholarly Publishing, and Malcolm Wheeler. More broadly, we wish to acknowledge a number of people who in various ways have supported us – and each in their own way continues to do so. Namely, David Adams, Charlotte Brooks, Andrew Capone, Olga Ciccarelli and colleagues at the National Hospital for Neurology, John Cobb, Harald Dolles, Helen Gibson, Dallas Hanson, Jason Lucas and colleagues at UniSuper, Di Nicol, Ian Roderick, Peter and Julie Scatchard, Stuart and Be Schonnel, Steve Smith, John and Sally Tisdell, Graeme Tonks, and Mark Wickham. Lastly, the influence of J. Forbes Munro, Emeritus Professor of Economic History at the University of Glasgow, is not without its import. The framing of his biographical business history 'Maritime Enterprise and Empire: Sir William McKinnon and his Business Network, 1823–1893' (2003, Suffolk: The Boydell Press) using (in his case) an entrepreneurship lens provided the template for the academic rationale of this book. Although inevitably not to his peerless standards, his approach to economic history strongly influences ours. We are deeply indebted to his example.

Stan Dibben & Mark Dibben
September 2018

INTRODUCTION TO THE ACCOMPANYING AUDIO VISUAL MATERIAL

While Stan Dibben's *Hold On!* had many photographs built into the chapters, we felt for *Enterprise on the Edge of Industry* that there was the opportunity to put together a yet more comprehensive compendium of photographs, as well as audio and film. This is available from the publisher (photo essays) and on the *'Hold On' by Stan Dibben* Facebook public group page (film and interviews). It does not substitute the book, it rather complements it, for it is perfectly possible to read the book without recourse the additional material and vice-versa. Taken together there is a purposeful overlap, for the additional resources tell much the same tale, and yet we have endeavored to ensure there are stories therein that either are not in the book or at least provide an extra twist to the tale.

I. Photo Essays – via the Publisher

The photographs are arranged as a series of 'photo essays' accompanying the chapters. There are some 350 photographs, of which most of those found in *Hold On!* can also be found here and yet, to keep *Hold On!* unique in its own way, there are photos in that book that are not be found here. Equally, too, there are many more photographs here than it was even remotely possible to include in *Hold On!*. As before, the vast majority are from the family's own collection. What has been uniquely available to us this time is of course the Cyril Smith collection. Cyril took a great many photographs when he was serving in the 50th Royal Tank Regiment. These we donated to the Tank Museum at Bovington in Dorset since that is now the spiritual home of 50th Royal Tank Regiment (50 RTR), within which Cyril spent the Second World War. One of their archivists, Katie Thompson, has worked closely with us to allow us to tell the story of Cyril's time in the war, a story that speaks powerfully to his life afterwards. In addition, Cyril had amassed a large number of other racing photographs that

Stan was not aware of at the time of *Hold On!*, and we scanned many of them. This has allowed us to significantly augment the racing photographs published previously.

That said, as with *Hold On!*, many of the photographs in this book and its photo essays are of unknown origin. Whilst every effort has been made to trace the rights holders, the passage of time has made this extremely difficult. As we have intimated, most of the photographs we know come from the authors' family collections, including those by Bill Salmond, who gave Stan Dibben a large number when Bill was employed by him. Where also known, the rights holders have been acknowledged in the captions accompanying the photographs. Those captions without an acknowledgement are most often the authors' own photographs, some of which have been used in publications by others; please accept our apologies for any errors. Thanks are due at least to Godfrey Andrews for all the old photographs of Ropley, Ralph Bonhorst, Berndt Bouillon, Theresa Browning and colleagues at the National Motor Museum in Beaulieu, Vin Cent, Sid Diggins, Harald and Monika Dolles, the late Tas Graham, Heinz Hertz, son of Willi Hertz the great German sidecar racer, and Cabell Hopkins for the *No Ordinary Passenger* film (not included on the Facebook page but available via the *New York Times* website), Davide Mallavasi, Miles McCallum, Michael Sid McCormick, Gert Meulman, Harry Mustard, Jeff Rush, Bill Snelling, Jake Sutton, Rex Svoboda, as discussed Katie Thompson and colleagues at the Tank Museum in Bovington, Noboru Torii and colleagues at NGK Spark Plugs in Nagoya, and Malcolm Wheeler and colleagues at Mortons Media Group.

II. Audio Material – via Facebook

When Stan was in Quebec in Canada during the latter stages of the Second World War, he spent a lot of his spare time playing trumpet and was introduced to a local dance band, the Al Bedard Band. He did a lot of gigs with them and they also did a private recording session. Some of this session was used as a backing track to the *No Ordinary Passenger* film by Cabell Hopkins. So there is the opportunity to put the whole session, six tunes, on as a little album. Admittedly, it's just a local band, it's a bit scratchy and it's in mono, the band has long since ceased to exist and the band's leader is no longer with us. But, well, why not? At the very least, it is a glimpse into a time long since passed and gives an essence of the Canada part of the story.

Over the years, Stan has given numerous interviews on various aspects of his life and career. We have chosen two, given twenty years apart to provide the listener a couple of perspectives. The first and most recent is a radio interview by Phil Jones, 'Slow Phil', for his internet radio programme the Sidecar Show in the Winter of 2016. The second is an interview extract by Dennis Skillikan for the Beaulieu Motor Museum in Hampshire on 30 August 1991, when we drove down with Andrew Mustard so that he could also do an interview with Dennis about his life and times, and particularly of course in the context of the fact that Andrew was the Project Manager for the Bluebird World Land Speed Record; the car is at Beaulieu. This latter interview extract adds another perspective on the chapter about Andrew, and on the chapter about the Bluebird Land Speed Record Project itself. We are grateful to Phil, obviously, and to Theresa Browning and Murray Weston for access to the Beaulieu interviews – as well as the now-retired Steve Vokins for arranging the recordings there in the first place. The Beaulieu interviews can be heard in their entirety at Beaulieu.

III. Film Material – via Facebook

While researching *Enterprise on the Edge of Industry*, we found in the darkest corner of the TV cabinet a VHS tape of the 1953 and 1955 Belgian Grand Prix, with their original commentaries. A shortened version of the 1953 film was used as part of a Castrol film entitled *On the Surface* but not with this commentary, rather with another commentary that spoke to the title of the film. DUKE Video have over the years done a great service by publishing a number of films of sidecar racing in the 1950s, such as the 1953 and 1956 Ulster Grand Prix as a part of videos telling particular stories. Insofar as our two films are concerned, however, we cannot remember seeing these films before and nor can we recall how we came by the VHS tape or who gave it to us. We felt the contents were simply too good to leave out, particularly since they would help considerably in telling the Cyril Smith story. We have therefore decided to include them and apologise for any unwitting breach of copyright in so doing.

Last but not least, when Stan was in Australia for the Bluebird World Land Speed Record Project in 1964, he filmed proceedings for himself – with the help of one or two willing assistants. It is a silent film that was edited when he got home by his friend Freddie Hawkin. It adds something special and new to the account that has not previously seen the light of day. Stan's written commentary of it is as follows:

00:00 Here we are preparing to travel to Muloorina from Maree, having arrived by train from Adelaide.

01:20 Setting off on the road!

02:00 Traveling from Muloorina to Lake Eyre, with detail of the difficult road conditions.

02:45 On Lake Eyre with the main camp flooded after rain.

03:00 Track Preparation: Me and my track crew dragging railway lines up the track to smooth it by 'shaving' the salt.

04:51 Putting the stakes in the salt to mark out the guide lines for the track

05:26 Bluebird Preparation: Andrew Mustard and crew preparing the car for a run. With detail of the parachute, wheel changing and fueling.

06:58 Charging the car's onboard systems via the special Land Rovers

07:18 Tonya Campbell with her husband Donald, as he prepares for a run complete with teddy bear.

08:00 Bluebird starts and sets off on a run.

08:27 I was often in charge of the radio and this is me talking to Donald in the car.

08:50 The return run, with Andrew in the Elfin as a 'chase car' as Bluebird returns.

09:15 Servicing Bluebird after the run with Donald in discussion about it.

09:34 The Homestead: the boys with their pet! They were fond of him and he was fond of them.

10:12 One of the many cockatoos resident at Muloorina and one of the homestead's dogs.

10:30 An emu at the homestead, one of the children, and many more cockatoos – one with a couple of the homestead workers.

11:24 The infamous ancient car complete with wooden wheels, of course, and cow skeletons.

11:36 The flora and fauna of Lake Eyre, including the river made by the artesian bore and a Wedge-tailed Eagle.

12:30 Sydney as it was in 1964, on the way back to the UK. Including many merchant and military navy ships, the harbor bridge and the downtown skyline.

15:00   The Pan-Am flight to Hawaii, inside their (nearly empty!) 707 complete with 'skylights'

15:25   Panoramic views of Hawaii with new hotel under construction, one with an outside lift.

16:18   The famous Hawaii surf.

16:35   Flying out of Hawaii, with a volcano in view, en route to LA.

17:55   End. [And then on to Winnipeg where we landed in a violent thunderstorm, the only time I have ever been worried in an aeroplane. From there to London, with a fabulous view of the Aurora Borealis.]

Stan Dibben aged 4 at the beekeeper Mr Barret's. The boy's connection to countryside would stay with him all his life

1

PRECURSORS TO LIVELIHOOD

1. Relatively Care-Free Beginnings

My father was the middle son of not exactly poor farmers. They were rental farming 1,200 acres at Manor Farm, Walderton, in Sussex. He served in World War One, a private in the army and was taken prisoner during the retreat from Mons in Belgium in 1914. On repatriation at the end of the war he joined the Metropolitan Police, J Division, at Barkingside. This was a time when moustaches were still very much in vogue both in the Army and the Police; all the pictures I have ever seen of him portray a tall man with a tremendous 'tea strainer tache.' He and my mother had a police house at 32 Tomswood Hill Barkingside Essex, where I was born on 5 May 1925, but he died in 1926 in St Thomas' hospital. The cause of death, I was told, was believed to be the after effects of chlorine gas and experimental injections received while a prisoner in Germany. He was buried at Barkingside after a military funeral. Unfortunately, the authorities held that his death was due to contracting Tuberculosis from policing the London slums, where it was rife, and denied my mother a war widow's pension. Of course, I never knew him.

Mother was a country girl from Hampshire, in the eyes of her in-laws not good enough for their son. On the death of her husband, she had to move from the marital home to live on a police widow's pension of 11 shillings a week. With my elder brother and sister, we returned to her parents' home in Ropley in Hampshire, and she earned a bit extra washing dishes in the local Chequers pub. Her father was the stationmaster at Ropley station, apparently, on what is now the Watercress line. I loved to see the 'living' steam engines, huffing and puffing their unforgettable smelling steam. He shaped the rather grand Yew trees that were still there when I last paid a visit. He died soon after we arrived and I never knew him either. My old maternal grandmother, a tiny gentle and caring old soul said to me when she was

1

crying one day 'Never mind love, if the Lord doesn't come he sends.' It turns out her husband wasn't the station master at all, but more of a general dog's body, porter, signalman, tree trimmer etc.

Ropley was truly rural then. Our home at No.1 Gascoigne Lane was a semi-detached brick and flint cottage, two bedrooms upstairs and one downstairs; a living room, kitchen, larder and just off the kitchen inside the back door a wood fired 'copper' for washing clothes. The bath was a portable galvanised tub that lived in the outside woodshed brought indoors when needed and filled with hot water from kettles. Of course, there was no running water. Drinking water was drawn up in a bucket from 30 ft down the well, cold, crystal clear and tasteless as water should be. Washing water was the rainwater collected in large metal tubs from the roof of the house, with fascinating bugs swimming about on the surface. Ice on the inside of the bedroom window.

We had a brick built outside toilet that was almost overwhelmingly, powerfully cold on deep-winter mornings. Mahogany seat, newspaper and/or paper shopping bag to use in the absence of unheard of toilet rolls, and the bucket of excrement to be buried in a hole dug in the garden. Of course, there was no electricity either, only a paraffin lamp and candles. Coal and wood fired black fire grate with oven for cooking and heating in the living room, supplemented in the kitchen with a small paraffin fired heater. A large 'copper' in the washhouse, with small fire place beneath, to do the clothes washing. No washroom complete without a mangle. That heavy spring loaded two wooden roller devices, through which the washed and still wet material would be squeezed through by turning a handle, thereby removing most of the water to hasten the drying time.

The big half acre garden was, like the surrounding country-side, full of wild flowers; saxifrage, sweet scented blue, white and pink violets, blue cornflowers all visited by a profusion of butterflies; red admirals, peacocks, tortoiseshells, brimstones meadow browns, little blue ones and the odd swallow-tail doubtless rarely seen today if at all. Plenty of stinging nettles too, black with caterpillars and later of course myriads of tortoiseshell butterflies. To this wondrous scene add a whole variety of songbirds. Across the lane opposite, in a small copse, red squirrels, rabbits and stoats. In the evening, rooks cawing their way home to roost. How I used to laugh at them leisurely flying above, suddenly flapping in frenzied panic when I raised and pointed a garden broom in imitation of a gun. No fools these creatures.

2. Connection to Countryside

At the back of our place lived Mr and Mrs Barratt. She was a Yorkshire matron with her ginger parkin cake and her thumping washing dolly, he was a retired dentist who had taken up bee keeping. His sign by the front gate read, 'We grow honey, take some home.' This tall man, always in his trilby hat, explained that each beehive had wooden squares in which hung frames where the bees made the honey. When one square was full another was placed on top and so on until the beehive was four or five squares high. This was what he meant by 'growing honey', adding, building up, 'growing', the number of honey comb frames of the bee hives. He used to take me around the garden showing me his bees at work collecting pollen. When the time came to harvest the honey, the frames would be taken from the squares. He wore a net over his head and shoulders and carried a large smoke puffer. He used to squeeze the blue, acrid smoke into the hive to make his bees sleepy. The frames would then be taken to his extraction shed – that's what he called it – where the frames were placed into a hand operated centrifuge and the honey, gallons of it, spun out. What joy it was winding the handle and dipping a finger in the succulent, sticky sweet honey. Sometimes Mr Barratt would be making small wooden boxes in which he placed sugar cubes to feed the queen bees. He posted these to other beekeepers. He was of some repute and used to broadcast on the radio; I was always thrilled to hear his voice coming out of the speakers. He taught me much about bees and about being in touch with Nature.

Regular pocket money for me was unheard of. Pennies could be earned in the late summer selling apples from the never-pruned Codlin and Bramley apple trees I fearlessly climbed, to the day-trippers from the Grey Green coaches stopped for refreshment at the Chequers Inn, 100 yards down the lane. The main road, now the A31, was being surfaced. What fun to be near the road rollers rattling, smoking and hissing steam! The Seddon lorries, too, with their own steaming smelly character. Many hours were spent sitting up in the trees watching the cars and motorbikes of all shapes, colours and sizes passing by.

I started school at five years old. Alresford Prep School, 'APS' said the cap badge. This was in West Street up an alley on the right-hand side, three miles from Ropley by the Aldershot and District bus that stopped by the Chequers at 8:15 and home again – 4 stops – on the 4 o'clock service. I remember how nice the driver was to me and Mother liked him too – perhaps that was why! This early childhood was happy but poor. I remember little about my brother and sister, probably because being older, they were away at boarding schools.

My father had been a Freemason and our education was paid for by them. I learned some family facts 80 odd years on, in the discovery of a half-sister who was adopted at birth and never knew either her mother or her father. He was, I presume, the bus driver. Unmarried pregnancy was a total disgrace then.

An early achievement was learning to ride a bicycle. I had found a frame on a rubbish tip and took it home. It had two wheels, no tyres, no saddle or brakes. Our garden had a bit of a slope to it, so I tied on a cushion for a saddle, pushed it up the slope, got aboard and free wheeled down the slope into the brick built outside toilet with bucket. Mother was on the 'throne' at the time and was not best pleased to be showered with bricks and very old mortar. By the time I had performed that a few times, I could balance and had even learnt to replace some of the bricks and mortar.

My old Uncle was a gamekeeper. What a good sharp shot he was. I saw him kill a rabbit from six or seven feet in an instant, before I'd even seen it. He'd kill almost anything for dinner, be it pheasant, partridge, rabbit, hare, pigeon, even rook. The only thing he'd kill and not eat was rat. He was also a very good carpenter and did work for the local builder. He used to breed pheasants for the local landowners which he released in Bighton wood. One day he said, 'Do you want to hear nightingale song?' We went up to a wood, Old Down, not far from home. We walked through the trees to a spot facing west where the wood opened out on to a field. It was a beautiful evening and we sat down on a bank in the warm, windless evening sun. 'Now keep quiet – not a sound.' We sat, for what seemed an eternity. 'Keep quiet.' Finally, my young patience was rewarded by a rustle in the tree above and then a symphony of trills and warbles, infinite in variety, the like of which I had never heard and have to this day never forgotten. Speaking of music, he also used to 'scrape' a violin. I remember looking inside it and reading a label I think said 'copi di Guaneri fecit anno 1680'. Mother sold it for £5 to a dealer in Kingsworthy near Winchester.

He taught me a lot of country skills. How to use a scythe to cut the long grass in the garden and a faghook for the short stuff like stinging nettles. Sharpening saws; those big cross cuts with a vertical handle at each end; cutting up big tree trunks for the fire indoors, him one end, me at the other. 'No lad, pull don't push.' The scent of the big grain saw dust; pine, elm, oak, horse chestnut; all distinctive, and not the fine dusty stuff usually associated with sawing wood. The 'billhook', that short sharp chopper for splitting the big logs already cut and split with an axe. Lessons, too, on the safe use of chisels, and wood planes which he had made, together with an assortment of tools and how to use them, without loss of fingers, and how to do general repairs to anything in need of attention. By contrast, another uncle who was not, from memory, any good at anything except voluminous consumption of beer down at the Chequers Inn. In fairness to him, he planted many of the trees now to be seen looking over the field opposite the Chequers Inn beyond the railway line, now tall and in straight lines, so I guess he was sober some of the time!

Two elderly, scary spinster sisters – Shadwell by name – occupied No. 2 Gascoigne Lane. When they died, my mother purchased both cottages from the owner Miss Wynn for the enormous sum of £400, with a loan on an interest only basis from a private lender. We moved out of a crowded No. 1 into No. 2. Milk was delivered by Mr Kingsland in his pony and trap: a two-wheeled cart drawn by a very lively pony. The milk, in a large urn, was dispensed into a family jug and half pound pats of daffodil yellow butter too were sold. The weather one weekend was atrocious with thunderstorms and rain sufficient to make the lane into a fast-flowing six-inch deep river. A clap of thunder … a scared pony … the urn no longer upright, spilling its milk into the flood while tall Mr Kingsland in his long white coat, stood ankle deep shouting in vain, 'Whoa! Stop!' I heard later that the horse arrived safely home on the other side of the village, with the cart and the empty milk churn. The following poem is by Margaret Suffolk, a friend of mine who has given me permission to include it. It is illustrative of my early childhood in the country and is a favourite of mine.

Through Eyes of Love.
I'm bored Nan, are you? Oh no, not me,
I'm watching a woodpecker in that tree.
I'm listening to the humming of a bumblebee
Making honey for someone's tea.
Why don't you come and sit with me?
There's plenty more for us to see.

A Jenny wren with his tail up high
Shapes of clouds that form in the sky.
The drone of a bee passing by.
The long slender wings of a dragon fly.
A proud little robin with a red breast,
Somewhere close she has a nest.
Her baby's first flight will be put to the test

Slowly and gently they'll do their best.

The tallest flowers sway in the breeze
Scattering pollen that makes us sneeze.
Pansies with faces that seem to please.
New hawthorn leaves known as bread and cheese.

A snail, a slug, a little grey bug,
A fly trapped in a web gives a final tug.
A little frog sits under a stone
He doesn't mind if he sits alone.
In a pond nearby his tadpoles have grown.
You may hear him croak but you won't hear him moan.
So, don't be bored my little one
With so much to see, it's so much fun
A new tale to tell when each day is done.

3. The Shock of School

All this happy, care-free country life, coupled with a gentle introduction to discipline at prep school, ended at 8 years of age with departure to boarding school, paid for by the Freemasons. Being without a father, the Royal Masonic Institute for Boys in Bushy, Hertfordshire was to be my destination by train to Waterloo, then underground train to Bushey and Oxhey Station.

On arrival I was totally overwhelmed …

This was not a happy time for me. I recall the housemaster in the junior school once say, 'Are you alright boy, why are you frowning?' Frowning at about 9 years of age? This was clearly not an unusually rough day. Bad manners and unruly behaviour were not tolerated. Guilty once at about 11 years old, of unacceptable manners, I had to write a hundred times, 'Where ignorance predominates, vulgarity conspicuously and assiduously asserts itself.' At 11 years old? I joined 3 pens together and wrote it all 33 plus one times. There was one major problem: all mistakes were in triplicate and so I had to do it all over again. Worse, the ingenuity was not appreciated and was punished by another 50 lines.

When I was 14, I had the cane once for displaying lack of respect for a senior prefect who had given me a rough time for beating him on a cross country run. My lack of respect was there for all to see in the form of graffiti. 'Ray is a bullying shit!' Pretty serious stuff from a 14-year-old. Four strokes for that and a repeat for 'Ray is a bigger bullying shit'. He was an objectionable character with protruding teeth, smelly feet and all. We disliked each other immensely. The wheals from the last caning were still evident three weeks later when we broke up for summer holidays.

Schools like this invariably had a cadet corps. The one at this school was the 10th cadet battalion of the London Rifle Brigade. Marching and arms drill was compulsory. Now I was only 4 ft 5 inches at the time and not exactly built for 'shoulder arms' using Boer War 303 Lee Enfield rifles, with me posing a serious risk of causing serious injury to the boy in the rank behind me. I was put in the bugle band which I thoroughly enjoyed, and soon became very proficient.

Learning to swim was unusual to say the least. Breaststroke on the bed every night before sleep time for about 2 weeks. It was still quite cold in early May, but the inevitable happened, the dreaded and fateful night when the housemaster said 'Swimming pool tomorrow. One length.' At 2 p.m. the next day, half a dozen other new boys and I went to the outdoor pool and lined up, completely naked, at the deep end. We were then commanded to 'Jump!' Those that did not were pushed. The length was swum by all, first time. God was I pleased to get out of that cold purgatory. It was a good school academically, but emotionally bankrupt.

The Junior School consisted of eight brick Houses, 'A' to 'H', 50 boys in each and each with 2 masters. Wood block floors smelt of floor polish and disinfectant. Two dormitories with 25 beds head to toe, blue bedspreads, large diameter hot water pipes, cold, almighty cold bathrooms where every morning complete submersion was 'The Wakener.' Thirty minutes' revision of the previous night's one-hour prep, a walk through the cloisters to a dining room which seated 400 boys and a master at the head of each of the 16 tables. To relieve the monotony of the regular breakfasts, fried egg sometimes, apple with cereal sometimes. My slice of buttered bread was cut into small squares, placed under my hot mug of tea to make 'toast', then spread with Marmite brought from home (I had one small jar to last the term). Delicious! The food was healthy, but monotonous: Monday dinner, beef, mashed potatoes, cabbage and rice pudding; Tuesday, cold meat, salad, bread and butter pudding (i.e. white bread soaked in custard and currants); Thursday, beef stew, mashed potato and swede (ugh!). With little variety, the weekly menu rarely altered but, being only just sufficient, it didn't produce fussy eaters.

There was chapel every Sunday morning and evening and a walk 'in crocodile', line astern, outside the school grounds around Bushey. On winter afternoons rugby or soccer, then evening prep. In the summer, cricket, swimming, and evening prep 6:30 to 8 p.m., then 30 minutes free time and bed. Once, just before leaving Junior School to join the Senior School – complete with its imposing clock-tower – I was playing cricket for the House Team. I had bowled out two masters and was opening bat. I stayed in the whole innings, scoring 45 runs. We lost and I was given a lecture for not scoring more! I remember saying to myself, 'Sod the cricket!'

The first film I saw at a cinema was *Good-Bye Mr Chips* with Robert Donat. All the boys in that film came from our school, me included. The trips by bus to Denham Studios fairly close to Bushey were exciting. I was chosen for a dormitory pillow fight scene … that was fun. I was also chosen to play a scene showing boys coming back from holidays. My part involved carrying a suitcase up some steps. I can't have been very convincing until someone put some house bricks in the case. I think I managed to perform OK but must have nearly had a rupture in the process. I often wonder how much money was received for all 30 or 40 boy film extras.

We had three holidays at home each year, three weeks at Easter and Christmas and six weeks in the summer, nearly always spent in Ropley. I remember one only Christmas spent with my paternal grandparents and uncle on the farm: Manor Farm at Walderton in Sussex: and only two summer holidays. These were fine breaks, riding the big shire horses, cutting harvest, milk, fresh full cream straight from the coolers, sometimes a squirt direct from the udder if the milker was feeling like playing tricks.

There were rides on the binders, those clattering, horse drawn machines with their flailing rotors beating the corn down on to the cutters, thence to be tied into sheaves and thrown into the harvested area. Sometimes the binder twine would break, bringing the whole operation to a halt. When all the corn was cut and sheaves stood up into stooks, the men with their pitchforks would throw them on to the horse drawn carts to be taken and built into stacks. Truly labour intensive hard work and poorly paid. At the end of the day in the field, a ride back to the farm, unescorted on the back of one of the massive, shire horses. Those gentle giants knew the way.

The one and only Christmas at the farm in Walderton, I remember a Christmas tree although I can't remember presents. Auntie Flossie, the wife of my father's youngest brother Monty loved to play the piano and insisted I accompany her, singing. Her favourite was a tune famous at the time called 'I passed by your Window one morning in May' sung regularly on the radio (and now kept for all time on YouTube!) by Frances Alda. Flossie's posh accent, which was very similar to Alda's own, was the opposite to mine and I enjoyed myself deliberately pronouncing 'passt' and 'winnder' which annoyed her. 'No, no boy – how dreadful!' My paternal grandmother would have little or nothing to do with her grandchildren, or at least not me. Never a hug, not even a hand held. Grandad, I remember more fondly. A bearded, taciturn but also kind, gentle and very much hen-pecked old man. The two trips down to the farm were truly memorable with the smell of a slipping clutch as we struggled up Harting Hill south of Petersfield in an Austin 7 Ruby. Uncle Monty, who worked on the farm, had a Brough Superior motorcycle in one of the sheds, although I never saw him ride it.

When war broke out, my mother wanted her youngest boy home to avoid the possibility of air raids, Bushey being so close to London, so although only 14 and at a school where most 'A' stream boys went on towards university, I left at the end of the summer term. The quality of education was high and had the war not been on I suppose I would have stayed. So, the end of school came and home I went from that awful place by train from Bushey, via Waterloo. I was dressed in a 'leaving suit', complete with trilby hat, which felt huge, ridiculous and embarrassing. It was thrown from the train window with much glee somewhere near Brooklands, the famous old racetrack. I was pleased to leave. I had no qualifications, but having received a very good education, and the acceptance, mostly without rancour, of imposed strict discipline. This taught the self-discipline that put me in such good stead many times in later life.

**

I. The Kindness of Miss Wynn

There clearly is a poignant connection to Nature and country life, lost to the vast majority of children today, but what strikes one most about this account is the poverty, the emotional and physical loneliness, and the reality of a fatherless upbringing. Stan was to all intents and purposes an only child, such was the age difference between him and his elder siblings. The seeds of this unfortunate set of circumstances were sown not solely in Stan's father's death, nor even in the no-doubt happy realisation of a third child three years after the first two, made by a couple deeply in love and settled with a stable job, good prospects and a good income. Reginald had gone against his parents wishes in marrying his village sweetheart on 15 October 1919. Rather, the precursors to the unfortunate circumstances that befell Mabel Dibben and her young children lie in the decision not to award a war widow's pension. Immediately after the war and into the mid-1920s, as Lewis-Stempel notes (2014: 274–91), public interest in the plight of the former prisoners of war (PoWs) was great. An exhibition of work by PoWs from the Ruhleben camp at the Central Hall in Westminster ran for the 28 days of February 1919 (Pope-Hennessy, 1919), and six hundred PoWs marched to the Cenotaph in 1926. By this time, however, the government faced a difficult problem in respect of PoWs, namely the cost of war pensions. PoW 'death rates in the Twenties and Thirties were five times than that of other veterans' (Lewis-Stempel, 2014: 283), let alone that of the general population. The government denied hundreds of widows such as Mabel Dibben, whose husbands had died in circumstances that could reasonably be attributed at least in part to their PoW experience, War Widows Pensions that would have guaranteed their economic futures.

Any reason not to award the pension that could be found was found. In Reginald Dibben's case, there was no denial of the fact he had suffered as a PoW. There was no denial that his succumbing to the Tuberculosis may have been in part a result of weakness caused by his years of imprisonment. Yet no amount of evidence or affidavits, no amount of public appeal, as evidenced by local newspaper articles about Reginald's case, would suffice. He had been passed fit to join the Metropolitan Police and, perhaps even more than this, he had, so the countering argument went, forgone the opportunity offered immediately to all PoWs on repatriation to apply for a pension on the grounds of brutal treatment through a 'Statement of Extraordinary Treatment by the Enemy of British Prisoner of War.' Most PoWs were in such a hurry to get home that, rather than take the time to fill out the necessary paperwork and then wait two days for a medical board – which would most likely have found in their favour at that time since the government's view on war pensions was quite different to what it became – they instead 'took the alternative: a gratuity of £2, a disclaimer to the effect that the prisoner was not suffering any war-related disability, and off home a.s.a.p.' (Lewis-Stempel, 2014: 278). Yet Reginald had gone to hospital on repatriation, stayed 7 days there, and no evidence of illness was found. He was thus passed medically fit and returned to active service, from which he was finally discharged on 22 April 1920, and having passed the necessary medical to join the Police, entered the police force in August that year. It seems *prima face* that the decision not to award a War Widow's pension was correct.

Like many hundreds of other widows, the result of not being awarded a War Widow's pension was not only grief but considerable poverty for Mabel Dibben and her family. They kept a roof over their head through the kindness of the landlady, Miss Wynn. When she became a police widow, Stan's mother had a pension of 2 pounds 2 shillings (120 pounds in 2016 terms, Historic inflation calculator, website) a month, to raise three children living with her own mother and two brothers in their rented cottage. To afford her own rented cottage next door even at a low rent she was forced to supplement her income working as a maid and cook in the house of one of the local gentry, a Lady Collins (later the wife of Lord Docker, owner of BSA), for a couple of pounds a month, as well as washing glasses in the local pub for 2 pennies an hour.

Stan would later add another pound a week most weeks from playing the trumpet in the dance band aged 15. This made the total household income in 1940, including his 2 pounds (40 shillings) a month from being a grocer's boy at the village shop, approximately 7 pounds 4 shillings (430 pounds in today's terms). That his Uncle was forced to supplement his job as a gamekeeper with other work demonstrates not only that village life had not changed substantially since the 1800s but that the reality of the 'lower' or 'working' classes has changed comparatively little in the many decades since the 1930s. That is, we find then – as so often now – a single parent family getting income from a variety of different jobs and sources and 'just about managing'. The difference between then and now is there was no electricity and no running water, the house being heated and lit by coal, wood and candles, and little or no public transport – much less a motor car.

According to Kelly's Directory of Hampshire of 1911, Ropley's major landowners are listed as follows: Winchester College; Magdalen College, Oxford; H.G. Holt; A.E. Scott of Rotherfield Park; B. Bond and J.C. Knowlman esqrs.; Miss Hagen and Miss Wynn. She lived not far from Gascoigne Lane, in a house whose front bank was regularly lit with glow-worms at night; Stan, with his abiding interest in Nature, was fascinated by them. Miss Wynn had inherited the cottages at Gascoigne Lane as part of a portfolio of properties from her father the Reverend John Wynne (Kelly, 1898: 410). The 1911 directory paints a picture of a village parish where the majority of the population are evidently renting. Although this is some 14 years before Mabel moved back to Ropley, little had changed by 1926. With the increase in traffic and the improvements in the roads, the market for rented property would almost certainly have been no less strong.

There was no money on Mabel's Windebank side of the family, and she had been ostracized by the Dibbens for not allowing Reginald's mother Sarah

Dibben to adopt the eldest grandchild she loved as her own having brought the young boy up, from the time his father had died to the time he left school at 16. In contrast, it seems Stan was the runt of the litter. Having inherited so much property in Ropley as the only daughter of one of the major landowners, Miss Wynn could afford to keep the rent of the cottage at a bare minimum, despite the opportunity of much higher returns at a time when Ropley was increasingly within commuting distance by train of London. Then, with remarkable foresight and generosity, she arranged for a private mortgage on the house (i.e. the two semi-detached cottages once the spinsters who had lived next door died and Mabel's mother and brothers had moved in) in Mabel's name, and for the repayments to be on the interest only. This was on a capital sum of only £400. A slightly smaller sized property on Gascoigne Lane sold for £810,000 in 2017; in today's figures Mabel paid about £26,000 (Rightmove, website; Historical UK inflation, website).

In short, Miss Wynn sold the two cottages to Mabel – on an interest only basis and thus never expecting to see the capital returned – for something approaching 30 times *less* than their actual value. This is an example of E.F. Schumacher's insistence that small communities, with strong human connection, can supportively work not to economic interest but to the interest of other more important measures of success, that transcend a traditional cost-benefit analysis (Schumacher, [1973] 2011: 30–1). Stan would later pay the mortgage off in full, ensuring the house was owned by his mother and preventing it from reverting to the by-then late Miss Wynn's estate – much to the annoyance of the trustee. Unlike Miss Wynn, the trustee had nothing other than an economic return in mind, in perpetuity. On the other hand, human values were clearly uppermost in Miss Wynn's thinking, in an environment where the village community and the people in it were evidently more important to her than the potential economic return.

Without these remarkable acts, it is doubtful Mabel and her youngest son would have been anything other than homeless. Nonetheless, life was still hard. She had gone from a comfortable living as a policeman's wife in London to a widow and single mother in a Hampshire village, cobbling money together to supplement a meagre police widow's pension sufficient to survive. Growing up without a father is bound to have an important effect on a young boy; it is apposite to explore in more depth how these circumstances arose. Even then, tuberculosis was not a disease to which a genuinely fit man in the prime of his life should have succumbed. Reginald was ill with it, on and off, for eighteen months before he died. He could not shake it. As we have already noted, prisoners of war succumbed to illnesses at a rate far higher than not just the normal population but other war veterans. 'In particular they suffered greater tendency to gastro-intestinal problems, bronchitis and enervation' and no serious effort had been made by the government to support them medically (Lewis-Stempel, 2014: 283).

II. The Long Arm of the War

For German prisoners of war interned on the Isle of Man, life was tolerable and they appear to have been well looked after (Richardson, 2013). For British prisoners of war, however, the experience by and large was indeed brutal enough (Moynihan, 2011; Yarnall, 1978), increasingly so as Germany's economy collapsed, to lead to the negative post-war survivability outcomes (Lewis-Stempel, 2014 and Paterson, 2012). Doitscsh notes (1917), the Prisoner of War camps were places of horror and death, and yet Mulford's own (1919) account seems particularly revealing. There was great care and kind treatment by the German medical staff 'who worked like Trojans night and day'. Most orderlies were 'PoW volunteers, 30 for 1000; 1 German doctor' and were 'given several privileges' as Interpreter. Once his hospital had been almost cleared, however, he explains

> I was told by the Doctor my services would be no longer required, so I proceeded to the neighbouring camp of Langensalza [of] 12000 prisoners ... the most unhealthy and sinister camp in Germany ... The Germans were the most brutal and ferocious I ever saw.
>
> In 1915, cholera [it was in fact typhus] broke out with appalling severity and the Germans, terrified, deserted the camp and left the wretched prisoners to their fate. 3000 of them died in all and the rest after 12 months of agony under conditions beyond description, were drafted out to other camps.
>
> By the end of 1916 I was well in touch with my people at home and was receiving a regular supply of food parcels so that starvations with its attendant horrors was spared me.
>
> The Germans [i.e. the local population] [...] were on the whole quite a decent crowd but cowed and tyrannized by the cursed system which held Germany together so long. They had long passed the stage of reflecting on their lot and simply did their duty in a stoical and resigned fashion which made one pity them.

Rockstuhl's German account (2013) provides us with a somewhat different rendering. Relying on a number of academic medical studies that had been undertaken post-war, he notes 'Between 1914 and 1918 27,707 prisoners were located in the camp Langensalza. Six out of every one hundred prisoners died (1,642 fatalities). Many of them died because of spotted fever [typhus], pulmonary tuberculosis, pneumonia, dysentery and cholera' (2013: 43). He further notes that typhus 'was a big problem not only in Langensalza. By July 1915, 21 out of 41 Prisoner of War Camps registered exactly 44,732 cases. 70% of the inmates in Cottbus fell ill, 45% in Langensalza and 40% in Kassel' (2013: 43). In regards to the assertion that the 'German guards, terrified, deserted the camp and left the wretched prisoners to their fate' (above), a somewhat more nuanced view is also provided by Rockstuhl, quoting a study undertaken in 1925 by Gustav Thauß (1925/2006: 273–4), who noted:

> In February 1915 spotted fever [typhus] broke out in the prison camp, a very virulent disease, which was almost unknown in those days in Germany. February 17th the first case was discovered. In fact, by February 27th the newspapers reported that only 13 men got sick with this pandemic disease and that in comparison to 10,000 men being in the camp that slim number gives no reason to be concerned. All officers and men officially engaged in the camp were located at Schwefelbad and Rasenmühle and so on, in order to have as low as possible a contact with the town. Soon the pandemic disease grew alarmingly. Because of the spotted fever diseases, a meeting with representatives of the concerned civilian authorities under the chair of the substitute of the District President, Oberregierungsrat Lewald, took place in the local town hall on Sunday 21 March 1915. At the request of the district president, representatives of the local garrison and the camp headquarters, headed by Oberst von Koppy, attended. Actions to be taken to fight the disease, especially to prevent it being spread among the civilian population, as well as further precautionary directives that should be issued were intensively discussed. Finally, a statement that could be published was agreed by all sides, that there is no reason for the civilian population to be worried.

The announcement was issued at the end of March by the local magistrate (Thauß, 1925: 275, in Rockstuhl, 2013) as follows:

> The residents of Langensalza are aware from previous announcements that the commandant's office of the prisoner camp thankfully strives to put a stop to the spotted fever that has unfortunately broken out in the camp, and especially to prevent it to be spread out to the civilian population. A total isolation of the camp has already failed – apart from anything else – because of the necessity of food supply. However, it is possible for each and every person to avoid direct contact with people working in and around the camp, especially by staying away from the camp and even from the locations where the military people who are on duty in the camp are staying (Rasenmühle, Wiegands Fabrik, Schwefelbad, Unterer Felsenkeller). Attention is especially drawn to the fact that all civilian staff working in the camp kitchen are instructed to wear a yellow brassard [arm band].
>
> Langensalza, 30 March 1915
> Magistrate Wiebeck

It was only once it was realised that the spotted fever was typhus, as opposed to other diseases such as cholera (which did break out also, due to the use of the local river for washing and cooking water) or Meningitis, that the outbreak was brought under control by a thorough de-lousing of the camp; typhus is spread by lice. According to Rockstuhl (2013), the precautions taken to prevent spread to the civilian population were partly successful in that 'only' 385 civilians died, while other deaths at the camp were from wounds received while at the front, exhaustion, pulmonary inflammation, pulmonary tuberculosis, dysentery and insanity, with may who died being later exhumed from the camp cemetery and repatriated after the war. The war's impact evidently extended far beyond the battlefield.

III. Reginald's War in Detail

Reginald had been a groom prior to his enlistment, aged 19, as a Regular soldier into the Hampshire Regiment on 11 September 1913 at Petersfield (and was a Lance Corporal in July prior to deployment). This was ten months before the assassination of Archduke Ferdinand that presaged the descent into world war, and some time before the military and political threat from Germany was widely appreciated among the general public whose attention was focused, if at all, on the distant Second Balkan War. Like many young men before and since, he evidently saw a better prospect of adventure for himself in the Army. In the event there was little adventure to be had in peacetime for he spent all his time with the Regiment's 1st Battalion, which remained in England up until the outbreak of war.

The Battalion left its encampment at Harrow by train for Southampton at twenty minutes past midnight on 22 August 1914 and was shipped to France, arriving at Havre at 11 p.m. on the 23rd. According to the 1st Battalion's War Diary, thirteen hours later it left, again by train, for Le Cateau. There it detrained at 3:30 in the morning of the 25th, whence it 'marched to Solesmes and took up position to cover the retirement of 5th Division' during the retreat to the River Marne. Precisely twelve hours after detraining at Le Cateau, it 'withdrew [from Solesmes] to Braistre, which village was held until midnight, when retirement was continued, in conjunction with the remainder of the 11th Brigade.' Unlike the more widely appreciated static trench warfare that was to follow, the early engagements between the two sides in World War One were very fast-moving, with the 1st Battalion Hampshire Regiment covering the retreat of the British Expeditionary Force from Mons, as the Germany Army pressed further and further Westward.

Twenty-four hours after leaving the train station at Le Cateau, the men were finally able to rest and eat, bivouacked at Le Coquelet. They were soon back in action. Indeed, 26 August, only three days after their arrival in France, was a particularly difficult day as the Battalion fought hard to cover the 11th Brigade's further retreat to Ligny. From 4 a.m. to 3 p.m. that day, the Hampshires ensured the German infantry were unable to advance but they suffered significant casualties in dead and wounded, as a result of heavy machine gun and artillery shrapnel-shell fire. Despite, or perhaps because of their success, the enemy attempted to work behind the 10th Brigade ensconced to the right of the Hampshire's position and so the Battalion was again ordered to withdraw, this time to Ligny itself.

Under further heavy shrapnel fire they held Ligny with gunfire support until 6 p.m. when they withdrew towards Ellincourt. At this point, it appears the Germans had either reached their objective for the day or, as a result of their own difficult experience having been stopped by the British, decided not to press farther forward. If the German infantry advance had been checked at the Battle of Le Cateau, not least as a result of the Hampshire Regiment's efforts, the ferocity of the day's engagements had left its mark on the Battalion with 9 killed, 131 injured, and 42 missing. The injured, including Reginald Dibben who had been shot in the heel, were gathered together along with the commanding officer at Ligny's schoolhouse and church. However, the lack of ambulances and the speed of the withdrawal towards Ellincourt meant that the majority had to be left behind (Atkinson, 1952: 11). They were still in Ligny when the Germans overran the town later that evening. Barely 72 hours after arriving in France, Reginald's fighting war was over, his prisoner war had begun.

According to an account of Jack Probert's experiences, an Australian soldier wounded and captured at Ligny after the Battle of Le Cateau, there followed some seventy-two hours of monotony, apart from being given soup and bread twice a day, the prisoners were largey left alone with the instruction not to leave the buildings they were in. 'A couple of young, overworked German doctors ... appeared regularly to provide morphia and direct orderlies on dressing the wounds of the more seriously injured men' (Probert and Probert, 2001: 59). Four days after their capture, however, they were marched to the railway station, loaded onto cattle trucks and sent on a three-day journey to Germany. By and large, although there was testimony of beatings and shootings and being left until last to be treated (Lewis-Stempel, 2014), and despite the confines of the trucks, it seems injured prisoners were not dealt with too badly. The farther they got from the front, however, the worse the treatment became as the shared experience of war was less likely between prisoner and guard – and local civilians (Lewis-Stempel, 2014: 33–52).

Reginald spent the vast majority of his time at Langensalza, one of the largest and most notorious PoW camps in Germany.[1] The people of Langensalza were themselves not proud of 'their' PoW camp which was in operation between 1914 and 1919. Nonetheless, nearly every family living in Langensalza or in the neighbouring villages were, almost inevitably given its size, directly or indirectly involved in the camp; fathers, grandfathers, children and grandchildren worked as guards. Many prisoners worked from 1916 in local businesses and agriculture within the region and by 1918 this amounted to 1,444 prisoners daily. The first prisoners, 350 Russians including 5 officers, arrived early in the morning on Friday 20 November 1914 (Rockstuhl, 2013: 5–8). According to Alfred Agert (quoted in Rockstuhl, 2013):

During the following few days 4,500 Russian soldiers were unloaded and brought into the camp. Because of their fur caps they cause quite a sensation among the local population. [...] Every barrack was soon filled with 1,000 men. There is mud between the barracks. Already there are vermin. A morgue and a cemetery have already been arranged. Ernst Weiß's mill provides power for the camp. There is a ten-meter-wide safety buffer zone around the camp. Nobody is allowed to enter this buffer zone.

The first PoW died on November 28th, 1914. His name is still known: Malaschenkow, a Russian soldier. Cause of death: suspected dysentery and cardiac insufficiency. A religious service was carried out for him by a Protestant priest. Catholic priests refused to bury prisoners with Russian nationality. The Catholic priest Voigt campaigned for better living conditions for French prisoners, 80 in total. In the town there emerged a growing fear of spotted fever [typhus] spreading into the town. Because of that worry among the inhabitants, the town council held talks with the military office. As a result, the guards were taken out of the local homes and received grouped accommodation around the area of the Rasenmühle.

As the cemetery was no longer big enough, a mass burial site was laid out at 'Langen Rasen'. In total 2,027 prisoners were registered as dead [during the camp's existence]. Causes of death: dysentery, typhus, mental illness and cholera. After cases of cholera became public, the commander of the camp ordered joint isolation for the nurses together with the sick prisoners. After the war ended 240 deceased British PoWs were reburied in Niederzwehren. During the last two years of war prisoners going to work were no longer guarded. More than a few prisoners took that chance to escape. Use of the water from the river Unstrut was forbidden because of the risk of infection. PoWs constructed the road from Alterstedt to Zimmern.

Again, according to Rockstuhl (2013: 8), Langensalza held 28,000 prisoners during the war, of which 12,200 were French, 9,400 were Russian, 3,500 were British, 2,300 were Italian, 180 were Belgian, 100 were Romainian and 27 were from the USA, with a total of 1,642 prisoners dying in Langensalza and buried in its two cemeteries (note the discrepancy between this figure and Agert's significantly higher number). The British did their best to maintain high standards at Langensalza, as an Australian William Barry recalled 'the first that I noticed was the clean and tidy way the Tommies were dressed. Every man wore a blue serge uniform cap with the usual military brass button and everything about them was spick and span and they themselves were the picture of cleanliness' (in Coombes, 2011: 286–7).

IV. Letters Home

Reginald, however, described the conditions in the camp during his stay there rather differently, in a letter written to the Secretary of the Hampshire Regiment's Help Committee published in the regimental journal after his release to an internment camp in neutral Holland on 22 January 1918 (Dibben, 1918).

> 16 March 1918
> Miss Burbury, – Thank you so much for your letter of congratulation. I am very happy indeed to be out of Germany; it really isn't a country for healthy living Englishmen, although of course it suits the Germans. I have only been in two camps in Germany, so I am afraid there is not much I can tell you, only what I have already read in the papers. The last camp I was in, which was Langensalza, was an awful place and considered to be one of the worst camps in the country. In the early part of 1915 something like two thousand died there with typhus, so that will no doubt give you some idea of the place and what it is like. The treatment there is still very bad, especially that of wounded men. From May last year till about September we had something like nine hundred new arrivals; nearly all were wounded. On arriving they were thrown into dirty old barracks without beds or blankets, some even remained there two or three days without food, except that which was given by the English Help Committee; in three months fifty of the nine hundred died, two-thirds from neglect and starvation. I have made a statement here [ie. in Holland] about the camp and the treatment which I hope will be published

in some of the papers, and will, I hope, help to open the eyes of the public, who still do not believe that prisoners of war are being treated badly in Germany.

I could tell you a lot about Germany, if time would permit; all I can do is thank the Committee who supplied the men of the Regiment so well, and I think I can safely say kept us alive, because I do not believe I should ever have come out of Germany without the help of our fine Committee. I hope and trust that they will continue to supply those who are still suffering extreme hardships in the hands of the Huns. Now that we are in Holland we do not require parcels of food and clothing, and I am sure we are all feeling the benefit of good air and fresh food.

Once more thanking the whole of the Committee for their hard work on my behalf during my long stay in Germany.

I beg to remain, yours truly,

R. Dibben, Corpl.

It stands in stark contrast to one received by Reginald's father William Dibben some eight weeks earlier (Harrison, 1918).

Dear Mr Dibben, – I have just arrived [home, having been repatriated] from Germany, and have been partly under the care of your son, as being interpreter to the doctor of the ward that I was in. When I was leaving the ward to come home your son asked me if I would drop you a line to say that he was in the best of health and spirits, and enjoying himself, for which I can vouch. He is a fine, big fellow, and you will be proud of him when he returns, which I hope will not be so long. Corpl. Dibben – for as such he is still – I recognised out there, and still has his stripes up, has quite an easy time of it, and is allowed anywhere in the camp or outside; he has as much freedom as any German that I have seen out there, and a far easier time. All that he has to do is follow the doctor round on his visit at nine o'clock, and sometimes in the afternoon at three o'clock, and interpret for the English prisoners, which were twelve in number while I was there. So, you can imagine what a time he was having. I think this is about all that I have to say, unless there is anything that you wish to ask me

concerning your son, which I shall be only too glad to answer.
With best wishes for a happy New Year.

  I remain, yours very truly,

  C. Harrison.

The difference might be explained in the quite differing perspectives of the authors. Clearly his work in the hospital gave Reginald a comparatively privileged existence that would perhaps have given greater emphasis to his capacity to observe and comment on the privations being suffered in the camp. We note his guesstimate of the number of deaths from typhus corroborates Rockstuhl's and is in contrast to Mulford's above, although he appears to have had a similar experience to the latter as a medical orderly.

Langensalza was a large military camp town which, according to Rockstuhl (2013: 145), was in effect

> a huge military hospital. The following buildings were converted into sickbays: the shooting club clubhouse; coffee house, the Reichshof [with its] sulphur bath facility, the former youth clubhouse on Erfuter Straße, the Logenhaus (today known as the Caritas Hostel), and later on the wool yarn spinning mill, the middle school's sports hall as well as a barracks.

Quoting Backhaus et al, Rockstuhl continues his decription of the PoW camp hospitals as follows.

> Of course, every prison camp comes with a PoW sickbay. Initially the military administration did not plan on sickbays solely for the prisoners. Every camp should have had only one or two barracks for mildly ill prisoners. It was intended that more gravely ill prisoners and the ones with chronic illnesses would be brought [into] into the reserve military hospital. Soon it became apparent that this would not work and that a hospital with entirely its own administration needed to be affiliated to the camps. The Ohrdruf camp had its own sickbay from the start. On the military trainings field, next to the army encampments, stood a nice and very modern military hospital but this only had a capacity of approximately 30 beds. So, it was further enlarged and extended with all kind of barracks and in the end there were some sickbay

divisions built up next to the newly built PoW camp. In Erfurt [again by contrast], there were immediately sickbay barracks constructed next to the prison camp.

Of course, from the beginning while these barracks were built they were determined for the intake of people with internal ailments or who were recovering from surgery. Attached to the barrack wards for surgery cases were the operating theatre and different rooms for bandaging wounds. Additionally, every hospital needed its own administration building with an examination room, furthermore a kitchen with its own pantry, as well as living and sleeping quarters for the German and foreign nursing staff. The many foreign physicians had to be accommodated in the military hospital or as close as possible. So, the sickbays of the different camps are completely different because over the period they diverged according to need. Very important and absolutely necessary is the fact that every hospital had one section with numerous small barrack wards specially for people with infectious diseases.

With the barracks itself it became apparent that hospitals with small barrack wards proved themselves more successful than the ones with one big barrack ward. It is especially for infectious ill people, necessary to have as many small wards as possible separated from one another. The isolation wards barracks built at Ohrdruf and in Langensalza were very exemplary in this respect. Each of that kind of barracks consisted of four completely separated wards with special outside doorways. Every ward has one bigger sick bay with 12 beds, a small one with 4 beds which could also be used as an accommodation for a special warden, its own bathroom and two latrines. The purpose of that is that the people with infectious diseases could not only be easily separated from the other ill people but from one another as well.

In sum, according to this German language account, Reginald may well have been volunteering as a medical orderly in a fairly comprehensive set-up. If the entire town had been turned into a hospital, this may also account for him being given a free pass out of the camp, once his camp rounds were completed. According to the first-hand account of an R. Preston, the prison hospital was called Saxe Thuringia, and was run with considerable efficiency. A bedridden

Australian who was persuaded by his fellow prisoners to say to the German doctor he was unwell was immediately diagnosed with tetanus and put in an isolation ward (Preston, 1980: 28). Prisoners were sent for 'working commandes' either to the Railway yards to shovel coal, to the sugar beet factories or to the salt mines in Bad Rastenberg, 'a dreadful place' (ibid.). The mine also mined gold and used an alluvial system designed by a New Zealander. There is some difference between Reginald's account and Preston's later recollections (1980), who recalled good treatment, usually enough food although the only meat was tinned blood, parcels from home every fortnight, and a 'Red Cross parcel from Denmark now and then', good medical care, and being allowed to strip and wash down after every shift at the mine. 'How wonderful it would be if English miners could end their shift and go home to their families clean and fresh – and this was 1917' (1980: 36).

Preston even had a gentle romance with one of the German girls, Mina, who worked at the mine 'If I was a young girl I could fall in love with you, but as it is I am too old' (1980: 35) he was told, after an embrace and a kiss on the cheek. How complete Preston's account is, however, remains open to question given the passing of the years between the occurrence of the events and the writing up of the account; it is certainly somewhat selective. Harrison's letter above, on the other hand, was written having only just returned home. That being said, he had spent his entire time in the hospital as opposed to the main camp; his perspective is perhaps both somewhat rose-tinted and particular. In addition, writing to a PoW's parents brings with it a responsibility to provide a positive rendition to ease their own suffering.

That Reginald at least witnessed suffering and had to deal with its aftermath is evidenced most poignantly in a letter he wrote to the widow of a private who died under his care.

Kriegsgefangenenlager Langensalza den 20th 12 – 1917

Dear Mrs Murphy,

It is with deepest regret that I write to inform you of the death of your husband Pte J Murphy 7th R. Inns. Fusiliers, who passed away on the 18th inst; He had been very ill for the last month with disentry, he also had a very bad wound which of course made him very weak.

Corpl. Ross and myself were with him when he died, and it was his wish that I should write to you, he asked me to wish you and his dear children good bye.

I have given his personal effects to Corpl. Ross who will take care of them untill he comes home.

Corporal Ross and I send you our united sympathies to you and your family.

I beg to remain

Yours very sincerely

Corporal R Dibben

What is perhaps of most interest from this account is the level of responsibility that evidently befell even regular soldiers once they were PoWs. It would be usual for officers to write letters to widows on the battlefield, but PoW officers were held separately from other ranks. So Reginald assumed the responsibility not only of caring for Pte Murphy but writing the no doubt difficult but necessary letter. Not long after this letter, in January 1918, Reginald was transferred to an internment camp in Holland, from where he would have been among the first to be repatriated after the war ended (Paterson, 2012). He was discharged from active duty in April 1920 and would appear to have stayed on as a Territorial soldier until 10 September 1925.

V. Conclusion: The War Widow

Thankfully Reginald's father William, the tenant farmer, seems to have cared for his widowed daughter-in-law and her children considerably more than his wife, Stan's paternal grandmother. According to one of his great grandchildren, the daughter of his eldest grandson and Stan's older brother Jim, William gave Mabel cash on his regular visits to Petersfield market where they would meet in secret (pers. comm. Sue Rivers with Mark Dibben, Feb. 2018). While this no doubt helped, Mabel still needed to wash dishes in the local pub; it couldn't replace the War Widow's pension. Armed with the knowledge Reginald was a well-respected medical orderly, we can now return by way of a conclusion to the question of Reginald's death and the decision not to award the pension to his widow.

There are some strange aspects to Reginald's case that are hidden in plain sight within the War Widow Pension claim. First, it was noted that on post mortem examination Reginald's lungs were normal. Ordinarily, TB is spread through the air with new cases contracting the disease by inhaling the bacterium that causes it. Despite the arguments made by the awarding committee, it would be highly unlikely that one could have TB in the abdomen and at the same time not have it in the lungs, were it the case that the TB had been contracted from living a city life as a Metropolitan Police Officer. Further, in the months before his death, he had both his testicles removed as they were infected with it, and he died of tubercular meningitis. This means that the disease had taken such a hold that it had spread to the cerebral spinal fluid. It is a horrendous way to die.

In addition, the post mortem examination revealed the TB was also in his bladder. In short, Reginald had urogenital tuberculosis. This is mainly contracted through 'hematogenous spread', i.e. through the sharing of blood either directly or through coming into contact with 'infected pathologic material' (Kulchavenya et al., 2016), such as used bandages. Reginald did say he had inoculations when in Germany. Rockstuhl (2013) lists one of the many causes of death at Langensalza as being pulmonary tuberculosis but as we have already noted Reginald did not die of pulmonary tuberculosis. If, however, needles used for inoculations were not perfectly sterile then he could easily have been injected with TB, however unintentionally. Further, it stands to reason that his work as a medical orderly would have brought him into regular contact with bloodied bandages. TB can remain latent in the body for many, many years before becoming active. In short, it is perfectly possible that his TB could have been contracted in the PoW camp and so it is highly likely that Mabel Dibben was wrongly denied a war widow's pension. Clearly, and as with many hundreds of other cases where War Widow's Pension was denied, the effects of this wrong decision were to reverberate down the decades.

Notes

Very little research has been published on the history of the World War One PoW camp at Langensalza. Only two books exist in German that discuss it, one by Gustav Thauß, *Langansalza als Garnisonsstadt 1704–1922* [*Langensalza as a Garrison Town*] was published in 1925 (reprinted 2006) and a book focused entirely on the prison camp by Harald Rockstuhl, *Gefangenenlager Langensalza 20 November 1914 bis 18. März 1919* [*The Langensalza Prison Camp, 20 November 1914 to 18 March 1919*], published in 2013. The latter book contains the chapter on the camp in Thauß's book. Rockstuhl also had access to some unpublished manuscripts, including that of Alfred Agert and Backhaus A. et al und Kriegsarchiv der Universitätsbibliothek Jena (1918): *Thüringen im Weltkrieg.*

Vaterländisches Kriegsgedenkbuch in Wort und Bild für die thüringischen Staaten [Backhaus A. et al and War Archive of the University library of Jena (1918): *Thuringia during World Wars. Patriotic war memorial book in word and pictures for the States of Thurinia*], Verlag der Literaturwerke Minerva R. Max Lippold, Leipzig, Band 1. We are grateful to Monika Dolles for translating the most pertinent chapters of Rockstuhl's book. These translations are to our knowledge the first time a comprehensive German account of the PoW camps has found its way into the English language; they are therefore an important contribution in themselves.

Stan's cat Tooter (left) and his Mum's cat Ginger. Tooter puss would catch rabbit and bring it back, which would regularly help make ends meet

2

SOCIAL ENTERPRISE
IN EXTREMIS

Corporals of the 1st Battalion, Hampshire Regiment, prior to deployment to France following the commencement of hostilities. Source: Colin Bulleid; Royal Hampshire Regiment Museum, Winchester

I. The Red Cross and the Local Help Committee Associations

Reginald Dibben's March 1918 letter to Miss Burbury, then-Secretary of the Hampshire Regiment Prisoner of War Fund (Dibben, 1918), in which he describes his time in Germany serves to reveal the significance of the 'Help Committees'. Reginald is clearly of the view that without their parcels of food and clothing, he and many thousands like him, would not have survived their incarceration. In comparison with the fighting in the First World War, comparatively little has been written about the PoWs and much less on the Care

Committees and Associations which merit only occasional mention. More has been written about the important role of the Red Cross, but they only contributed one-third of all the relief aid sent to PoWs (*Prisoner of War Journal*, 1918, 12: 137). How and why did the Care Associations and Regimental Prisoner of War Fund Committees come into being, and what can we learn about the nature of social enterprise during the First World War from the study of one example, the Hampshire Regiment, to which Reginald owed his own life?

Probert and Probert (2001: 69) offer some insight.

> At the beginning of the war food and clothing relief was the responsibility of separate Red Cross organisations in each of the Allied countries. There was no centralisation. So British prisoners … received parcels directly from their relatives, from various regimental societies, and even from their 'godmothers' – charitable women who made it a practice to send parcels to British prisoners whose names they had secured from local regimental committees. Not unexpectedly, abuses of the latter occurred – addresses of godmothers were sometimes traded among the prisoners, the market price of the address being determined by the quality of parcels received. Some prisoner received as many as twenty parcels a month from different godmothers, and would auction or sell their contents to less fortunate fellow prisoners … in their early letters, men requested mainly food, tobacco and clothing. Warm clothing and boots were at a premium as the Germans supplied only those in desperate need of replacement clothes.

While this reveals some of the 'entrepreneurial' creativity that ensued to ensure survival on the edge of the world's first experience of industrial warfare, it is also suggestive of the demands being placed on them by the realities in Germany.

PoW Associations sprang up across the UK, either linked officially to named regiments or formed by people either as collectives of individuals linked to towns or counties, or simply by wealthy individuals such as Lady Garvah's Prisoners' Fund (Miss E B Gibbes 99/81/1). This was a spontaneous response to the news that filtered back, quickly, from the Continent of the large numbers of prisoners of war (PoWs) that were being captured. The small entirely independent self-organising associations, funds and help committees who were of sufficient monetary size were eventually collated by law under one nationwide, so-called 'Central Care Committee'. This was made up of representatives from each of the local and regimental Associations; Miss Burbury was the official representative of the Hampshire Regiment Prisoner of War Fund on the Central Prisoner of War Committee. How might we explain the spontaneous self-organising that preceded centralisation?

First, in a time before the National Health Service, local philanthropy to support the poor and needy of a community was commonplace; there was no more impoverished and needy group of individuals than the PoWs languishing in prison camps in Germany, Austria and Turkey. Second, with a large proportion of the male population at war, and thus the vast majority of prisoners being the sons, fathers, husbands or brothers of the women at home, establishing Associations of this sort was a natural response of these women to do something to support their relatives – and even strangers. The Women's Institutes movement sprang up in the UK in 1915 'to revitalise rural communities and encourage women to become more involved in producing food during the First World War' (The Women's Institute, website). It is no coincidence that the care committees and associations were run almost entirely by women, and that one of the most important roles carried out was the organised sending of food parcels. As but one example of the close connection, the first Treasurer of the Women's Institute, Alice Williams, worked for one of the French associations, the French Wounded Emergency Fund, being awarded the Medaille de la Reconnaissance Francaise by the French Government for her work (The Women's Institute, Alice Williams, website).

During the period April 1916 to September 1918, the Australian Red Cross 'furnished free to troops in England and France, and prisoners-of-war, goods and entertainments valued at £192,005 Sterling' (Scott, 1936: 725).

> A department of the Australian Red Cross for the supply of parcels and comforts to Australian prisoners-of-war in Germany was established in London in 1915. Mr Fairbairn was placed in charge of this work. He paid a visit to Switzerland to inspect the methods of the Bureau de Secours aux Prisonitiers de Guerre, and decided to work through that agency as far as possible. The bureau made a special feature of its weekly supplies of bread to prisoners-of-war, and it was found that bread baked in Berne

reached the prisoners in much better condition than that baked in England. The bread sent from Berne to Australian prisoners in Germany cost £18,263. The supplies sent to prisoners in Germany through this bureau reached their destination in 98 per cent of cases. Good working relations were established with the commandants of many prisoners' camps in Germany, who, on the whole, facilitated the processes superintended by the bureau. Mr Fairbairn, however, concluded that the food and clothing supplied to Australian military prisoners were insufficient. He therefore arranged for the sending of extra supplies, which were provided by the Australian Red Cross. It was rather more difficult to ensure that supplies should reach Australian prisoners-of-war in Turkey, but Mr Fairbairn got into touch with the United States embassy in Constantinople, and arranged for the forwarding of money through its instrumentality. After America came into the war in 1917, this channel of communication was closed. During the war, 395,595 parcels of food were sent to Germany, Turkey, Holland, Austria, and Switzerland at an approximate cost to the Red Cross funds of £176,000. As the total number of Australian prisoners-of-war was 4,353, it is evident that the Red Cross exerted itself to send as much food as was permitted by the regulations. In addition to the food supplies, 36,369 parcels of clothing were sent, together with such supplies as tooth brushes, playing cards, tobacco, cigarettes, and-for entomological warfare-insect powder. Further, the Red Cross accepted the responsibility of spending money on behalf of the prisoners, for such permitted articles as were asked for by them; and it had as many as 3,000 private accounts to keep for the maintenance of this very useful service (Scott, 1936: 706–7)

In the early part of the war, the German PoW hospitals were well-supplied and patients reasonably well looked after but, as the war progressed and the blocked took effect so supplies dwindled along with the care (Coombes, 2011). The Red Cross played a very significant part in the support of PoWs, and their part in the war is well documented (see e.g. Coombes, 2011). There is no doubt that the 'parcel system ensured the survival of British and French other-rank captives in Germany, particularly those who were among the 1.5 million prisoners of war working for the German war economy by 1918' (Jones, 2011: 264).

As Grant (2014) notes, however, in the absence of a social welfare system, the First World War saw thousands of charitable organisations spring up in support of life on the home front as well as soldiers and prisoners of war. Almost every single large town appears to have had a war association of some sort. The War Charities Act 1916 was an attempt to bring these charities under some sort of governing body, the Director General of Voluntary Organisations, to prevent fraud.

According to the British Prisoner of War Journal, the rules relating to the types of parcels that could and could not be sent were strict. For example, relatives could send a parcel once a quarter but it had to be through the Post Office, it could not have been packed by an authorised Association, nor could it bear a Red Cross Label (1918, 1: 11). By 1918 the Central Prisoner of War Committee (CPC) had representation on its board of all the authorised Associations, including Miss Burbury, the British Red Cross and the Australian Red Cross (1918, 2: 13). Regimental Associations often worked without subsidy from the CPC (1918, 12: 138). Packing for Australian PoWs was done close to the Old Bank, Headquarters of the CPC, and was overseen by G.A. Stephen, brother of the Bishop of Tasmania. As many of the contents as possible, including jam and biscuits were of Australian origin (1918, 3: 33). All Australian PoWs were corresponded with by a Mrs Chomley, the 'first capture' parcel always included clothing, and all repatriated Australian PoWs came through London to the Australian Red Cross. Caring for PoWs became a massive undertaking with 12,000 parcels being sent to Germany in the Autumn of 1917 alone (1918, 5: 59). To organise distribution of parcels, each of the main camps had their own help committees (1918, 10: 114).

II. Mrs Barlow and the Hampshire Regiment Help Committee

The Hampshire Regiment's help committee or prisoner of war association, entitled the 'Hampshire Regiment Prisoners of War Help Fund' was the main mechanism by which the Regiment's PoWs, among them Reginald Dibben, were supported during the war. Based on the PoW-related entries in the *Royal Hampshire Regiment Journal,** we can discern its growth, its financial and

---

*   The journal entries were found by the volunteer staff of the Hampshire Regiment Museum, copied into Word and forwarded by e-mail without page numbers. We are deeply grateful for this research; it would have been churlish to ask them to

personnel challenges and the ever-increasing amount of work it was asked to carry out as it sought to support an ever-growing number of PoWs. The first entries in the Regimental journal about it are from 1915, and are letters from two officer prisoners of war, telling of the challenges of learning languages and the daily routine of camp life. There is no information as to when the Association was set up, but the March 1916 Issue notes that a Mrs Barlow had been running 'the Fund single-handed'. The April 1915 Issue contains an article entitled 'Rules regarding Correspondence for Prisoners of War'. This provides the first explanation of the organizing system being put in place in the UK to support PoWs, as follows.

The following has been issued by the War Office:

1–Letters, postcards and postal parcels should be addressed as follows: (Name, initials, rank and regiment), British Prisoner of War, in Germany (or Austria–Hungary), c/o General Post Office, Mount Pleasant, London.

When the place where the prisoner is confined is known, the words, 'At …' should be inserted at the beginning of the third line of the address. It is recommended that parcels should not be sent unless the place of confinement is known.

2–Communications should be limited to private and family news and to necessary business communications, and should not be sent too frequently. No references to the naval, military, or political situation, or to naval and military movements and organisations, are allowed. Letters or postcards containing such references will not be delivered.

3–Friends of prisoners of war are advised to send postcards in preference to letters, as postcards are less likely to be delayed. If letters are sent, they should not exceed in length two sides of a sheet of notepaper, and should contain nothing but the sheet of notepaper. Letters and postcards may be written in English (though letters in German are probably delivered more quickly). On no account should the writing be crossed.

4–Letters cannot for the present be accepted for registration.

---

revisit it for pagination. In writing this analysis, therefore, we only refer explicitly to the Issue month.

5–Postage need not be paid either on letters or parcels addressed to British prisoners of war.

6–No letters should be enclosed in parcels, and newspapers must not on any account be sent. So far as is known, there is no other restriction on the contents of parcels; tobacco may be sent and will be admitted duty free, but foodstuffs of a perishable character should not be sent.

7–Remittances can be made by money order to British prisoners of war. No charge is made for commission. Instructions as to how to proceed can be obtained from post offices. The transmission of coin, either in letters or parcels, is expressly prohibited. Postal orders and bank notes should not be sent.

8–Postal parcels will be insured without charge.

9–It must be understood that no guarantee of the delivery of either parcels or letters can be given, and that the War Office accepts no responsibility. In any case considerable delay may take place and failure to receive an acknowledgment should not necessarily be taken as an indication that letters and parcels sent have not been delivered.

10–So far as is known, prisoners of war in Germany are allowed to write letters or postcards from time to time; but they may not always have facilities for doing so, and the fact that no communication is received from them need not give rise to anxiety.

Even at this comparatively early stage, therefore, the War Office looked to at least provide what reassurances it could to relatives both in the attempt to assuage anxiety for PoWs from whom no correspondence was received and also in respect of the practicalities of automatic insurance of parcels. Importantly, there is quite detailed oversight of the process, with strict parameters being set to ensure correspondence could be delivered. There is also clear evidence of censorship for all outgoing mail, even although the word 'censor' itself is not used.

The April 1915 issue also contained an entry on a 'Mr L.J. Austin, FRCS, who was arrested by the Germans on 18 August, after only two days in Belgium' and who had written a book, *My Experiences as a German Prisoner,* detailing his experience of life in the camps which was available for sale for 2 shillings. He had been interred with 1st Hampshire Regiment officers but, unlike the soldiers, as a civilian he had been able to return to England in January 1915. The May 1915 Issue contains an editorial that suggests not only that the Regiment was not confident of knowing the whereabouts of its Non-Commissioned Officers (NCOs) and men, but also that it had concerns for their wellbeing as PoWs. 'Friends or relatives knowing of any NCO's or men of the Regiment who are prisoners of war in Germany are asked to forward the regimental number, rank, name and address of such prisoners to the OC Depot, Hampshire Regiment, Winchester, with a view to some assistance being given them.' The August 1915 Issue provides evidence that those concerns were well founded, in the publication of a letter written on 11 June from a Sgt. H J. Jeffrey, informing the Regiment that another prisoner, a Pte Maynard had only received one parcel since his imprisonment and that, as a result, 'he is the most unfortunate of us here.'

Sgt Jeffrey asks for food and cigarettes for the unfortunate Private, and a shaving kit for himself. Clearly mail from Germany was being received by the Regiment within six weeks. The next PoW entry is in the November Issue, and consists of a second letter from Sgt Jeffrey.

> Sennelager, September 19th
> Madam, – I beg to thank you for the parcels containing shaving kit and comforts.
> Already it has proved very handy, as several of us use it and it is doing yeoman service. All the men of the Regiment are well and cheerful, and deeply grateful for all the Ladies of the Regiment are doing for us. Thanking You again.
> I remain
> Yours very respectfully
> SERGT HJ JEFFERY,
> 1st *Hampshire Regiment.*

Unlike those written by the officers published earlier in the year, which contain no addressee, these letters, from an NCO, begin with 'Dear Madam'; apparently the officers were communicating directly with the Regiment, while the NCOs and men were communicating with Mrs Barlow. It is clear too they were keenly aware of the help and support their female relatives at home were providing.

By March 1916, some sense of the extent and nature of that help becomes apparent. The Fund was supporting 170 men from the Regiment in Germany. The mechanism was that each man was 'adopted' by friends of the Regiment, and receive[d] a parcel weekly.' Some focus had by now been established in that not only had each been sent 'complete outfits of clothing' but, at a total cost of around £30 per month, also a weekly supply of 4 lb of bread. This was through an arrangement with Le Bureau de Secours aux Prisonniers de Guerre in Berne. To the cost of 10 shillings per man monthly, it was also supporting 25 men in Turkey through a separate source, Lady Burghclere's Fund. In Bulgaria, the numbers of PoWs was less clear, but somewhere between 60–120, and support at this point was just beginning with 'a trial parcel [was] being sent to all whose addresses we have [from the] letters [that] have been received from several of the men.

Beyond this, however, the March Issue is mute as to the particular details of the help being provided, noting only that the 'amount expended from the Fund in 1915 was £263 14s 4d, and the balance in hand on 31 December was £155 7s 7d.' This is a not inconsiderable sum of money (£263 is over £24,000 in today's terms; Historical UK inflation, website). It is, however, clear that the size of the task had perhaps understandably outgrown the capabilities of one person. As a result, 'a small working committee has formed itself, consisting of Mrs Barlow, Mrs R.D. Johnston, Capt. HGF Frisby, and Capt. EWN. Wade; Mrs Barlow remaining Hon Secretary.' The entry is written by HGF Frisby, Captain, Hampshire Regiment; the regiment itself has for the first time become directly involved in the care of its NCOs and men.

Mrs Barlow's work continued unabated. According to the June issue of the regimental journal, she interviewed the American Chargé d'Affaires to Bulgaria in London, and discovered that conditions for the prisoners, which once were 'wretched', were now improving. 'The majority of our men are at Philippopolis, where they are under British officers, who are allowed to arrange and manage things more or less in their own way.' The financial burdens on the Fund for the caring for all these men in Bulgaria were eased when a Lady Victoria Herbert, undertook 'to provide for thirty-five men, and [by] Mrs Knowles' Fund, which [had] undertaken sixteen, besides other individual adopters.' That is to say, at this point in the war, the role of wealthy women was not inconsiderable. In addition, the Editor of another military journal, 'Khaki', had 'sent the Fund since January 1st forty-nine cases of provisions, which [were] repacked in 11 lb boxes for men in special need.' June saw an improvement in the level of communication on the ground with prisoners in Bulgaria, thanks to the efforts of Mrs Barlow. The July Issue of the journal was noting that men were now gratefully receiving parcels of food – notably bread through the Bureau De Secours – clothing twice a week and letters once a week.

The Fund was also bolstered with further external support for Hampshire Regiment prisoners from a Lady Burghclere, who was sending through the American Embassy in Turkey 5 shillings per fortnight to the PoWs in Constantinople. The challenges for the Fund in supporting PoWs in Turkey were being exacerbated by the fact that no parcels were getting through, so the Fund itself contributed additional sums so that each man received 5 shillings per week. The plight of Hampshire Regiment PoWs had by now evidently struck a chord among the local people in Hampshire; there were so many donations received it was impossible to print thanks to each donor by name. Further, it was not only civilians who were contributing, the NCO's and male and female clerks of the Army Pay Office in Exeter had, by June, donated a total of £15 (£1,400 in today's terms, Historical UK inflation, website) for Hampshire Regiment PoWs in Germany. Evidently, the Fund was now more explicitly organized, with subscriptions and donations now being primarily sent to 'Captain Frisby, the Treasurer, RMC, Camberley' (i.e. Sandhurst).

Further assistance from private individuals was noted in the September Issue, with additional parcels having begun to be recently sent fortnightly to some of the Hampshire PoWs in Turkey by the aforementioned Lady Herbert. In June a Mrs and Miss Andrews had 'packed the last consignment of clothing for men in Germany, a very considerable undertaking.' This arrived relatively quickly; 'the first acknowledgment of its arrival is to hand (July 30th) from Münster.' The Editor of *Khaki* provided a further generous gift of groceries, Messrs Cadbury provided chocolate, and Messrs Horlick 'two gross tins of lunch tablets.' Private companies were now aware of the needs of the Regiment's PoWs. A further £3 was forthcoming from the Army Pay Office and 'several very generous donations, amounting in all to £20, [were] received from Mrs Faith, whose son, Captain T Faith, is at present serving with one of [the Regiment's] Service battalions.' The wives of soldiers on home guard duty in the UK were sparing thought for the PoWs. These donations allowed the Fund Committee to focus its attention ever more on Bulgaria, sending forty-nine extra parcels to Bulgaria including groceries, soap and towels. Further, on the evidence of men working there indicating they were in particular need of support, 'special boxes containing biscuits, cocoa, potted meat, and milk tablets [being] been sent to Friedricksfeld in Germany, which is the base camp for men sent to work in Russia.'

Meanwhile, the expectations on the organization were by now becoming ever more apparent to the Working Committee. Having only been established to support prisoners from the two Regular Batallions, it was now responsible for all but the 4th Batallion for which a Mrs Bowker had assumed responsibility. As a result, an appeal was made in the September Issue of the Regimental Journal for 'any ladies connected with or friends of the members of our Service and Territorial battalions, who would be willing to "adopt" a prisoner or contribute to the Fund.' Any whose offer was not immediately taken up were put on a 'waiting list' so that as soon as anew prisoner was identified, they would be connected with an adopted 'Mother'. Again, Mrs Barlow appears to have been the driving force behind this initiative, as 'full particulars of the "adoption system" [could] be obtained' from her. The significance of women in the support of PoWs of the Regiment, and indeed more generally, is once more strikingly apparent.

III. Centralisation, and Local Public Appeals for Money

The January 1917 issue records a visit by a Colonel Jackson to Hampshire Regiment PoWs. This visit demonstrates both the extent to which a very different moral code was in operation in World War One than was to exist perhaps ever again, and also just how important parcels from home were in supplementing meals that were described as 'too light'. The next entry relating to the organization of PoW support is to be found in the March Issue. The 'Depot Notes' therein record the thanks of Mrs Middleton and Mrs Beckett to audiences 'at the Regent Theatre during the performances of a recent week, who so generously contributed towards the funds for the Hampshire Regimental Prisoners of War ... The total of money collected was £55.' March was notable for the following article, which was in response to the need to establish a formal Association for the work of the Fund to continue under the new arrangements passed by Parliament and which officially (if not in practice) had came into force on 1 December 1916. All the work of the many and varied funds and help committees in the country were to be amalgamated into a smaller number of Associations. Importantly, each Association was to be of a larger size and, along with the British Red Cross, would have a formal responsibility to send a requisite number of parcels to the men they were responsible for each and every fortnight.

An Appeal to the Men and Women of Hampshire

Lord Selborne, Hon Colonel – Hampshire Regiment, has, in the terms of the following letter, issued a strong appeal to natives and residents of Hampshire to support the fund of the County Regiment, which supplies much needed food and essential comforts to men of the regiment now confined in enemy prison camps. The appeal runs:

'I do not think I need remind you how hard is the fate of British prisoners of war belonging to the Hampshire Regiment in Germany, Bulgaria, and Turkey, or that there is a real danger of their insufficient nourishment. Every battalion which has been on service, whether in Flanders, or in Gallipoli, or in Greece, or in Mesopotamia, has upheld the magnificent traditions of the regiment, and the number of prisoners is comparatively few; but I think you will agree that it should be a point of honour with us to see that the lot of those men is alleviated as far as possible. As you may know, the Hampshire Regiment Prisoners of War Fund has been supplying parcels of food and essential comforts regularly to the men of the regiment. New regulations have now been issued by the Government under which parcels are only allowed to be sent to prisoners of war either through the British Red Cross Society or some authorised Association. There is a strong feeling in Hampshire that the Fund which has been associated with the Hampshire Regiment should continue to be the means of sending parcels to the men of the regiment who are prisoners of war, but to enable this to he done a large sum of money is needed. Three parcels have to be sent every fortnight, costing 6s each, in addition to bread from Switzerland costing 7s per month, so that the cost of maintaining one prisoner of war is £2 3s each month. The total sum which will have to be raised by the Hampshire Regiment Prisoners of War Fund for the ensuing year is £7,500. Permit me to ask you to send a contribution to Major HGF Frisby, Hampshire Regiment, 'Bathurst,' Park Road, Camberley.'

This change in approach, i.e. the establishment of a centrally organized system based in London was in response to the plain fact that, despite the remarkable generosity of the many hundreds of small donors and 'sponsors' of individual PoWs, and despite the 93 so-called Regimental Care Committees established by June 1915, the coverage remained patchy. Not all prisoners were being supported adequately while some were getting too much and the Army was concerned it did not have adequate oversight of the information contained in letters being sent out (Lewis-Stempel, 2014: 90). As the PoW population in enemy hands grew with the progress of the war, so the War Office decided this was placing un-meet-able demands on the self-organised informal funds and societies that had sprung up around the country. The more formalised, we might say corporatised system, in which the emotional responses of individual donors was replaced by a more objective approach, was seen to be the only solution. Certainly, it is clear the Hampshire Fund was well organized, particularly after the Regiment itself became formally involved with the establishment of the Working Committee but, nonetheless and as has been shown, it too was short of the needful in both people and monetary funds. Lord Selborne's intervention was, it turned out, a successful attempt to create the necessary critical mass to be able to continue to support the Hampshire Regiment PoWs directly from the Hampshire community under the new centralized system, by establishing a Hampshire Regiment Prisoner of War Association formally recognized by the War Office in London.

Before the Association was established, however, the contribution of the Fund to the welfare of the PoWs, as well as the logistical challenges it faced, was made starkly clear in an article written by Mrs Barlow as Honorary Secretary in the April 1917 Issue.

> Under the present system three food parcels are sent to each man once a fortnight, and 7 lb of bread weekly. Those who have so kindly assisted in the past by 'adopting' individual prisoners have generously responded to the request that they would now subscribe towards their parcels instead. The parcels have cost on an average 6s each.
>
> During December there was a complete stoppage in Germany of the delivery of all parcels, which resulted in none being received before January 10th, since when we have had 170 acknowledgments, and the men seem, on the whole, well

pleased with the new parcels; we are altering one or two items at their request.

In addition to the parcels the Fund sent, during February and March, ½lb of tobacco and 200 cigarettes to each man. The present regulations permit each man to receive 2 lb of tobacco or 100 cigarettes fortnightly. Any friends and relatives can have a permit to send smokes by applying to the Hon Secretary, Mrs Barlow, 2, Gloucester Walk, Campden Hill, W 8, and it is hoped that they will do so, as there seems to have been some misunderstanding, and the men expected to receive smokes in their parcels. At the present price of food, it is impossible to send any cigarettes in the parcels without reducing the food supply, which of course must not be done.

The dispatch of all parcels is being done at 20, Denman Street, London Bridge, and we shall be glad to hear from anyone who will offer to assist in the packing of the parcels, as after April 1st this will be done entirely by voluntary workers.

During March an appeal has been made to the County by Lord Selborne, on behalf of the Regimental Prisoners of War Fund, and it is hoped that sufficient money will be subscribed to ensure all the prisoners being provided for entirely.

The centralized packing system was clearly working, although Mrs Barlow whose husband was a Lt. Colonel in the Regiment, had moved from Camberley to London fortuitously to be closer to it. Nonetheless, the monetary challenges being faced even with the centralized system had necessitated a switch to an entire volunteer packing force and, as with the local packing arrangements that had existed previously, there was a need for more people. The food situation in Germany was clearly serious and the money problems are evident too in the consequent necessity to arrange 'smokes' separately and this caused consternation among the PoWs who were expecting them, and the bureaucracy of the permit process was not helping. At this stage, too, it was not certain the Hampshire Regiment would have its own Association as the required financials were not yet in place. Despite, or perhaps because of, the new centralized system it seems Mrs Barlow was once again working essentially alone, under difficult circumstances.

Of the parcels themselves, according to the April Issue they were made up as follows, demonstrating the wide variety of products that needed to be sourced, purchased and packed regularly.

CONTENTS OF THREE PARCELS

3 Large Tins Milk	½ lb Cheese
1 lb Tea	½ lb Raisins
1 lb Sugar	2 lb Beef
1 lb Cocoa	1 lb Mutton
1 lb Margarine or Dripping	2 Tins Fish
1 lb Oatmeal (Rolled Oats)	1 lb Biscuits, variety
3 lb Bacon	3 Bits Soap
1 lb Dried Lentils, Peas, or Beans	2 Puddings
2 lb Jam	½ lb Chocolate
A Little Curry Powder	**Total cost 18s**

According to the list of recipients noted in the April Issue, over two hundred Hampshire Regiment prisoners, in over thirty separate camps, had received at least one parcel since December 2016, amounting to over 600 parcels received in total. This does not take into account parcels sent and not yet received, and is astonishing organizational achievement, particularly when set in the context of the 'stoppages' in Germany, and bearing in mind also that the centralized system was packing for all military PoWs, not just the Hampshire Regiment. Despite being the only prisoner listed as being at Langensalza, Reginald Dibben had acknowledged receipt of six since December 2016.

According to the June Issue, the needs of PoWs had by now reached the ear of the 'comforts' fund for the Regular Hampshire Battalions, for it had sent 'over 1,800 parcels of clothing to prisoners of war' since August 1915, along with food parcels. This was in addition to the many tens of thousands of 'comforts' items (including socks, mittens, shirts, candles, Oxo squares, enameled mugs and stationery packets), sent to the troops on the frontline. Meanwhile, the PoW Help Fund, the main subject of this discussion, had been encountering quality problems with the packing of the parcels being sent, and had drafted in 'ladies interested in the Regiment' to support members of the Committee who had taken over the job from 1 April. There was also an increase in the supply of food being sent, with each fortnightly parcel now including a very popular 3 lb of bacon. Since the packing had been done by only one person in February and March, it is not surprising given the range of different items being included and numbers of parcels being sent that there were quality issues. Mrs Barlow had apparently been quick to solve the problem, once she had heard back from prisoners that the parcels were not up to the usual standards. This challenge of food supply and labour was ever-present. Rather than have parcels packed especially for the Hampshire Regiment a further change was made, to a standardised Central Prisoners of War Committee set of parcels with the following contents:

'A' Parcel
1 lb beef 1
½ lb vegetables
1 tin rations
½ lb cheese
½ lb tea
½ lb Nestle's milk
½ lb sugar
½ lb margarine
1 lb jam
1 lb biscuits
1 tin sardines
50 cigarettes

'B' Parcel
1 tin sausages
1 tin herrings
1 tin Oxo cubes or Marmite
1 lb biscuits
½ lb cocoa
½ lb cooked ham
½ lb dripping
1 tin baked beans
½ lb Nestle's milk
1 tin syrup
Knight's carbolic soap
Pepper, salt, mustard
50 cigarettes

'C' Parcel
1 tin beef
1 tin salmon
½ lb ration biscuits
½ lb tin milk
½ lb tea
½ lb sugar
1 tin fruit
1 tin Oxo cubes
1 lb grape nuts or Force
½ lb figs, dates, or chocolate
1 tin potted meat
½ lb margarine or dripping
Small suet pudding
1 piece soap

'D' Parcel
1 tin beef or rations
½ lb ham
1 tin sardines
1 tin baked beans
3 soup squares
½ lb tea
1 lb sugar
2 lb tin milk
2 lb brawn, paté or camp pie
½ lb biscuits
1 lb dripping
½ lb currant biscuits
1 tin marmalade
50 cigarettes

This did not solve all the problems, for the warmer weather had brought the challenge of the bread sent from Berne arriving 'mouldy, and therefore a form of bread-biscuits has been substituted during the summer, which it [was] hoped will [and did] prove more satisfactory.' The War Office, too, were forcing changes for parcels sent to Germany such that it was now 'impossible for friends and relatives to send the extra parcel that was allowed at the commencement of the present scheme.' This meant that Mrs Barlow's cigarette permit service was in much demand, as the only extra now allowed were cigarettes. Prisoners were themselves supporting the cost of this for those families unable to cover the cost themselves, and the June Issue notes in particular that 'owing to the kindness of Captain NE Baxter, himself a prisoner in Germany, we have been able during the past two months to send the full amount permissible to each of the men whose relatives are not able to provide his smokes.'

Not only were the Hampshire Regiment Prisoner of Help War Fund's committee members having to deal with problems in Germany but, again according to the June Issue of the Regimental Journal, Bulgaria too was a continuing source of logistical difficulties. 'There has been a bad block parcels to Bulgaria; but Lieut Gilliland has reported the arrival of 1,200 parcels in the camp in one day, and we hope to hear that many of ours are among them.' Turkey remained problematic also, for even if money sent 'through the kindness of Lady Burghclere seems to be delivered fairly regularly …, [t]here has been a long stoppage of all parcels to Turkey, but we are sending them again now.'

The November Issue contains a 'Report of the Hampshire Regiment P.O.W Help Fund', in which the number of Hampshire PoWs is understood to be '213 in Germany, 76 in Bulgaria, 20 in Turkey (taken in Gallipoli), 49 in Turkey (taken at Gaza).' The switch to the standardized parcels on 11 May were not liked by all prisoners, the original Hampshires-own ones 'having contained more solid food, though less variety.' One advantage of the standardized parcels seems to have been that they got 'the preference in transit' not only in Germany but also at home, where 'the delay in the arrival of the earlier parcels [was] due to our own post office arrangements, over which we had endless trouble.' It seems it perhaps wasn't the enemy that had been causing the most logistical difficulty. By this stage in the initiative, they were receiving over 900 'acknowledgement of parcels received' postcards a month.

Medical parcels were not dealt with by the Central Committee once the system was centralized, but rather by the Hove Invalids Committee Fund, under the care of a

Major Widal, one of the doctors from the camp at Wittenberg. Each case we have reported to them has been very promptly and sympathetically dealt with. ... From the Hove Committee the following medicines etc., have also been despatched: [...] 9400 L.-Cpl. Dibben (to whom we used to send Angier's Emulsion), cod liver oil and malt, and a tonic.

According to Texas State University's Virtual Tour of Pharmacy Artefects (website), Angier's Emulsion was used to treat, in addition to constipation(!), influenza and other respiratory tract infections. Reginald Dibben was clearly suffering from health problems long before he returned to the UK.

Mrs Barlow's efforts earlier in the year in respect of the Bulgarian situation seemed to be paying off, for 'with one exception, every single man got his blanket sent out in November 1916.' The situation in Turkey, on the other hand, was still problematical with very few parcel-acknowledge cards being received and urgent requests 'to send money immediately for the assistance of ... 49 men' were being addressed with the Hampshire PoW Help Committee 'endeavoring to send £1 per month to each of them through the Foreign Office. The cost of this [was] undertaken by the Isle of Wight Territorial Active Service Fund.' Once again, different funds and associations were working together to support individual Regiments' PoWs.

Lord Selborne's Appeal in the March Issue to the men and women of Hampshire for £7,500, to guarantee that the Fund be recognized as a formal Association under the 'corporatising' War Office regulations had met with the necessary response. While they had hoped at the outside to receive £3,000 a year in subscriptions[, t]he actual sums received [were] as follows: –

For the first half of the year	£3,262 12 7
Result of the Appeal circulated throughout the County	£4,070 0 0
For June 1917	£481 16 2
For July 1917	£479 2 10
For August 1917	£379 17 1
For September 1917	£380 18 3

	£9,324 7 8

(The sum for the first half year includes several large sums from funds that had to be closed under the new system.)

The centralization scheme, which also created a minimum size hurdle had required some creative accounting to arrive at the nonetheless remarkable sum of what, in today's terms, would be considerably more than £500,000. It had also potentially cut off donors focused on particular contributions, who could no longer target their philanthropy in the way they had. Still, the local community had dug into its pockets and come up with sufficient money to guarantee the Fund's recognition under the new scheme. The committee, however, sounded a note of caution. 'Though this sum greatly exceeds our expectations, it is only sufficient to meet the expenses of the present year, as the cost of food is now so very great.' Preparations were being made to make another County-wide appeal, and this despite the fact that the contributions of many regular subscribers to the Fund had in fact increased over time. The Committee was particularly grateful to

the following for their quite indefatigable efforts in raising money for the Hampshire Regiment P.O.W. Help Fund: –

Mrs Bell, of Brockenhurst, who has organized all the parishes in the diocese, and started branches at Lymington and Hythe (Southampton).

The Southampton P.O.W. Fund.
Women's Liberal Association, Bournemouth.
The Church Army P.O.W. Fund.
The Isle of Wight Territorial Active Service Fund.
The Army Pay Department, Exeter.
The Mayoress of Londonderry's Fund.
Eling Parish Council.
East Hendred P.O.W. Fund.

These major benefactors to the Fund consisted either of local groups of women in villages and towns, of which it should be noted only Mrs Bell's Brockenhurst, Lymington and Hythe arrangement was the only one actually in Hampshire, or other Army organisations. Again, the extent and inter-connectedness geographically and institutionally, is remarkable. It would be understandable, for example, if a fund based in Northern Ireland paid exclusive attention to the PoWs of the many Irish Regiments who served in the British Army during World War One.

IV. Miss Burbury Takes Over

Mrs Barlow's work with the Committee appears to have come to an end in December 1917, for the Secretary of the Committee in all 1918 correspondence was a Miss Dorothy Burbury of 15 Melbury Road, Kensignton. With the fourth Christmas of the war long past, she provided the February 1918 Issue of the Regimental journal with the 'General Report of the Hampshire Regiment Prisoners of War Fund, 1 February 1918', noting the numbers of prisoners had now reached 233 in Germany, 75 in Bulgaria and 63 in Turkey. As usual, socks were in most demand – from the Germans as well as the PoWs themselves; socks, as well as soap and tobacco seemed to be most likely to be pilfered from the parcels before the prisoners received them. The parcel acknowledgement postcard system was not entirely reliable since many were being stopped by the German authorities on censorship grounds. Nonetheless, from October 1917 to February 1918, 3,201 cards had been received by the fund Committee, which was therefore confident was less than the number of parcels being received by the men. In Bulgaria, parcels were now arriving with greater regularity and were supplemented by monthly money orders. The situation in Turkey, however, had not improved. With the exception of the money sent to the 17 men taken prisoner in Gallipoli through Lady Burghclere's Fund, 'the distribution of which is reported regularly', the Committee had not yet heard of the delivery of any of the money it had sent directly to the other 46 taken in Gaza. The Turkish problem was so great that 'the whole system of despatches of food and money to men in Turkey is being re-organised.'

The change of Secretary brought no change to the financial challenges, with the cost of food parcels and cigarettes rising. While subscriptions to the Fund for the four months October 1917 to the end of January 1918 was over £2,400 (£152,000 at 2017 in today's terms, Historical UK inflation, website), including 'a grant of £180 from the Central Prisoners of War Committee in December ... the present income from subscriptions [would] not meet the increased expenditure.' The news from the Hampshire Regiment Prisoners of War (Regular Bns) Clothing Association, acting 'under authority from the Central Prisoners of War Committee, to whom they are solely responsible for the care, in a clothing sense of all non-commissioned officers and men of the Regular Battalions of the Hampshire Regiment, who are unfortunately in the hands of our enemies as prisoners of war', was rather better. The totals for 1917 of dispatched clothing parcels were 1,748 to Germany, 542 to Bulgaria and 45 to Turkey, with each parcel sent half-yearly containing one complete set of essential clothes as follows:

Boots	pair 1	Vests	2
Shoes	pair 1	Cardigan	1
Socks	pairs 3	Gloves pair	1
Drawers	pairs 2	Towels	2
Shirts	2	Handkerchiefs	3
Trousers	pair 1	Cap	1
Jacket	1		

In addition, one of the parcels sent each year would also include an overcoat and a pair of braces, with each parcel being individually addressed and wrapped in waterproof paper covers; parcels to Bulgaria and Turkey were additionally wrapped in a canvas cover. With regards to clothing, the 'acknowledge postcard' system appeared to be working more effectively, with a 98 per cent return rate. Clothing was just as strictly monitored by the Central Prisoners of War Committee under the auspices of the War Office. On no account could extra be sent beyond the allotted two, even if it were known that a prisoner had not received his parcel, so limited was the clothing available in 1917. Perhaps just in time for Christmas for some, from 15 December 1917 these rules were relaxed slightly, so that 'if the Committee have good reasons to put forward that parcels have not reached their true destination, they may apply for authority from the Central Prisoners of War Committee to send other articles.'

In contrast with the food parcels, the clothing parcels drew on the regular Army clothing supply at the Barracks in Winchester and so no additional funding was required, with all the packing work 'done voluntarily, and for love of the men of the Regiment' from there:

[E]very one of [the parcels] is packed in two covers, each bearing a red cross label pasted on with the address of the man written in block letters, and in addition written in like manner on each of the covering material, paper, or canvas, the latter carefully sewn up and the red cross label stitched on; further, an acknowledgment card is enclosed in the parcel giving the address of the recipient and the contents in detail on the one side, and the address of the individual to whom it is to be returned to at Winchester. Every package for Bulgaria and Turkey requires a separate way bill. The books, records, and work of the Committee have been inspected four times during the year by Travelling Censors from the Central Prisoners of War Committee, and those officers expressed their satisfaction as to the good order and correctness in all, and whose expressions have been verified by letters from the Central Office.

Unlike Mrs Barlow's experiences with the post office earlier in the war, there was 'no hitch in the work with postal authorities' in the UK. This may have been at least in part due to the evidently strict routines put in place with regards to packing and addressing the parcels. Clearly, too, the Central Prisoners of War Committee paid very close attention to the work of the Associations that came under it. By the April 1918 Issue, greater information was available in regards to the prisoners held in Turkey. Mrs Barlow's attempts to 're-organise' matters for the Regiment's PoWs there had had little effect, for the great detail of the account serves only to confirm the difficult circumstances. Food was more likely to be able to be bought from what money could be sent, than it could ever be obtained from parcels – which were still not getting through (see also Paterson, 2012).

V. Ramping-up the Aid to Meet the Ever-increasing Need

Fund raising was a key aspect of the work of the Hampshire Regiment Prisoners of War Fund Committee, and an article in the June 1918 Issue of the Regimental Journal demonstrates completely that genuinely entertaining ways had by now been found to garner additional income.

A charming entertainment, which in all respects was a most gratifying success, was given at the Guildhall, Winchester, on Thursday afternoon, May 23rd, in aid of The Hampshire Regt Prisoners of War Fund. Miss Jean Sterling Mackinlay consented to give a song recital, assisted at the piano by her brother, Mr Kenneth Mackinlay. The young lady is a daughter of Madame Antoinette Sterling (Mrs Mackinlay), the famous American contralto vocalist, who for the last thirty years of her life had her permanent residence in this country. There was a splendidly filled room, there being very few empty seats either on the floor of the hall or in the gallery. The audience included several wounded officers, and about 100 wounded men tickets for the latter being provided by the kindness of friends, many officers of the United States Army were also present, the CO and one or two others being with the Mayor and Mayoress in their private box. NCO's officiated as stewards, under the direction of Major HBO Coddington. The following ladies were programme sellers: Mrs Middleton, Mrs Thurn, Mrs Dolphin, Mrs Stevenson, Mrs Tompson, Miss Andrews, Miss Coddington, Miss D Edmeades, and Miss Westmorland.

In the interval, Colonel Westmorland went on the platform and, on behalf of the Regiment, thanked Miss Jean Sterling Mackinlay, and the audience for rallying in such numbers to help so worthy a purpose. Adding a few words with regard to the Fund, the Colonel said that but for the parcels sent to them, the prisoners of war would be starved. Each parcel now cost 10s, and as they averaged three a fortnight to each man (in Germany and Bulgaria those in Turkish hands are sent money from the Fund), that meant 30s a fortnight each. The parcels last year came to £7,500, and this year they calculated they should want an income of £10,000. The concert was closed by the band playing 'The Star-Spangled Banner,' 'God save the King,' and the Hampshire Regimental Marches. The bookings were in the hands of Messrs Teague and King Ltd who also kindly lent the Broadwood Grand, the result of the concert being that the sum of £161 has been handed over to the Treasurer of the Fund.

What is perhaps most striking about this entry is the number of agreements required for the concert to be put on, all with the understanding that proceeds should go to the Fund. Of course, £161 is over £10,000 in today's terms, while the £10,000 required for 1918 amounts to over £630,000 (Historical UK inflation, website). This is indicative not just of the costs involved but of the very serious nature of the undertakings that the social enterprise – for that is what the Fund was – was responsible for, run by a Committee of half a dozen volunteers.

By August 1918, the number of Hamsphire Regiment PoWs stood at 344 in Germany, 75 in Bulgaria, and in Turkey 14 captured in Gallipoli, 43 captured at Gaza and 45 captured at Kut, making a total excluding officers of 523. The parcels reaching prisoners in Germany were now a very sizeable number, with 4,101 acknowledgment cards having been received by the Fund Committee in the three months since 1 May. This is particularly remarkable since from a number of the camps 'none of the cards may be returned, and from one camp only one may be sent each month.' By this late stage of the war, the parcels seemed to be taking between one and a half and four months to be received. With the very large numbers of prisoners in Germany by this stage, changes were made to facilitate the transport of food parcels, with four larger parcels being sent each month at a cost for food per man, including the bread from Switzerland of £3 7s 6d a month (over £190 in today's terms, Historical UK inflation, website).

It was only at this point in the war that the Fund was able to count the service to Bulgaria a success, the parcel post having reopened in June 1918 and reliably so; six 10 lb parcels were being sent a month, each costing 10s, all of which were received according to the acknowledgement card system. So reliable was the service that the British Help Committee at the Plovdiv camp, asked the Committee to stop sending money and instead send a full complement of parcels. The same could still not be aid of Turkey, with £2 per man per month still be required to be sent through the Geneva Red Cross Society in view of the fact that parcels were still not arriving in any reliable manner.

July and August 1918 had seen two changes, reported in the August Issue of the Regimental Journal, to simplify the care of Hampshire PoWs. On 8 July, the 1/4th Comforts Fund, which had separately been caring for members of that Battalion captured at Kut three years previously, was amalgamated into the Hampshire Regiment PoW Fund 'for the purpose of simplifying the appeals for money for all prisoners of war of the Regiment throughout the county.' Further, from 15 August, it took over responsibility for the Kut prisoners from the Central Prisoners of War Committee itself, so that all prisoners of war of the Regiment, of Regular, Territorial, and Service Battalions were thenceforth in its care. This ensured that there was 'only one Fund in the county sending parcels and money to the prisoners of war of the Regiment, wherever they may be interned.' To facilitate the coordination, two members of the 1/4th Committee were co-opted onto the Fund's Committee. Clearly this was a pragmatic solution to the challenge of ensuring all Hampshire Regiment prisoners were dealt with equally and thus equally effectively. Care of the very sick and disabled in Germany and Bulgaria was, however, retained by the Invalids' Comforts Fund at Hove, who were continuing to deal with their care 'most promptly.' General medicines for the prisoners in Turkey, to cope with malaria and the effects of the heat, such as quinine and opium tablets, were sent in food parcels.

The August Issue of the Regimental Journal reports that the sum of £18 5s (over £1,100 in today's terms, Historical UK inflation, website) was sent to the Hampshire Regiment Prisoners of War Help Fund by twenty seven NCO's and men of the Regiment now interned in Holland, among them Reginald Dibben. The financial concerns were growing ever more pressing, however, with the cost of food parcels continuing to increase and the number of prisoners needing to be cared for also rising. As Dorothy Burbury noted:

> It now costs this Fund close on £20,000 a year to feed the men alone (clothing being provided by the War Office). This is more than double the whole cost of a year ago. To meet this, we are trying to start local funds all over the county, similar to those already doing such splendid work in the New Forest districts. Mrs Middleton, Harestock, Winchester, has most kindly consented to organise the county with a view to collecting funds. Local funds have already started in Winchester, Broughton, and Ringwood, since the last Report was issued.

A second appeal that had been sent around the county in the spring, in anticipation of these challenges had, however, not been as successful. It brought in about £2,500 (over £150,000 in today's terms, Historical UK inflation, website), and though still a sizeable sum it amounted to half that garnered from the first Hampshire-wide appeal the year before. Either there was donation fatigue, or the costs of the war were telling on the people of the county and they were thinking of the future peace.

By November, the financial situation was so severe that Miss Burbury paid special attention to it in an article in that month's Issue dated 13 November, i.e. two days after the cessation of hostilities. '[A] house-to-house collection [was] being made in Winchester, and it [was] hoped that a considerable sum will be collected.' Further, she noted that in response to the spring appeal, £50 had been donated by the 36th Recruit Distribution Battalion, and the Sergeants' Mess of the 53rd (YS) Battalion TR, Hants, had been contributing a monthly basis for cigarettes and tobacco.

> In response to the appeal for funds sent to all battalions last spring, the following sums have been received up to the present:

8th Battalion	(1st instalment)...	£57	14	3
10th „...		£55	4	0
3rd „	(Sergts .)...	£2	1	9
15th		£74	1	4
10th „	(Officers).....	£6	2	6
3rd „...		£100	0	0
8th „	(2nd instalment)...	£57	2	11
17th		£25	0	0

(The above is given in order of receipt.)

The officers and men of the Hampshire Regiment itself were digging deep into their own pockets (£373 amounts to over £23,000 in today's terms), to support their captured colleagues.

Money, however, was not the only problem. Just as the war ended, so the support of prisoners still overseas became more pressing and more difficult. This is not least because the focus was now inexorably turning to simply getting the prisoners home, a logistical exercise of its own sizeable proportions. It was a challenge was to keep track of prisoners as they were first released and then repatriated. From the point of view of the Hampshire PoW Fund, the pressure to get troops back home to their families meant the Committee knew little of the numbers who had arrived home, or indeed where individual PoWs were. The situation in Germany was very chaotic although around 75% of British PoWs in Germany were repatriated by Christmas, far higher than PoWs of other nationalities (Paterson, 2012: 53). Having been sent to Holland in January 1918, Reginald Dibben was one of the first to get back home. This prompted Miss Burbury, the Secretary of the Committee, to put out an appeal to the families asking them to inform her when they knew. Of course, as soon as there were no longer any PoWs, so there was no need for a Fund, and it was wound up on 7 January 1919.

The final period of the war was extremely hectic, for this was the period when, with German's economy almost collapsed, there was perhaps greatest need for support. In the seven months from 1 June 1918 to 7 January 1919 the Fund had spent £9,500 (£604,200 in today's terms). A report appeared in the March 1919 Issue of the Regimental Journal, noting that with a small number of exceptions of individuals supported directly by the Central PoW Committee, all Hampshire Regiment PoWs had been supported entirely by donations from Hampshire and the Isle of Wight and from other interested parties. An amount of money had even been donated to fund a welcome-home party, but 'owing to various difficulties the plan has had to be abandoned' and so the donations, 'together with the balance of the General Fund, which amounts to £240' was handed over to the Hampshire and Isle of Wight Military Aid Fund, which continues to support ex-soldiers of the Royal Hampshire Regiment to this day.

At the national level, following its establishment in December 1916 the Central Prisoner of War Committee in London grew such that it finally employed 700 workers of which 300 were volunteers. These were organised into Departments including Military Records, Office Records, Parcels, Finance, Military Clothing, Special (bread), Journal, and Stores (1918, 12: 151). The administrative costs of the running the CPC were covered by a grant from the War Office, which meant that all donations going through it were able to be sent on to the prisoners. The results achieved were documented in the December issue of the British Prisoners of War Journal as follows (1918, 12: 137–8).

> Total expenditure on supplies to PoWs including the work of all the Care Committees and local Associations throughout the country, amounted to 6.5 million pounds. Close on 9 million food parcels and 800,000 clothing parcels had been dispatched to prisoners. ... One third of the 6.5 million was from the Red Cross & The Order of St John, and two-thirds were directly contributed by the public ... An expenditure of 4 million pounds passed through the books of the Central Committee in the two years of its operations, about 20,000 pounds a day ... 2,500 letters a day were received and the Finance Department alone was dealing with 700 communications a day. During the two years of its existence, it received 178,341 letters containing remittances [to prisoners] amounting to £2,060,978 ... 2.5 million parcels were dispatched from the packing room of the Central Committee alone.

To put some perspective on just the monetary figures of these numbers, setting aside the remarkable feat of organization implicit in the success of the central fund, a two-year expenditure of £4,000,000 pounds in 1918 is the equivalent of £254,400, 000 in today's terms, about £1,272,000 a day, while direct remittances to prisoners through private letters of £2,060,978 is the equivalent of £131,078,200 in today's terms (Historical UK inflation, website).

VI. Conclusion: The Invaluable and Largely Untold 'Good Work' of Women

To conclude, it is clear that until the War Office took over control of PoW parcels in December 1916 through the establishment of its Central Prisoners of War Committee, the Hampshire Regiment's PoW Fund (and we presume all the individual regimental PoW funds across the country) was directly responsible for the care of prisoners in Germany, Turkey and Bulgaria. As the number of prisoners grew, so it actively grew its volunteer force who both provided items for the parcels and packed them. This gave them some staffing issues but these appear to have been quickly addressed. The driving force behind the Hampshire Regt's Association up until December 1916 was self-evidently Mrs Barlow of Camberley whose contribution, the Editor of the Hampshire Regimental Journal recognized in June 1916, was so significant that 'without her we fear our Prisoners would have fared badly – Ed.' Also of note are the large numbers of other donations, particularly of money, not only from private individuals but even other parts of the Army.

The very success of the help committees in identifying a need and doing what they could to meet it overtook the local capacity to meet that need as it grew exponentially; this necessitated a centralised bureaucratic approach. Reginald Dibben's experience of corporatisation, the structuring of small entities into one major unit focused dispassionately on the delivery of certain strategic goals was, as we have seen, unfailingly positive. Even after the War Office centralized parcel packing and dispatch in London, the Fund was still working actively and successfully to secure funding for the Regiment's prisoners and of course pay for the parcels being packed for Hampshire Regiment PoWs centrally in London. Ultimately, and by its own admission, the amount of work became too much, and on this basis the War Office decision to centralize all the hundreds of Associations across the country to one organization was correct. Nonetheless, the sheer numbers of prisoners the Hampshire Regiment Association helped during the war, the sheer numbers of parcels and within that the numbers of individual items sent in, packed up and sent out in the absence prior to December 1916 of any formal support mechanism, can only be seen as a remarkable, nay astonishing achievement.

What is perhaps most clear from this study is the amount of community support for the prisoners of war. For the Hampshire Fund to have raised around £30,000 in less than four years, over £19 million in today's terms, the vast majority from 'the men and women of the county', is significant enough from a largely rural population. When one then considers the Central Prisoner of War Committee figures, which are tantamount to the total funding from across all the UK Funds, the mostly private support of the prisoners of war in World War One is astonishing. This is at a time long before the welfare state, but it perhaps is an indication of the inherent willingness among the population to support those in need even when not personally known to them; a successful welfare state requires significant tax levy from an electorate. It also speaks directly to E.F. Schuamcher's focus on human value and local community being the central pillar of social and, from that, thus economic wellbeing. The role of women in the development and running of not just the Hampshire Regiment Prisoner of War Fund but, indeed, all of the 'help committees' in the country, is of course worthy of note. It would not have happened without their leadership or their dedication to even the smallest detail, which was of course unpaid. They were doing, in Schumacher's concept of it, 'good work'.

In short, there is no doubt the women behind the help committees were providing what he would have described as 'necessary and useful goods and services'. Further their remarkable initiative was 'enabling [them] to use and perfect [their] gifts as good stewards' of the community, and it was '[doing] so in service to, and in cooperation with others' (1980: 3). What is more, they were doing this 'in conditions of human dignity and freedom' ([1973] 2011: 38) from the edge of a war that had denied human dignity and freedom to the people for whom they were doing it. It is thus somewhat difficult to argue against the idea that here too, then, can be found a cumulative beauty in the multiplicity of small actions taken by the (mostly) women of the 'help committees'; small is beautiful even and perhaps all the more so *in extremis* ([1973] 2011). That it was unpaid is of course irrelevant to Schumacher's arguments. What they were doing, therefore, was an example of the epitome of 'good work'; they were attaining 'given ends with the minimum means' ([1973] 2011: 42), making a genuine difference not just to peoples' lives, but to their very chances of living. Without the leadership of women, and the work of women within the help committees, many hundreds of thousands more soldiers would most likely not have returned home.

When his father Reginald died of tubercular meningitis, his mother brought the young family back to No. 1 Gascoigne Lane; no running water or electricity but vegetables from the garden were an important source of food

3

EARLY WORK LIFE

Gilbert St, Ropley.

Harding's Grocers, 1910. Essentially unchanged when Stan worked there in 1940–41, and where he learnt the principles of customer care and true business ethics

1. First Experiences of Work and War

My first job after I left school was on a farm. First day, 4:30 a.m. in early February. I was 14. The farmer was a hard-headed north countryman. I had to let out and feed the chickens and then go up to a 100-acre field which was covered in heaps of manure waiting to be spread. So, I started. After about an hour and spreading two or three heaps of incredibly smelling pig muck, I thought 'My God, I'm going to be doing this for ages.' My education can't have been totally wasted. I timed the spread time of the next heap, counted the remaining heaps, length by breadth of the field, about 300 x 20 minutes ... Oh no! ... 100 hours came up in the sum in the dirt. Fortunately, an adult appeared on the scene and the task seemed less formidable. Mother could not stand the stink when I arrived home ... I bathed in a galvanised bath in the kitchen and changed my job pronto!

I next found work in the grocery/bakery shop up Gascoigne Lane in Ropley. It's not there anymore. It was run by two Harding brothers, Charlie and William. I used to deliver bread and groceries around the village on a tradesman's bike with a large wicker basket in the front. When groceries were done I served in the shop until 4 p.m., then was off with William in a big maroon Chevrolet van, to deliver goods and groceries in the outlying villages, usually arriving back at the shop by 10 p.m. One elderly, wealthy old lady gave me an order including 'black treacle'. 'It must be Fowlers West Indian, young man.' 'I'll do my best, Ma'am, but there is a war on you know.' The lady thought a comment like that from a young upstart was the height of impudence and she said so in a well-educated stentorian voice. She was very angry when on my next visit there was no black treacle. Neither was she amused when I said, 'It was probably on that ship that was reported sunk last week.' The war was a distant thing in the villages then.

Rats in the flour store were a serious problem. The method of control was for me to go up into the loft, bung up all the rat holes in the felt lining under the corrugated iron roof, except one, and beat the felt with a stick. This would force the rats to evacuate their space through the one open hole. Out they would come, running over my feet, squealing and fighting each other, to be grabbed by Ratty, an expert terrier. He would kill them with one bite – a dozen rats and more in quick succession. My reward was a hot baker's twist, platted lengths of dough baked to perfection with real daffodil-yellow butter.

At 15, this baker's boy, cycling around on a tradesman's bike with sweet smelling hot freshly made uncovered bread in the basket, fearlessly watched the Battle of Britain air battles, dog fights as they were then called, between RAF Spitfires and marauding German bombers. They weaved a pattern of bright white trails in the clear azure blue 1940 summer sky, accompanied by staccato bursts of fire from the 8 wing mounted Spitfire's guns and the chatter of return fire from the Luftwaffe Junkers 88s, Dornier bombers and ME 109's. One day I remember seeing a couple of aircraft, mere specs way above, falling away with smoke pouring from them and no parachutes to be seen. I wondered and wondered what happened to the crews. These dogfights were exciting, yet somehow ghostly so vertically distant.

I anxiously awaited my 18th birthday when I could volunteer for flying duty in the RAF. Spitfires.

At about 10:30 one evening, William and I were on our last deliveries and there were a couple of almighty 'crumps'. Two bombs had been dropped not far away, we knew not where. We stopped at our last gate. It was very dark. I stayed in the van and William disappeared up the drive on foot. He was a long time but eventually he came back for more bread. He had fallen into the bomb crater. He couldn't possibly deliver the first lot; they were still in the bomb hole. I remember him as a tall gentleman in every Victorian sense. He allowed me to drive the van a few yards sometimes, 'Not with the engine on of course!' He was as pleased as punch some 12 years later when my motorcycle prowess became well known, and used to tell people, 'I taught him how to drive you know.'

I had by this time procured a nice new Dawes, drop-handle bar racing bike, purchased in Winchester 10 miles away and ridden home. One afternoon on a hot summer day in 1940, a 'dog-fight' took place and a Junkers 88 had been shot down, crashing in a field at West Tisted, and I remember rushing off with adolescent speed on my bicycle to see the remains of the plane and crew.

On arrival at the scene in the corner of a field with lots of trees near-by on that sweet-scented summer day, was the scattered remains of what was once a bomber. A few of the locals had already arrived and had covered up most of the human remains. I say most, because I was looking for the odd, very strictly forbidden souvenir and found a small electric motor alongside a finger, I left it where it was – the finger not the motor – and cycled off home with my memento in my pocket. Dismantled and re-assembled, it stayed in the hall-stand drawer untouched for years after my initial fascination.

Thinking back, I must have been incredibly callous at that tender age, with no feelings for the German crew, doubtless due to the propaganda laced general war reports on the radio and in the daily *News Chronicle* paper. (No television then of course.)

Ropley village hall, decorated with a profusion of paper chains flags and flowers, held dances in aid of the Free French and other causes, on most Saturday nights. My mother was involved in these events by way of preparing sandwiches and being in charge of the cloakrooms. I became quite proficient at the dances of the time, waltz, foxtrot, quickstep, St Bernard waltz, Okey-Cokey and all. On one such occasion the lads and I were standing by the stage, passing comments about the musicians and I said, 'Well the trumpet can't be that difficult with only three valves … I could do that easy.' The trumpet player heard my bragging and said 'OK, play "Cookhouse" at the interval.' I was embarrassed when at interval time he announced that, 'There's a young man about to play for you.' He was so impressed with my 'Cookhouse' that he offered to teach me. Thus, began a relationship with Frank Kendall, an ex-military band cornet player.

He told me he had played in Spain and the USA with Paul Whiteman, and Austria with Marek Weber. He was certainly an expert with great technical ability and within six months I was playing second trumpet alongside him. It was wonderful experience and my sole consuming interest. I began deputising for him when he thought I could cope and he introduced me to his agent in Winchester who ran various small groups and paid 5 shillings a night. Frank said 'Sex is like music: listen, feel, learn, love. Then play.'

2. Mid-Southern Utility Company

16 now, and I had started an apprenticeship with the Mid-Southern Utility Co. who were the electrical distribution people in the area, eventually to become a branch of the Southern Electricity Board. My wage was 10 shillings for a fifty-two and a half-hour week with an extra 6 days a week for my bicycle. On many occasions I would cycle 10 miles to Winchester or one of the local villages to play in a band, cycle home at midnight and be up again at six thirty to cycle the three miles to work in Alresford. It was hard going but rewarding. After a year or so, I discovered that the agent was charging £1 a night for my musical services, (20 shillings to the £1) and still paying me five, but it was 50% of what I was getting for the week's work as an apprentice and a lot easier. It was my first experience of commerce.

I met girls too. I had no experience of talking to them let alone any other activity: I found controlling that ill-disciplined, disobedient male appendage with which I had been blessed, well-nigh impossible. Well, my old grand mother told me to 'find one as easy as an old shoe'. Thus far I have never found one that fitted her description, not even a well-fitting slipper! Betsy, the post-master's daughter, was gorgeous. We used to meet up in the woods and, with much amusement, watch the mating antics of insects and wild life in general. Truly learning about the birds and bees. I got stung once! She was much stronger and more sexually urgent and confident than me. She scared me to death. Her father, the local postmaster, disapproved to such an extent that he visited my mother threatening her with a Sword of Damocles if he heard of further assignations.

It was 1941, and at this time the army was in the area in vast numbers. We entertained some at home. One was the proud owner of a 250 cc over-head valve OK Supreme motorcycle. He was a real motorcycle enthusiast and used to take me for rides. What a thrill. Eventually he taught me to ride it around the garden, around the fruit trees, over the potato patch, doing my best to avoid the hysterically cackling chicken running wild.

The war was well and truly on. Food rationing, 2 oz of butter per person per week, about the same amount of cheese and of course, the national loaf was the sole choice of bread. We were more lucky than many, in that we could shoot pigeons, kill chicken. Even my old cat, Tooter, would bring home the odd rabbit. Vegetables were all home-grown and I spent many hours digging and planting them. Such bliss after those dreadful loveless years at boarding school. Tooter wasn't musical. She used to climb on my shoulder when I was practising and bite lumps out of my ear. Poor puss!

Riding my bike home one Saturday lunchtime, I called into the Shant Inn for a thirst quencher to find all the occupants staring at their half-filled glasses through steamed up hastily donned gas masks. The air raid warning had been given by the Air Raid Precaution (ARP) car rushing past with hand bell ringing. The imbibers had mistaken the warning for a gas attack and were somewhat surprised at this young lad ignoring the warning. I wondered at the time whether I was wrong or were they. Thank goodness I was right. The gas attack warning rattle was never needed.

Cycling home from playing trumpet at a dance in the village hall at Bighton one still tranquil summer night at about 1 a.m., I came to the bridge over the railway line (now the Watercress Line) just east of Ropley station. To my surprise I was commanded to 'Halt! Who goes there?' The Home Guard were on duty. This was the time when an invasion by German troops was anticipated.

'It's me, Jack, you silly old bugger.'

'Who is me? Advance and be recognised or I'll fire.'

Oh God! I dismounted and cautiously moved towards this obviously jittery sentry.

'You could've been shot you know I've got one up the spout. ('Up the spout' meant the gun was loaded.) There's a war on you know and you could easily have been a German parachutist.'

After a few minutes chastisement, I was allowed to proceed. Real Dad's Army stuff.

At night, German bombers would fly overhead, sounding low enough to see. I used to throw stones in the air in the vain hope of hitting one! Sometimes the rat-ta-tat of night fighters would wake us from sleep. On one occasion a bomber released its deadly load a mile up the road in a field trying to get away. Tooter was on my bed and hastily got beneath the covers. A few noisy nights later more bombs came down in a field at Bramdean a couple of miles away as the crow flies.

The electrical work was fine. By the age of 17, I was wiring houses, fixing meters, mending cookers, and connecting the mains to houses. Rural electrification was in full swing and we were busy. My tradesman was a big Canadian who had come over on holiday with his wife in the summer of 1939, and was stuck in the UK unable to get a passage home.

Big Bob Kemp was a good teacher, capable of doing most things electrical as far as the electrical supply industry was concerned. He was given a 600 cc-side valve docile Ariel motorcycle to use as his transport, complete with steel grill on the back for carrying the cash boxes when emptying the 'pay as you go' meters. It was strictly forbidden for me to ride pillion and I was expected to ride my bicycle to the daily work with him. Ha! Some hopes of that. Bob would leave the works yard, with his tools strapped to the rear grill and make for the café up the street. I would join him, have a cup of tea and a bun for the grand price of one old penny. He would remove the tools, I would sit on the grill, the tools would be transferred to the tank and we would proceed to the job with me riding pillion, right foot on the kick start, left foot sharing the rider's foot rest. I rode many hundreds of illegal miles like this. The boss knew of course but did nothing about it. There was a war on and people had much more serious things to worry about than a young lad-riding pillion and enjoying himself, even if there was the risk of falling off and or ruining his manhood. Bob was a good safe rider and never once was there the slightest feeling of insecurity. Bob needed an assistant and I needed the lift! We had fun he and I.

Wiring the Tichborne village hall Bob said, 'I'll take up a floorboard, you go under, I'll drill holes and you can push the wire up through. I'm going to get some fags first.' Two hours later he returned to find wire poking up through some holes but not all of them. 'You there Stan?' A muffled voice replied 'Yes. Where have you been? I've been stuck under here for ages.' My overalls and pants had been pierced by a rusty old nail and I tried to take them off. Imagine Bob's surprise when, in his torch light, he saw my naked backside with pants around my ankles. 'Goddamn Laddie! What are you doing? I suppose I'll have to take up three or four boards to get you out.'

Bob was off work on one very rare occasion and I went to his home for lunch. On opening the front door, at the end of a long hallway was Bob, trousers down, stooped over a large bucket of water, splashing his nether regions. He had used some Sloanes liniment, the potent lotion of the day for pulled muscles, and it had splashed where there was no pulled muscle. His little wife in the kitchen was in hysterics!

The show room door was in a recess off the pavement and next to a lively pub. It was the norm when opening up on Monday morning to scrub the recess and floor mat to remove the stench of urine put there by weekend drinkers. The manager said, 'I'll soon stop that!' He acquired a motorcycle magneto, joined it up to a small electric motor and wired it up to the chrome doorframe. Came Monday morning, no urine stench, and a few minutes after opening a young man came in to report that he had had a shock off the door. The shock wouldn't have hurt him other than give his manhood a jolt. We had no more problems of that nature.

Meter reading was hectic. In town I would read about 200 a day, in the country districts probably 100. No calculators then. Consumption had to be calculated and entered on the customer's meter card. I was reading the meter at Ropley church, which was situated high on the wall in the vestry behind the organ, and meant climbing to see it. The vicar, Rev'd Geldart, came in and was merrily talking to himself when, for fun, I dropped the thick heavy meter reader's book from my great height, making sure that it fell flat to have maximum audible effect. The poor man nearly had a fit and gave me some talking to. We had a bit of a laugh when he phoned to complain to the boss.

I was entrusted with the job of filling the manager's 350 cc Ariel Red Hunter motorcycle, and was allowed to push it down to Hankin's garage having first cleaned and polished it. It wasn't long before I was sitting astride, coasting down and pushing it back. And then of course the obvious; starting it and riding it. The only other motorbike I used to see regularly was a parachutist's folding motorcycle that belonged to the voluminous lady next door. She would use it to get to the shops and would drape her skirt around it as she carefully sat on the saddle. You couldn't see the bike at all, just hear it screaming underneath her as she revved the tiny engine before dropping the clutch and setting off up the road, the engine struggling with the heavy burden. Wheeeeee – neowww – put, put, put, put, put. I lost count how often I saw this spectacle but was in stiches every time.

The Methodist Hall in Broad Street had been taken over by the army. Bob and I were detailed to wire up the boot repair machines and extra lighting.

Situated on top of a ladder inside the hall, I hit my thumb with a hammer resulting in some language I had certainly not learnt at school. The ladder began to shake; I began to wonder if HE was in attendance! On looking down I saw an elderly lady who was demanding my immediate descent. It was too dangerous to stay aloft so down I came and received a very stern lecture about the use of such language in the House of the Lord. 'Do you read your portion of the Good Book every day young man?' 'Oh yes of course' said I. Bob, now an interested bystander, said in his loud Canadian voice 'You Goddam liar', emphasising the second word particularly heavily. The enraged lady, no doubt a respected pillar of society, chased me relentlessly for weeks, which had me crossing the road to avoid her lectures whenever I saw her. If Bob were here now he would still be laughing his head off.

There was no sympathy for those who were plain rude or didn't pay their bills. I remember an ex-Indian Army Colonel who barked 'Come here, boy, when I'm talking to you!' Which received the reply 'Pardon? Are you talking to me? Well you'd better come here then.' Five or six weeks after meter reading, was 'cut-off' time and Bob or I would have the job of collecting or disconnecting. On one occasion, a member of the House of Lords, The Right Honourable the Lord Templemore, was overdue and I was sent around to do the necessary. I strode up the front door of the mansion in Old Alresford, rang the bell and was confronted by the butler. He took one look at me and said in his most arrogant tone of voice 'Tradesmen around the back' my instant reply was 'I'm not a tradesman, I'm an apprentice'. Since no money was forth coming, I did the necessary up the pole, with climbing irons, and disconnected the supply. By the time I got back to the office, there was some heated conversation going on the phone and I was sent back to reconnect. The cheque was there but no reconnection fee so, obeying instructions, the premises remained cut off from the electricity supply and the whole process started again to be eventually sorted out by the chief engineer himself. 'Well-done lad, you were only obeying my instructions'.

This was summer time and harvesting was in full swing. When I had some spare time, I would be in the near-by fields making stooks from the sheaves of corn: No combine harvesters then. My work in the electricity supply industry was classified as a reserved occupation which meant that I would not be conscripted into the armed forces at 18 years of age, as was the norm. Arial dogfights had now become occasional occurrences but my urge to fly Spitfires had not diminished. I volunteered for RAF aircrew, was interviewed and rejected. I knew not why. Imagine my chagrin when no more than two or three days later I received my call-up papers from the Royal Navy. I didn't fancy that one little bit, so I sent them back by return of post with a letter enclosed pointing out that I was in a reserved occupation. The reply was immediate. 'You volunteered for active service. The Senior Service Royal Navy has priority need for electricians. Report immediately to RN barracks Gosport forthwith using the rail passes enclosed or be arrested by the RN police.' Oh God!

The day before my call-up into the RN, I was chasing rats in a cornfield across the 2-inch stubble. They couldn't run as fast as me in those conditions, and one turned and grabbed my ankle through to the bone. On my first days in the Navy, square bashing days, I poured neat iodine into the wound rather than report sick. It healed, but the scar remained for many months and other recruits couldn't understand why I didn't report sick. 'Just for that!' I remember saying. Thinking of rats reminds me of the occasion when cycling home at dead of night from a dance band engagement, I was startled to see in the moonlight, hundreds of the creatures crossing the road en route from one field across the road to another, compelling me to a rapid stop until some minutes later the road was clear. Scary, but atmospheric at the same time!

3. The Navy

The training barracks in Gosport was to some an intimidating place. The first day was spent getting uniforms, service number: that all-important string of digits never to be forgotten, and repeated every payday, 'Cap off! PMX634892 Sir' and generally getting sorted out. On retiring and lights out, I was surprised to hear young men, never before away from home, crying themselves to sleep. For me a disturbing sound, remembering my first nights at boarding school and I took some time in the dead of night trying to give them some comfort and confidence.

The square bashing, the endless marching up and down the parade ground, being bawled at by an instructor, was no problem. My army cadet training at school stood me in good stead and came swimming instruction time I decided that I was a non-swimmer and needed lessons. I was in fact a strong swimmer and accustomed to cold wet purgatory, but yes, swimming was better than square bashing. Came the final lesson and passing out parade, I was classified the most improved rating in the class, with an excellent learning achievement. As part of Gosport training routines was guard duty during the night getting used to 'on board ship' hours and staying awake, with the threat of 'death if caught asleep' emphasised by the instructors, metaphorically speaking of course … I hoped!

I was posted to the shore based electrical school at HMS *Vernon* in Portsmouth. I learnt more about electricity in the 8 weeks here than I had in the previous two and a half years as an apprentice. I was given the rank of 'Wireman', seven days home leave, then told to report back to HMS *Victory* (no, not Nelson's old ship) the barracks in Portsmouth. Here I saw, for the first time in my life, homosexuals, in a group, lots of them! They had been conscripted by age to active service like the rest of us and called into the Royal Navy. The accommodation as on-board navy ships, consisted of 'mess' decks; tables seating about 30 men. There was row upon row of them with provision to sling individual hammocks. At the far end of the mess deck, I noticed two tables different from the rest. These had table cloths, flowers and properly laid out cutlery. I said to a colleague 'What's going on down there?' He explained the homosexual facts of life by telling me in Naval parlance about the 'golden rivet', and said 'Don't get involved with that bunch of queers'. Attitudes were different then and the Navy obviously felt that these men were best kept together ashore until the end of the war. I must say that never once during my time in the service was I ever aware of being approached by another matelot with sex in mind. (Matelot is the French word for sailor, and was used extensively as a slang word for Naval personnel during the war).

The next posting came just two days after my arrival in the barracks and I found myself heading on the train to Liverpool to board the troopship SS *Strathmore*, the pre-war cruise liner. I'd had some misgivings about seasickness, but this ship was so big it could never roll, certainly until well clear of port. It was not until we were a few days out that I learnt of our destination, Malta. It rolled and pitched. God how it tossed about. We were headed due West and my geography told me that we should by now be heading due South.

Not so. We were soon in convoy headed what seemed to me to be all over the place and eventually, after numerous alerts and depth charges going off, the fantastic sight of our destroyer escorts rolling like demented corks, we ourselves, rolling and pitching with waves breaking over the bows. After about 12 days, we were sailing through the Straits of Gibraltar into the calm blue Mediterranean. How enchanting the warm sweet sea air never before experienced and dolphins riding our fluorescent bow wave. Is there really a war on? We continued eastward with warnings of enemy action in the form of radio-controlled bombs and enemy submarines, and eventually entered the bomb battered Grand Harbour in Malta. If memory serves me well some 15 days out of Liverpool. What now, I wondered. At least I hadn't been sick.

Waiting and more waiting. Having a few drinks down the 'Gut' (Straight Street) in the capital Valetta. Waiting. More drinks. Rescuing my drinking partner from the cellar of a bombed house into which he had fallen. He was too far down for me to reach him to pull him out. Only one thing for it. Off with my bell bottom trousers, lower them down to him and haul him out. Then a couple of days in the sick bay with suspected sand fly fever (it wasn't), followed by some work in the bomb-devastated harbour working on ships and ship-to-shore electrical installations. Then, at last, a posting. A motor fishing vessel was leaving for Algiers and I was to report immediately.

This was some trip! A crew of less than a dozen with me, a passenger, a few days out, terrible seas, off the island of Pantellaria at sundown steaming all night and off Pantellaria at dawn. The 'heads' (latrines) were right up for'd. Have you ever tried doing a six-second roller coaster, hanging on with one hand and having a pee with the other, up and down 20 ft waves? I wasn't sea sick but very pleased to arrive in Algiers, where we were billeted in the Lycee (school) close to the Place Emir Abdel Kadder in town.

This was just a short walk from the dockyard where I was to report at 7 o'clock next morning. The walk under the shopping arcade and across the town square with the statue of a man on a horse, and down to the dockyard workshops took about ten minutes, pestered most days by Arab youths for some of our pretty meagre rations. My work was challenging and interesting, repairing and charging batteries, small and very large, servicing electric motors, often rewinding field coils and armatures, again both small through to enormous. The long serving Chief Petty Officer was a man of great knowledge and more importantly to me, the young one, very compassionate and almost fatherly.

A group of us went up to Surcouf, a beach West of Algiers. It was my first experience of going through a swarm of locusts. These huge grasshopper-like creatures, millions of them battering the bus windscreen. On another trip to this beach (it hadn't been long since some of the North Africa troop landings had taken place here), I was sitting with my hands behind my back digging into the sand when I became aware of what was obviously a hand grenade. We all moved, very, very quickly to a safe distance. After some minutes we all slowly crept back to have a close look. The pin had not been removed. No Bang!

One morning I was instructed to go to the Commander in Chief's office to wire up some bells there. After about a month, I was summoned back to his office to rectify a fault. 'When I press this button, my secretary arrives. Fine. When I press this button my Royal Marine sentry appears. Fine. Now, when I press this one'. He demonstrated and there was complete pandemonium. Dozens of navy personnel appeared with all speed. He smiled. At least he had a sense of humour. 'Fix it young man!' A simple fault rectified in minutes, but he still had me walking in fear and trepidation.

Algiers had an outbreak of some sort, Bubonic plague I think it was, the one that devastated London in 1665 and was sorted out by the Great Fire of London. We were unlikely to have a fire of those dimensions in this city, and so we were all inoculated, and it was the most uncomfortable one I had ever experienced. I felt like death for days, heavy limbs like lead, but certainly not excused duties. Here, in my spare time, I was able to start playing trumpet again and playing in a group for officers' mess dances. ENSA, the wartime entertainment group that travelled war zones entertaining troops, arrived on one occasion with one of my trumpet playing idols Nat Gonella. It was some thrill for this young man to hear him perform.

On the 22 November 1944, and 11 months since my arrival here at HMS *Hannibal*, as this base was called, the time came for me to be posted back home to HMS *Vernon* thence to the pre-war girls' college Roedean at Brighton. All the girls had departed, but some of the signs remained much to the amusement of we matelots. 'If you need Matron, Call'. Roedean had been taken over by the Navy to be used as an electrical training school. The comfort enjoyed, after the bunks with the feet in tins of paraffin to deter the bed bugs in Algiers, was much appreciated. The electrical course on gyrocompass, ship's telephones, gun-firing circuits, instrument repeater circuits, certainly did wonders for my ability and general confidence. There is no doubt that forces training is far better than one can get in civilian life was proved to me yet again.

Back to barracks in Portsmouth, now promoted to Leading Wireman, and the wait for my next adventure. It came in the form of the battleship HMS *Nelson*. She was quite old by this time and in refit so there was much work to be done but life on a large battleship reminded me too much of boarding school. Worse, in fact, because you couldn't get anywhere on the ship without the appropriate pass. Thank God it was not to last any more than a few days, for I made a few intentional telephone repair 'errors', such that those officers picking up a demanding phone got a deafening blast in the ear. I was sent back to requalify! The officer in charge asked why on earth I had been sent back. 'Dibben, the percentage you qualified at is such that –' He paused and, most perceptively, realisation dawned. 'Ah you don't like big ships, do you?' to which I replied, 'I don't like big ships, sir.' His reply was immediate and kind. After all, he could have had me charged; intentional damage to a warship was a serious offence. 'Well then, seven days leave and you'll be re-posted.' Rather than report back to Roedean, I was to report to Portsmouth Barracks and then to I knew not where, other than I was to catch a train to Liverpool.

Another troopship, this time to Canada, where I was to commission a Landing Ship Tank (LST) being built at Levis on the opposite side of the St Lawrence to Quebec City. I was there for 11 months and had the time of my life. I was billeted in Canadian navy barracks doing nothing. This was all because I had my trumpet with me, and practising one day laying on my bunk, a loud authoritative voice boomed 'Who's making that God-awful noise up there?' It turned out that the owner of the voice, a Canadian navy officer, had contacts in the city and I soon found myself playing with the local Al Bedard band. Regular gigs at the Salle de Variete in down town Quebec and others further afield. I was in heaven and earning money too, the like of which I had never seen. Having been in Algiers for such a long time, my French was quite good and improved no end there. Both victory days, Europe and Japan were spent there. I could not have found a better place, or people, with which to end my war service. It had to end of course, and eleven months after my arrival, I boarded LST3524 headed down river to Boston and then on to Gibraltar. As we steamed past Quebec, a small launch came alongside to deliver a packet for 'Laddie Dibben'. Al and the band had made a collection for me and presented me with an expensive Tissot watch. I wondered if I would ever see Francoise again. I received a letter from her ending 'mille lecs d'amour' but she forgot to put her address on. I had lent my navy mate $40. 'I'll pay you back.' I never heard from him again either.

This shakedown cruise was fine. The flat-bottomed ship had a strange motion slipping and sliding down the Atlantic rollers. With all the dangers of U-boats and enemy action gone, a new ship with no more than a few teething problems, life was easy. Sailing merrily along on a fine sunny day with stern portholes open, a large Atlantic roller washed over the deck pouring gallons of water into the seamen's quarters. We had been well and truly 'pooped.' It was a rude awakening for those who had imbibed not only their own daily rum ration, but also the tots of others kindly donated. Gibraltar was good. Sailing in dinghies off Algeciras, a bit of shopping for the odd present made easier with the money from my trumpet playing in Canada, some hockey, a few drinks and then off again headed for the Clyde.

The trip back was pleasant enough, although in the middle of the Bay of Biscay I had an experience – which I never forgot. My 21st birthday occurred, and with it an invitation for drinks in the officer's mess. The ship was rolling about quite a lot, and Purser's rum as served to the officers, was a good deal stronger than I had tasted before. After numerous tots, the last thing I remember about my birthday was trying to retrieve a cigarette end, which, in my efforts to deposit in an ashtray, had dropped between loose cushions. Apparently, I was carried down to the gyro compass compartment which I had taken over as my personal sleeping quarters, and didn't wake up until passing Ailsa Craig, the rock one sees when entering the Clyde into Scotland, some 800 miles or so later. Some hangover. Never again! Neat navy rum (neaters) at that time was potent stuff especially for a near teetotaller! That declaration has never been broken to that extent, and in similar circumstances I have always looked for a pouring place other than my gullet.

Thinking back, my residence in the gyro compass room was made in the interest of trumpet practice. Chromatic scales arpeggios, triple tonguing et al. were not appreciated when transmitted up the voice pipe to the wheelhouse and the bridge, and an instruction to desist was soon received. My cure; five or six pairs of socks, clean ones, stuffed up the appropriate orifice. Practicing continued without further complaint. Once at anchor in the Gairloch, along with a few dozen other LSTs, instructions were issued to put these vessels into a state of care and preservation. This became my occupation. After some months LST3524 had been done, then a move to LST3513. This was very frustrating since, as a 'hostilities only' member of the Royal Navy, my desire was demobilisation. Evenings ashore were spent having a couple of beers in Helensburgh or more interestingly, by train to Glasgow and a trip to Barrowland to listen to the Jock McGregor dance band. Very good it was too. I even had the chance to sit in a couple of times. Practising continued in the gyro room.

Demob papers began to come through but never mine. After a very frustrating 10 months, instructions to report to Portsmouth for release from the service came through and Civilian Street was now not far away. My 'To whom it may concern' papers issued on my release, refer to me as 'the backbone of the electrical party' and I must assume that was the reason for the delay in my release. On 16 August 1946, I was once again a civilian, dressed in my service issue civilian suit headed on the train to Ropley.

My war had been always interesting, occasionally very scary, certainly challenging. I had learnt more about electricity than I would have as a civilian apprentice. On occasions it had been dangerous from U boats and bombers. Remembering the time in Algiers when for some weeks the staple diet had consisted mainly of dried egg and gherkins, never again would I be fussy over food. Financially the war service had been disastrous. My Post Office Naval Savings book shows that from issue in 1944, I managed to save £22 (about £870 today), which was my total worldly wealth. Training and experiences had taught me much about self-discipline, and how to accept the status quo without rancour. I had learnt much about the way to 'make do and mend,' of little practical use in this age of designed obsolescence producing products planned to fill the ever-diminishing rubbish tips. Compared to tens of thousands of the armed forces personnel, I had been extremely lucky. It was over and a new life beckoned.

4. Canada as a Civilian, and Back to MSUCo

My apprenticeship still had to be completed by one more year at the Mid-Southern Utility Company, at £1 per week plus the same 6d per week for the use of my bicycle. I did it and got my indentures calling me a fully qualified electrician. I was effectively a full-time electrician and my old mate, Canadian Bob Kemp, was still there not yet able to return home and living with his diminutive wife in Alresford.

The electricity supply industry was soon to be nationalised and this branch came under the new Southern Electricity Board (SEB). I was announced as one of the apprentices of the year and invited to attend the Electricity Board's summer school to be held in Magdalen College in Oxford, chaired by the new SEB boss, Sir Henry Nimmo. The industry was now pretty well a union closed shop. 'To be more efficient'. At last conference day question time, I said that 'I failed to see how it was more efficient, when in my district of Alresford, which had been run efficiently with one chief engineer and his assistant, one electrician, one apprentice and two labourers, we now had, since nationalisation, additional staff of meter readers, van drivers, meter fixers, overhead linesmen, installation inspectors etc etc'. These comments, from a very junior non-union employee, didn't go down at all well, and on my return to work, I was told in no uncertain terms to choose what I wanted to be and join the union! I decided to go back to Canada and see how it was out of uniform.

The plane ticket was 14 weeks' wages, £94 one way. We took off from Northolt airport, (Heathrow was still in its infancy) flying in a DC4, the 4 engined version of the old war time workhorse Dakota. Landing firstly at Shannon to refuel and a meal in the airport. My new acquaintance was a young Irish lad. He complained bitterly to the waitress in the restaurant when served with a miniscule portion of fish after the soup, 'Where's the bloody spuds?' He was soon back to normal after a couple of whiskies and a steak and chips main course. We boarded our freshly refuelled DC4 bound for Gander in Newfoundland at a cruising altitude of 7,000 feet. After about an hour, peering down at the clearly visible white topped waves I had been tossed about on so recently aboard LST3524, it was announced that we were diverting to Reykjavik Iceland due to head winds. The aircraft seemed inadequate. We arrived after a welcome whisky induced nap, had a fantastic never to be forgotten breakfast and my first ever taste of real coffee, and took off again bound for Gander in Newfoundland.

It's mighty cold up there in February. Clearly visible snow-covered Labrador and my confidence was slightly dented when the plane's heating system went haywire. The pilot announced his apologies and said not to worry, it's only another hour or so before we reach Gander. Thank God for the bottle of Irish whisky bought in Shannon airport. By the time we reached Gander, two of the engines were tethered, we were unable to land because of fog and made our way to an emergency landing strip at Mingen in Quebec province. The whisky central heating was working very well, but had a serious effect on my personal navigational ability. The plane repaired, we arrived at our destination Toronto without further ado, some 36 hours after leaving Northolt.

I found accommodation in a hostel, and on the first evening, a request was made by a visitor for a pint of 'O' group blood for his wife in childbirth. It transpired that he didn't have the necessary cash! Without hesitation I volunteered, had a test, gave the blood and to my immense surprise, received $40. My first job was in a car radiator factory soldering copper pipes: easy, boring and I left it after a week. Next job was much better: Northern Electric, wiring a large new factory building in down town Toronto. This was OK except I wasn't doing any wiring. The main task was using a pneumatic drill punching holes through very thick reinforced concrete floors for the electrician to do the wiring.

By this time, I had found digs; a room with a bed, no food nor drink. I was, in late winter, in temperatures 10 to 15 degrees below zero, bloody cold, going down town in a street car (tram) for breakfast before starting work. I found new digs, but they took nearly half my weekly wage of $40. It was certainly less strenuous giving blood. Before I left England, a distant relative asked me to look for her brothers Frank and Bill Humphrys: spelt with a 'y' she said. One was a brick layer the other a barber. She knew not where they were in Canada and I put it out of my mind. One lunch time, I went to a barber and was chatting away, when I suddenly realised the name on the mirror was Bill Humphrys. I said after a few minutes 'Have you heard from your sister Bess lately?' The poor man stopped snipping and said, 'Who the hell are you? I haven't heard from her for more than 20 years'. He went over to see her. It was some reunion I believe. I never saw or heard anything of them again.

At last, spring had melted the snow; it was warm; how I hated the cold! I was playing trumpet again in the odd group and being paid too. The next job was wiring work with Northern Electric in the big telephone exchange in Adelaide Street I think it was. This was more like it. I'd met Helen too; gorgeous. I'd not had a girlfriend since 1942/3 and she eventually became my sister-in-law in a successful and lifelong marriage. News of their affair reached me when I was in Algiers and I was not a happy matelot at that time. Now Helen, a real dusky beauty, who had a red rose in her hair the first time I saw her, came from Jackson's Point not very far from Toronto. She, like me, was in digs and we had many happy times together. Things were fine I thought. She went home one-week end and never came back.

I phoned Al Bedard in Quebec City hoping that I might make a move back to where I had had so many happy times during the war such a short time ago. 'Sorry Laddie, there's only work here for French Canadians now.'

I caught a train to New York to see a few big bands and had a ball. Les Brown and his 'band of renown' at Birdland, a very young and up and coming Frank Sinatra singing with one of the Dorsey Brothers bands complete with organised screaming teenage fans, Duke Ellington, trips down 52nd street to visit the numerous clubs where every night the best jazz musicians like Coleman Hawkins and Billie Holiday were performing. One evening Dizzie Gillespie was playing what was the new Be-Bop style, which to me was a screaming unmelodious cacophony. I didn't like that at all; not tuneful enough for me. Now Harry James, my favourite trumpet player, was a different story altogether.

A week or so later saw me on board the SS *Ernie Pyle*, a former liberty ship bound for Southampton, and spent much of the pleasant voyage playing trumpet on deck to some American students en route to Europe. Great, slightly inebriated fun. I arrived in England with not enough cash to buy a rail ticket and hitched lifts home to Ropley. The Southern Electricity Board was looking for staff and I started where I had left off.

My trumpet playing was my chief interest, and gigs all over the county came on a regular basis; Alresford, Alton, Petersfield, Midhurst town hall and most of the village ones too, not to forget playing in a band in the Winchester Lido formed mainly from musicians in the King's Royal Rifle Brigade I think it was, stationed in the town. Good experience this … I was enjoying life, riding the Southern Electricity Board Ariel motorcycles in my own right and owning firstly a BSA C11G, a small 250 cc side valve, which was very quickly worn out and replaced by a 350 cc overhead valve MAC Velocette. It was my pride and joy resulting in dire warnings of death from the village locals and family. I still remember the registration number AMW 137.

The Velocette became my transport with trumpet on my back to my dance band work, so much easier than cycling home at midnight, often in excess of 12 miles, and motorcycling soon became my hobby after joining the Alton and District Motorcycle Club. Saturday afternoon football in the Ropley village team soon became un-interesting, with club nights on Tuesdays and club-organised events at weekends. A Lands End run, map reading events, marking trials sections, where competitors were penalised for putting a foot on the ground or stopping in a special section of usually wooded area, and going to scrambles (now known as Moto-Cross), whetted my appetite for competition. My Velocette was really unsuitable for trials even with its rear tyre replaced with the larger spare tyre from a relative's car, and was with some reluctance replaced with a proper trials bike, a G3LC Matchless. Now I was having fun!

After some fairly good performances I was introduced to Ralph Venables, the doyen of trials reporters for many years. He used me on occasions to accompany Dick Kemp, a local rider of repute and a works supported Royal Enfield man, to try out trials sections for events he was organising. He would ask me to keep riding through his constantly changing section until I fell off: it would then be Dick's turn to ride through until he fell off. Thus, was a section born.

I got to know some ex-army despatch riders who had formed a trick riding team and had fun practising with them. Top man on a pyramid of riders on two machines, riding solo side saddle with right foot on left footrest and right hand holding left side of the handlebar. Another stunt was the rein ride. Here, the rider stands on the saddle steering the machine holding rope tied to the handlebar necessitating a fixed throttle. Fine in a flat field, not so good when performing at a horticultural show with the crowd surrounding a sloping enclosure. The throttle was set to plonk slowly up the slope and was of course much too quick going down. The turn at the bottom gave the seated audience a bit of a fright and me a bent Matchless and dented ego. It was good too to attend the Speedway final at Wembley Stadium doing the same thing, but this time not falling off.

Summer 1949 came and a club run to the Isle of Man TT races. I had listened enthralled to Graham Walker, father of Murray Walker of F1 fame, giving radio commentary on the TT races in his never to be forgotten gravelly voice. It was magic to my ears. I went again in 1950, and did a few mad Sunday laps of the course when the roads were open, and I was hooked. Restless on return to work after the holiday of my life in Canada, a change was needed. Without risk, I would stay as I was, without adventure I would stay parochial. Time to move on.

***

I. Ropley – Village Business in a Time of War

This was a time before supermarkets and before mass movement of people by car; people still walked to the shops. This meant that village shops assumed tremendous significance for local communities. Ropley's history dates back to the Bronze Age. It was on the Pilgrim's Way between London and Canterbury, and had a long history of being self-supporting. The population of Ropley parish being 1,090 in 1932 and while, by the outbreak of World War Two, it had a growing commuter community working in Alresford and Alton (Ropley, website), its main industry was still agriculture. There were two village shops, one in Ropley, and the other in Ropley Dean, the hamlet that had grown up around the railway station. This meant that each of the two shops were likely supporting upwards of 400 people. The shop Stan was employed in at 15 years of age, Hardings, was in existence at least in 1910, as the photograph on the front cover attests to, but it seems to date back farther than that.

Although there are two bakers in Ropley listed (with no street names) in the Post Office Directory of 1855 (Kelly, 1855: 128), T. Purver and W. Hunt, only Mr Hunt was also a grocer (and tailor). By the 1898 edition of Kelly's Directory of Hampshire (the publisher of the previous Post Office Directory who had assumed naming rights), there was only one grocer and baker (and draper) in Ropley, Read Bros listed in Gilbert St. (Kelly, 1898: 410). By the 1911 edition (Kelly, 1911: 481–2), Stan's grandfather William is listed as a farmer in Ropley, and so too a Mr William Harding at Chases Farm. Also listed are

Harding Bros, Grocers, Gilbert St. (adjacent to Chases farm). In 1911, there are 31 private residences listed and 62 commercial enterprises. Of these, 19 are farmers, 2 are poultry breeders, 3 purveyors of agricultural machinery and 'parts', 1 'agricultural machinery owner', 4 hosteliers of various sorts (including the Chequers Inn), 3 grocers, 2 builders, 1 timber merchant, 1 coal merchant, 1 bootmaker, 1 plumber, 2 bicycle retailers and repairers, 1 blacksmith, 1 saddler, 1 steam thrashing machine manufacturer, 1 motor engineer, along with assorted other professions such churchmen, physicians, and council inspectors.

At North Farm, Stan was earning 7 shillings and 6 pence a week (when the average adult wage was 5 pounds), but muck-spreading and feeding chickens paled after only a couple of months. For example, he got into trouble for letting the chickens out by mistake and had to spend an hour rounding them all up again for market. On his way home one day he was passing Hardings the grocers in the village, called in and asked if there was a job. He was in luck. The elder brother, Charlie kept the shop while his brother William did the deliveries. Stan was earning the same as he was at the farm but found this job far more congenial. Adding up long triple-columns of goods ordered in pounds, shillings and pence to determine the amount owed by a customer was straightforward enough. To do this one is working in three bases at the same time, not only the now-standard base 10 multiples we find today in the pounds and pence currency (ie. 100 pennies in the pound with the pound itself in base 10), but also bases 20 (shillings in the pound) and 12 (pence in the shilling; 240 pence in the pound). To be able to run one's finger down a list of takings and put the answer straight in at the bottom is a task of mental arithmetic likely impossible for the vast majority today, but it was taught at the RMIB as a matter of course. Long hours were spent learning how to do it, and practicing it. When Charlie Harding saw Stan doing this he was impressed, 'That's good, boy!' Such an ability was not usual for a 14-year-old village lad, and certainly not one who'd just wandered in off a farm. He raised his pay to 10 shillings, knowing he could trust him to do more than stack shelves.

At the time of Stan's employment at Hardings, the bread oven was quite old with the so-called 'bakehouse' and store in the back half of the ground floor of the building and the grocers in the front half. Since Read Bros are listed as grocers in Gilbert St. in 1898, it is fair to assume the Harding Bros bought the business. Charlie Harding lived above the business while William lived in Ropley Dean. Since Harding does not appear as a Ropley entry in the 1898 Kelly's Directory, it is difficult to determine with any accuracy the connection if any between William Harding the farmer in Gilbert St. and William and Charlie Harding's shop fifty yards up the road. However, since the fresh vegetables sold in the shop were locally sourced, it seems probable that the two businesses were in some way related.

It is however clear that Harding Bros served a local clientele, some of whom were undoubtedly wealthy but many of whom were farm workers and other labourers living in accommodation owned by the major landowners. Even at the outbreak of war when Stan joined the business (Feb. 1940), the opportunity for their customers to make regular trips into the local towns for groceries was slight; there remained a close reliance on the business by the residents of the village. With conscription for National Service in 1939 leaving the villages almost without adult men, this reliance will have only increased. The importance of the local grocer for local communities was such that, along with other trades such as electricians in the electricity supply industry, theirs was a reserved occupation exempt from being called up. All this was immediately evident in the fact that the Harding Bros shop itself was always busy throughout the day. In addition, Stan spent every morning delivering fresh bread around the village on the shop's bicycle, and he and William spent three afternoons and evenings a week delivering groceries to customers unable to walk to the shop from the farthest reaches of the village and its environs. They often did not get back to the shop until half past ten at night.

With such a reliant and reliable customer base, a view informed by 21st century marketing wisdom would most likely suggest that the Harding Bros had no need to pay much attention to developing or maintaining good customer relations. However, like many of their fellow grocers at this time, the brothers took the opposite view and paid great attention to their customers' needs. This was in terms of ensuring reliability of the products sold and their continuity of supply as far as possible, even in wartime, as well as the timely reliability of delivery to those customers unable to come into the shop. Without this supply, people could literally go hungry. Stan quickly understood that, with this reliance on the business, there came a responsibility not to extract maximum profit from a customer base unable to shop elsewhere. To do so would have been to take advantage of the situation and inflict unnecessary pain on local people of limited means. Furthermore, it never occurred to them to up the prices. Living in the village themselves, profit came some way down their list of priorities; the focus was on adequate profit sufficient to make a living and maintain the business, not excessive profit for its own sake or for single-minded personal gain. Despite the oligipolistic nature of the local grocery industry, the focus was unremittingly on customer service. This was a lesson Stan never forgot.

II. Rural Electrification – The Case of MSUCo

The historiography of the electrical utility companies 'unfortunately resembles that of electrification, in that the rural dimension has been largely ignored' (Brassley et al., 2017a: fn 40). While there has been work done that a) investigates the market behaviour of local utilities at the beginning of the gasification and electrification of the UK (e.g. Millward, 1991); b) recognises that electrification was not universally welcomed (Luckin, 1991); and c) examines the development of the industry around the political innovation that was the Central Electricity Board (Hannah, 1979), there has only been one study of the electrification of an area of the UK, namely Moore-Colyer's study of rural Wales (2016). Yet, while it recognises the importance of small utility companies in the process, even this is largely focused on the various companies' responses to Legislation and their relationship to government. As Brassley et al. observe (2016b),

> there has hitherto been little further academic investigation of this vast, protracted, and sometimes contested undertaking. We know little about the timing or geography of rural electrification, about the providers, beneficiaries or indeed losers. The decision-making process that led to electrification remains unclear: how much local input was there? When, and to what extent, did local authorities become important players? [...] To what extent were relevant Whitehall departments such as the Ministry of Agriculture able to influence decisions, or did policy statements such as the Scott Report of 1942 remain largely aspirational?

In other words, an in-depth study of one electrical company during this period is called for, since it may provide useful insight into these questions – especially when furnished with an inside account. If the company under study was also responsible for the electrification of the many army camps that sprang up in the South of England prior to D-Day, we may also glean some insight into the nature of the relationship between private utility companies and the coalition war government in enabling the war effort.

Brassley et al. give a thorough summary of the industry during the 1930s and 1940s as follows (2017b):

> The national grid was completed in 1933, but, in the words of the McGowan Committee in 1936, 'the problems arising in connection with distribution are entirely different in character from, and far more complex than, those arising in connection with generation.' They were later described as 'almost chaotic', and arose from the large number of electricity undertakings, of very different sizes, and the associated variability in tariffs and charging systems, which was one of the main reasons, it was generally felt, holding back growth in demand, especially for the use of electricity for heating and power. The Second World War led to further rationalisation and concentration. A national voltage was established in 1945, and a report produced (probably for internal use) within the Ministry of Agriculture in September of that year discussed 'the belief that electricity is a social service which should be provided by right to every citizen', although it noted that 'there may be some justification for this opinion but the satisfaction of such a demand will depend on the readiness of the urban population to bear part of the cost of distributing electricity to rural areas.' The same report noted that while the private undertakings had distributed 54 per cent of their surpluses on interest and dividend payments in 1937, the public companies had only needed to use 27 per cent of their surpluses for interest payments and were therefore in a much better position to expand services.

The Mid-Southern Utility Company was one of the many hundreds of utility companies that Brassley et al. (2017) refer to, and that sprang up in the UK to take advantage of the new technologies of gas and, later, electricity (Hannah, 1979). When Stan joined as an apprentice on 5 May 1941, his sixteenth birthday, according to the Directors Minutes Books*, it had already

---

* The MSUCo Directors Minutes Books are held at the Hampshire Records Office and were consulted there in January 2016 and May 2018. The following account is based on the information contained therein. The Minute Book consulted were, by library catalogue number, 19M65/B1 – 1872–1881, B25 – 1937–39, B26 – 1939–41, B27 – 1941–44 and B28 – 1946–49 (www. http://calm.hants.gov.uk).

been in operation for 69 years, having been established in January 1872 with John Aplon in the Chair, and two others Mr Frederick Eggar and a Mr John Lightfoot to take advantage of gas supply opportunities in and around Aldershot in Hampshire. Thus, its focus, unlike many who were city-based, was on a largely rural part of the country. This meant it was not so heavily subject to the pressures of municipal (ie. town council-owned) competition. The minutes of the company throughout these years show a business growing substantially with a steady flow of contracts and a constant redistribution of shares as individuals came and went and as the business profits grew. By 1937 the business had grown to such an extent that even the minutes (though not the accounts) were separated into Districts.

Even by 1937, according to the Engineer's Report within the minutes, the vast majority of the work was still gas installation. By 1940 there was very significant growth in revenue, due at least in part to the demand for electrification of army camps. Electricity revenue in 1937 amounted to £187,119 while in 1941 these had risen to £323,333. The electricity distribution network was developed sufficiently to make electrification of the rural towns and villages cost-effective. Gross profit for the two years, £80,330 and £54,293 respectively, suggests a large increase in costs but it was only in 1938 that the business factored in depreciation.

Gas supply to the towns was still a sizeable part of the business, however, and profits there also increased, from £23,201 in 1937 to £34,192 in 1941. That said, electricity was the main growth area. The budget for 1941 forecast a 17% increase in sales of units of electricity over 1940, and this was achieved. The increased growth in the retail electricity market yielded small increases in profit from £42,971 in 1938 to the £54,293 of 1941 (£3 million pounds in today's terms, Historical UK inflation, website). The decision to invest further in electricity supply was based on the calculations of MSUCo's Chief Engineer who argued to the board at a meeting on 1 May 1941 that a 34.7% per annum return could be realistically achieved. This was based on a connection cost per new consumer of £96 and a forecast income from that connection of £25 per annum. The company expected to see a profit from each new connection within 4 years and a minimum annual return of 25%. Despite the infrastructure costs associated with it, electricity supply away from the major conurbations was now reliably making money.

At the time Stan joined the company as an electrical wireman apprentice in No.6 District Alresford on 5 shillings a week, salaries of the Electrical

Department amounted to £11,500 per annum (around £642,000 today). In fact, the business immediately pre-war and during the war under J.A. Braddock was paying what would be regarded today as comparatively small directors' salaries of £702 (around £39,000 today) in 1939 and, with exceptional war expenditure costs to cover bomb damage of £4,844, this had fallen slightly to £635 (around £35,500 today) by 1941. Throughout this period, the business was continuing to pay £500 (around £25,700 today) per year to the executors of the original founders. The directors also agreed Stan's wage for 1941 would be £12 whereas his boss, the area electrical engineer Mr Duffy, would be paid £310. The company's chief engineer was paid £680, while the company's accountants, Deloitte, Plender, Griffiths & Co. were paid £800 a year for their work.

All in all, these sums were sufficient to cause the directors concern in terms of their capacity to remain a private company in the face of growing calls for nationalisation of the industry. A special meeting of the directors, ten days after Stan joined the company, on 15 May, saw a proposal to secure special status through the tabling of a Bill in Parliament – the Mid-Southern Utility Bill – but this was withdrawn. It is difficult to ascertain the detail of the discussion, as 4 pages of the company minutes appear to have been removed. Suffice to say the question of the company's independence was highly sensitive at a time when there were increasing concerns in government about the profit taking of private utility companies (Hannah, 1979). A report to the company directors by Deloitte Plender, Griffiths & Co on 31 July 1941 regarding excess profits demonstrated that MSUCo was indeed prime example of the sort of company that was causing concern, for it now had seven subsidiaries that it had bought up over the course of its history, including Associated Utilities Ltd, Alton & District Utility Co., Amesbury Electric Light & General Supply Co., Basingstoke Gas Co., Downton Electric Light Co., and Petersfield Electric Light & Power Co.

Despite the fact that pricing was now managed by the Board of Trade, 1941 saw the beginning of a protracted argument with the Government that would last right through until nationalisation in 1948. Of more immediate concern in 1941 were heavy summer thunderstorms in June and August that disrupted supplies in the Alresford District, there were air raid damages to electricity supplies, and the Essential Work Provisions for Reserved Occupations directive of 26 June 1941 restricted companies' employment practices. Not only that but the Transport and General Workers Union were in discussion with the company in July, which led the company to join the Federation of

Gas Employers 'to hold the union at arm's length'. There were bright spots, it was paid £3,000 by the War Department for the supply of electricity to three army camps in August. It also agreed to supply Yarwood Farm in Ropley at a cost of £678 in August, which included subcontracting out the 11,000-volt line provision to Callender's Cables; Stan worked with the Callender's cable jointer on occasion. This was based on a £100 per annum revenue from the farm. Interestingly, at 14.7% annual return, this was considerably less than the 25% annual return on new connections that the company had decided upon in June, and suggests the company was sympathetic to the needs of rural business customers. Certainly, the longer than desired return on investment was offset somewhat by the amount of immediate income forthcoming from the War Department.

Union representatives were making their presence felt on the ground, visiting local depots and shops. Stan took exception to the union tactics of demanding he join the Transport and General Workers Union, which he found threatening and bullying. The unions had been amalgamating to increase their power, and as far as Stan was concerned even at 16, were more political party than trade unions. In a remarkable demonstration of self-confidence – he ignored them. The directors, on the other hand felt they could not do so; they agreed the company should become associated with the respective employers' side of the Joint Industrial Council for the Electricity and Gas Industries. In a board meeting on 19 September 1941, it was noted this was received with satisfaction by the TGWU and the Ministry of Labour, and that 'it appears likely that necessary negotiations on wage problems will now be conducted in a more reasonable atmosphere.' When faced with the combined weight of the TGWU and the Government, the directors had sought sanctuary in what was, in effect, an employers' union of their own. As employers' associations focused on the utility companies had existed since early 1919 (Hannah, 1979: 265), it seems MSUCo was a reluctant signatory that had guarded its independence as a private company until it became patently not in the interests of the business to continue to do so. Following a lengthy negotiation, the directors agreed that the 'technical staff of the Electricity Department were to be brought into line with the Salary Schedules of the N.J.I.C. [National Joint Industrial Council] for the Electricity Supply industry as from 1 January 1944, following negotiations with the Electrical Power Engineers Association.'

Throughout the war it stands to reason the War Department was a major customer. As further examples, in September 1941 it followed up its

June contract with another twice the size, £6,200, for Air Force and Navy supply; in four months it had spent the equivalent of half a million pounds in today's terms with MSUCo. Not only this, in November it received a grant for electricity supply of £1,958 10s 9d from the Board of Trade, and in December it agreed to take on the work supplying electricity to the pump house for 'an oil pipeline'. Stan worked on this top-secret project, reading the six meters at a place designated 'Pluto', that was preparatory for the D-Day landings. (He would leave his pushbike at the main gate at Micheldever Station and went in, and was never once challenged for his pass by the entrance guards.) Clearly, and despite the government concerns over excess profits, the company was trusted sufficiently to work on critical war infrastructure. Not that the Government had much choice for, in effect, MSUCo had by now a virtual monopoly on electricity supply in the central South of England. Indeed, such was the amount of war work from June 1941 that the company was forced to temporarily decline new civilian business.

In the case of MSUCo, and perhaps contrary to the norm suggested by Bassley et al. (2017; above), it seems that the cost of rural electrification was being born almost entirely by the rural population. There is no sense within the minutes that the expansion MSUCo presided over during the war years was being much subsidised; every electrification project was put to the Finance Board as a fully costed business case. There seems perhaps little doubt that as a private company MSUCo was being more efficient than its public equivalents in the cities, but at what cost? As an apprentice, Stan was earning 10s a week for a 52 ½ hr week, which went up in half a crown increments a year to a pound maximum plus, of course, the 6d a year for the use of his bicycle at work. Two years were spent in Alresford before getting called up, three years in the electrical branch in the Royal Navy where he had learnt more in his first electrical course than he had the two years previously. When he got demobbed, knowing more than the chief area engineer Mr Duffy, he was still on a pound a week and had to do another year to get his indentures.

Mr Duffy, a Scotsman, would give Stan 5 shillings and he'd get two boxes of watercress for Duffy to take up to head office in Aldershot for the usual weekly conference, pick up the wages and bring them back to Alresford on Friday. The Alresford branch territory encompassed an area up to within 3 miles of Winchester at the A34 and then up to Alton, North as far as Micheldever Station and South as far as Bramdean. Stan spent all his time with the electrician, Bob Kemp, a Canadian, to learn solely through experience as an electrician's mate. Quickly, however, Stan was left to his own devices, particularly when it came to the quarterly meter reading. As a 17-year-old, he would spend the best part of one month in every four out in the area on his bicycle every day reading meters; the engineers, Duffy and Deveral, would not get involved in that basic work. Nor did they spend any time teaching their apprentice. Once Bob Kemp had taught him to wire houses he was left to his own devices to do it, at seventeen. We may wonder whether this was a one-off or was an example of regular practice in the company's other Areas.

The directors continued the practice begun pre-war of redistributing shares; perhaps now with the added scrutiny of government, there was a need to make the stock ownership more transparent. One example can be found in Table 1, which is copied from the Minutes verbatim and concerns the transfer and transmission of stock on 21 August 1941. Items of note include the transfer of stock from the company's original London bankers Westminster Bank to their London lawyers De Zoete and Gordon; it seems by the war the company had transferred its banking affairs to Barclays. Further, the directors seem keen to redistribute shares owned by the Executors of the original owners to named individuals. Another transfer of note is to Eastern & South Africa Telegraph Co. Ltd. Finally, and highlighting a major concern of the Government and, indeed, the London Stock Exchange, the shares are almost all preferential. That is to say, profits of the company were distributed to these stockholders first, over and above Ordinary shareholders. The directors seem to be selecting very carefully those who would benefit from the business' success.

Transferor	Amount	Stock	Old Cert No.	Transferee	Amount	New Cert No.
Westminster Bank Ltd. 41, Lothbury, E.C.2.	£2,000	4% Deb.	092	De Zoete, H.W. & o'ers.	£2,000	0414
Clarke, Exors. Of Miss M.E.W. do.	£100 £100	" "	18 17	Vestey, R.A. & o'rs.	£200	0415
Elliot, C.E.M.	£200	"A"	3	Elliot,C.E.M & an'r	£200	73
Phillips, Dr. P.P	£1,000	"C"	93	Eastern & South Africa Telegraph Co. Ltd.	£1,000	540
Fladgate,Sole Exor.of Miss M.	£200	Pref.	2105	Fladgate, E.W.	£200	4705
Pirrie, J.	£5	"	749	Pogbee, C.A.	£5	4706
Hulbert, J.N.	£5	"	3602	Vine, H.A.E.	£5	4707

Knight, V.T.	10	Pref.	2420	Tite, H.H.	5	4709
do.	10	"	2882	Whiting, A.E.	5	4710
do.	10	"	3790	Smith, P.V.	5	4711
do.	10	"	2532	Warner, H.	5	2
do.	5	"	575	Ruffell, F.W.	5	3
do.	5	"	1005	Stround, G.C.	5	4
do.	5	"	3467	Streadborough, H.W.	5	5
do.	5	"	1831	Butler, A.H.	5	6
do.	10	"	97	Kingshott, F.	5	7
do.	5	"	3060	Young, C.F.	5	8
				Swain, H.	5	9
				Fry, H.W.R.	5	4720
				Gaines, F.J.	5	1
				Greenwood, W.C.W	5	2
				Kemp, R.E.	5	3
	£75				£75	
Chadbourn, L.	5	Pref.	1552	Avern, G.H	5	4724
	18	"	3318	Williams, T.O.	5	5
	2	"	3421	Bolton, R.J.	5	6
				Bennett, S.G.	5	7
				Volans, M.A.	5	8
	£25				£25	
Jackson, J.P.	20	Pref.	4164			
do.	25	"	2318			
do.	20	"	1745			
do.	30	"	3457			
do.	25	"	3706			
do.	30	"	2919			
	£150			Jackson, J.F.	£150	4729
Gillespie, Exors.of Mrs H.D.	416	Pref.	4584			
Hollas, Mrs.K.	£1,500	"	1666	Kaynes, J.M.& an'r	£1,916	4730
	£1,916					

Table 1. Mid-Southern Utility Co., 1941 Directors Minute Book, page 143: Finance & General Board. 21st August 1941. Hampshire Archives and Local Studies, No. 19M 65/B27

The company continued to extend electricity (and gas) supply on an as requested basis, both to civilian users and military users throughout 1942. Yet throughout 1942 also, the directors were in another protracted discussion with the Government through their accountants, this time in respect of whether their own fees could be free of tax as they had been paid, or whether they should amount to payment for a contract under the 1941 Finance Act and thus should be taxed. This was an important issue, in the light of the company's books for 1941 which reveal electricity revenue alone as £848,418 with depreciation of

£44,795 to leave a balance of £691,631; the risk to the company from being too large, and too successful in the eyes of the wartime Government was not without its significance. The company's business continued to be highly successful through on into 1943, such that by 30 March 1943 it had a cash statement alone of £53,648 (in excess of £2.4 m in today's terms).

The Parliamentary discussion that had presaged the withdrawal of the original Mid-Southern Utility Bill had noted with growing concern the disconnect between its profits and its dividends, particularly the payment of dividends to ordinary shares. In mid-1943, the directors sought the advice of their long-since relied-upon political advisor and financial fixer, one Arthur Collins of 13–15 Old Queen St, Westminster SW1. Collins appears with increasing frequency in the Minute Books as the war draws to a close and the spectre of nationalisation looms; from the correspondence, he seems to have had an inside line to Ministers, was also working closely with other utility companies as well as coal mining businesses, and the directors invariably acted directly on the advice they received from him. The financial structure, reorganisation of capital and the relationship of profits to dividends, however, were not the only source of concern during the Summer of 1943. On 17 August, the directors discussed the 'misuse of gas by Canadian units at the Marital Quarters at Blackdevon' and this had reached such proportions that they had begun the process of seeking legal remedy to recover the losses. The difficulty was that it was not possible, for reasons that are unclear from the Minute Books, to ascertain precisely how much gas had been 'stolen.' In the end, they reached agreement with Canadian Army as to the amount that should be repaid.

In January 1944, the directors were now concerned with the repayment of Mortgage Bonds that had been taken out many years previously to finance expansion of the business in the 1930s. Despite the accumulation of profits, the directors were reluctant to repay the Bonds and sought a two-year extension from the Government. On 4 March 1944, they got the answer they did not want. The company received instruction from the Government's Capital Issues Committee that it would not be allowed to postpone 'for a period of two years the maturity of the £125,000 Mortgage Bonds as [it had] proposed. The maturing bonds should be duly paid off from the Company's internal resources.' Yet again, the directors were able to, frankly, get away without paying the Bond holders, for they not only managed to avoid paying the sum back from savings but even delayed the process and until mid-1948, when they secured a loan through Barclays to repay the Bonds to holders, that loan secured against the new nationalised British Electricity stock. Which is to say they kept the private profits of MSUCo intact and placed the liability for the repayment on the newly nationalised industry.

With the Minute Books for the period late 1944 to early 1946 missing from the Hampshire Archives, it is not possible explore MSUCo's activities in the run up to the end of World War Two, but it seems reasonable to surmise that it continued to expand its utility supply to rural customers and continued with work for the War Department. It is also reasonable to suggest that the directors – who by this time included Harold Read of Deloitte, Plender, Griffiths & Co – spent considerable periods concerned with arguments concerning the company's size and profitability during that time, for yet more disputes are discernible in the 1946–1949 Minute Book. The first of these was with local government. Their financial adviser Arthur Collins wrote a letter on 17 July 1946 to 'F.A. Ricketts, Secretary, Mid-Southern Utility Co.' with regards to an 'ongoing dispute with the Alton and Petersfield Local Authorities [...] regarding the accumulation of profit' and a requisite 'reduction in carry-forward.' In it, he reports a meeting he had had with the local authorities and their lawyers, in which it was clear that MSUCo was going to be forced not only to agree a reduction in carry-forward amounts to the next tax year but also to agree a reduction in prices over and above the ones its directors had themselves suggested. Worse, if not agreed to, Collins noted, they would 'have been imposed upon us, I think, by Parliament', in the light of the fact that company's 'revenue has been increasing at the rate of about £50,000 a year for the last two years.' Clearly, by this stage, the director's view of the business was in stark contrast to that of all levels of Government.

Matters appeared to improve in October 1946, when MSUCo secured agreement from the Alton and Petersfield Electricity Company and the Local Authorities to absorb that company's 'undertakings'. However, this was blocked by the national Government. Arthur Collins wrote again to the MSUCo Secretary F.A. Ricketts on Friday 28 March 1947, saying 'There is no chance of securing the [Alton and Petersfield Transfer] Order we seek. [...] I would have liked, and in normal circumstances taken every possible step, to approach the Minister direct, but at this time I am afraid it is hopeless'; the view of the Government by this time was that MSUCo was too profitable and in any case, it was now focused resolutely on nationalising the entire industry, so the takeover was – in its eyes – unnecessary.

Indeed, the passing of the Electricity Act later that year sealed the fate of MSUCo. It was only a matter of whether the entirety of the company would be nationalised in one fell swoop or not. Again, Arthur Collins was consulted. His view written in a letter to F.A. Ricketts in September 1947 speaks powerfully to the culture of the business:

> [T]he interests of the shareholders come first, and that even if the choice to be made left the staff at some disadvantage, I should feel it my duty to ensure that the shareholders got what I believed was beneficial to them. ... If I could see that by a complete transfer [of the business to government ownership] the staff would derive great benefit then I should make a special point of it ... I do not however perceive that if complete transfer took place, the staff as a whole will have a better chance of maintaining their positions and their livelihood under the new management.

As a direct result of this advice, on 9 October 1947, the Chairman Thomas A. Ruddock and the rest of the MSUCo Board resolved to retain the gas and water businesses. They agreed with Collins' view that the gas and water businesses could continue separately as a sizeable going concern and thus that the prospective rate of return for shareholders as a private company was greater than would be achievable were all the company's interests transferred to national ownership. As a consequence, at the Mid-Southern Utility Co. Annual General Meeting on 26 February 1948, the Chairman informed the shareholders that, with the passing of the Electricity Act 1947, only the electricity side of the business would be nationalised. This was to be achieved by what in effect was an exchange of stock at an agreed transfer price from MSUCo shares to British Electricity Shares. According to letters written by the accountants Deloitte, Plender, Griffiths & Co. on 19 April 1949, MSUCo's electricity interests were converted to British Electricity shares to the value of £1,517,830 [£56,463,276 in today's terms]. Although they disputed the value as being too little, the final work of the 'Directors of the Company [was] to transfer with effect the 1st May 1949 British Electricity stock to those stockholders who have already made application for transfer.' With that, after 77 years of continuous operation, first as the Aldershot Gas & Water Company and finally as Mid-Southern Utility Company, the Minutes end.

III. Conclusion

In sum, the Directors Minutes of the Mid-Southern Utility Company for the period that Stan Dibben was associated with it are dominated not by the continual and regular development of the gas, water and electricity supply businesses across the company's territory. This is not to say that this topic is not a continual subject of discussion, evidently carefully developed through consistent business cases with the emphasis on genuine profitability in each case. Herein lies, along with highly lucrative government contracts during the war, the tremendous profitability of the company; the development of rural electricity supply in the South of England was purely on commercial grounds rather than the public interest. Further, prices were maintained as high as could be got away with, even in the face of government control and concern. Nor are the Directors Minutes dominated by the other standing business items such as Area Reports, electricity, gas and water Supply, Staff Pay, as well as holiday pay and allowances, and individual pension requests from salaried staff reaching retirement age – all of which appear to have been agreed to.

Rather, the Minutes are dominated by one dispute with Government after another. If it is not in regards to tax, it is absolute profits, or financial structure, or dividends to shareholders, or even the takeover of other companies. On the one hand, the MSUCo directors seem to have been running a very efficient and profitable business in their own interests and the interests of those who had preferential shares and yet, on the other hand perhaps because of this strategic commercial focus, their thinking was, apparently, increasingly at odds with the wishes of government both national and local. It is therefore difficult to avoid the conclusion that MSUCo was most likely one of the major examples of commercial excess in the eyes of the government of the day that, just precisely, led to the decision to nationalise the industry.

What is absolutely crystal clear is that the company was using Stan as cheap labour. We can only wonder whether this was an exception wrought by Mr Duffy, or a wider company practice. After being demobbed in 1946, Stan had re-joined MSUCo to finish his apprenticeship. Soon Bob Kemp returned home to Canada and so Stan spent his time doing the electrician's job. His time in the Navy meant by this stage he knew just as much if not more than almost anyone else in the shop, and he could be trusted to do the job. Dozens of postwar prefabricated houses were being put up in the area as a replacement for bombed out housing stock, and he wired most of them. He also wired Alresford railway station. As a senior apprentice, Stan was paid £1 pound a week, up in half a crown (2 shillings and sixpence) increments yearly from the 5 shillings starting weekly wage when he had joined. Bob Kemp had been earning £6 a week but Stan wasn't unhappy about it; he was busy and enjoyed the work in and of itself. Nonetheless, this is a clear example of using apprentices as cheap labour, something the union movement was keenly aware of (Hall, 1985).

He was, though, already aware that there were perhaps better prospects. Stan went back to Canada in search of happier times. Canada postwar, however, was quite different from Canada during the war. It is clear even as a trained and qualified electrician, being a foreigner there was no possibility of him taking jobs qualified Canadians could have – in the music business too. Even his girlfriend gave him the cold shoulder without telling him. By this time, Stan's mother was living on her own and so both the push and the pull to return to the UK was powerful.

He returned to Ropley in August 1948, took up his former post at the now-Southern Electricity Board, and immediately attended the first Southern Electricity Board Summer School as the Apprentice of the Year. It was held at Magdalen College in Oxford and on the final day of the event Sir Henry Nimmo, the Chairman of the Southern Electricity Board, declared the industry would be more efficient now that it was nationalised, and suggested to the audience that they would already have seen the efficiencies coming through. Stan raised a hand and asked the following question:

> Our little office down in Hampshire where I work had a Chief Engineer, an Engineer, a General Electrician, myself as the apprentice plus two Labourers. As Mid-Southern Utility Co, the electrician and I did all the tasks required, including the job of reading meters, and we were never behind on work. Now as part of SEB, we also have a meter reader, insulation inspector, wireman, overhead linesman and a van driver. How can things be more efficient?

Sir Henry replied by suggesting Stan talk to the area manager after the conference. When he got back to the office the Chief Engineer, a Scotsman called Mr Duffy, said that Stan had blotted his copybook. The union idea of 'one man one job' had taken hold and he was to choose what role he wished to do. He was immediately confronted by local union leaders, too, expecting him to join up and finally choose one specific job. Stan's experience of the union movement was of very aggressive bullying to become part of the Transport and General Workers Union, into which a number of the electrical unions had merged in the 1930s. It might seem puzzling that he would be subjected to such conduct.

However, Alan Fox's remarkable 'History and Heritage', in which he explains the 'social origins of the British industrial relations system', offers some insight. As a result of Churchill's wartime coalition government, official union hierarchies were deeply involved in administering government policy in the social and industrial spheres. 'This created possibilities of the rank and file becoming exposed to unofficial grass roots leadership by disaffected militants' (1985: 361). They were clearly a strong presence still in the immediate post-war period. As a skilled manual worker in the postwar nationalised electricity industry, there would have been a closed shop agreement with rigorous demarcation lines [we are grateful to Professor Frank Burchill for pointing this out in conversation, August 2016].

Unionism and the closed shop extended beyond the electricity industry into almost every aspect of employed life. Stan was being paid £1 pound from the £5 fee that his agent charged for his services playing trumpet in Winchester. That said, he wasn't worried about the money – which means of course he was likely being exploited, for he really should have been paid at least £4. On the other hand, he could find no work in Birmingham as a trumpeter because he was not part of the Musician's Union. Of course, had he been a member of the Musician's Union when in Ropley he might have seen more of his fee in his pocket, and he would have found work in Birmingham. That aside, Stan would not be bullied and did not flinch when confronted with the ultimatum as to 'what did he want to be', and indeed called their bluff by saying he could always go back to the farm.

Others of different character, more acquiescent, more willing to tow the line for a quiet life, would not have turned their back on what was a hard-won trade, and would have stayed in the SEB for the rest of their lives. It was, after all, a guaranteed job and many did just that. In the decade or so since he had started work as a famer's boy he had learnt much about life, and about work, what he wanted and more importantly too perhaps, what he didn't want. He didn't want to be stuck in a hierarchical regime that he concluded was replete with narrow-mindedness, as he saw it. He sought freedom from the village too, and new opportunities, and was prepared to give up his trade as an electrician to achieve it. As we've noted already many would have stayed put but, unsurprisingly in that light, he resigned and moved to Birmingham to join BSA, and live his dream.

This Deed of Apprenticeship made the

Twenty ninth day of *May*. 19 *41* . between MID SOUTHERN
UTILITY COMPANY whose Principal Office is situate in Victoria Road Aldershot in the County
of Southampton (hereinafter called " the Company ") of the first part *Mabel Mary*
Dibben of 2, Gascoigne Lane Ropley in the County of Southampton
Widow
(hereinafter called " the Guardian ") of the second part and *Stanley John Dibben*
of 2, Gascoigne Lane Ropley aforesaid
(hereinafter called " the Apprentice ") of the third part
WITNESSETH as follows :—

1. THE Apprentice of his own free will and with consent of the Guardian hereby binds
himself apprentice to the Company to learn the trade of a*n Electrical Wireman*
in the Company's shops or works for a term of five years from the *Fifth*
day of *May*   19*41* .

2. THE Apprentice and the Guardian as surety for the Apprentice jointly and severally
covenant with the Company :—

(a) That the Apprentice will during the whole of the said term excepting the usual holidays
diligently and faithfully serve the Company and to the utmost of his power and skill
attend to the Company's business faithfully obey all lawful orders and requirements of

Stan Dibben's Deed of Apprenticeship, 5 May 1941

4

INTO THE
MOTORCYCLE INDUSTRY

Stan Dibben building his first racer in the BSA factory Gold Star shop, Birmingham, 1950

1. The Gold Star Life at BSA

Once I started motorcycle events, maintenance and tuning became an absorbing hobby. In stripping my newly acquired G3LC matchless trials bike, (on the kitchen table), I had found a new and challenging interest. Reading the 'Blue un' and the 'Green un,' Motorcycle and Motorcycling respectively, increased the interest to the point where the motorcycle industry was where I wanted to be ... not as a fitter in a shop, but in the factory. I remembered Sir Stanley Adams, who was a big voice in General Electric I think it was, had said to me when I was 16 and repairing, on my own, the electric cooker at his mansion 'Young man, you really must get into industry proper when this wretched war is over.' So, a contact was sought, and Bert Perigoe, the competitions manager at BSA, was mentioned by Ralph Venables during a conversation about trials riding. I thought, 'Right, that's the man I'll write to,' and write I did, with an immediate reply, 'Yes, we have work you can do building Gold Stars. You start immediately; your accommodation had been arranged in Ombersley Road, Small Heath.'

The 1950s Gold Star assembly shop was manned by just eight men under the supervision of Sammy Jones, ex New Imperial TT rider. All of us total enthusiasts, including the Gold Star tester, Lol Statham. One of the first changes necessary was to the lodgings. Ombersley Road digs were a prime example of one lodgee getting out of bed when another, on night shift, got into the one vacated. The food too was primitive to say the least. My war time experience and school meals had certainly removed any 'fuss about food' complexes I might have had, but a large oval dish full of tripe with boiled potato all the way around the rim, was a bit 'off-putting' after a cold wet ride the 130 odd miles up from Ropley on a winter Sunday afternoon. Birmingham is very different to Ropley.

One of my colleagues at BSA, Stuart McLeod, said he would try and get me into his digs, 202 Charles Road, Small Heath. Walking distance from the Armoury Road factory, it was the place for motorcyclists. Geoff Duke, Bill Nicholson, David Tye, overseas riders in transit, all stayed at some time or other. Mrs Pearson and husband Jim looked after us well. Large Mrs P, whose bra I remember extended the full length of her kitchen table, threatened in a jocular way to wrap it around my neck when I passed a cheeky comment about it. Jim, who always cooked the breakfast, was a quiet man. A fellow lodger, a rotund 18 stone Irishman called Walter, was the butt of practical jokes. He used to gobble his food in order to get the armchair by the fire. A red chilli pepper in his tomato soup calmed him down a bit and had him pleading for water. Doans backache kidney pills in his tea in the evening had him going to the doctor in the morning because 'something terrible has happened, me water was green this morning ...'

Walter was a bit of a Guinness man and came in too often under the influence. He and I shared a room way up in the attic. A whole tin of Andrews

94

Liver Salts in his chamber pot under the bed and the effervescence spraying his manhood, had him standing from the kneeling position in double quick time. A tug on a loose end of cotton from one of his fly buttons had a similar upstanding effect. Poor Walter, he was as good as gold, but not a motorcyclist! He was not all together inept at getting his own back, like the evening when I went out with him for a drink and he put salt in my whiskey!

Life at BSA was good. I was building road Gold Star motorcycles, trials and racing ones, even International 6-day event ones for the likes of Fred Rist, the UK team captain. At weekends, I used to go home down to Ropley, sometimes on my Matchless G3LC trials bike and more often on a machine from Len Crisp's experimental department. A 650 Gold Flash, a B31, B34, even a Bantam – all needing mileage. I was riding in weekend trials too. I won the newcomer's award in the Calcutt Trial, my first event since arriving in the Midlands riding my Matchless. It caused quite a stir and much comment in the factory the following morning, and even more a few evenings later at Birmingham Motor Club. Stuart McLeod had become almost a big brother influence. He was a well-educated articulate Geordie and our discussions on solo racing with the IoM in particular, encouraged me to have a go.

My first race machine had been a wheelbarrow wheel at the age of about eight. I used to hold the spindle each side and with body almost parallel to the ground, push it as fast as I could around the house and garden. It was great fun when on holiday from that Masonic Institute for fatherless boys. The cuts and bruises from crashes were totally ignored. I had a word with Sammy Jones, my Gold Star Shop boss. The hire-purchase on a 350 cc racer was arranged. Stuart and I built it in our own time. The frame lugs were lightened, gearbox run in, engine prepared with extra care and the only all black painted Gold Star ever to leave the factory was built! Lol Statham, the tester, declared it to be a good one. My first race was an event at Chelmsford. I fell off trying too hard but there was no serious damage to bike or man. Next one was at Eppynt – not quite so disastrous but still trying too hard with careless abandon – and so on to other meetings, improving all the time.

Stuart and I began to visit the Cherry Orchard Café right in the middle of Birmingham. It was owned by Olga Kevelos, the well-known and accomplished trials rider. I got to know her very well on my regular visits, made with Stewart McCleod, my colleague in the BSA factory Gold Star assembly shop. Olga's stories were never ending and varied in the extreme, and so well presented in the tribute to her. She was invariably modest, and with genuine interest in hearing my war time activities. New to the industry, I learnt a great deal on those evening visits and was introduced to many in the trade. Real coffee, laced with a tot or two of brandy, always a good conversational lubricant. Olga was a lovely person, and I felt greatly honoured to have met her on so many convivial occasions. Rex McCandless was also a regular visitor to the Cherry Orchard. The designer of the Norton featherbed frame, so named by reason of the vastly improved handling and at the time, superior to any other Norton. It was suggested that it should become the standard Norton frame for the whole range of models. Objections had been raised by both Design and Financial Directors. Rex thought I would be just the man to test and report on the new proposed models. He asked me to accept a job in Norton's experimental department ... Oh yes please!

2. Testing – and Racing at Norton

My arrival in Bracebridge Street, the Norton home, was met with antagonism in certain quarters. Comments like 'You will find that the low speed handling is too heavy', 'You will find vibration periods unacceptable,' and a host of other objections. My reply made to all in a visit to the drawing and design office was that, 'I understand my job is to ride and report my findings, not ride and confirm objections made.' I was not too popular in some quarters. So LOK622, the pre-production model 88 500 vertical twin, was soon put to use in the form of 400 miles a day, every day, come what may. There were those who disbelieved the daily mileage, so I sent a postcard at my expense from the furthest point of my enjoyment-Portsmouth one day, Aberystwyth next day, Lake District ... and so on. There were no more doubters!

Sometimes I'd do 200 miles in the morning, change barrels and pistons and do another 200 in the afternoon. Often I'd go from Bracebridge Street in Birmingham to John Avery Motorcycles in Oxford for coffee in an hour – thence to Ropley and back via Portsmouth, Salisbury and Worcester! What a life! Speeding south from Birmingham towards Oxford on one of the many 400 mile a day joyous Norton 88 test rides, phenomenal avoidances became essential. Somewhere in the vicinity of Stratford on Avon and full of the joys of the job, there on both sides of the road heaps, many of the largest heaps of manure imaginable. In those days, out of town speed limits non-existent, traffic minimal and my approach speed to these soft obstacles in the order of 90 mph. Rapid speed reduction and trials riding experience; both boots and 'dab coat' well manured; preceded the encounter around the next corner of a herd of very slow-moving circus elephants on their early morning exercise. My report to the factory on my day's work complimented the road handling of the 88. Mrs P. my lodgings landlady, was astonished at my smelly arrival. 'Where on earth have you been?' she asked. 'I've been speeding along a trunk road.'

After some 48,000 miles a few alterations were made – some to move the vibration period – some to strengthen the frame, but all very minor. During this period, 1952, I had made an entry on my Gold Star for the Manx Grand Prix in September. Norton were happy to let me take my annual holiday to compete. My immediate boss at Norton was now Joe Craig, the highly successful race and development manager. 'God.' I said to him, 'Would you please consider finding me a 350 Manx racer for the coming Isle of Man meeting?' 'No, no,' says he, 'ride your Gold Star' after a few more requests. 'The press knows me as the Featherbed tester, what are they going to say?' Finally he relented and said, 'Ok, but you must build it in your own time,' just three days before the event started. Stuart McLeod, who was still at BSA, was smuggled into the holy of holies at Norton and working all night and, raiding the 'works' race machine store, a very good 'standard' 350 Manx was ready.

Joe Craig gave me a final instruction, 'As a novice, if you return a lap quicker than 30 minutes, I'll take the bike off you!' Some thought Joe was a hardened old bugger but he clearly wasn't as hard as his reputation. Many laps were covered on my Gold Star, learning the course when the roads were open, with Peter, Deemster Kneale's son riding pillion, the much-appreciated teacher. Came the race, I did as I was told, almost. I did a lap in 28 minutes, lost 10 minutes on one lap changing a spark plug in Kirkmichel, lost count of the laps and did eight instead of the required seven, but what a difference in the way the featherbed handled compared to my Gold Star. I'm sure the one after the seven was the quickest. My friends all had 'one over the eight' in the evening.

On my return to work, 'God' was impressed. With long nose and chin to match, a caricatureist's dream. At work, usually dressed in suit and tie, unlike most of the ideas men of the industry who were happier in work-worn overalls. He had been a competent road racer pre-World War Two but, surprisingly, I never saw him sit astride an ordinary road going motorcycle, and more surprisingly not even one of his Norton works racing machines. His considerable forte was 'suck it and see', with much information coming from his works racers and testers. A dour man of dry humour who could display a quiet laugh, one day outside the factory in pouring rain, a motorcyclist riding a German BMW motorcycle stopped.

'Excuse me sir, could you give me directions please?'

'Well now I could I suppose, but you don't want to be starting from here!'

Joe thought it was hilarious.

He let me make further entries at Thruxton where I surprised many by winning my heat in the 350 and finishing well in the final. After a good performance at Silverstone soon after, says he, 'Will you no make an entry for the 500 class at Blandford as well as the 350? You can use LOK622.' This was the 48,000-mile pre-production prototype. Well, this was not competitive and I said so, 'Well, will you no go up to Frank Cope's the Triumph dealer in town, buy a pair of Triumph GP cams, get Harry Salter (the race department machinist) to copy the profile on to Norton Dominator cam blanks ... and see how you go?' I did, and both went very well. I had a minor contretemps with John Surtees in the 350 and ended up in the 'coal yard' with two broken ribs. John won the Senior 500 cc race on a Manx, listed in the entry as 'Norton 490 cc'. I kept out of his way this time, finishing 11th at a speed of 74.18 mph on No.44, a certain 'Norton 490 cc' (Dibben, 2012: 34–5). The very first 'Dommie Racer.'

Getting to the meeting had not been a case of putting the bikes in a van and driving there. Came this race day, I loaded the two machines onto a model 16H 600 cc side-valve Norton sidecar. This was the float, the factory work-horse, and comprised of nothing more than a wheel attached to a frame with a few planks of wood on which to carry goods. So I set off at 5 a.m. for the day's work some 180 miles each way, no motorways then remember. I arrived back at the Birmingham lodgings sometime after midnight with two broken ribs, sore, too elated to be tired, and keen to get back to work on Monday to tell them all about it. Life doesn't have to be easy to bring happiness.

Back at the works, I was now trusted to go to the Motor Industry Research Association test track with race machinery and works riders like Ray Amm and Ken Kavanagh, and I began to learn how to ride a racer. At this time, we were trying out trailing link forks instead of the Norton Road Holder telescopics. These were fabricated in the experimental workshop by Bob Collier, to be used at this stage of development on the prototype Ray Amm 'Kneeler'. Feeling full of confidence, I began to think of the 1953 season on Norton machinery with growing excitement and gratitude. What a shame nobody in the works ever even hinted at my possible future, and it wasn't until some years later that I was told by my then Managing Director ... but more of that later.

Unfortunately, in that respect, one day I was told to report to the Motor Industries Research Association test track, MIRA, to meet Mr Eric Oliver, the World Champion Sidecar rider of considerable repute. 'He needs some ballast' said Joe Craig. On arrival Eric said, 'I want you to watch the swinging arm rear suspension and tell me what the movement is'. Not too difficult I guess on the banked circuit. So! I put my feet in the nose of the sidecar, rested my head on my right arm by the rear wheel and did as I was asked. After about half a dozen laps, we stopped, I told Eric what was happening, end of testing I thought. Oh no!! I'd like to go round the road circuit, and you'll have to ride the sidecar round the left handers. That was a bit different and strenuous to say the least. It was a good day, a new experience. End of story, or so I thought. Thinking no more about it, I went back to work.

Imagine my surprise when visiting the Motor and Motorcycle Club in Birmingham, to be greeted by strange looks and comments from friends, 'are you sure you know what you are doing?' – 'You must be mad!' – 'Have you really thought about it?' … 'What the blazes are you talking about?' 'What the hell are you talking about?' said I. 'Well, you are passengering Oliver next year in the World Championship Series.' 'It's the first I've heard about it,' I said. It was a flattering position to be in. In today's parlance, a bit like being involved with Steve Webster or Dave Molyneux. Or indeed, given Eric's authority in the sport and the enormous popularity of sidecar racing at the time, with the Mercedes Grand Prix team. Given that I would be racing a 500 cc solo as well, of course I agreed. My self-confidence in matters motorcycling was such that doubts or fears were never in my mind. My confidence in all matters motorcycling was such that doubts or fears never entered my mind. With hindsight it was probably a mistake, but it lead to some great experiences, and changed not only my career but also my whole approach to life in general.

***

I. Working on the Edge of the BSA Factory

There is something remarkably bold about writing to the Competitions Manager of a major corporation out of the blue asking for a job. That the reply was immediate probably suggest Stan's name had already been mentioned. To get into the Gold Star shop was not easy; the recommendation must have been glowing. The first lodgings found by the company were clearly the basic slot for young working-class men and the hot bunk system, more commonly found on Navy submarines, coupled with the very basic of food, indicates the owners were extracting the maximum from the establishment. The move to 202 Charles Road suggests the people in the Gold Star shop were part of the small cadre of people in the industry, outside of management, who were on the inside. 202 was known in the industry and getting a room there was not easy either. Becoming a regular at the Cherry Orchard Café, too, was a sign Stan had quite quickly got himself into the right circles.

Joining BSA was the first time Stan had been in a large factory, and he was surprised at the general atmosphere. The tendency was for groups of workers, almost invariably men, to walk into work together, work together and then walk out of work together. It seemed people tended not to mix with people from other parts of the factory. Neither did people seem to travel to or from work on motorbikes. There were lots of families working within the heavily unionised corporation, so while there was a family atmosphere, it only existed in small groups. The key rule was that if you were 5 minutes late clocking in you would lose 15 mins pay but if you were 5 minutes late clocking off you'd not get anything extra. The corporation was felt to be sufficiently 'distant' and impersonal that a culture of pilfering had built up among some; taking bits from stores for home projects was regarded as a perk of the job.

According to sources within the Friends of the National Motor Museum at Beaulieu, all the Directors Minute Books of the AMC group companies, including BSA and Norton, were burnt when AMC went into receivership (pers. comm. 21 Jan. 2017). Unlike the Mid-Southern Utility Company, therefore, little can be discerned beyond first-hand accounts, what literature there is almost invariably focuses on the motorcycles and the motorcycle racing. One exception is Bert Hopwood's autobiography 'Whatever Happened to the British Motorcycle Industry' (2007) which provides an executive management account of the various companies he was involved with, including BSA and (after Stan left the company) Norton. Some hint of the distance between senior executives and the shop floor can be gleaned from Hopwood's observation that 'management meetings at Armoury Road [BSA] took on the appearance of a grand council of a government department at times', coupled with his view that even middle management should become involved in product development only at the point when 'irrevocable decisions will have been made' (2007: 96–7). Further, although, at times, we went through the pantomime of discussing certain new projects at enormous gatherings it was only, I think, for the purpose of enabling the lower strata to feel more involved. I am thankful that the real and lasting decisions invariably were made during meetings where seven or eight only were present, although even this number seemed a crowd. (2007: 97)

It is little wonder the 'lower strata' felt the corporation to be sufficiently distant that stealing was not even frowned upon by the gate guards.

Such lack of loyalty was not the case in the Gold Star shop, where eight people assembled bikes and, under Sammy Jones (from the small pre-war motorcycle manufacturer New Imperial), that had a more close-knit family atmosphere. Jones would hand out job sheets to the individual builders in the morning, each man would go to the stores and collect all the pieces required, including pre-completed engines, take it all back to a bench and assemble it. One bike was built per person per day. Unlike the standard production machines, the Gold Star range were all hand-built at the time, and every one was road tested by the Gold Star's own road tester. (This is by and large the same way that Norton builds its machines today.) Each member of the team would support each other if one needed help on a particular machine they were building.

The wages were paid every Friday in a pay packet with cash in it, handed out personally by Jones. With one exception of a visit from the sales manager to the Gold Star shop, Jones was the only manager Stan saw. He was a small cog in a big engine. BSA had a sales and service force working in the field, but there was an oligopolistic attitude to the business, where the competition was deemed rather irrelevant. There was strong resistance to any attempts to improve production and even design quality; a 'free for all – and friction generating – system' seriously endangered the future of the company (Todd, 2012: 89).

While much of this post-war large production line factory culture is well known, what is interesting to note is the complete separation of the hand-built shop. It was in a building far away from the main factory, behind the administrative offices. The dozen people employed there, including two test-preparing staff responsible for fuelling, oiling and running engines up, never mixed with the general factory employees; there was no need to. All this allowed the development of a culture that was different from the rest of the business, focused particularly on building the Gold Star product as a high-end brand within the BSA portfolio. Clearly, the management understood the need.

Stan saw an opportunity to ride motorbikes down to Ropley for the occasional weekend, in the experimental department. He asked if they had a mileage bike he could ride to Ropley with, and they agreed to the request. His newcomers motorcycle trial award was proof enough to the experimental department, very early on in his time at BSA, that he could ride their prototypes. During the two and a half years he was there, Stan rode a wide variety of pre-production and experimental machines, providing feedback on his return to the factory after the weekend. As his reputation among the cognoscenti grew and he came into contact with more of the influential people in the industry, notably, through his time at the Cherry Orchard Café, so the job at Norton came up. Rex McAndless needed someone who was clearly capable of doing a great deal of riding but who was not known at Norton and thus not likely to be influenced against the Manx frame by people the drawing office there

II. Handling the Politics at Norton

Going from BSA to Norton, Stan was expecting to find a factory but found a small building. It was of course a much smaller company, a Small and Medium Sized Enterprise (SME); the footprint of the factory was less than one-tenth the size of the BSA's Armoury Road site. The entrance to the Bracebridge St. factory in Birmingham was at the left-hand end of the building. At the right-hand end of the building was a roller-shutter door, rarely opened, that gave access to the experimental department. The building was only the width of one street, between Bracebridge St. and Aston Brooke Rd. Largely unchanged from 1912, walking in the entrance there was a small foyer, with the Managing Director's office off that on the right and a public door into the Sales Office. Walking through the foyer, one was met by a line-up of newly made bikes ready for road test, then there were four relatively relaxed production lines (very few bikes ever came back for warranty repair) laid side-by-side parallel to the main entrance. To the left of the lines was the stores and the engine assembly and test department. This had separate access to the experimental department at the back of the building behind the production lines.

The Managing Director's and other management offices were to the right of the production lines, with the drawing office upstairs above them on a landing. The race department was situated on the landing opposite, above the engine department. Walking straight through from the foyer, past the new bikes, beside the stores and engine department and out the back door onto

Aston Brooke Rd led you to R.T. Shelley. This was a wholly owned subsidiary of Norton that did all the machining work necessary for Norton's to assemble the machines, including frame making. Not having welding expertise, it could not build the McAndless frames needed for Featherbed Manx racers or Dominator road bikes, which was subcontracted to Reynolds Tube Co., who were the 'the leading experts in tubular welded structures' at that time (Sprayson, 2012: 24). The politics surrounding the McAndless frame revolved around having to pay royalties for its use and the fact that it exposed the technological limitations at R.T. Shelley, which did most of the engineering while Norton concentrated on machine assembly and experimental development. In time, R.T. Shelley would make most of the components for the AMC group, which exploited its ownership of the firm (Hopwood, 2007: 153) to demand ever-decreasing prices substantially below cost; there was little investment. The experimental department consisted of three people, Bob Collier who was in overall charge, Harry Salter the engineer and Stan. In the same area, the two brothers Charlie and Arthur Edwards built and prepared the race machines along with a specialist engine polisher Bill Stuart, who did all the fine porting. The race department stores were upstairs in a small permanently locked room. Joe Craig was located in the drawing office, which was essentially off-limits to all bar a small handful of people, of whom Stan in his experimental tester role was one.

The solution to the office politics regarding mileages ridden of sending postcards from the furthest point was simple and effective, and typical of his approach to things, simply providing irrefutable evidence. As his reputation grew within Norton, and as he came into greater contact with Joe Craig, Norton's legendary competitions manager, so he was entrusted with more experimental work beyond the 88 Dominator. Craig's decision to allow him to ride a Manx Norton at the Manx Grand Prix was a strong signal of approval. Having Stan build it in his own time, i.e. out of office hours, was an open invitation from Craig to build the machine with whatever works parts he wanted. The paternalism, inherent in the suggestion that if he rode it too quickly the bike would be take off him, is indicative of a more caring side. It also demonstrates that in Craig's mind the machine was owned by Norton; it was an unofficial works entry.

It was not generally known at Norton that the company was owned by Associated Motor Cycles by 1952, and certainly Stan knew nothing of it, because the two businesses, AJS-Matchless in London and Norton in Birmingham, were kept separate except for the very senior board. While management at Bracebridge

Street was distinct from the rest of the people, nonetheless, the feeling was of a small family. Whether or not this was a function of its physical size as a place, it was much closer-knit with (at least ostensibly) nothing remotely 'corporate' or corporatized about it. The business was sufficiently small that pay was not the responsibility of department managers, instead the weekly cash was handed out by one of the clerks in the finance office. Comparing the Gold Star shop to the experimental department at Norton's, they were both close-knit groups of people working together. The key difference was that the Gold Star shop was always busy building machines to order, whereas the experimental department at Norton was fairly quiet, working on single projects most of the time. In direct contrast to the Norton experimental department BSA's equivalent, which in itself was equally non-corporatised, was located in a separate building with ten people working there and was a permanent hive of activity.

In sum, Stan's time in the British motorcycle industry at its postwar height, and particularly his time at Norton, nonetheless shows evidence of the impending decline. Namely, the secret takeover of Norton by AMC due to a lack of funds, the politics associated with resistance to change and improvement, inherent in the McAndless frame arguments in the drawing office, and the chronic underinvestment in new engines and technology generally. Nonetheless, Stan's experience of it was somewhat different. He was working in the best departments at BSA and Norton, admittedly as much by chance as by design. His growing reputation as a skilled solo rider had seen him move from simply road testing a prototype production machine at Norton to testing new racing motorbikes such as the Kneeler and, in what amounted to another attempt to reduce the frontal area to increase speed, the so-called 'Low Boy'. This featured a conventional riding position but modified petrol tank and frame. This machine, intended for 1954, was criticised for being too cramped by many of those who rode it. The reason was that it was in fact built to fit Stan,* a sure sign the intention was for him to be riding for Norton in the future.

His straightforward thinking evidently impressed the multiple Sidecar World Champion Eric Oliver during the test of his sidecar outfit, but how can the 'order' to ride as a sidecar passenger with Oliver be set in the context of being thought of in the race department as a future Norton solo racer? A year spent under the tutelage of the acknowledged master racing motorcyclist, learning the

---

* This was demonstrated at the Sammy Miller motorcycle museum in July 2016. Miller argued it was too small and showed how he could not fit inside its fairing, whereupon Stan stated it was built for him and, to prove the point, climbed on the machine and tucked in behind the fairing exactly.

circuits, learning what was involved in racing at the highest level, and riding his own solo machine in supporting races, would have been seen as perhaps the very best possible introduction to World Championship level motorsport. So began what was intended to be a year's sabbatical from the factory. Narrow-minded thinking and management reluctance to reward success would prove otherwise.

A recent picture of a very original Norton 88 Dominator 500 cc twin, the type that Stan did all pre-production development on while at Norton Motors, Bracebridge St., 1951–52

5

THE BUSINESS OF
SIDECAR RACING

Eric Oliver and Stan Dibben's race van painted with sponsors logos, and caravan at
Spa Francorchamps in Belgium, 1953

1. Learning Race Craft

1953 was the year that finished my solo racing aspirations. I'd been making
great strides with Norton factory support, riding the 350 Manx, and building
and racing at Blandford in October 1952, the first Dommie Racer. Testing at
MIRA with the likes of Ken Kavanagh and Ray Amm, I was on a very fast
learning curve. But saying yes to Eric Oliver – even for a year's secondment to
his employ – changed all that.

I joined Eric in the Watsonian Sidecar factory to work on the sidecars,
prior to our first race at Silverstone. One outfit was the conventional 'bolt-on-

to-the-motorcycle' sidecar, the other a double skinned fully streamlined outfit fabricated by Ben Willets, the ace sheet metal worker, with the rider kneeling in rather than sitting on the motorcycle. After some test rides at Silverstone with the conventional outfit, I began to get the feel of things. Handholds clearly had to be tailor made to suit my body dimensions on both outfits. After modifications had been made at Watsonian, and more Silverstone practice, we were ready to race.

We had long discussions about riding the sidecar. He said, 'You're called a passenger but you'll have to be more than that.' He proceeded to explain the finesse of weight distribution, movement timing, keeping eyes open for the opposition's activity, race craft etc. He made it very clear that I wasn't just there for the ride. How right he was.

Eric had served in World War Two with distinction on Lancaster bombers as a Flight Engineer in the Royal Air Force on many raids over Europe. He did many tours over enemy territory at a time when crews were lucky to get away with but one. Immediately after the war, his engineering prowess was very much to the fore in the preparation of racing machinery, both mechanical and aerodynamic, when the design and preparation of racing sidecars left much to be desired. Before the war his racing was almost entirely on grass track, with wins at Brands Hatch when it was just a grass track! In the immediate post-war years, he was unbeatable; before I joined him he had already won the inaugural 1949 World Championship with Denis Jenkinson, who won fame as a sports journalist after winning the Mille Miglia navigating for Stirling Moss. Eric had also won the World Championship twice, in 1950 and 1951 with the Italian Lorenzo Dobelli. He was no slouch at racing solo motorcycles either, when the opportunity arose.

His racing experience was such that he could dictate how a race would be run, for Eric always had a pre-race plan. We would sit down and plan how to dictate the race, and the plan was nearly always made to work. I discovered there was no better teacher of the skills required to ride a racing sidecar, and he recognised that the historical use of the word 'passenger' was, in the racing context, defamatory. After the first race we did at Silverstone, where I was introduced to the art of sidecar riding, we proceeded down to Pau in Southern France. This was the life, the atmosphere was fabulous and the people wonderful. We won at Pau, and I learnt a great deal, in particular about not stepping off the back under acceleration! We won there, but I fell off the solo!! Eric said, 'You can't afford to fall off the solo, Stan. If you get hurt, it'll ruin our sidecar chances'. I realized then and there that my serious solo career was more or less at an end. I did race the solo at most of the continental circuits, but was never really trying. Still, it was good fun.

Back to England for repairs to my solo Norton and another race which again we won. A few days later, on the road again bound for Mettet and Floreffe circuits in Belgium. At Hockenheim, in Germany, a few races later, we knew we were going to have considerable difficulty with the factory BMW race team led by Wiggerl Kraus/Bernhard Huser, Wilhelm (Willi) Noll/Fritz Cron, Walter Schneider/Han Strauß, Fritz Hillebrand/Manfred Grunwald and Wilhelm (Willi) Faust/Karl Remmert. Their team leader was to be allowed to win. Their strategy would obviously be to pass us on a left-hand bend; (we were slower with the sidecar on the left), then to be held back by the three other team members, allowing their team leader to get far enough away to be impossible for us to catch.

Race craft came in here. In our customary pre-race discussion, Eric told me that the works BMWs would gang up on us. We will let them do it until the last left-hand corner before the finish. We will then approach the corner on the 'wrong' line, fool them, and take their corner off them. So, on the appropriate lap, depending how far their main man was in front, we would enter the last left on the extreme left of the road and keep going straight to a later left peel off point, keeping the three team members from passing, leaving us to take care of their leading head man. The element of surprise was such that the three ran into difficulties, we as planned passed the main man by slipstreaming and won by a half a wheel. Very exciting for all concerned and essential too that I was fully aware of what to expect, so that I could perform as required.

There's a lot more to sidecar riding than being mere ballast and just holding on!

2. The 1953 World Championship Rounds

Throughout the whole year, the races were almost invariably hard fought with the opposition from the BMWs now becoming more interesting, but it was 1952 Norton World Champion Cyril Smith with Les Nutt in the chair who always proved the most serious and concerted opposition. The first Grand Prix of the year was the Belgium Grand Prix at Francorchamps. It was decided to use the fully streamlined outfit, the first fully streamlined sidecar ever raced and forerunner to all the modern ones. It was unique because the driver kneeled rather than sat on the machine. It stood no higher than your average desk, had the petrol tank in the sidecar and used a special air intake at the top of the fairing to stop a vacuum forming between the windscreen and the driver. All very sophisticated stuff that was designed by Ben Willets at Watsonian at Eric Oliver's initiative, Eric having ridden the Norton solo kneeler. It was intended to allow us to easily beat the opposition and, by changing engine and rear wheel sprockets, we had it geared 'long' so that it would do 140 mph. Conventional sidecars at the time were lapping at more than 90 mph. We were looking for the 100 mph lap with that estimated top speed. It looked beautiful too, resplendent in Norton Silver and British Racing Green.

For about a mile down the Masta straight and into the Stavelot corner, both not now included on the current circuit, things were very, very interesting. To see the air pressure distorting the streamlining panel fixing rubbers only inches from my face was an education. The trouble was that the fairing on the sidecar itself was wrongly shaped and so it created lift at terminal velocity. With hindsight, this was clearly due to the difference in airflow around the sidecar compared with the bike. I seem to recall Eric saying that the streamlining had been tested in the wind tunnel at Bristol, but, if so, it was obvious from the way the outfit behaved that the problem hadn't been picked up. A look at the photographs of the machine shows the problem was rather staying us in the face, as it is clear that the sidecar fairing was very 'unclean'. The lift problem necessitated right lock to get the chair down and then left lock to get the outfit straight, and then right lock and so on: a massive weave. Very exciting at 140 mph plus. This was all a little too entertaining, though, so we didn't use it in the race. We did use it later in the year to win at Brands Hatch and Silverstone, and our friends Jacques Drion and Inge Stoll finished third with it at the Italian GP at Monza, albeit with standard gearing so that it wouldn't be so inclined to take off.

The race and win at the Spa Francorchamps circuit, in front of a huge crowd, was a thrilling event, even with the conventional outfit. It was a race-long dice with Cyril Smith and Les Nutt and we just got to the finish line in front by about a second. This circuit which is not now used in its old form was, along with the 22 km version of the Nürburgring and the Isle of Man TT circuit, one of my favourite circuits. The French Grand Prix at Rouen with a circuit of only 5.1 km followed Spa in the Grand Prix calendar. The usual struggle with Cyril and Les was expected and occurred. They had serious suspension problems in the race but still managed to finish second behind us. Our new lap record was 73.99 mph with a race average of 71.96 mph. I was enjoying the continental experience but it was good to be heading home, for a bit.

The next World Championship race was the Ulster Grand Prix, held for the first time (for the sidecars) on the 7.5-mile Dundrod circuit in Northern Ireland. The same battle with Cyril and Les occurred, and after a near 80 mph average we retired with a broken sidecar axle, so they went on to a well-deserved win with a race average of 77.79 mph. We had the honour of the fastest lap of 79.17 mph. This meant the championship was very close and we headed back to Europe for the Swiss Grand Prix at Bremgarten near Berne. This 16-lap, 72-mile, tree lined event was a sidecar rider's challenge, needing extra rapid movement about the sidecar to keep the whole thing balanced. This turned out to be a more comfortable win with the Smith/Nutt combination being caught behind one of the German teams for a while which must have held them back a little as they finished nearly 30 seconds behind us in second. Eric and I must have got our team-work fairly well honed by now too, though. We'd discuss everything carefully after each practice session and not only did it produce the win but we broke the lap record, previously held by Frigerio and Ricotti's Gilera outfit, by over 5 mph.

This event was not without additional interest for me in particular. I had parked our Austin Three-Way van and its caravan in the market place while attending the prize giving, got back to it afterwards and went straight to bed; Eric stayed in a hotel at that event as his wife Mildred had travelled over for it. I woke up in the morning to find myself surrounded by market stalls with the windscreen covered in police stickers. After heated discussion with the local on-the-spot authority, it was agreed that I would be allowed to move away from the market on the understanding that I called in at the local police station to pay the necessary fine. I moved but decided not to stop. I must confess to some trepidation when crossing the border into Italy a few hours later but got away with it. I certainly didn't have enough cash to pay the police in Berne or at the border control, and Eric and Mildred had anyway gone on ahead in the car. No computers then, to hastily pass on information!

The drive on down to Monza in Italy ended up being a nice short break. Cyril and Les were following me to make sure all was well and we stopped for the night at Lake Maggiore where we had a swim, hired a rowing boat and went fishing the next day. And so to Monza – the home of Italian motorcycling and the masses of Italian race fanatics, and the Grand Prix des Nations. The atmosphere here was unbelievable in its intensity, just as it is today. The meeting was nearly cancelled, however, because of a hiatus caused over start money. The British works teams, Norton, Matchless/AJS and Velocette had all withdrawn, leaving it to the European manufacturers in the solo races. The sidecar event was unaffected, and the tension increased because the Italian fans were now expecting a clean sweep of the major classes; only the 125 cc class had been won by anything other than an Italian machine. It was not to be.

The sidecar World Championship rested on the result here. Whoever won between Eric and I, and Cyril and Les, would win the title. For the whole 16 laps the pair of us swapped places, sometimes in the Lesmo curves at the back of the circuit, sometimes coming out of the Parabolica, the last corner before the start and finish straight, or on occasion down the straight itself past the grandstand. Eric and I had our usual lengthy practice discussions, and we decided that if necessary on the last corner we would peel off early into the corner with minimum weight over the back inducing oversteer, which should upset the opposition's thinking and give us the edge entering the last dash to the finish. We managed it by the smallest whisker over the line, and this determined the 1953 World Championship for us rather than Cyril and Les. It was the best finish to a Grand Prix that season and denied the local fans the Gilera win they had so hoped for. To give you some idea of how close the racing was, both outfits equalled the lap record of 91.16 mph. We were both right on the limit. I don't know what happened to the Gileras but Jacques Drion and Inge Stoll came third on our kneeler, as I mentioned earlier; they were nearly a minute behind by the end.

3. The Continental Circus

Driving around Europe between each race weekend was always an eye opener. The war had only been over for seven years. I was horrified to see the damage our bombers had caused, especially in Cologne and Stuggart. Having said that, the food was good, so was the drink in moderation; the degree of fitness necessary dictated that. Never once was I subjected to bad words or ill feeling in Germany. Race meetings were held all over France, Belgium, Spain, and Italy, truly a Continental Circus and very enjoyable.

So it was that, aside from the Grand Prix, the other international and national club events all over Europe, that began before the first Grand Prix and continued on after the last one, were also a wonderful experience. The Mettet circuit was a surprise. I had never imagined spectators standing 5 or 6 deep on the pavement at the side of the road on which we were racing. Rushing by at speed with hundreds of foot-filled shoes just literally inches away from my face; I was learning more about the psychology of riding on a racing sidecar than I had ever imagined! It wasn't much different on the solo at Mettet, except that the shoes were replaced with faces, and gave the impression of wearing a patch over one eye. Quite an experience at 100 mph. We won the sidecar race but I can't remember where I finished on the solo. I do recall Australian Tony McAlpine wondering why my Norton was so much quicker than his. It wasn't the machine, it was the weight it had to carry! Tony was great fun, but weighed probably 50% more than my fraction over 60 kg.

The next weekend found us just over a mile away at Floreffe. A fast 8.4 km circuit with a few cobble-stoned roads. We were leading the sidecar race but retired with engine failure. Clearly winning was not a foregone conclusion. The solo race was fun. The sidecar responsibilities were such that I couldn't risk falling off through trying too hard, and the solo racing therefore became a high-speed exercise rather than a race. I was amused when passing a slower rider to see him poking his tongue out at me, and the said muscular organ was rapidly flapping up and down in the wind. So *this* is the 'Continental Circus'!

Ironically, with sidecar racing so very popular in Germany there was no German Grand Prix in 1953. The event had been planned to take place at Schotten, but all the major works supported riders refused to race there because the tree-lined, narrow and slippery course was considered too dangerous for the now 'super-fast' machines. I was taken around the old circuit by the Classic Grand Prix organisers in 2007 and, although difficult, it was certainly not as demanding as for example the Isle of Man TT circuit now is with the truly high-speed motorcycles in existence now. So I have to conclude the objections were more financially expedient than the safety related.

An incident occurred at Solitude, when a spectator moved forward to the edge of the track on a left-hander to watch as the leaders approached, no doubt thinking that the motorcycle rather than the sidecar would be nearest to him; driving on the right as they do on the Continent, the BMWs had the sidecar on the right. The only problem with that assumption was Eric and I were leading the race! He occupied the grass verge that I needed to hang out over. I had no choice but to brace my shoulders and hit him side on. To do otherwise would have meant a sidecar-over-bike incident with serious injuries to both driver and I. It hurt I can tell you! As a result we ended up finishing second. I never did hear what happened to the spectator. Enquiries I made after the race as to his condition were fruitless and my multiple bruising soon recovered. I've never forgotten it and I sincerely hope he was not seriously injured.

We also had a serious crash at the Nürburgring circuit where we were surprised and completely caught out by a corner that had been dry on the earlier laps but was now wet. We could reliably drift the outfit almost to the curb in the dry but with it now wet of course we overdid the drift and thumped the curb. The sidecar went over the bike trapping Eric under it, while I went sliding up the road on my back, feet in the lead for a few seconds until I was passed by the howling mob on both sides. By the time I had got to my feet, Eric had righted the outfit and was calling for me to get back on board. I did, but the damage to the sidecar made it impossible to proceed. I was bruised but this was quickly cured by two very large German brandies in the pits. I have many emotional memories standing on the podium in front of thousands of fans, particularly in Germany. Despite the still quite recent hostilities between the two countries, it must be said that there was never any animosity between nationalities in the racing circles, only sincere friendships.

One minor problem resulted, though, from the Nurburgring crash in that Eric had damaged his elbows. That meant he couldn't drive and flew back to England for 'rapid running repairs'. I had never driven a car or any four-wheeled vehicle in my life before but anyway ended up driving the van and caravan down the autobahn and over the Swiss Alps to the next event at Aix les Bains in France! Cyril and Les agreed with Eric that they would follow me to make sure I was alright; there was a good deal of camaraderie and friendship despite the close racing. My amateur attempts at manoeuvring the van and caravan around the mountain corners, they told me later, were mighty close to the edge and had them perpetually sucking their teeth expecting me to disappear at any moment. Another very quick learning curve!!

Our last event in 1953 was in Casablanca. By this time I was doing all the driving, and have fond memories of driving all the way there and back from Birmingham to Morocco. The drive through southern France, Spain and Morocco, driving in the Austin van past the Arab nomadic enclosures, Rabat, in the heat of the African summer was a unique experience even for me, remembering my war-time adventures down there. It was a good adventure and a fitting way to end the season. It was nearly our last ever. The circuit surface was good, but lined with massive palm trees and deep sand. At one point in the weekend we ran off the road on the exit from a right-hand corner, and I was very lucky not to have been suffocated by flying sand and decapitated by an unseen palm. It was a unique way to end the season. The Motorcycle journal would later say in their 27 January 1955 issue that 'The Oliver/Dibben 1953 season partnership was regarded as the most successful in the sphere of Grand Prix racing.' It had been some adventure.

After, as I recall, something in the order of 32 international starts, 29 wins, one second place, one retirement and one prang – and 32 record laps, the fabulous year ended with a presentation at the Royal Automobile Club (RAC), Pall Mall in London, where Eric received his gold championship medal. I got a silver one, shaking hands with a man who even got my name wrong. No wonder I'm not famous! Interesting to note, too, that I rarely if ever saw the name of the 'passenger' in any motorcycle and sidecar event mentioned in the 'Motorycling' or 'Motorcycle' journals that year.

4. The Reality of the Sidecar 'Passenger's' Lot

Back in England after a season's racing on the Continent, well I passed my driving test first time! But I was dismayed not to receive a letter of congratulations for the World Championship from family or friends; except Stuart McLeod of course; and with no bonus payments from anyone; not Norton, Watsonian, Continental tyres, Fosatti chain, Castrol; not a thing, not even a phone call. It's not quite correct to say that I did not receive a bonus payment. At the Earles Court motorcycle and cycle show, I was doing a public relations job on the Watsonian sidecar stand and visited the Girling stand where the stand manager said 'Stan, you deserve a bonus after that performance. Here's £40, but don't tell anybody' After the show, there were a few club dinners to attend, which were great fun. The World Championship medal presentation at the RAC in Pall Mall was interesting. Eric received his gold one and I my silver one; a clear indication of the lack of official regard for the efforts of the man in the chair. They even got my name wrong when presenting me with the medal!

So it was not difficult to decide that, although exciting and good for one's ego, sidecar racing was not worth the very considerable risk to life and limb (my compulsory life insurance premium was 10% of the total benefit: i.e. £100 for £1,000 of cover), and I hoped to start again where I had left off. I wanted to get back to racing my solo motorcycles. With the £143 savings from the season in the bank (the taxman had £40 of it later). January 1954, found me back in the Norton factory, no more sidecar racing intentions, intent on restarting my solo career. It never happened. For about 2 weeks, I was again in the experimental department and beginning to settle down to some serious work under Joe Craig, when I was called into Managing Director Gilbert Smith's office. I had asked for a rise from £7 to £8 per week and was asked why, when I wasn't even married. I answered 'I thought you would pay me for what I did, not on the basis of need. That Mr Smith is communism.' He was livid, so was I. To say I was disillusioned would be an understatement. To say I was bloody angry would be totally accurate. It's no wonder that the star riders of the time accepted rides from MV, Gilera and Moto Guzzi. I learned later that many had been treated in similar fashion. In Stuart Barker's book *Barry Sheene 1950–2003*, the double World Champion talks at length of the iniquitous attitudes regarding money in the UK motorcycle racing scene. Manufacturers were always pleased to advertise race successes but were not always supportive in helping up and coming riders get to that level.

Being now unemployed, I sold my BSA Gold Star racer and bought a 125 cc James motorcycle for transport and got a job selling motorcycles at Handlays, the famous Bristol St. dealer in the centre of Birmingham. The first thing they did after I joined them was put a big photo of me up on the wall of the shop. It did the trick; my first week paid me £22 wages and commission. This was alright!

Then Cyril Smith (not related in any way to the aforementioned Gilbert Smith) phoned me. The 1952 World Champion, with whom I had been friendly when working at the Norton factory where he was in charge of the production testers, was without a 'passenger' for the 1954 season. His man, Les Nutt, had joined Eric Oliver since I had declared no intention to continue. So Cyril expressed an interest in my teaming up with him. I was still in lodgings, and the Sunday lunches coupled with an offer of £40 per week guaranteed, made the decision to resume sidecar racing pretty easy, and we proceeded with work on a new fully streamlined outfit. It looked good and we had our first win at the first race of the year at Silverstone, beating my old mate Eric by a wheel, much to everyone's surprise. Cyril's too, because our sidecar had been drifting out of Woodcote corner every lap, but on the last lap it didn't. Eric was poised to pass on the inside as I knew he would, he couldn't, there was no room, demonstrating that the driver is sometimes controlling what the sidecar rider (passenger) is allowing the outfit to do. Teamwork.

Cyril was a superb driver and just as quick as Eric on right hand corners, but his stature and short arms inhibited his speed around left handers: he couldn't clamber about onto the sidecar like Eric could. Cyril had not been used to much sidecar rider control of the outfit on corners, but he soon realised the benefits. I had learned much about riding a sidecar, had given it much thought in the process, and discovered just how much control could be exercised. Sidecar riders on race machines not only need to be very fit and self disciplined beyond the norm. They need to have an understanding, to achieve maximum speed, of precise timing, optimum weight position, leverages, wind resistance, traction control, and with their activities planned and agreed with the other member of the team, the driver, after practice.

In late-January 1954 Eric Oliver, Cyril Smith and I had been invited to the Isle of Man to try out the Clypse course. It was proposed to bring back the sidecars, and we were asked to try out this new circuit. It was fun having the roads closed for us in January and going the wrong way up the long climb from Brandish corner to Creg ny Baa. It was cold but energetic. This road race circuit was going to be demanding. It was used, from 1954 up to 1959, for the smaller capacity motorcycles as well as the 'chairs'. A good deal warmer in June than January.

I raced with Cyril with much success and plenty of frustration with engine failures. We had fantastic performances particularly at Nürburgring and Francorchamps. He was good to be with and I actually ended up staying with him for three seasons, 1954, 1955 and 1956, with no more than a few minor mishaps. One in the Isle of Man resulted in a broken nose and 15 stitches to re-attach my top lip after an argument with a rearranged bank. After returning to Birmingham, I went to the Birmingham Accident Hospital to have the stitches out, my own GP having refused. There was the same response there, saying that if I was prepared to risk my neck in the Isle of Man TT races, I should go back there to have the stitches out. Mrs Pearson, my landlady was horrified to see me taking them out with nail scissors and tweezers. The character at the hospital was given a few facts of commercial life in no uncertain language. At that time, Birmingham and Coventry were supplying the world with more than something like 70% of its motorcycles and an even higher percentage of sidecars.

At Solitude in '54 I met a lovely German girl, Gisela, who kept me entertained. At Solitude again in 1955, the speakers yelled 'Herr Dibben zum Telefon bitte.' I went to the race office and answered straight away. On the phone was Gisela. 'Can I come and see you Stan?' 'No Gisela, not this year.' 'Oh, why not?' 'I've got my English girlfriend with me.' The conversation went on for a few minutes before I ended the call. Walking back to the pits I received numerous boos and cat-calls from all and sundry. Imagine my surprise to discover the loudspeakers had stayed on and the whole telephone conversation had been heard by thousands! Imagine too the other rider's comments when walking back to the pits; 'You lousy sod.' It's a small world, though, for I met her by chance 10 years later in a milk bar in Hawaii, where she was working for an American Service man's family.

Nürburgring again 29 May 1955, this time with Cyril Smith. We overdid it a bit in the banked Karussell corner and came out of the banking. It is a left hander and I was hanging out as usual when, suddenly, I found the sidecar way too far above the road. By dropping my whole body down onto the road, I got the outfit back to where it was supposed to be. We won the race and got the fastest lap, but I finished it with a rough pair of two-piece leathers having started the race in a nearly new one piece. An excursion from the track later that season over a ditch and into a cornfield, coupled with the necessary acrobatics, left me with a hernia. At season's end, I went into hospital for repairs, and at the same time it was considered necessary to have my nose opened up to assist breathing. A sub mucus re-section. Whilst in the post-operative state, I had a visit from the Managing Director of the Perry Chain Company, American Bill MacLeod, whose products both Cyril and I had been using on the sidecar and my solo. The conversation resulted in my joining the company on 1 January 1956. Thus ended my racing. Or did it?

I was in the Isle of Man working for Perry in my new capacity as trade baron Peter Tye's assistant at the 1956 TT races in June, having 'retired' in January, when a very deflated Cyril Smith came up to me. 'Have you got your racing leathers with you? I can't get on with my new man in the chair. He will get me killed.' I sent for and duly received them from my digs with a note from Mrs P 'You must be mad'. The Clypse Course was no place for an inexperienced sidecar rider. I did the rest of the major races with Cyril that year, flying out to do the Grands Prix events. Perry management were very accommodating but also very concerned, and said so. As in 1955 we broke the lap record at Spa (99.29 mph) but retired with engine problems, and just as in the previous year too we were very competitive all season but the Norton motor was no longer up to the job. By the end of that year, I'd had enough sidecar work, and thankfully Eric Bliss was available and rode with Cyril for the remainder of his career, with some notable successes.

One or two solo race opportunities came along in the form of production road machine races like the 500-mile races at Thruxton on the factory 250 cc Ariel Leader and the following year on the Ariel Arrow. An opportunity arose to do the Barcelona 24-hour race at Montjuich Park. The machine was to be a factory Velocette Venom owned by Mike Tompkinson, the Hereford motorcycle retailer. He drove us down in his black and yellow 1926 Rolls Royce.

The Barcelona taxis were black and yellow too, and caused much laughter on occasions. Howard German and Phil Heath made up the team of three. We came away with a couple of trophies for our efforts, and there, I determined to end racing for good, out of consideration to Perry Chains who had treated me with the respect and generosity I had never known from an employer.

***

I. The Popularity of Sidecar Racing in the 1950s

Sidecar racing today is undeniably a sport that has declined markedly in popularity since its heyday in the 1950s and 1960s. Engines have been repositioned to be behind the driver in 'long chairs' and, even in more traditional 'short chairs' where the engine remains in front of the driver as it used to be, dimension altered to give far greater stability. The machines are faster but the 'thrills and spills' are fewer so that public allegiance has shifted to solo bike racing, notably road-derived 'Superbikes' and the race-only machines of what has come to be known as MotoGP – the current equivalent of the 500 cc World Championship of yesteryear – as well as various types of car racing, notably Formula 1.

The affluent elements of today's society, coupled with the car manufacturers and high-end technology and luxury goods companies, not to mention the occasional soft drink manufacturer, lavish money on the aforementioned Grand Prix car racing in particular. This is so to such an extent that with the advent of television, and particularly now on-line and pay-per-view television, and with the motorcar firmly established long-since as infinitely more popular than the motorcycle as the mode of transport of choice for the masses, Formula 1 is undeniably the 'blue riband' of motor sport. Indeed, it supports a thriving industry based largely in the UK. The substantial drop in the popularity of motorcycles, hastened too by ever-increasing concerns as to their safety or otherwise has led to a concomitant drop in the popularity of motorcycle sport, notwithstanding a recent resurgence of motorcycle road racing (as opposed to racing on specially designed circuits) most notably focused around the Isle of Man TT races. This is not to say that motorcycle sport does not have a strong and loyal following, but comparatively speaking it is far smaller than it was and when set against the popularity of car racing.

Gone are the days when the sidecar was the default mode of transport for the average man in the street and his family, and we shall explore this further below. Sidecar racing too has suffered a considerable drop in its popularity, such that it has only a comparatively small band of loyal followers. This has led to three things. First, there is lower prize money since fewer people are thrilled by sidecar racing, are not there to provide the greater revenues that would warrant it. Second, there is less sponsorship from companies aiming to advertise their product through the sport, and there is less demand from television companies to broadcast it – all comparative to solo bike racing and much more so comparative to car racing. This has led to a drop-in income – instead of a growth in income – for those teams who aim to make a living out of the sport. Indeed remarkably few sidecar teams today are able to do so. Third, as a participant sport, the cost of building or purchasing a new sidecar outfit amounts to much the same if not more than a Formula 3 car. Further the demand for new racing sidecars is considerably less than the demand for new F3 cars, so the economies of scale are not there. It follows, this has knock-on effects for the second-hand market also. In sum, in spite of the remarkable efforts of a few dedicated people to develop the sport, for example Helen Gibson and others in the Isle of Man who ensure burgeoning grids of outfits, sidecar racing is very much a minority sport.

In the 1950s, by contrast, European 'race-goers' flocked to 'internationals' – i.e. not just those events that counted towards the World Championship each year – to watch top-class professional sidecar drivers and their riders battle it out on road circuits that today would be described as ludicrously lethal. Nonetheless, to be able to make a living as a professional sidecar racer, it was essential to earn start and prize money on as many weekends as possible; two, three and sometimes even four times a month. This financial aspect drove the 'circus' whereby all the regular teams would arrive, each in their own time, at a race venue and make camp, do the event, strike camp and move on to the next meeting. From late spring to early Autumn, they would therefore be criss-crossing the Continent during the weeks so as to be racing at the weekends. Further, the five years 1952–1956 witnessed advances in machine design that would permanently change the sport, and that still be seen clearly in the outfits of today. Such was the pace of development in this period that some of the advances witnessed in machine design of that time even presaged some of the more recent advances in solo racing motorcycle design. This was particularly where the focus was on using technological innovation in the chassis and streamlining to overcome power disadvantages of British engines in particular that, conversely and by complete contrast to the German and Italian engines of the time, had suffered from a thorough lack of development.

Motorcycle racing had restarted in a bleak post-war Europe in 1949, but the focus of manufacturers was very much on solos rather than sidecars. It was left to individual drivers, such as Eric Oliver in the UK, to come to their own agreements with the motorcycle manufacturers to adapt solos for sidecar use; Oliver and his rider Denis Jenkinson, of later Mille Miglia and journalistic fame, won the inaugural World Championship with a Norton-Watsonian outfit. That said, the Italian Gilera marque invested in a works team of two outfits and very nearly won the World Championship in 1950 and 1951; only the genius of Oliver and his Italian rider Lorenzo Dobelli kept them at bay. By 1952 BMW were beginning to invest seriously in the sport, and their ongoing investment would soon result in a dominance that would extend almost unbroken for 30 years to 1974. By 1952, then, with a full complement of sidecars filling the starting grids and with all three of the major manufacturers of the day, Norton with Eric Oliver, Gilera and BMW, directly (as opposed to merely offering engines and frames for sale to privateers) involved, sidecar racing had finally emerged from the shadow of the Second World War.

Thus the events of 1952–1956 were of especial importance to the sport. Genuine competition among the teams was most evident, transformational innovation was most apparent, and public interest in the sport was high for they could see a direct connection between the sidecars being raced and the sidecars they rode. The 'front-exit' design of the sidecars meant that the riders' work in balancing the machine through corners was much more apparent, their having to move backwards along the sidecar to 'get out' on left handers and 'over the back' for right handers (with left mounted sidecars; the opposite for right mounted ones). Since the wheels and tyres used were still at that time much the same size and width as solo tyres meant that their 'acrobatics' took place amid much high-speed drifting of the outfit. In the 1950s, sidecar racing was much more exciting to watch than solo motorcycle racing. By complete contrast to today, sidecars then were *the* motorcycle racing spectacle.

II. Watsonian

The business of sidecar racing, however, is not just about the sidecar rider, the driver or even the motorcycle manufacturer. For there to be a sidecar at all, there has to be a sidecar manufacturer. In the UK there was only one manufacturer that was seriously building sidecar outfits for international road racing – Watsonian. Stan found Watsonian to be a friendly place, and the experimental and race development shop was similar to the culture BSA Gold Star shop. Although he was being paid by Eric Oliver at £10 a week, he worked with Ben Willets on the standard sidecar he and Oliver would use in the 1953 season – and of course the kneeler. This was built by Watsonian and designed by Ben Willets using similar basic principles to that which guided the kneeler solo. Eric Oliver had been a apart of the world speed record team that had used the kneeler solo at Montlhéry in the winter of 1952, a machine that Stan, too, had tested in his role as chief experimental tester at Nortons.

An excellent article appeared in The Motor Cycle on Thursday 2 July 1953 focused on the technical aspects of the kneeler, reprinted in the January/ February issue of Classic Racer 2014 by Malcolm Wheeler (Wheeler, 2014). The timing of the original publication was intentional for it coincided with the machine's debut at the Belgian Grand Prix that very weekend. Copies of it and its competitor journal Motor Cycling which came out the same day and also had an article on the machine would have most likely been rushed to Spa next day, in time for the event on the 4th and 5th. Perhaps most notable, in the light of the stability issue, was the fitment of a 'sidecar undershield [...], a smooth surface beneath the sidecar chassis [...] to cut down wind resistance' (p. 6).

While this of course presaged all recent chassis development not only in sidecars but also racing cars, when coupled with the shape of the sidecar fairing quite obviously to the modern eye created a shape very akin to an aeroplane wing, as opposed to a shape the opposite of an aeroplane wing, right in the middle of the machine. This produced forces strong enough to distort the fairing and force the inch-long rubber attachment bolts completely out of shape, one squeezed fat, the other stretched thin, bolts that could not be compressed at all ordinarily even with a vice. This effect had not been witnessed in the wind tunnel tests, we may presume because it had not been felt necessary to produce wind speeds of 140 mph; the effect of the streamlining at smoothing airflow could be produced at far lower speeds. There is some irony in this because, as the article notes, aeronautical principles were used in the design of the machine fairing, with ducting designed such that 'the main air stream flowing past the outlets will exert an extractor effect and so will suck spilled air through the duct, thereby reducing the drag [in a manner] similar to that employed on aero-engine radiators' (p. 6).

In addition air was 'directed onto the cylinder head by means of an internal scoop' from the air intake built into the sidecar fairing (p. 7).

But for that one aerodynamic oversight, the machine was a great success and, with a redesigned fairing was campaigned by Eric Oliver and Les Nutt in 1954 as their only outfit, employing a very narrow special mini-fairing for short circuits to cut down the weight. It was of course revolutionary and established the principle for all sidecars particularly from 1960 onwards when kneelers became the norm. Before then, the adoption of the enclosed kneeler principle was slow to take effect, partly because of the need for a completely different chassis to a 'sitter', for which it was possible to modify a solo frame sufficiently and thus reduce cost. Watsonian were also heavily involved in the development of a different approach to racing sidecars that was effectively a half-way house in-between a traditional 'sitter' and a 'kneeler' that Ben Willets developed with Cyril Smith. This design is discussed in detail in Chapter 7; suffice to say it yielded advances that were in their own way significant, pre-dated similar advances in sidecars and solos by 50 years, and were undoubtedly effective.

Stan found Watsonian to be quite different to Norton, not only because there he had been involved with the Featherbed frame that was heavily resisted by the Norton design shop and that had involved numerous arguments, but it was a more family atmosphere at Watsonian that allowed the experimental shop to be more open to truing genuinely new ideas. The family atmosphere was evidenced by the offer to repaint Stan's Peugeot 202 from a light green to a dark blue after he bought it at the end of 1954, which they did free of charge. The new ideas came not only in the kneeler, for example, but also in pioneering the use of glass-reinforced plastic to make sidecar bodies. Stan helped Willets make the first one in the winter of 1952/3 and remembers it as an awful, messy and itchy job, because of the glass fibre's effect on the skin. The Watsonian Director's Minute Books for the period 1949–1956 show incidental expenses as ranging from £655 in 1949 to £637 in 1956. There is a notable dip in 1952 – £509 and 1953 – £518. Perhaps interestingly as the sidecar rider, Stan never received any bonuses at any stage of his racing career. Indeed they were never mentioned; Watsonian saw themselves very much as working for the driver – and as early as 1951 were paying Eric Oliver £6.10s a week for the privilege.

By the time Stan Dibben first went into the Watsonian factory in November 1952, the company had been in business for forty years. The first meeting of the Patent Collapsible Side-Car Company Ltd was held on 20

January 1913, with the name changing to the Watsonian Folding Sidecar Co Ltd as a result of a 'Special Meeting of the Company' on 14 September that year (Watson, 1913–1963). While the change of name reflected the controlling interest in the company of its two main shareholders George and Thomas Frederick Watson, nonetheless, the venture's fortunes at this time hinged on the patent that enabled a sidecar to be bolted to a motorcycle and hinged, indeed, to allow it to be parked up in much narrower confines than with other sidecars of the time. This made it attractive to families living in the cities where narrow lanes were a major feature of the industrial housing. The focus at this stage of the company, therefore, was in providing a mode of transport to the masses, and this continued right through to the immediate postwar period, when Stan was working in the factory.

At the March 1921 Annual General Meeting, Thomas Watson had taken over as Chairman and by 1936, the company was able to issue a dividend of 10% less tax on the employee preference shares with an additional remuneration to T.F. Watson of £550 (ibid.). The company, now named Watsonian Sidecar Co Ltd, grew significantly during the Second World War, with sales increasing from £54,311 in 1938 to £85, 212 by 1944; they enjoyed a sales increase of £9,986 in 1944 alone. What is interesting is that 1940 saw a dramatic drop in sales and revenue which, according to the minute books, was 'mainly due to the change in the type of manufacture due to the intervention of war conditions' (ibid.), which required that the company dip into its reserves having made a loss of £1,069. By 1941, they had turned things around and made £5,229 net profit on a turnover of £31,550 compared with a turnover of £29,030 the previous year. The war affected the company in a manner similar to Mid-Southern Utility Co: There was an initial drop in revenue due to a collapse in consumer confidence and a shift to war work. This was then quickly recovered as a result of the increasing military demand (in this case) for sidecars and other war-related equipment able to be manufactured using the same tools and techniques, such as fire trailers.

By the 1950s, and now under the Chairmanship of Ron Watson, the company was benefitting from the post-war boom in motorcycle sales, with the small inexpensive mass-produced family car that would replace the sidecar as the main mode of transport for the masses still some way over the horizon. The company was at its absolute zenith during the 1950s, arguably the world's leading sidecar manufacturer. Indeed, the sales, gross profit and net profit figures for the eleven years 1952–1962 make for interesting reading, as follows.

Year	1952	1953	1954	1955	1956	1957	1958	1959	1960	1961	1962
Sales £	391416	445699	469164	447117	<u>239436</u>	322084	299596	n/a	335077	283214	227449
Gr. Pr £	163928	171563	183478	172329	100871	99322	94419	n/a	112103	100461	69031
Nt. Pr £	92268	97216	103534	98495	34290	35990	39811	n/a	51530	44026	10527
NP/S	23.5%	21.8%	22.1%	22.0%	14.3%	11.2%	13.3%	n/a	15.4%	15.5%	<u>4.6%</u>

The drop-in profit percentage in 1956 may have been due to the company taking over Swallow sidecars in that year. Three other factors no doubt affected sales. First, the Suez Crisis caused a fuel shortage. Second, by this stage British Norton Watsonian sidecars were no longer winning Grand Prix. This was also the year that the company started to mass produce the glass-reinforced plastic sidecar bodies, which took longer to make but in the long run expected to be cheaper to manufacture and did not suffer from the corrosion problems of the all metal bodies. The loss in profit percentage in 1957 can be explained too by the learning costs of this new manufacturing method being absorbed. The growth in sales in the late-1950s and early 1960s can in part be associated with Watsonian winning the contract for the RAC sidecar roadside repair vehicles and by the Watsonian sales being augmented by the demand for Swallow sidecars. By 1963, however, sales had fallen again to £177,128 and by 1963 they made a sales loss for the year of £460, which worsened again to £1,260.

By this stage, however, the Morris Mini had begun to replace the sidecar as the cheap family transport. Sales and particularly profits in 1962 were a far cry from what they had been a decade earlier, but the very small profit *percentage* is hard to explain. What is clear is that the good times were over. Steib sidecars, the largest Germany manufacturer, founded in 1913 and Watsonian's largest competitor, actually stopped production altogether in 1965 it can reasonably be surmised for the same reasons. Although the company survived until 1989 by focussing on agricultural equipment, it no longer exists. Of course, on the sidecar side, it always faced competition from Ural who gained access to the original designs as part of war reparations and continue to manufacture sidecars successfully. There is an irony in this since today Watsonian is now an official agent for Ural, selling their combinations alongside the sidecars they make themselves. While at first glance there would appear to be direct competition between the two, the market segment each occupies is by and large quite different. Ural only import motorcycle and sidecar outfits already assembled as complete entities geared towards on and, importantly, off-road touring, whereas Watsonian sell separate sidecars for subsequent fitment to a wide range of solo motorcycles aimed at the road user. In this sense the two manufacturers' products, when taken together largely dominate the entire sector. This is important for Watsonian as a retail business; it offers a one-stop shop for sidecar sales and service.

Watsonian survived the 1960s by relying on the many years of financial reserves it had built up, and by reducing the size of its workforce. The 1970s were a time where the mainstay of the business was in the manufacture of fibreglass roofs for Land Rover. When this ceased, more drastic measures were needed. The company closed its Birmingham factory and moved to its present location of Blockley, near Moreton-in-Marsh, with only a dozen staff. It had gone from a major fixture of the motorcycle industry to a small firm on a trading estate in the Cotswolds but, crucially, it had survived – and in a way that would allow it to prosper as a small business. In 1988, it merged with Squire sidecars as an inevitable restructure of the British sidecar industry, since sales of sidecars had continued to contract. In 1999, the company was approached by Royal Enfield with an offer to become the official importer of Royal Enfield from India. At this stage, Royal Enfield were manufacturing a machine that was almost unchanged from the version that had been sent to India to be manufactured for the Indian Army, the original British company having long-since disappeared, and Watsonian saw this as a way of further diversifying their business to provide another income stream. Over the 14 years of this association, Watsonian used its own manufacturing expertise to provide much advice to Royal Enfield in improving the product, and developed a wide range of 'special' versions of the 500 cc single, including, Trials endure and Clubmans café racer models. Although these were popular – they harked back to the romantic era of the British Motorcycle industry, from a business point of view they proved costly to make, as a lot of manufacturing and rebuilding work had to be done to create them.

The decision not to renew the contract the company had with Royal Enfield to be the official importer in 2013 is instructive of how the culture of Watsonian remains largely unchanged from its earlier times, and instructive of how the company has been able to remain in business. When Royal Enfield brought out the fuel injection engine to replace the carburetted version this included a move from a separate gearbox to a gearbox integrated with the engine, but there was a component problem. Royal Enfield sent new components to be fitted under warranty to solve the issue, but this meant that all the bikes Watsonian had already sent out to dealers had to be recalled, the engines removed from the frames, the faulty components replaced with the new components, the engines reinstalled in the frames and the bikes sent back to the dealers. As Ben Matthews noted (pers. comm. with Mark Dibben, 7 June 2016)

> The dealers were very understanding, and we had 25 people working to do the warranties and they did a great job. Luckily, we had a spare building here and we turned that into a factory of sorts and although Royal Enfield covered the parts, they expected us to cover the labour. That ended up being near-enough £100,000. It changed the company too, because I had to be a man-manager with over 30 people to think about, as well as rushing about the country picking up and delivering bikes. Quite apart from that warranty issue, we were really working very hard. That was okay at the time because we thought we were doing really well. Until the costs were added up, and we realised weren't making much money at all.
>
> None of us enjoyed that time and Royal Enfield really wanted us to scale up. So we decided not to renew the importer contract but just remain a dealer for them, as a side-issue – if you'll excuse the pun – to the sidecars. We had thought ten years ago the sidecars really were going to stop, that there wasn't enough market for them, but that's changed. We're making as much money now as we were as the RE importer and there are only 6 of us here now. It's a much nicer place to come to work in the morning, and we have control of our own products.

In short, Watsonian has resisted the urge of what E.F. Schumacher described as 'giantism' witnessed in the motorcycle industry. It is likely Watsonian would have succumbed to the debt that would have been necessary to meet Royal Enfield's growth expectations. Remaining small and doing good work focused on the enjoyment of artisan scale hand-built manufacture has allowed it to quietly prosper as a small business, in a similar manner to the equally traditional car maker Morgan.

In a similar manner to Morgan, too, most new models such as the Meteor and Zanzara models are updates of old models to suit current market demand, in this case the re-cycled drop-tanks from the World War Two Mosquito aircraft that the company turned into sidecar outfits. However, the new Flight model designed for contemporary enduro style motorcycles such as the BMW GS range, and its new 'Barefoot Caravans' venture, demonstrate that despite or perhaps because of its small size, the company retains a capacity for innovation. Further, its strategic shift away from being the Royal Enfield importer and the intentional downsizing of the business has allowed it to act quickly to adjust to market demands, building from its past, to remain profitable.

In sum, the history of Watsonian is replete with examples of shrewd business decisions such as this; they are surely the reason it continues successfully manufacturing sidecars to this day. Despite the enormous changes witnessed in the motorcycle industry over the century of its existence, during which motorcycles and motorcycle and sidecar combinations have gone from everyday transport for families to expensive leisure products, Watsonian has held true to its origins. The values that Stan Dibben witnessed when working at the company in the winter of 1952/3 are intact. By remaining a small person-centred company, it has survived where others have not. That it does so in the era of cheap motor cars and many competing high-end leisure activities counts as a remarkable achievement, one that perhaps even surpasses its achievements as the pre-eminent sidecar manufacture of the 1950s.

Watsonian are the premier sidecar manufacturer, still in existence today. This is their 1937 Lilleshal Sports model. Source: Watsonian Archives

6

THE SIDECAR RIDER

World Champions Eric Oliver and Stan Dibben, racing the first ever fully streamlined kneeler sidecar outfit in 1953. Stan is as far out as he can get, with his arms straight and with his knees drawn up as far as possible. This ensures maximum weight acting outside of, and forward of, the sidecar wheel to prevent the sidecar from lifting due to the g forces of high speed cornering.

1. What Makes a Sidecar Rider

It is little known that sidecar racing has produced more British World Championship winning teams than any other sport since 1949. Of course there is the driver too, but what makes a racing sidecar rider? By which I mean professionals, not those only doing it for fun. It's a serious business and addictive. There is psychological aspect in connection with inner strengths. Love of everything connected with the activity; it's analysis. Above everything, self discipline. There is understanding, the willingness to learn, the ability to concentrate totally and act under extreme pressure and stress, from which comes self-confidence, along with the ability to work within, and debate within, the team.

There is a technical aspect also. The ability to anticipate, analyse, and understand every probable and possible scenario, performing at speed the actions required related to traction, G forces and balance, and therefore understanding precise weight distribution and placement. Putting into action lessons learnt during practice sessions. Remembering at all times that exhibitionism is not conducive to success. Lastly, there is a physical aspect. Height as required to facilitate movement. Body weight kept under control by sensible diet, no, or minimum alcohol consumption and hard work. Obesity becomes ballast and means poor power to weight ratio, and the lack of the required ability to 'time' and move precisely as required.

Why is there such poor TV and media coverage? F1 car racing has good general public interest because the public can relate to their four wheeled cars. There are no modern three wheeled cars. Why is there massive interest in Wimbledon when the vast majority of spectators have most likely never held a tennis racket? The TV and press coverage centres on the massive endeavour needed to win to which the public can relate. And football. I suppose spectators can relate to kicking a ball, to the prevalent cheating, lack of discipline and intimidation of those in authority. Crowd hysteria too plays a part. National pride, too, has a bearing on sport.

Why then such poor media coverage on sidecar racing? The effort needed to ride a racing sidecar is appreciated by those in the sport, although there are a few who find it expedient for financial or egotistical reasons not to acknowledge the effort.

Although sidecar rider names have in general and recent years been published, the misnomer 'passenger' is still used. The activity is often laughed at by many, using expressions like 'you must be mad', and jocular names like 'a bit on the side', 'swinger,' or 'monkey'. How can general public interest be generated with these sort of inherent jocular but nonetheless derogatory terms? Of course, the simple fact is that, unlike in its heyday when I was racing, sidecars are rarely seen on the road today and so cannot be 'connected to'; people have no concept of the ultra high-speed Olympics athleticism involved in modern 190 mph sidecars.

2. What is it like to Ride a Sidecar?

There is a 'family' feeling within the fraternity. Camaraderie of the sort found in the active armed forces. A shared understanding of the risks, and a mutual understanding of the sense of achievement. There are no 'losers' among those who do not win.

The dictionary definition:

> *Ballast. Anything carried on a ship or vehicle to give stability.*
> *Passenger. A member of a group or team who is not participating fully in the work.*

It seems one is taken for a ride, and not a metaphorical one!

Have no doubt, the word 'passenger' in the context of sidecar racing was and still is a misnomer. Sidecar rider, or as they are known in Germany, *beifahrar*, is a more accurate description. Certainly in the early days of the sport, the passenger was just that. He or she sat in a wicker basket, suitably attached to a solo motorcycle, and simply went for the ride. The only reward? Either a thrill or a cure for constipation!

In post war years things changed – and how! 'Passengers' they were no longer. More correctly they were sidecar riders possessing special abilities and exceptional levels of physical fitness and self-discipline. Unfortunately in the UK, the 'passenger' tag had stuck, with the rewards, and more importantly, the recognition sadly reflecting the word. The eminent road racer and journalist Fergus Anderson wrote in 'The Motorcycle' 17 April 1952 'I take a dim view of even coupling the passenger's name with that of the driver. You can take any normally active person and he will quickly learn to be as good as any other.' I knew Fergus quite well and by the time he and I had a few discussions in 1953 he had come to very different conclusions. Is it any wonder that passengers were seen in such poor half-witted light.

Allow me in a few paragraphs to take you back to the 1950's and attempt to give the feel for what was involved in being a high-speed road racing sidecar rider. No longer is the norm sitting and leaning to counteract the 'g' forces. The sidecar, an aluminium sheet covered with a 1 cm thick vinyl covered foam cushion (I dispensed with the foam as it added just added weight), with a 2 cm high ridge across the back on which to place one's shins and assist in keeping toes off the road when laying prone on the fastest parts of the circuit. Shortened big toes very painful. Lightweight boxing boots offer some brief protection but it still hurts to bounce your toes on the road at 140 mph! The platform, usually covered with oil from an exposed primary chain lubricated by total loss drip feed oiler, quickly becomes a skating rink, even more so when racing in the rain.

The sidecar is (or should be) tailor made and individually suited handhold positions are of paramount importance, if the regulation minimum 60 kg weight sidecar rider is to achieve the speedy and precisely timed movements of Olympic standards necessary, to have a significant bearing on lap times. To achieve this precision, hours are spent in the workshop moving around the sidecar platform finding the handholds without looking for them, eyes closed. It's necessary too to learn how to use the forces of gravity to lessen the workload. Time the movement too late and you need muscles like a champion weight lifter to counteract those G forces, move too soon, and run the considerable risk of going into orbit. Get it totally wrong and run out of road at best, or end up upside down both alive if lady luck is with you, but doubtless with an irate driver.

The golden rule: Never let go with both hands at the same time. Not always easy in a tight left right or right left 'S' bend.

Course examination on arrival always meant looking at the verges of the left handers. There might be a stone hidden in the grass where I wanted to put my shoulder. Boulder to shoulder hurts! Pre-race discussions involved race tactics based on what we thought the opposition would do, and we were usually able to work the plan. A tough 'no quarter given or asked sport' this.

Line up on the starting grid; fastest in practice at the front. Dead engine start. Goggles down (full-face helmets not thought of yet). All is quiet. Very quiet. The starter's flag drops, push like hell, usually about three strides, the engine fires, leap aboard. Noise like thunder, exhaust pipe just a foot or so away, sidecar trying to get away from you. Haul yourself aboard by grabbing the right handhold behind the driver's left leg, reach out with the left hand for the handhold up in the sidecar nose and pull yourself into the prone position hoping that the outfit behind doesn't put its front wheel between your legs! Make a mistake and end up with a bloody nose and a few missing teeth. Hang on to the handhold positioned in the nose of the sidecar fairing. Up through the gears, a left-hand corner approaches.

Tuck the knees up by your chest, move hands to the handholds; one at time remember; slide out left enough to balance the outfit before the apex of the corner, a bit more if the sidecar lifts, a bit less if the outfit goes into over-steer. The essence of team work. Round the corner, slide back in, all movements as smooth as possible. This is an outfit balancing act remember. Head now down behind the front fairing, keep it out of the wind, head up can lose 200 or 300 rpm. Count off the seconds now before the next manoeuvre. It's a right hander. To drift or not to drift that is the question. Where's the opposition?

Before brakes go on, right hand grabs the handhold by the driver's left leg, left hand joins right hand and then let's go. Standing up now for maximum wind brake with one foot forward for control. At peel off point before the apex of the corner, left hand joins the right one which moves immediately to the hold under the driver's right leg. Head and shoulders now behind the driver's back, rider's ear too close to the megaphone exhaust for comfort. Feet now positioned to control drift; as near as possible to the rear wheel for maximum adhesion, or on the move as much as necessary towards the sidecar mudguard to promote or control drift. Coming out of the corner now and the right hand joins the left which immediately reaches forward to grab the one under the front fairing; let go with the right hand and dive into the prone position for the straight. Split second timing here. Get it wrong and end up running up the road faster than an Olympic sprinter at best, or major facial disfigurement. We are not leading the race. Another left approaching, it's bumpy; watch your feet in the primary chain, slide out, stones and dust pepper your face now inches from the sidecar in front A bank on the left with loose dirt. My shoulder rubs it sending a shower of dust and stones over the outfit behind. It drops away! Smoke from the squealing tyres from those in front; hot hot exhaust gasses fill my lungs. Sidecar lifting, out further now, both arms straight shoulder and hips scraping the road and very close to the outfit in front.

Be prepared for deceleration to avoid running into it. Speed about 95 mph. Left arm taking the strain to avoid being thrown forward and off the front. That's better, now we're in front. No more stones and dust in my face. Must get a good facemask, a handkerchief not really good enough. (Full-face helmets would later solve this problem!) Slide back in, don't put your foot into the primary chain, and resume the prone position with right ear inches away from that whirring chain. Deafening noise from the single cylinder 7,000 rpm 500 cc Norton engine. Only another few laps to go, another 40 or 50 corners, before the chequered flag, another race over. Cruise back to the pits and the blissful silence. Take the cotton wool out of my ears and be left with the tinnitus still with me after 50 years.

That was what an uneventful race was like. Sometimes things weren't quite as straightforward!

3. Racing after Retirement

If you get addicted to the sidecar racing game – perhaps I should say 'when' not 'if' – you end up not being able to say 'no'! In 1957, Golden Jubilee Year, it had been decided to discontinue using the Clypse course for the TT races in the Isle of Man, which meant that the sidecars would be racing on the main thirty-seven and three-quarter mile course after many years. Eric Oliver had been asked to open the roads after the Senior 500 cc solo race to see what sort of lap times could be expected. He phoned me. 'Will you do it with me? You are the only one I can think of who knows the way around.' Both Eric and I had raced solo machines around the course and we looked forward with much enthusiasm to the opportunity. Our lap times no doubt resulted in the 'chairs' racing on the main circuit. I couldn't resist the chance to go round there. It is a fabulous place.

I rode once with Pip Harris, one of the best UK sidecar drivers. He found himself at Scarborough with an empty 'chair'. I was attending the meeting on behalf of Perry Chain Co, so it must have been 1958. It was certainly interesting. I think we came third. Not too bad, and I found I still enjoyed it. Came 1960 and the inevitable 'Will you do it with me Stan?', this time from Eric Oliver. I was going to be there in my capacity as assistant to Peter Tye, so with his reluctant blessing I was able to say to Eric 'Sure I will. It will be part of the history of the TT races and I'll be proud to do it'. This was the year when the sidecar TT had been brought back to the big circuit from the Clypse course. Eric and I had been retired from racing but we both felt that, since we had both ridden solos in the TT, our course knowledge was such that we had a very good chance of winning. The machine was a fully streamlined outfit, very fast, with an Earles type front suspension that looked a bit like the rear suspension bolted on the front. This system had been used on solo racing machines by BMW and MV Agusta and so I thought it should be sound enough. The standing start practice lap was way up on everybody else and we were really enjoying ourselves on the flying lap.

Our discussions on how to take certain corners were being put into practice. Barregarrow was a real challenge. We had made a special trip by car to have a look at this very fast left hander. Eric reckoned it was flat out in top gear if all the road could be used. No room for me to get out in the customary fashion because of the wall, which was right up to the edge of the road. On top of this there is a hump, over what I think is a bridge, at the apex of the corner. The front wheel would drop over the hump and cause the sidecar wheel to lift. I suggested we use all the road and I would simply get out as and when I could, keeping my left ear next to the wall as it receded. Helmets then were 'bone domes', the protective shell, such as it was, started above the ears and all you had covering your ears was a bit of leather. With a bit of right steering, we agreed we should be okay, and we were. It was flat out, and gave the marshals there a bit of a fright. I remember seeing them scatter, and one of them told me all about when I met the in the pits a couple of days later. Apparently, the marshals couldn't see the approaching bikes from where they were positioned, but only hear them. They would listen for the sound of the revs dropping as the rider eased (lifted) off the throttle; this was the sign the rider knew there was a corner in front of him on the approach. Only we had taken it flat out. 'We heard you coming. We knew it was you – it had to be. But you just *kept* coming. Not even a lift. And we just thought 'Christ! Olly's forgotten where he is.' He laughed, 'You sod!'

The first practice lap was fairly quick at 79.71 mph, the quickest of the session by an incredible 7 mph. The next one, a flying lap, was going very well indeed, as we rushed up the mountain part of the lap. We got as far as the left hander above the corner known as Guthrie's Memorial, and that is the last thing I remember until waking up in Nobles hospital. Sadly, that was the end of our 1960 TT. The front forks had broken off the bike complete with wheel and fairing, and I wonder if our antics at Barregarrow had started the fork problem. Eric ended up yards off the road with a badly damaged back. I escaped with nothing more than concussion and a few bruises. I had been caught up in the wire and brought to a relatively gentle stop. This had happened at about 5 a.m. in the morning. I remember nothing about the incident. Peter Tye came into the hospital round about 8 a.m. I remember the worried look on his face.

I suffered no apparent serious injuries, but Eric's back injuries were more severe. Within 24 hours, I was back to my product support job with two generous black eyes and plenty of bruises, and had to settle for watching the rest of the TT from the pits. Our speed to the point of the crash was such that we should have won the race by a fair margin. It's still a major disappointment to me, a great Isle of Man TT enthusiast to this day. The long Spa Francorchamps circuit in Belgium, now not used at all, and the big Nürburgring circuit in Germany, now no longer used for Grand Prix, are real favourites of mine, but the Mountain Course on the Isle of Man is the Mount Everest of racing circuits. It has been castigated by many due to the number of fatalities over its long history. I am always saddened by untimely deaths and even in very recent years some of those have been friends, the wonderful and talented Dwight Beare to name but one. The TT and Manx Grand Prix events are almost always over-subscribed.

Many more apply to ride there each year than the organisers will accept. We might well question the experience of many at the lower end of the field who are there to experience riding extremely quickly on public roads, rather than to be competitive insofar as the races themselves are concerned. Nonetheless, it's enduring popularity with racers and non-racers alike, as well as the spectators, is a function of the 'Mount Everest' challenge the course represents and, for all the careful preparation, there will always be mishaps both human and mechanical. Certainly there is no room for error, but the throttle goes in both directions and must be used with disciplined self-control. As for me, many years later when in hospital for a gall bladder operation, it was discovered that one or two internal organs weren't quite where they should have been. The surgeon told me afterwards they had needed some slight repositioning and, after asking me several questions, put it down to the accident at the 1960 TT. Funny, I never felt any discomfort at the time.

Only twice more did I race on sidecars. Some twenty years after my last TT, in 1978, Eric phoned me to join him in two vintage races. 'Nobody seems to be able to beat those 3 wheeled Moggies any more. So I've got this mad idea.' By 'Moggies', Eric meant the vintage Morgan 3 wheeled cars that always raced in the sidecar events in the 1950s, and were never a problem then. It seemed that in the vintage scene they were very much a force to be reckoned with, I think because of access to more modern engine parts. Anyway, Olly thought this needed sorting out and his 'mad idea' consisted of a typically fastidiously prepared girder forked (the vintage date cut-off that year was 1949, so telescopic forks weren't allowed), methanol burning, high compression long stroke engine. The first event at Mallory Park we won without too much difficulty. I hope that doesn't sound too conceited. I remember Eric saying to me 'are you sure you are happy to ride with me again? I've had a couple of heart attacks you know.' I didn't have any concerns there, we could handle it, 'You are more likely to have a problem of that nature in the paddock waiting to go out on the circuit, and we will be stationary then.' We didn't do the second round at Cadwell Park (I'm near certain it was, because it was such a trek to get there being Lincoln that we'd have needed to stay overnight), so the next and last event was at Brands Hatch and we went very well.

One of Eric's favourite tricks had always been to rush up the inside of the opposition and take the corner off them. He hadn't forgotten it. We dispatched two moggies in this fashion, one at the sweeping right hand corner after the start and one at the next corner, the hairpin at the top of the hill. Both tried to turn in, only to find we had dived underneath them and were already where they needed to be. The inevitable happened: They slewed sideways and tipped upside down. Typical Olly, he would take no prisoners! We were leading the race until Eric missed a gear change approaching the last corner and much to his incredible annoyance, we came 'second to a Moggie!' He was so cross with himself he wouldn't go up on the podium. The Master of Ceremonies waited and waited but to no avail; we had gone straight back to the pits. Olly was insistent. 'No,' he quietly insisted, exhausted. 'We didn't win. We don't deserve to be there.' Our fastest lap had been a mere second or so slower than when we had last raced there 25 years earlier. With a combined age of 123 years, it could have been worse!

4. Why Do It? – And Where?

I was often asked and often wonder myself what the attraction was in the strange activity. Both my drivers Eric Oliver and Cyril Smith have long-since left this earth. On his retirement from sidecar racing, Eric tried his hand at sports cars with many victories. He raced these probably mostly for fun, but still with that well-known determination to win. He also ran a successful motorcycle retail business. Sadly, he died on 1 March 1980 after a lengthy and frustrating illness related to an earlier heart attack. Cyril became my father in law and there is so much more to be said about him that he is the subject of the next chapter. Suffice to say here that both had served their country in World War Two with patriotism and great distinction. It was therefore not surprising that despite ever-outclassed Norton machinery and in Cyril's case in particular, poor Norton support such that he had to pay for all his Norton engine parts, neither would take up offers made by 'foreign' manufacturers. Although rather more so for Cyril than Eric, there was definitely a patriotic element to both their racing. It wasn't just for the fun of it for either of them, of course, but standing on the podium Eric's pride was more in the personal achievement and the reward that followed, Cyril's pride was in and for something else. For Cyril it was primarily patriotic.

In my case, of course, I look back to the moment Joe Craig, my boss at Norton, told me Eric Oliver needed a bit of ballast. As a young man, I suppose I just couldn't resist the chance to be involved with an already three-time World Champion. I raced sidecars because I was willingly coerced. What did it take to perform at World Championship level? Without doubt it was the most life-threatening form of racing. Thrilling, physically very demanding, great self-discipline and self-control, the ultimate in mutual trust and excellent for adrenaline production. Courage? I never thought of it in that way. The bikes you were racing against are all going in the same direction, usually, and all going at the same speed, roughly. They're certainly not coming straight for you as they are on the open road. I think W.B. Yeats, in his poem about the Irish Airman, probably got it about right, 'A lonely impulse of delight led to this tumult …' I daresay it's just in the genes of some young people to take risks and seek thrills with a healthy disregard for their own safety. There was also the mental challenge. I think Rudyard Kipling's 'If' captures this aspect perfectly with the lines 'If you can force your heart and nerve and sinew to serve your turn long after they are gone, and so hold on when there is nothing in you except the will which says to them "Hold on!"' I have met many motorcycle and car racers, and the best are often quiet, thoughtful, even methodical people. The traits they all share are determination and, above all, an unshakeable confidence in their own ability. No doubt skydivers are the same, but that's something that has never tempted me – I don't like the inevitability of the sudden stop if the 'brakes' fail! At least with a motorbike you stand a chance.

After I had retired at the end of 1956, I was asked to draw up a proposed bonus schedule for all motor sport activities for consideration by the controlling body within the industry, the British Motorcycle and Cycle Industries Association, of which all major manufacturers, wholesalers and retailers were members. This was 1957 and I fully engaged now as assistant competitions manager for the Perry Chain Co. For the first time I included sidecar riders (passengers) in the bonus schedule. The meeting was attended by most of the directors in the motorcycle industry; Norton, AJS, Matchless, BSA and all. Imagine my feelings when the Perry Chain Co. representative at the meeting Howard Gibbs told me that my idea had been turned down out of hand with the comment 'Sidecar riders; passengers you mean. Nonsense! If we agree to that, we shall be expected to pay mechanics in respect of wins!' What an arrogant insult, indicative of no appreciation of the risks, skill and guts involved. Howard was a good man and embarrassed to relay such a message. Did they think sidecar riders (passengers) were all illiterate, ignorant idiots?

5. Les Nutt

Racing sidecars before the Second World War were little more than wicker baskets with the – yes aptly called – 'passenger' sitting in them unable to influence proceedings very much. By the 1950s, racing sidecar design had progressed such that passengers they were no longer, but the name and therefore the concept had stuck. Their status was reflected in the low amounts of prize money. While Formula 1 drivers are ever-increasingly cocooned in their specially designed machines with protection built into the design, we sidecar riders are out on the edge with only our leathers between us and the tarmac. Modern solo riders have knee and even elbow sliders but there was certainly no such thing in the 1950s. We'd have needed hip sliders. Sidecar events have surely provided many exciting and dangerous moments, However we aren't generally considered for sport-related awards. I'm afraid bravery and skill just aren't enough. Sidecars are nowadays only associated with the odd 'crazy' family, all trussed up with the kids in the sidecar and Mum on the back-riding pillion. Or even better, Dad on the back-riding pillion! I can assure you they are having a lot more fun than the vast majority of the people travelling along in their shiny air-conditioned boxes. Still, sidecars have very little status as modes of transport in the today's world. Along with status comes glamour, and I don't think we sidecar racers are a glamorous lot really. More gritty than glamorous. The solo boys often look upon us as 'unhinged.' However, a very special arrangement exists between driver and rider in a successful team.

In any era, it is tempting to make comparisons of ability and style. Some sidecar drivers and riders are perceived to be better than others are. Some do stand out above the rest. In sidecar racing, sidecar drivers have always been the main focus of attention in the media. Yet it has always been the case, too, that the very best drivers know and understand the crucial role played by their sidecar riders in their success. Clearly the main focus of this book are the exploits of its first author. To focus on the 1950s, the World Championship successes of the BMW teams from 1954 have kept the German sidecar riders, such as Fritz Cron, Karl Remmert, Hans Strauß and Manfred Grunwald, more readily well known. However, it would be most remiss not to mention immediately other sidecar riders of the 1950s era who were undeniably world class, even if the machines they were riding were increasingly being outclassed. Perhaps we should mention first Inge Stoll, the superb female sidecar rider who was tragically killed along with her driver Jacques Drion in a racing accident. Her abilities as a sidecar rider were well recognised within the 'circus', but were unfortunately ignored by the media somewhat in favour of her gender; clearly, this did her a tremendous disservice. Other names from the first years of the World Championship must include Denis Jenkinson. He won the inaugural World Championship in 1949 with Eric Oliver and became well known as a motor sport journalist and navigator for Stirling Moss in winning the Mille Miglia. He was to some extent instrumental in what was to become the basic design of the 1950's sidecars. Max George partnered the all-time supremo of Australian sidecar racing Bob Mitchell, and Lorenzo Dobelli won two World Championships with Eric Oliver in 1950 and 1951. Eric Bliss raced with Eric Oliver in 1955 and with Cyril Smith in 1957 and 1958, and at the TT in 1959. With Cyril in particular, he achieved some fine results, perhaps most notably a second at the 1957 Italian GP at Monza.

Bob Clements was Cyril's rider for much of the 1952 season, they developed the high-speed drift technique together that allowed them to be so competitive that year, and that Cyril would use with Less Nutt in 1953. It shouldn't be forgotten that Cyril and Bob won the German Grand Prix together, which put them at the top of the World Championship standings. Bob retired immediately after that meeting, however, when he received a telegram from his wife threatened to divorce him if he didn't return home immediately. Pip Harris' regular rider Ray Campbell, too, was clearly world class; together they achieved some excellent international podiums and top-five results particularly in 1956 and 1957.

Perhaps the most underrated of the British riders at World Championship level, though, is Les Nutt. Les only did three full seasons on the Continent 1952–1954, but rode with Eric Oliver in 1947 and 1948 in the UK as well as the occasional overseas race, and again in the UK during 1950 and 1951 when Eric was partnered in Europe by another world class rider, the Italian Lorenzo Dobelli. Les stayed at home out of loyalty to the garage where he worked and, but for this, could easily have been riding with Eric Oliver when he won his three successive world titles 1949–51. He went on the continent in 1952 with another driver he rode a lot with at his local Cadwell Park circuit, Jackie Beeton. Jackie released him to ride with Cyril Smith for the Italian GP as a result of his own machine going through a bad patch of reliability (Nutt, in Hawtin 1993).

Since neither Les nor Bob Clements did the full season with Cyril Smith in 1952, that year was the first in which two riders' names were recorded as winning the championship alongside Cyril, but no F.I.M. (Fédération Internationale de Motocyclisme, the official world governing body of motorcycle sport) World Championship medal for the sidecar rider was actually awarded. Further, Les and Cyril finished equal on total points won with Eric Oliver and I at the end of the 1953 season, losing the World Championship by half a bike's length as we have seen. Further still, Les was denied a near-certain World Championship in 1954. Having won the opening three rounds of the World Championship at the Isle of Man TT, the Ulster GP and the Belgian GP at Spa, he missed the German GP at Solitude as a result of the accident he and Eric Oliver had at Feldberg that left Eric with a broken arm. It broke again during the Swiss GP and, although they managed fifth despite this, it put paid to the season (Louth, 1983). In sum then, Les Nutt was without doubt the World Champion sidecar rider England never had.

6. Comparing the Modern Era with the 1950s – and with Formula 1

Modern sidecars are clearly different from those of 50 years ago, and rider athletic activity not perceived as being so vital – in fact it's still remarkably important, but I would argue that there has never been a motor sport activity where risk to life and limb is greater. I have had the chance in recent years to ride modern racing sidecars and that experience, coupled with conversations around the world with riders who have mastered both front exit and rear exist sidecars gives me some sense of what they are like and what the differences are. Conversations with people like Gloria Gates, 11 times New Zealand South island Champion who (along with her partner and driver Colin Hooper, sadly killed at a race at Ruapuna), has done so much to keep the sport alive in that part of the world, and Paul Woodhead the triple World Champion with Steve Webster. It's a somewhat similar, somewhat different skill. The accelerative forces of 200 bhp and modern wide sticky tyres would make it very difficult to get forwards to lie prone having been 'over the back', for example. But then all that power puts a premium on correct use of the rider's weight. The influence able to be exerted on left handers isn't so great, but there's still a reasonable amount you can do on right handers. Although considerably safer than those of 50 years ago, it is obviously not possible for modern sidecars to match the safety advances made in F1 cars. Today's F1 car racers would demand ten times their current earnings to race the F1 cars of the 1950s, let alone those first mid 1950's fully streamlined 140/150 miles an hour outfits of Eric Oliver, Cyril Smith, Willi Noll et al. Perhaps rightly so. Sponsorship was non-existent in the UK, for the rider at any rate. I am told by Annette Daykin, rider for her late husband Robin, that even today riders often have to pay their way more than be paid, contributing their share of the petrol and entry fee for example. Well, rightly so – as long as the prize money is given back in similar measure.

As you know, my favourite circuits without doubt were the Isle of Man, the big Nürburgring and the long Spa Francorchamps circuit not now used for major motorcycle racing events: too dangerous. Floreffe and Mettet, both Belgian circuits too. There was also the wonderful Solitude near Stuttgart. Berne, in Switzerland was a fast, fine and challenging arena. I would have found the current short tracks not to my liking. Although there was more risk to life and limb, I preferred the pure road circuits rather than the short multi lap races with their flat out for a few seconds, brakes hard on, a bit more flat out and so on and on and on and on 'earoling' to the chequered flag. More space if you fall off, but I found their stop-start, stop-start feel more tiresome than rewarding. Around and around and around. There never seemed to be anything much to them, nothing to really catch your attention. Where would you prefer to go snorkelling? Endless lengths in a swimming pool, or the Great Barrier Reef off the coast of Australia? Sure, there may be sharks, but that just comes with the territory. And they're only reef sharks. Most of the time.

Today we see champagne squirted by the litre over winners on the rostrum. What a waste! I never experienced that sort of cooling down. Standing up there on the rostrum, helmet and goggles off, sweaty, ears ringing to the point of deafness, feeling the anticlimax of dangers overcome and success over opposition. Proud too with the Union Jack flying and the National Anthem playing, honouring our achievement, often an emotional experience with feelings of patriotism not so long after World War Two. Then the prize giving dinner and dance now with friends who, only a short while ago, had been the opposition and would soon be again. I even found myself playing trumpet with the band on the odd occasion.

To quote Bob McIntyre in his book *Motorcycling Today 1962*: 'I must confess that as a ticket buying spectator, I would prefer watching sidecar races to solo events. The chariots are a wonderfully exciting spectacle and I don't think race organisers allot sufficient races for the sidecars. The prize money for the winners is smaller than for solo class winners. Sidecar drivers should be put on an equal footing: they certainly give value for money. Undoubtedly the greatest I have ever seen was Eric Oliver'.

Sadly sidecar racing is not now run alongside the major solo motorcycle races. I know of no valid sport, much less 'spectacle', reason. Sidecars were replaced by the mini as the cheap ride to work and family transport. Long gone are the days of the 'double adult' sidecar. Consequently, the general public cannot relate to this form of transport in any way and there are therefore no commercial spin-offs. Having said that, I can well imagine the oohs and aahs of television viewers that would come from watching the performance of sidecar riders of the era, racing with a video camera suitably placed on a top-flight rider's helmet. It would certainly have confirmed the misnomer and given the current health and safety people forty fits!

7. It's a Matter of Trust

Which brings me back to the question I have often been asked: 'Why do it?' The answer usually comes in the form of another question, 'Why not?', to which the reply is often 'But it's so dangerous!' True, it has its risks, but the risks are all relative. Still I can think of no other sport where two people are more reliant on each other for their safety and success than sidecar racing, and in circumstances too where verbal communication is impossible. It all comes down to trust. It turns out my son's early academic expertise was in this very subject; his observations have been instrumental in my better understanding why I, and other sidecar riders, are able to perform in such a highly dangerous activity.

Trust is a complicated subject when given adequate thought. It concerns a positive expectation regarding the behaviour of the other person in a situation entailing risk for you – 'interpersonal situational trust.' More specifically, this trust will be based around a shared professional understanding of the situation. Considerable knowledge, intensity and comprehension of a host of detailed situational cues, enable rational assessments under well-understood circumstances to be made and communicated in action by both parties, very rapidly. The success or otherwise of this, time after time, leads to a level of trust felt by one party for the other party and vice versa, manifest biochemically in fact through neuropeptides. Yes, you really do *feel* trust! It is too often perceived that the one in the sidecar must trust the one manipulating the brakes and throttle. I would argue from experience, not so. In the case of both the driver and the rider of a sidecar outfit, the trust they each have for each other, when the partnership is working, is more than they have for their own respective spouses. They have to … Perhaps this is one of the reasons the Birchall brothers have been so successful in recent years, they are clearly brilliant in their respective roles and there is an absolute connection.

By contrast, it must surely be crazy for a driver to take aboard ballast, i.e. without proper consideration of a sidecar rider's ability. I suppose it is often done because 'It'll be fun', 'I've always wanted to have a go', 'I've always wanted to do it', perhaps for journalistic experience. Well it might be more possible now for a bit of fun – not anywhere near the limit of course – with the comparative lack of movement available or necessary in modern rear exit sidecars, but a 1950s front exit sidecar platform, slippery with oil, takes some riding at over a hundred miles an hour. Will they be able to ride it properly and not merely hold on for dear life? Folly, too, to ride on a sidecar without considering everything about the driver. Blind trust?? Can he forget where he is going? (My experience with Cyril Smith at the Nürburgring in 1954; we worked out a solution.) And what about the machinery, will it break? (My experience in the Isle of Man in 1960; a bit late for a solution!)

Thinking about the trusts involved helps demonstrate that, ever since the beginning of the World Championship and even a bit before that, the word passenger has been a misnomer. Rider or *beifahrer* as the Germans call them, is a far better description of the task. After all, the rough driving may be done by the sidecar driver, but the fine steering is done by the sidecar rider!

***

I. How to Enjoy Riding a Sidecar

A more detailed account that explains the role of the sidecar rider, that inevitably repeats in different ways what has been said above, may yet prove to be instructive in the art of racing sidecars.[1] Clearly it is a tremendous thing to race a sidecar outfit. Nowhere else in motorsport, and perhaps in sport in general, is there such an intimate reliance on one's sporting partner. That reliance is made more remarkable by the fact that for the most part the one cannot see what the other is doing, and they cannot speak to each other while it's all happening. Both parties have to have absolute trust in the other, or serious accidents will be the result. Second, it should by now be clear that this sidecar game is addictive. Once it gets under your skin, the joyous lunacy of it never leaves you. It is tremendous fun!

A sidecar outfit – be this a front exit or rear exit, vintage or modern – is designed in such a way that it absolutely requires two people to get the most out of it, the driver and the rider. Obviously the driver is the person who is in charge of the throttle, brake and steering, and that input is well known. There are some challenges in comparison with being on a solo motorcycle such that, as a rule, you have to 'drive the bike around the sidecar' and 'coast the sidecar around the bike' in order to get it to go through corners. If we assume the sidecar is mounted on the left of the motorcycle, this means you drive the bike through left handers, otherwise the sidecar wheel would lift and the whole machine would go upside down. Or at least it would, if you didn't have the rider in the sidecar to stop it. And coast it through right handers, otherwise the machine will have a tendency to want to go straight on, taken in that direction by the effect of the sidecar wheel which of course is fixed in the straight-ahead position and is not self-steering. Or at least it would go straight on, if you didn't have the sidecar rider over the driven back wheel to add more weight to the machine and allow it be driven quite early out of the corner. Remember that (just as with a car) the inherent stability comes from the fixed wheels and what they're doing, not the steerable one(s) and what it's (they're) doing.

Clearly the driver does the steering and power application to put the machine where it needs to be, but thereafter it is the person in the sidecar who does much of the fine tuning. This is achieved by sometimes quite subtle use of body weight in different positions to, for example, stop the machine drifting, to promote drift, to ensure an early application of power on the exit of a corner, and of course to ensure the maximum possible speed can be carried through a corner. This is the work of a gymnast who has to have quite a bit of situational awareness of what is going on with the opposition around them, to be able to anticipate what is needed. A rider who masters this will gain the confidence of their driver very quickly and the team will – as long as the machine itself is reasonably competitive of course – most likely enjoy a lot of success. They will certainly enjoy themselves.

The sidecar rider – notice we're not calling them 'passengers', much less 'swingers' or 'monkeys' or any other derogatory term! – has to be physically fit and agile, but not necessarily very strong. It is a common misunderstanding that sidecar riders need brute strength. In fact, it is the driver who has to be quite strong, particularly in the upper body, in order to cope with not only the acceleration and braking but also the lateral g-forces involved in cornering, and the strength required to turn the handlebars. The rider on the other hand can work with the g-forces when moving around, particularly on front exit sidecars. If a rider finds s/he is fighting the lateral g-forces when cornering then s/he needs to have another think about the timing of the moves s/he is making. Clearly one has to hold on when accelerating but also under braking because the g-forces can be immense, especially with modern high-powered machines with wide, sticky tires.

With front exit sidecars in particular, where there is a bit more room to move about, it is possible to make life a lot easier in coping with braking. On the approach to left handers in a left-hand sidecar, of course you are usually lying flat (prone) on the sidecar and so you can brace with your arms. If you are changing direction right-left then you can use the braking forces to help you forwards and vice versa, accelerative forces left-right. Admittedly it takes a bit of effort to go left-right under braking and right-left under acceleration (the other way around for a right-hand sidecar). So you need to be able to find the handholds so that you don't miss them. Stan used to practice for hours on the bike in the garage, until he could move about with absolute confidence, blindfolded. You'll be too busy to go looking for them; your hands need to find them almost instinctively. Ideally, the outfit should be made-to-measure and the placement of the handholds exactly where you need them to be. Clearly this is not often possible, which makes being able to find the handholds where they are with absolute certainty, all the more important.

For right handers under braking, when you are kneeling at the back of the sidecar, you have got nothing in front of you to hold on to, all your handholds are to your right, and so there is a risk of being pitched forward. Stan found the way to brace for braking in this situation is to have my right hand over the back of the machine on the handhold located somewhere behind the driver's right foot, and my left hand on the handhold located somewhere behind the driver's left foot. To do this, one is in a semi-kneeling position. He then put his left foot forward so that, with a straight left leg, the heel of his left boot is 'dug into' the sidecar platform. Clearly if you are riding a right-hand sidecar it is the right leg that is straight, the heel of the right boot that is 'dug in'. This will provide all the bracing you will ever need and, with you hands on the correct handholds already, you can still move over the back of the machine as the brakes come off and before the strong lateral forces come on.

Moving with the forces and not against them is a key to both not becoming too fatigued and being in concert with the outfit; it allows the transfer of weight to be smoother and thus more effective. Some drivers like to feel the rider move, there being a slight 'nudge' this way or that. If you are right on the limit of adhesion such a 'nudge' can pitch the machine into a spin, but in any case, the best riders move so fluently and smoothly that they are never felt. Stan once rode (briefly!) with a driver who kept shutting off, worried he had fallen off, because the driver couldn't feel him move. This was dangerous obviously, because Stan was liable to be pitched overboard with such unexpected engine braking. He had to tell him 'If you don't feel me move, I've moved!'

Getting over the back wheel for right handers (or if the sidecar is on the right, for left handers) is not simply about allowing early application of the throttle on exit because of the extra weight over the rear wheel. It is in fact more about fine control of the outfit through the corner. Depending on what is needed, this is about preventing or promoting oversteer or understeer. To prevent oversteer, ie. the back of the machine becoming 'tail-happy', your feet are placed as close to and as parallel to the rear wheel as possible. Stan never braced himself using his feet against the sidecar wheel. All this does is transfer most of one's weight to the sidecar wheel, which is not where it needs to be. This is because weight is transferred through your feet, so the closer your feet are to the rear wheel the more weight is on the rear wheel. This prevents oversteer and stabilises the bike.

In contrast, to promote oversteer, or promote drift through a right hander (with a sidecar mounted on the left), you move your feet further and further away from the rear wheel and nearer the sidecar wheel, as far as necessary to achieve the drift you want. This is also one way of avoiding understeer, because the front of the bike will tend naturally to turn in, but when on the limit of grip, it will promote a two-wheel drift. Another way of correcting understeer on right handers, particularly on the limit of grip, is to keep your feet parallel and close to the rear wheel but move your body as far forward over the back of the bike as possible, so that your head is probably in line with the driver's hips. With rear exit modern sidecars, this is the most effective way of correcting understeer through right handers.

Remember too that in fast, slight right-handers, it may not be necessary to actually get over the back of the bike at all, but instead remain semi-kneeling with your upper body still in the sidecar itself. At the other extreme in fast tight right-handers, then you are all the way over the back. There is infinite room for adjustment between these two positions as required by the corner and the circumstances of the race. For example, you may be able to allow the machine to drift on exit, but also stop it drifting. In one famous race at Silverstone in 1954, Stan knew he could stop the outfit drifting on the exit of the last corner (Woodcote – a fast right hander), if he wanted to, but he left the door open by letting the outfit drift every lap. As he and Cyril Smith got there on the very last lap, he knew the opposition would try and come up the inside to overtake us, so he stopped it drifting and shut the door. They won this, the first race they did together, beating Eric Oliver and Les Nutt on the re-streamlined kneeler using only a 'dustbin' front fairing on a more traditional outfit.

As you exit corners, use the g-forces to help you back into the sidecar. As the lateral forces diminish and the accelerative forces increase, there will be a precise moment where they almost cancel each other out – almost a moment of 'nothing'. This is the best time to change hand holds, particularly when doing fast left-right or right-left changes of direction. You never let go with both hands. That said, with front exit sidecars, there are very rare occasions where it is necessary to dive forwards in a change of direction. But you don't want to get the timing of that manoeuver wrong!!

Left handers on a front exit sidecar with the sidecar on the left (and vice-versa for sidecars on the right) provide further opportunities for the rider to influence proceedings. There is less freedom of movement with a rear exit sidecar but the principles are much the same. If the corner is of quite shallow radius, only a left kink, you may either not need to move from the prone position at all, or you may need to get out left but forward of and still close to the sidecar nose and with your legs straight behind you. That is, just enough to correct understeer as the bike is driven through the corner. At the other extreme in a very tight but fast left hander, you would be looking to move quite early so that you are not fighting lateral g forces and so that you can move in concert with the entry, apex and exit. This requires careful positioning of the hand holds so that you can 'rotate' all the way out and back in again. The sidecar rider's effect on the sidecar wheel is in part a function of the leverage you generate by being 'all the way out', but it is also a function of where your legs are. To get the most effect both to stop the sidecar wheel lifting and also to prevent understeer, draw your knees up so that they are almost in the nose of the sidecar.

Between these two extremes, prone but forward of the sidecar on the one hand and 'all the way out' with the knees tucked up on the other hand, is an infinite range of adjustment depending upon the requirements of the corner and of the circumstances of the racing. For example, if you are in danger of another outfit darting up the inside on a left hander, 'all the way out' is useful, but on fast and slight corners, the less wind resistance you can generate the faster the bike can go. It may be, too, that there is too much weight forward and you're getting the back of the bike drifting out in oversteer. In that case your legs would need to be further back. It's all a question of adjusting what you are doing to suit the mix of issues you are dealing with, but what has hopefully been indicated is that there is a tremendous amount of adjustment possible both on left and right handers. The range of adjustment isn't quite as great with a rear exit sidecar and also the g-forces are greater with wide and sticky tires, but the basic principles are the same.

By way of a conclusion, when it comes down to it, successful sidecar racing is all about complete understanding and cooperation between the driver and the rider. A lot of thinking and talking about what's going to happen and what is needed before the race, will reap dividends in the race. Your lives as well as your successes are in each others' hands. Get all this right and it is not only a great thrill but also confidence inspiring and a source of immense satisfaction. One counterintuitive thing, the real art of racing is to win as slowly as sensibly possible. Many people have crashed or retired through mechanical failure while being well in the lead. Quite apart from the expense and the embarrassment, championships can be lost that way. You really ought to go quicker in practice than in the race. It's good to know how quick you can go if you need to. If you're not at the serious end of the game, and even if you've come last, when you know you've got the best possible out of yourselves and the outfit, that's reason enough to be more than happy with the day's exploits. At whatever level, it's all about having fun. Onwards and upwards – so long as it's fun.

Notes

This section was written by request, for use at an American sidecar racing school, in February 2018.

Cyril Smith and Stan Dibben, Aintree, 1955. Stan has his left foot forward and his arms locked, braced against the braking forces, prior to 'going over the back' for the right hander

7

C.J.H. SMITH: OF TANKS AND SIDECARS

Cyril Smith, Italy, 1943, with some of the tools of his Quartermaster trade. Source: Tank Museum, Bovington

I rode with my father in law Cyril Smith, the 1952 World Sidecar Champion, during the 1954, 55 and 56 seasons. I knew he had worked in the Norton factory at Bracebridge Street, Birmingham, in charge of the production test department in the late 1940s, early 1950s. The Cyril we all knew in the racing world was a man of great courage and determination, happy to help without question those around him when needed, and never given the respect he deserved either for his abilities or his successes. I knew he had been at El Alamein during the war, but that was pretty much all I knew for he didn't speak of his war experiences to any great extent. In fact, he had a distinguished war record, having volunteered for the Army before the outbreak of hostilities. He fought not only at El Alamein but in the other horrendous battles in North Africa as part of the Eighth Army under General Montgomery, then on to the invasion of Sicily and Italy, and then the fighting in Greece.

He was Mentioned in Despatches when a Corporal (Acting Sergeant) and later went on to be probably the youngest Squadron Quartermaster Sergeant in the British Army, before being demobilized after the end of the war in 1946. Much of his wartime activity can now be found in the archives of the Tank Museum at Bovington in Dorset. This indicates that he had a very rough and dangerous time during the war. According to family lore, he saved the life of a Gurkha who had had his stomach blown open, by dragging him bodily out of a minefield and he was given a Gurkha Kukri knife in recognition. This was a rare honour of the type attested to us recently by the staff at the Gurkha Museum in Winchester (pers. comm. Doug Henderson and Christine Bernáth, 11/9/18): Kukris were not given to soldiers outside the Gurkha Regiment lightly. Cyril was very proud of it; it meant more to him than the Mention in Despatches for distinguished service that he was awarded for his work repairing tanks. The Kukri was very, very sharp indeed – both he and I cut our hands on it. And it came with two smaller knives, apparently for cutting the ears off the enemy dead as proof. The knives, too are now in Bovington's care. It is clear he was greatly thought of by his colleagues.

Cyril was a Birmingham man to his boots. The total Brummie, accent and all, and proud of it. And why not? This beer-drinking, hard talking character would never fail to give help and assistance when asked by his fellow racers. He was a pipe smoker, mingled with the occasional woodbine – not for him filtered cigarettes! – and a good man, a good mate. After he stopped racing he found work in Redcar on the North-East coast of England and moved with some reluctance from his native Birmingham, with his equally reluctant wife Irene. A phone call one evening informed me that he had driven cross the Penines to Keswick in the Lake District, and had been found dead in the very hotel where his daughter, my wife, Kathleen and I had spent our honeymoon. The mate I had risked my life with so many times on the racetracks had committed suicide at just 43 years of age.

Such a tragic event had a dramatic effect on life in general and left so many questions unanswered. His daughter to whom he had been so close was, like so many children in such circumstances, naturally wracked with irrational guilt. In the days when problems were kept 'in the family', and before counsellors were regarded as being able to make a healthy, positive contribution to everyday life – rather than being 'just for the daft' – I think it is fair to say she probably never got over it. I don't suppose I was much help. I'm sure many people say amongst other things that I, too, can be a stubborn sod at the best of times. I very quickly adopted the view that Cyril was a selfish bastard for what he did that night. Without doubt Cyril was a man of considerable substance whose tenacity and loyalty was never truly acknowledged or understood. My views about his suicide changed, along with society's I suppose, and clearly those who commit suicide are at their wits end. Nobody commits suicide 'lightly', even if they may commit suicide impulsively, consumed by overwhelming despair or a feeling of being a hopeless burden to others. Kathleen long maintained that Cyril's death, from an overdose of sleeping tablets, had been 'a cry for help', a mistake. So getting 'underneath the surface' to discover what might have driven my best mate over the edge has remained a profound hope of mine. Since Kathleen's death, much of his background has come to light.

***

I. Knowing Your Own Way

There is a memorial to Cyril J.H. Smith on the Isle of Man, organised by Helen Gibson, in the form of an oak tree planted by the Samaritans in Sulby Glen. It stands alongside others to commemorate the lives of TT racers who have committed suicide. On it is a brass plaque with the inscription 'The courage to know the pain of knowing'. On 1 September 1945, a poem was dedicated to Cyril 'in appreciation of the fine work he has done in the Desert – El Alamein – Tripoli, Sicily – Italy and Greece' (Hunter, 1945), an extract of which is as follows.

> *In times when things have struck us pretty hard,*
> *And 'Jerry' pressed down on us with lines of steel,*
> *Fighting tooth & nail & boot, with nothing barred,*
> *Old 'Smudge' was there with Faith we all could feel. [ctd.]*

Born on 2 January 1919 in Birmingham to working class parents, Cyril John Henry Smith was the eldest of three boys. The second brother Leonard who was a year younger was killed when his ship, the cruiser HMS *Neptune* with a crew of 764, sank with the loss of all but one when the flotilla it was leading steamed into an unknown German minefield off Tripoli on 19 December 1941. The youngest of the three brothers, Dennis, was born in 1927 and was too young to be called up for hostilities. The family were Quakers and, as such, pacifists. Yet Cyril refused to declare himself a Conscientious Objector and in fact volunteered on the 2 February 1939.

He remained close to his mother, a well-respected midwife, and the two remaining brothers got on well after the war, their respective children playing with each other when they were seven and eight and lived in Birmingham's Marston Green. Yet volunteering nonetheless seems to have placed an irrevocable schism in the family, for father and son were to remain effectively estranged for the rest of their lives. Arguments about joining up or not evidently brought Cyril and his girlfriend closer together in the summer of 1938, for Irene fell pregnant and they quickly married. She shared her boyfriend's dislike of his father, and would bring forth a pained expression from him whenever she suggested he was just like him. 'Oh, please don't say that. Anything but that!'

Irene apparently supported him joining up despite the fact that by then she was seven months pregnant. Apart from the occasional brief periods of leave while his regiment was in the UK up to May 1942, he was not to see his wife and daughter again until his return from fighting in the Greek Civil War, as part of the 'thin red line of black hats' (Hamilton, 1996), in the Spring of 1946. As was usual for those who volunteered as the conscription process was beginning, his Army record card was altered from volunteer to 'Duration WS' – i.e. service for the duration of the war – the original enlistment details having been rubbed out and written over (all Army record cards were written in pencil). This evidently did not change his father's impression of things, though it will have pleased his wife, who complained of being lonely while he was away; she formed a strong friendship with a former boyfriend whom his young daughter associated with as her father until Cyril returned home.

II. Tanks

It appears too from his Army record card held at the Tank Museum in Bovington, Dorset that, on Armistice Day 1939, Cyril was posted to the 50th Battalion of the Royal Tank Regiment – '50th Batt. RTR. 11/11/39'. As such, he would have been one of '47 men posted to the regiment, the first draft of other ranks' received that day (Hamilton, 1996: 14). 50 RTR was then in work up at Bristol before a move in May 1940 to Llandwrog, North Wales and then to Blundellsands near Liverpool in October where they received their first deployment of tanks. The first year had been spent in training and guarding local sites of military importance such as airfields. The first half of 1941 saw the regiment moving around the country, first to Swindon for training on Salisbury Plain and then Crowborough in Sussex. Following an inspection by HM King George VI on 1 May, it left for embarkation at Glasgow the next day, forming a part of 23rd Armoured Brigade which itself was part of the 8th Armoured Division. The Regiment left the Clyde along with the rest of the Division on 11 May on the troopship SS *Mooltan*, arriving at Capetown on 6 June. They left again on the 7th after a night's encampment ashore and arrived via the Cape of Good Hope at Port Tewfik, now Port Suez, on the Suez Canal in Egypt on 5 July (Hamilton, 1996: 14–25).

Cyril was part of the 'Echelon', the wheeled (lorries and jeeps; logistics and communication) as opposed to the tracked (tanks) part of the Regiment, attached to 23rd Armoured Brigade Workshops. He evidently showed a prowess for the logistical aspect of keeping the Regiment battle worthy as he was soon promoted to the Quartermaster ranks, specialising in tank repair and, later, recovery from the battlefield. According to S.D. Hamilton's catalogue of 50 RTR personnel honours and awards, he was one of only 4 members of its Echelons to be recognised formally for their actions (1996: 261–5). Upon arrival in the Middle East, the regiment's tanks were refitted at Geneifa where No. 4 Base Ordinance Workshop was located, and we may presume Cyril was involved in that. They were made ready by 15 July, and the regiment was sent into action on the 22nd, at 'an area of Ruin Ridge ([...] part of Mateiriya Ridge), south west of El Alamein railway station, in support of the 9th Australian Infantry Division's 24th Infantry Brigade' (Hamilton, 1996: 29). As such, they were part of the reinforcements brought up in the defence of British and Commonwealth forces' positions in what has come to be known as the First Battle of El Alamein, during which the German Eastward advance across North Africa to the oil fields was finally stopped.

In their first battle at El Alamein, 23 tanks were damaged, 10 of which were recovered. From this moment onwards 50 RTR gained a strong reputation within the British Eighth Army, itself rejuvenated under its new General Bernard Montgomery's leadership, as a first-class armoured regiment. It was used extensively in North Africa, Sicily and Italy, fighting in every major battle with the Eighth Army from El Alamein in July 1942 to the River Sangro in November 1943 – the only armoured unit to be able to claim that distinction. Indeed, 50 RTR 'spent 95% of its overseas deployment in contact with the enemy' (Hamilton, 1996, frontispiece). Similar levels of casualties in men and equipment were sustained throughout. Cyril was increasingly involved in tank recovery and repair work as a Quartermaster Sergeant, having his own Wight Scout car as a utility vehicle, a lorry and a crew of fitters for the purpose.

The Squadron Echelons were kept busy as part of 23rd Armoured Brigade Workshops after El Alamein, too, repairing tanks and recovering captured German vehicles as the pursuit of Rommel's Afrika Korps forces Westwards across the North African desert gathered pace. As Kennett and Tatman ([1970] 2003: 98–100) note, 'during the period 23 October–22 November 1942, [consolidated returns] show totals of 1,244 tanks recovered and 1,007 repaired' by the Eighth Army Corps of Electrical and Mechanical Engineers (REME) crews. (At this stage in its history, the REME was just in the process of being formed, and men were still regarded as being part of the Armoured Divisions, of which the Battalions and their Echelons formed a part.) The Echelons had a long difficult job in transporting the tanks across the desert from Tobruk in readiness for the assault on Tripoli in January 1943, due to poor weather. The transporters became bogged frequently and had to be winched up the hills. They also encountered many mines and blown bridges, the work of the retreating German forces (Hamilton, 1996: 81–3). Cyril told Irene after the war he had been injured by shrapnel in the desert when a mine had exploded. There is a photograph of Cyril in the desert in company with a fellow Sergeant, and with his left arm in a plaster cast. While he was not wounded sufficiently during the desert campaign for him to have been X2'd – 'evacuated behind regimental aid posts', i.e. to hospital – no record of such an evacuation being entered on his record card for that period, it is during the advance on Tripoli that this event is most likely to have occurred.

February 1943 saw 50 RTR as far West as Tunisia, where they captured the town of Ben Gardane, which was central to Montgomery's plans for the Eighth Army's farther advance (1958/2010: 157). B Squadron, of which Cyril was a part it seems for almost the entire war, was the first to enter the town. On the 20th B Squadron again captured a town, this time Medinine. In each operation, a tank had been lost to mines but there had been no casualties. There then followed a month as part of the defences at Medenine, which was Rommel's last North African counter-offensive, before they were readied to attack the German Mareth Line on 22 March (Hamilton, 1996: 86–9). This was 'one of the blackest, yet greatest days in the regiment's long and arduous active service in Egypt and North Africa' (ibid.: 90), for the regiment lost its Commanding Officer (CO) killed while at the same time leading the head-on assault on the

Mareth Line in what became known as the Battle of Mareth. The Regiment suffered high casualties in men and tanks but were ultimately successful in diverting enough of the Afrika Korp's attention away from its flanks that the New Zealand Division were successful in their 'left hook' and were able to link up with the 4th Indian Division. Outflanked, the enemy retreated from its most heavily defended position in North Africa.

The regiment was described at the time by 23rd Armoured Brigade CO Brigadier Richards in the following terms: 'I have no hesitation in saying there was no finer unit in the army than the one John [Cairns, CO] led into action on 23 March; his was the star battalion of the brigade' (Hamilton, 1996: 90). With a new CO, the regiment proceeded on, playing a large part in the subsequent Battle of Gabes Gap. Then, with the German forces defeated in North Africa by the end of May 1943, it re-equipped with the new American Sherman tank, gained 181 new recruits and re-supplied in June, in readiness for the invasion of Sicily on 8 July. Immediately upon victory in Sicily, there then followed the invasion of Italy on 3 September.

Throughout all this period, Cyril was sending postcards home. As was customary, postcards were often made from photographs. All of his wartime memorabilia was given to the Tank Museum, at Bovington in Dorset by the family. This includes two fully annotated photo albums. Many of the photos have notes on the back, such as 'Looking at this, sometimes I wonder if you'll still love me', 'To my dear wife and daughter, with all my love, Cyril', and 'Drunk! Sorry. Love, Cyril' There are also a handful that are of German soldiers. They are all from odd positions, such as from below and pointing up, at a distance, with sand in the foreground, and all printed using the same photographic paper as the others in the collection. One such is of a large tent in the distance, with three Germans standing around it, and one other dead under a sheet. Another is of a gun emplacement with two German soldiers manning it. The captions written on the back are usually 'Typical Germans'. Perhaps the strongest thing that stands out from reviewing the photos in the collection is the sense of camaraderie. A Sgt Hunter features quite prominently as 'The best Sgt in the 50th'. A number of other photos are of the crew of Cyril's White Scout Car, with 'some of the lads' as a caption on the back. Sometimes there is an outside shot either cooking or brewing tea 'before going up to the Blue', which is to say before going up to the front itself. Others are taken 'inside the back of the White' and one is taken from within the White in Italy, entitled 'Avoiding shellfire' – which can be seen ahead through the truck's windscreen.

III. The realities of tank recovery

The recovery teams, of which Cyril led one and of which there were only seven for the whole of the Eighth Army, each had a 3-ton truck and a White Scout Car and were entirely self-contained thus allowing recovery and repair of vehicles at all times and in all weathers (White, 1944). Major H.E. White's account of the activities of the 23rd Armoured Brigade during the North Africa, Sicily and Italy campaigns while he (and a predecessor) was its CO, gives a good insight into the work of the Echelons (White, 1944). Where a large number of tanks were put out of action, 'a crock dump is formed and the workshops move up to the crock dump'. At El Alamein, the Forward Detachment of the Recovery Section, 'was continuously shelled and bombed.' In Africa, where very great distances were covered, the Recovery Section 'travelled with Main Bgde HQ., and casualties were recovered from day-to-day battles, and crock dumps formed, for Workshops to move to. The backloading distances from Workshops to 3rd Line Workshops [i.e. base workshops] were normally very long.' Further, during the Mareth and Wadi Akarit battles, 'two complete teams … were sent forward.'

Sicily presented a completely different logistical challenge in tank recovery (Kennett and Tatman, [1970] 2003: 184–5). For each battle, various service teams would be sent forward to recover and repair tanks as quickly as possible. 'Due to the nature of the country, casualties of Sherman tanks from ditching and bogging were as many as the battle casualties. The movement [of the battle] was fast. Most of the casualties had to be towed by tractors … [and] as many as five service teams were out at once.' To save backloading, as far as possible 'tanks were repaired in situ', i.e. where they had been put out of action or become bogged or ditched. By contrast, in Italy (White, 1944: 13),

> due to the slower movement forward [of the battle], Workshop locations had to be decided by suitable locations of hard standing where possible. The actual recovery of tanks is more difficult, as invariably, due to the mountainous nature of the country, the casualty is under observation [by the enemy] during the day. Hence most of the recovery is carried out at night.

Due to the speed of the North Africa campaign, the Workshops had not able to recover tanks back to the '3rd Line', i.e. the main Workshop based far in the rear, so the forward teams were carrying out significant repairs and rebuilds in the field, 'in addition to normal 2nd linework'. Over two thousand vehicle repairs were carried out during the time 23rd Armoured Brigade Workshops were operative in North Africa, Sicily and Italy, of which some 900 were tank repairs, the others including trucks, light vehicles and guns. In just one month, 16 October to 15 November 1942, i.e. during the Second Battle of Alamein and the pursuit West across the desert, the total number of tanks recovered was 178 with 121 repaired (White, 1944: 21).

Following the Battle of the River Sangro in Italy, 50 RTR's Commanding Officer (CO) took the time to write up the Regimental War Diary October 1943–January 1944. His conclusion was that this period was the 'most fatiguing, if not the hardest fighting operation of the regiment's history' (Wilson, 1999: 162). Judging by the relative number of photographs in Cyril's albums, Italy was a particularly eventful period. The following (Wilson, 1999: 188) is the CO's summary of the vehicle 'casualties' for the period. It gives a sense both of the severity of the fighting and of the work being done to get vehicles operational again.

	Tanks	Carriers	S. Cars	B.Vehs	Totals
Repaired in Field Minor	128	21	10	6	165
Major	24				24
Repaired in A Echelon Minor	48	28	22	24	122
Major	74	32	34		140
Repaired in B Echelon Minor		4	12	46	62
Major	5	6	16	14	41
Totals	279	91	94	90	554
Bogged and towed out by Unit	73	12	6	72	163
Bogged and towed out by D8 Tractor	17				17
Totals	90	12	6	72	180
Knocked out by enemy action and 'Brewed Up'	10			1	11
Knocked out by enemy mines	17	1		1	19
Drowned	1				1
Totals	28	1		2	31

Appendix A to 50 R. Tanks Report on Operations.
Statement showing work carried out by Unit Technical Staff 23/10/43–5/1/44

Clearly, the recovery teams were working in difficult conditions for many months without let up. To get tanks recovered, repaired and back in the line as fast as possible required a good deal of quick thinking and innovative approaches to problems. In its own way, therefore, this was very much a work of 'enterprise on the edge' of battle. It was not unusual for repair crews to work 24 hours straight by eating and sleeping 'on' the tank being repaired (Kennett and Tatman, [1970] 2003). Cyril was awarded a Mention in Despatches, which was 'gazetted', i.e. published in March 1944; he told Irene after the war that this was for 72 hours' work repairing tanks. Given the 'many months' delay (Hamilton, 1986: 261) between the action for which the awards were recommended and their being gazetted, the award's March 1944 publication suggests this was most likely to have been at the time of the Battle of Sangro River in November 1943, during the Italian campaign. That is, during the very period enumerated by the CO above, when tanks were not only being damaged in battle but also bogged and ditched due to the poor ground.

During this period too, B Echelon came in for repeated attacks from the Luftwaffe, which killed 2nd Lt Pritchett, age 21, on 9 December 1943 (Wilson, 1999: 156). Not only were they dealing with the enemy but they were also dealing with the weather. According to the War Diary (ibid.: 160), on 1 January 1944, 'Snow in the B echelon area was four feet deep. There was a heavy rain storm before the snow, so that the ground was waterlogged and almost all B vehicles were immobilised off the roads.' Further, throughout much of the New Year period, it seems B Echelon was utilised as the main harbouring point for 50 RTR tanks in the Italian campaign (ibid.: 161).

IV. A case of unintended consequences?

Further, as a part of his War Diary, the CO Colonel J.C. Sleeman, provided a pithy analysis of the managerial, leadership, and logistical realities of the Regiment, under 'Section D – Administrative'. This was his observations and recommendations to higher command, and it reveals in some detail the challenges experienced by Quartermasters and their crews of fitters in the recovery and repair of materiel. All in all the report contains 76 separate topics of which Section D contains no less than 43, ranging from the supply of rum at one extreme to tank strength, ammunition and reinforcements at the other. Some of these are worth quoting directly, for they give a sense of battle from the standpoint of management, as follows (Wilson, 1999: 180–8).

50. Supply Vehicles for Armd Regts.
(A) The difficult going recently encountered makes the

provision of a suitable supply vehicle an urgent consideration. Throughout the day tanks edge forward, in support of infantry, over ground quite impassable to B vehicles, and when the time for replenishment arrives they are often quite 'ungetatable'. It has always been felt that a tracked supply vehicle is the only answer, which could at least go where tanks go.

The scale need not be large, two per Sqn being sufficient to enable tank requirements to be ferried from A echelon to the tank harbour. A tank chassis bearing a body similar to the old artillery dragon would be satisfactory – ensuring a reasonable cross-country performance and some protection for the crew and commodities. This unit has had no experience with the half-tracked White Scout Car, which might prove satisfactory. Replenishment has often had to be carried out within a few hundred yards of the forward defence lines, which, to say the least, has been a hazardous performance.

(B) All B [[supply]] vehicles should be of the 4 wheel-drive type – others should be regarded as obsolete.

51. Fitters Vehicles.

The present establishment of fitters vehicles (White Scout Car) is entirely inadequate. Fitters visit their squadrons every night wherever they may harbour, and to do this they are provided with vehicles quite incapable of crossing even moderately bad going and offering no real protection to the technical staff. It should be possible to provide each squadron with a tank chassis bearing side armour and a form of superstructure which could be converted into a fitters workshop, enabling even major repairs to be carried out 'in situ' rather than, as at the moment, returning to B.1. echelon area.

[…]

53. Ammunition.

(A) A.P. Before the Sangro battle, tank holdings were made up to 130 rounds. The additional quantity being H.E. After the

Sangro battle, owing to the number of enemy AFVs met and engaged, the proportion of ammunition carried was amended to 6 HE, 3AP, 1 Smoke.

(B) DA HE [Delayed action High explosive] This has proved the most satisfactory ammunition for houses. But it must be realised that the Italian houses are well-built, and it is not our job to destroy towns or villages.

(C) Ammunition Expenditure:

	23 Oct–4 Nov 1943	5 Nov–4 Jan 1944
75 mm HE	1421 Rounds	3780 Rounds
75 mm AP	195 rds	1177 rds
75 mm Smoke	77 rds	336 rds
2 inch HE	6 rds	16 rds
2 inch Smoke	115 rds	104 rds
0.45 inch TSMG	4900 rds	400 rds
0.300 inch Browning	15,325 rds	242,075 rds
0.303 inch Tracer	1600 rds	550 rds
0.303 inch Ball	6640 rds	4096 rds
Signals White	4 rds	2 rds
Signals Red	4 rds	nil
Signals Green	4 rds	nil
0.38 inch Pistol Rev	60 rds	nil

The tank strength during the above periods averaged 30.

54. Replenishment.
8 Indian Division has operated over the most difficult country, generally with poor communications. During the whole of the operations on the central sector the replenishment of tanks has been most difficult. Bad tracks, sometimes no track at all, bad going, few bridges, and shelling of essential maintenance routes added to the difficulties.

When B squadron [[Cyril's squadron]] were near Montefalcone, in front of Celenza, we replenished by mule train, each mule carrying about 10 rounds of 75 mm or about 4 tins of fuel, and although sure, it was rather slow.

During the river Moro operations, we have had to use a ferry service of carriers and 15-cwts, the tracks being so bad that 3-tonners were not allowed to use them, and as squadrons were at times carrying out static artillery shoots with HE, this meant an almost continuous service over a timed one-way route. The recce tp carriers cannot be spared for this work. Adequate vehicles should be issued – see para 50.

55. Water.
More powerful pumps are required, capable of drawing water from deep wells. In addition, large capacity tanks are required, as water is normally a problem. Something of a 30-cwt chassis is considered necessary.

[...]

57. Ration Holdings.
Ration holdings must be on a more generous scale than hitherto. It is entirely inadequate for tanks to live hand to mouth being rationed only every other day. If all tanks could be guaranteed to make squadron harbour each night it would not be so difficult, but with bad going, mines, etc, it means that every tank must be visited every other day with rations, which, though desirable, is often quite impractical. Owing to the difficulty of delivery, etc, it is recommended that 4 days, exclusive of the unexpired, be carried and, if possible, delivery to crews in boxes.

It is suggested that duplicate sets of boxes of suitable design and strength should be an issue in order that full may be exchanged for empty – or, at least some reasonable ration containers on the line of the housewives set of jars (jam, tea, sugar, etc,) should become normal tank equipment, actually fitted in the tank.

Experience during active operations over the past 18 months has proved that to treat armd regts as a bulk number of men, as for infantry units, is wrong. Army ration scales appear to be based upon an eighth of an ounce of something per man, which on communal feeding is quite satisfactory. But to cut down tank or vehicle crews such ingredients as syrup, jam, pickles etc is really quite ludicrous. This of course points to the AFV pack ration, which, especially during operations of this type, is the only answer. The Americans can do it, even down to individual men, which shows that it can be done.

58. Cookers.

5 Corps Catering Adviser has been provided with a design from this regt for an electric tank cooker, with a clamped-on kettle, worked off the Homelite. This would enable tank crews to have a 'brew-up' actually in the tank. Crews in recent operations have not been able to have any hot food whatsoever for as much as 24 hours.

The existing situation regarding the issue of the No. 2 tank cooker is unsatisfactory. Even when new, a large proportion fail to work, and with difficulty in obtaining spares, even serviceable ones become the same. It is rare to get any spares.

Great difficulty has been experienced in obtaining spares for Hydro-Cookers, and even with the most careful maintenance and nursing they go wrong, principally for lack of spare burner rings. This must be rectified.

59. Rum.

Rum issues always appear to be authorised very late in the day, often after dark, when all crews have turned in, making its issue either impossible or more of a nuisance than a boon. It is felt that if a rum issue is going to be necessary, it could be arranged much earlier.

It is felt that sufficient quantities should be carried by AFVs to tide them over two or three issues. These being authorised in the field by the regimental commander. If he is trusted with equipment valued at nearly two million pounds, surely he can be trusted to authorise a few shillings worth of rum.

60. Reinforcements.

(A) Insufficient provision has been made in the scale of reinforcements provided to cope with the increased number of sick evacuated during winter operations.

(B) Officers. Unless officers have actually fought in an armoured regiment prior to being commissioned, they are not fit to command a troop on arrival at unit from OCTU.

Time and equipment, therefore, must be available for training before an operation.

Owing to the high proportion of officer casualties suffered during battle, it is essential that a unit is well stocked with trained officers prior to operations.

E.g. Officer casualties of this unit between 4/11/43 and 10/1/44 are shown below:

Killed	6
(W.E. – 33 include Att M.O.)	
Wounded (include 2 att	16
Battle casualties evacuated	3
Courses in UK	2
School Instructors (ME and NA)	4
Kong Service abroad	1
Average absent – wounded, sick, courses:	9
Total	41

[The above casualty figures are confused and include people on courses and some counted twice, so in the table below I have listed officer casualties again.]

(C) Other Ranks. This unit may be more unfortunate than some, but the fact remains that since May 1943 when it converted to Shermans, only 10% of reinforcements received have been trained in Shermans. Of 37 ORs who arrived on 8/1/44 all had only a fortnight's Sherman experience.

OR casualties between 4/11/43 and 10/1/44 are shown below:

	Officers	Other Ranks
Killed	6	21
Wounded	16	52
Sick	?	85
Total	22	158

61. Training.

(A) A unit must therefore be given the following facilities:

Before battle 1) Be made up to full strength in officers and ORs, including 1st reinforcements immediately it is pulled out of the line. Actually, owing to sickness rate, number of attached would be welcome.

2) Time for training.

3) Equipment for training.

4) Suitable training area.

During battle 1) Be kept up to strength in trained personnel.

2) Hold additional to W.E. equipment in B echelon area for training purposes.

Unless this is done, there comes a time, if casualties are heavy, when the unit has used up all trained personnel. This period has been reached by this unit. Only 38 crews are now available. A unit should hold at least four Shermans and two carriers during operations in B echelon area for training purposes.

More instructors with recent practical experience are required at Training Establishments, Schools and Depots. Too many inexperienced [or those classified as] not required in unit, still stock these vital centres.

Units should hold a surplus of 1 officer and 29 men to cover the establishment required for the recce troop carriers – see para. 13.

Although this is meant to read as advice from the field, and genuine requests for more support, the impression it would give to a superior may well be of 'bellyaching' at best. It may even have been received with a growing annoyance. Higher up in the report is the following Section 42 (Wilson, 1999: 180).

42. German Tiger Tank.

On several occasions we were informed that Tiger tanks were reported at a certain place and that we were liable to encounter them.

The Sherman tank is out-gunned, out-armoured and out-sighted by the Tiger tank. The same applies to the Sherman tank in relation to the Panther and the Ferdinand.

Until we receive a better tank, the best antidote I can give is:

All our energies and thoughts must be devoted to attaining such rapidity and accuracy of fire that, in spite of our lighter guns, we should quickly attain 'fire mastery'.

This means that the rate of our fire must so dominate that of our opponent that the Tiger will be unable to use his heavier armament effectively, and that our best protection is the accurate and rapid fire of our own guns.

Battles are lost and won by men and not by machines.

This is nothing new to the RAC, who, unlike other services, have had to make do with inferior weapons practically throughout the war.

Such a note would be in danger of putting those in higher command who read it 'off-side', however much the information contained was acknowledged to be accurate.

Another part of Section D reads as follows, and is a chilling note in itself (Wilson, 1999: 187).

70. Identity Discs.

Identity disks are not proof against fire. Another substance should be issues to tank crews.

A great many of the British made Valentine tanks were vulnerable to catching fire ('brewing up') having been hit by even relatively light projectiles. The tanks crews gave them the nickname 'Ronsons' after the cigarette lighter, the Germans nicknamed them 'Tommy cookers'. The American Sherman tank was less prone to this problem but it still occurred. It evidently prompted this note regarding what the Americans call 'dog tags' worn by all soldiers. For identity disks to melt, the heat must have been significant, the task of identification of the bodies impossible. Quite apart from being a hell for the tank crews themselves, this also suggests the tank recovery crews will have seen some horrendous things.

It is evident Section D also reveals a range of supply and training problems, and significant recommendations such as developing the cooking facilities in the tanks, which were adopted (either directly or coincidentally) post war. We have quoted it at length, though, to give a sense of the general tone of the account. It is noteworthy, for it has a distinctive 'feel'. That is, one of a CO engaged in providing what he believes is valuable advice and requirements for his regiment but that comes across on occasion as a critique of the administrative systems and policies in place in the Armoured Brigade. While it no doubt reveals the challenges faced even in Italy (let alone the Desert before that) by 50 RTR, from a management perspective a natural immediate conclusion that might be drawn by those in high command from reading this document, is that the regiment was struggling.

It is important to note that it may not have been, but once a management impression is formed then the facts of the matter rather cease to be of relevance. After all, other RTR Battalions in Italy were engaged in similar operations and under similar pressures. What is clear is that within days of the report being written, the regiment was ordered to hand in its tanks and was rested. Less than a month after it, the CO was replaced. After another three months active service in the Italian campaign, the regiment was informed it would be relieved. It handed back its tanks for the final time on 16 May, and left for the Middle East on the 28th to commence training for an entirely different task. By October they were in Athens (Wilson, 1999: 204). The speed of decision making and the drastic change of role are such that it is worthwhile attempting to explore these decisions in more depth.

It is unusual for a regimental CO to write up such a comprehensive report, replete with observations and recommendations. We need to consider the possibility that Col Sleeman was asked to do so. 50 RTR was recognised as the best tank regiment; what better case study to consider? Which is to say, the statement of facts and the blunt requests for better support inherent in the report, no doubt further to verbal reports similar in nature, may have been requested. Whatever the case, the subliminal message that the regiment was struggling seems to have been heard. Further, many of the recommendations in Sleeman's report, such as the provision of the capability to cook within the hull of the tanks rather than outside, were subsequently taken up post war. It is clear from the War Diary, though, that none of the immediate requests for additional men and materiel seem to have been dealt with, nor was there any immediate rethink in what was being expected of 50 RTR and by extension other tank regiments. This may simply be because no more resources were available of course; to improve the lot of 50 RTR would have been to disadvantage others.

According to Hamilton's official history of 50 RTR, as a territorial regiment it had a quite informal approach, which was almost certainly different to Colonel Sleeman's as a regular officer and he may not have fitted in. He 'sadly never gained the respect or trust of the regiment … After the war John Sleeman became a very efficient high-grade staff officer' (Hamilton, 1996: 198). As Montgomery notes (1958/2010: 85–6), some officers are not suited to certain leadership roles but excel in others; Eisenhower in his view was far better suited to staff command and did not excel as a field general early in the war. Montgomery by his own account 'kept command appointments in [his] own hand, right down to and including battalion or regimental level' and was clear that 'if having received the help he might normally expect … from his immediate superior, […] a man fails – then he must go' (ibid.: 85). He would do this very quickly when the occasion warranted it (Montgomery, 1958/2012: 113) and frequently did so by sending regular officers home. His decisions in these matters have come to be seen as wise despite the ill feeling they caused (Barr, 2004: 257). Hamilton certainly makes the point that 50 RTR was Sleeman's first command, that it 'could not have come at a more difficult time than at the height of the Sangro battle; the pressure on him to succeed and to follow orders which he did not always agree with, must at times have been very severe' (1996: 198). Further, that he was perhaps treated unfairly by the regiment (ibid.). What is clear is that within three weeks of the report, Sleeman was relieved of command and posted back to the UK to be an Instructor at the Staff College.

While Sleeman's departure came at the very end of Montgomery's time in charge of the Eighth Army, by this stage the General's approach to matters would have been deeply infused within all its Divisions and Brigades, as he had 'acted early to bend [it] … to his will' (Barr, 2004: 257, also Royle, 2010). Further, Montgomery himself later acknowledged the administrative challenges the Eighth Army experienced in Italy, particularly in regard to 3rd line workshop availability and ammunition (1960: 127). That said, it was not unknown for him to replace individuals who had expressed one point of view, with others who expressed the same point of view whom he then believed (see Barr, 2004 and Royle, 2010). What is certain is that all this came at some cost to the regiment for, while all bar one of the other tank regiments of 23 Armoured Brigade followed Montgomery back to the UK and thence to Europe, the 50th Royal Tank Regiment was sent to Greece, and to the completely different task of peacekeeping. This is a task normally assigned only to infantry regiments. Evidently two simple management decisions were taken very quickly, namely to extract the CO from the field by posting him to a staff position back home, where his insights could be put to better use in informing new officers' thinking, and remove the regiment from frontline war work as soon as practicable. All in all, such decisions can be explained managerially on the grounds that, on the basis of the reports received, there was a clear risk to all concerned in doing otherwise and they were bound morally and as a matter of dutiful responsibility, to act on the reports received.

It should be pointed out that 40 RTR, 50 RTR's sister regular battalion, also found itself deployed to Athens, along with 2nd Battalion the Parachute Regiment and 11th Battalion Kings Royal Rifle Corps and later the Royal Dragoons. Yet *prima face*, for such a regiment as 50 RTR whose excellent reputation had always preceded it, that had uniquely been involved in every battle since El Alamein, not to have gone to Europe seems odd. This is especially since it had been regarded as the 'the finest unit in the army, the star battalion of 23rd Armoured Brigade' (Brigadier Richards, in Hamilton 1996: 91 and above), which is tantamount to saying the best fighting tank regiment in the British Army, and thus in all probability the world, at that point in the war. We have sought to explain managerially why this may or may not have occurred. The CO clearly demonstrated he was better suited to staff appointments and this was borne out in his subsequent career. Management responses often underpin command decisions (Pratten, 2009) and, in this case, the responses in regard to the regiment itself seem in many ways to have been the opposite to those explicitly sought by the CO, the 'middle manager' seeking to improve matters for his men. In sum, the decision not to send 50 RTR to Europe is, on the evidence of its War Diary, an excellent example of the law of unintended consequences in management.

V. Greece

This is not to say Greece was an easy assignment, although the regiment would doubtless have suffered far higher casualties had it been part of the European campaign. Greece was in effect a counter-insurgency operation on behalf of the Greek Government against the communist 'terrorist' groups ELAS and ELAM, which were engaging in what largely amounted to – and eventually became after British forces left in 1946 – a civil war. Politically, this was to ensure the Communists did not gain a foothold in Western Europe, and as such the operation was emphatically not without its importance as it amounted in effect to the first of the Cold War. It was also dangerous and involved at times some very serious street-to-street fighting; 27 officers and men were killed or missing believed killed, 62 wounded and 2 held prisoners of war. After the worst of the fighting had concluded, the Supreme Allied Commander, Mediterranean Theatre, Field Marshal Sir Harold Alexander addressed the regiment on 17 January 1945 as follows (Hamilton, 1996: 233):

> I realise you have had a particularly difficult task, which you
> have done extremely well. A tank man without a tank is like
> a cavalryman without a horse. You are all highly skilled tank
> technicians, but the experience you have gained will prove very
> useful. I am very grateful to you. It is now very obvious ...
> [that] if British troops had not taken the action they did, then
> there would have been large scale massacres in Greece. A good
> stout-hearted brigade on the spot prevented this. The Greek
> people are grateful to you. The test of a good soldier is if he can
> overcome a difficult situation however he is equipped. You all
> proved yourselves to be good soldiers. I know you will all be
> very glad to get tanks back again, and I hope to have you back
> with me again ...

That the regiment was deemed to have succeeded in this operation says much for the fundamental quality, training and indeed camaraderie of the men. Alexander's hope that the regiment would return to the main theatres of the Second World War was not to be fulfilled however. The regiment spent another year keeping the peace in Greece, still largely as an infantry regiment, with men returning home in greater numbers from January 1946 onwards. Strangely, 'unlike every other unit involved in the Greek Civil War ... the regiment was denied the battle honours "Athens" and "Greece 1944–1945"' (Hamilton, 1996: 235). Nor was it afforded the usual courtesy of returning home and being disbanded in the UK, even as a territorial as opposed to a regular regiment, for it was disbanded in Greece on 30 April 1946. We can only wonder why this was, for both decisions surely did the men of the regiment a disservice. It is difficult to draw any other conclusion than that it had 'blotted its copy-book.' Or, perhaps more accurately, had its copy-book unwittingly blotted for it.

VI. Cyril's War in Verse

Only very rarely were the dangerous and life-threatening experiences Cyril must have gone through ever mentioned once he returned to the UK. It was almost as if those experiences were to be kept solely for the 50 RTR reunions he would attend occasionally. His focus in the stories he would divulge was on the mechanical rather than the dangerous. Getting out to the damaged tanks, and getting them mobile again was recalled with a great deal of pride in the accomplishment of the small team he led. 'Crawling on your guts in the sand to fix tank tracks is no joke,' he noted on the back of one photograph. Yet, as is often the case with military folk, he would downplay the danger of the work through a casual dismissiveness of it. Clearly Cyril was liked, respected and highly valued. He left B Squadron which evidently he had been a part of from the start, at the beginning of September 1945 when 50 RTR had been in Greece for eleven months. Such was the regard in which he was held that a poem, an extract of which was presented at the beginning of the chapter, was written in his honour on behalf of the other non-commissioned officer and enlisted men of the Squadron.

> ### So Long [50th RTR] 'Smudge'
> *Tonight our hearts are full of deep felt grief*
> *The knowledge of a friend, now passing from our view*
> *The fact that 'Smudge' is leaving us; before you leave*
> *We'd like to say just what we think of you.*
> *In times when things have struck us pretty hard,*
> *And 'Jerry' pressed down on us with lines of steel,*
> *Fighting tooth & nail & boot, with nothing barred,*
> *Old 'Smudge' was there with Faith we all could feel.*
> *When things looked grim & tanks were off the track,*
> *When shot and shell were falling like the rain,*
> *Our 'Smudge' comes smiling through from somewhere at the back,*

And with his handy hammer, he gets them back again.
The one who pulled us from the mire,
When all we had left was our faith in God
The man who turns out, although still under fire
And smiling still, he quickly does his job.
Tonight our Friend, we wish you well, we cannot say goodbye,
Because no matter where fate leads, in our hearts you'll never die.
Your name will stay on every lip, your smile in every heart,
So here's Good Health, a hearty trip from the pals from whom you part.

Sgt. T. Hunter
Good luck 'Smudge' in your new undertaking.
From the S.S.M., S.Q.M.S., Sgts and men of 'B Squadron' 50th
R.T.R.
1st Sept. 1945
Dedicated to Cyril J.H. Smith in appreciation of the fine work
he has done in the Desert – El Alamein – Tripoli – Sicily – Italy
and Greece.

The fact the poem was written at all, let alone its contents, perhaps says more than anything about Cyril the military man. Sergeants don't routinely write poems for each other! The contents themselves summarise beautifully in verse the foregoing account. We have taken the trouble to give such a detailed account, and to render the poem in its entirety at this point, to allow the reader to reflect on the verses further to having read them at the beginning of the chapter. And perhaps gain a deeper sense than might otherwise be conveyed of what lay behind the words, the meaning they must have had for the author and the men – and the poem's recipient himself. Precisely what the 'new undertaking' was to be is unclear, but his record card shows him as 'evacuated on medical grounds behind the regimental aid posts' on 8 November (he had also been X2'd on 12 January 1944 during the regiment's period of rest after Sangro – most likely as a result of the actions which led to him receiving the Kukri from the Gurkhas; see above). He did not return to active duty for ten days. Why this was and how it came about are lost to history – along with the nature of the 'undertaking' itself. Cyril never spoke of it.

VII. Sidecars

Cyril the civilian was a slightly different character to Cyril the military man. He returned home from Greece in February 1946 and was placed on the reserve list in June, becoming part of the REME reserve from 1 January 1952. When at last he got back to Birmingham to his wife and daughter, it was the first time he had seen them in 4 years. The toddler was now a 7-year-old. She repeatedly burst into tears, not because she had missed him, but because she didn't know who he was and was frightened by this strange man in the house.

He ran a garage with his younger brother and started getting involved in sidecar racing, winning the inaugural British Grasstrack Championship, and the Hutchinson 100 in 1950. He got a job with Norton Motors in charge of the production testing; this was a pretty casual operation compared to the work he had been doing in the Army. His work in the factory was entirely on the production side, whereas Stan Dibben's was experimental and, despite the factory's small size, the two activities were quite separate. Being in charge of the production motorcycle testing is evidence of the same leadership capabilities that were evident in the Army, but he was at this stage in his life putting food on the table. His first experience road racing a sidecar was in fact as a rider with none other than Bill Boddice driving. In 1951, he took his sidecar to the Belgian GP at Spa, as did many of the British sidecar drivers for an overseas jaunt. His diary entry for that weekend, 30 June–1 July 1951 reads:

> B.G.P. 4th
> 22 X 42 – 17 X 44
> Max RPM 6400
> Money 4000 FR
> Bob Paid

Clearly he was working out 'engine X rear wheel sprocket' gearing options and the money was certainly there, but he made sure his sidecar rider Bob Clements was paid his share, 'a third for Bob, a third for me and a third for the bike.' After a race long battle with Pip Harris for the final rostrum place he finished 0.3 seconds behind to take a very creditable fourth, as he noted in the diary, in his very first race on the Continent. On the strength of this sojourn, he persuaded his wife to allow him to take leave from Norton and go on the Continent full time for 1952. In a postcard he wrote to her from the docks at Dover he wrote of his gratitude, promised he would make money from the adventure, and make her proud of him. In the notes at the beginning of his 1952 diary are entries relating to how much the venture was costing and how much he was being paid.

For example, it cost £11 17s 6d to paint the race van with the sponsors logos. Rarely are there entries that identify how much he was paid at each race, but he was paid 1,000 DM for racing at Nuremburg on 17 August. The winnings are rather tallied up in pounds against costs. Equally so, there is nothing in the 1952 diary about gearing or where he finished each weekend. Clearly the racing was 'under control' mentally, whereas the business of being a professional motorcycle racer for the first time needed some writing down – understandably so. While he was winning, it is evident from his diary the venture made the money he had promised Irene, and the World Championship ensured he kept his other promise to her. Yet while he was away winning the World Championship that year, Norton's Managing Director Gilbert Smith sacked him and then the accounts department sent him a bill at the end of the year for the bits he had used.

Stan got to know Cyril during the 1953 World Championship season and found him to be tough on the race circuit but gentle off it. There were fairly strong words if people were cheating, such as using over-sized engines. He thoroughly disapproved of all forms of cheating. He came across as a genuine straightforward character who would go out of his way to help people in the racing paddock; he would give more help to others than they would often give to him. He has been described as somewhat mercurial (Mitchell, 2012), and this was likely borne of a heightened sensitivity to others and perhaps an insecurity; he would adjust his external persona to fit in with the people he was with.

VIII. Racing Performance vis a vis Reputation

There was, however, no limitation to the help he would give to others, where possible. For example, he leant his 1954 sidecar outfit to Bill Boddice, the person who gave him his first introduction to road racing, to race at Cadwell Park (pers. comm. Michael Boddice with Stan Dibben, Apr. 2018). It has to be said that the help was not always reciprocated. He was remarkably patient, but was always saddened by the lack of integrity he felt he'd witnessed: There were times he felt thoroughly used and let down having done his best for people who then focused on their own needs and ambitions. In many respects, then, his sense of generosity and kindness did him a disservice in the cold world of business and racing. This was none more so, perhaps, than with Norton themselves. He was deeply hurt when they sent him the bill for 12s 6d for parts and sundries, after he had won the World Championship as he saw it 'for them'. And equally too by the dismissal in some quarters of his 1952 World Championship because he had a works engine, when he did not. He was a privateer. There has been much written in the press that Cyril had full works support in 1953 because people felt he must have had as the World Champion, but this is not the case. Even the commentator for the film of the 1953 Ulster GP mentions 'Cyril has the 1953 spec engine, Eric the 1951 version' but this statement was the wrong way around. Until 1954, only Eric Oliver had full factory support from Norton. (He was employed by Watsonian also, but there is no corresponding evidence in the Watsonian archive that Cyril was.) Cyril did have the loan of a current spec works Norton engine for the 1954 Belgian GP, but only after Eric crashed heavily at Feldberg in 1954 effectively ending his race-winning career, did Cyril routinely have access to current year works engines and parts. He invariably had to pay for them.

On the Continent, Cyril's talent as a sidecar driver was well-recognised; he appeared on the cover of the French magazine Moto Revenue in August 1953. His nickname in the UK was the same as it had been in the Army, 'Smudge.' On the Continent it was 'Le Lion'; the word has the same connotation in French as it does it English. The top German sidecar pairings, as well as Eric Oliver, held Cyril in very high regard. However his ability and achievements have often been dismissed particularly in the UK on the grounds, for example, that he 'only' won one World Championship and, say his detractors, only then because Eric was out of action for the first part of the season following a crash in France that broke his leg. People often forget that Cyril too had a very bad accident in 1952, at Mettet, where he fractured his skull. Like Oliver, he came back shortly afterwards to win, and he was never off the podium all year. They also forget that the 1953 World Championship was decided by a bike length at the last race at Monza, Oliver and Dibben first, Smith and Nutt second. That is, one bike length's difference across a season of hard racing when both Eric and Cyril were fully fit.

Which is to say, Cyril Smith was one bike length away from being a two-time World Champion. So close was the Monza race that the two sidecar pairings had shared the lap record at 2'34.5, 146.723 kmph, and so close was the championship between them that they were actually tied on 32 points at the end of the year, with the championship being determined by the points from the best three finishes. As Stan Dibben has said repeatedly Cyril Smith has rarely been given the credit he deserved. In an absolute classic race at the 1953

Belgian GP at Spa Francorchamps that left even the third placed BMW pairing of Wiggerl Kraus and Bernd Heuzer over a mile and a half behind, the Oliver/Dibben and Smith/Nutt pairings swapped the lead throughout the 8 lap, 70 mile race. Eric had only gained the lead, finally, on the very last corner and won by just a second. In sum, contrary to today's somewhat established view, Cyril was a very close match for Eric.

In a tribute to him in the front pages of the *Motor Cycle Year Book 1953*, Cyril was described as 'the only man with enough of what it takes to follow in the Eric Oliver tradition,' having won the 1952 World Championship 'through sheer driving brilliance and grit' (Chamberlain, 1953: ii). Further, after Eric stopped racing consistently following his 1954 accident at Feldberg, it is fair to say that through to the end of 1956 only Cyril was capable of seriously challenging (as opposed to following) the increasingly dominant BMW pairings. It should be said that in 1957 Pip Harris too was driving at that level. As well as driving brilliance and grit, Cyril did it through technical innovativeness in developing streamlined sidecars (Mitchell, 2012), along with Ben Willets at Watsonian, to overcome as far as was possible the power limitations of his Norton engine.

Cyril suffered numerous engine failures, including at the TT in 1954 when he and Stan had caught Eric Oliver's streamlined kneeler after a poor start only to retire, but this was particularly from 1955 onwards. His reputation has understandably been tarnished as a result. People questioned his engineering. Yet Cyril's engine building was described as follows by George Wilson in the November 1952 issue of Motor Cycle, 'a standard 490 cc Manx type built with all the precision at his command', components were a 'perfect fit. Valve and ignition timings were accurate to the nth degree. The internals were polished until they looked as if they were chromium plated' (Wilson, 1952: 585). This is usually the description used for works engines which, to repeat, Cyril only had secure access to from 1954 when he was given a new outside flywheel engine to use at the Belgian GP. The flywheel sheared off in practice, exiting via the sidecar and disappeared into the hedgerow. Stan Dibben, who spent many hours in the Smith workshop helping him to prepare the machines, never had any doubts about Cyril's engine building. The problems Cyril often had with his engines were purely and simply from over-revving. Whereby the valve collets holding the valves together with their respective springs, thus allowing each valve to open and close, would become detached. Immediately this happens, a valve will drop in on top of the piston, causing complete engine failure.

Without doubt, he had a tendency to ignore the engine rpm red line, to 'wring it's bl-dy neck!' as his daughter would often shout from the pit wall. As early as the opening Swiss GP at Berne in 1952, this was through necessity, as Wilson noted (1952: 586):

> By now, Smith had hopes of a win in spite of the Gilera's superior speed. But by using the Italian's slipstream wherever possible, his Manx engine was being grossly over-revved ... [Although] engine peak was 6,200 rpm – the rpm indicator frequently read 6,800! The engine lasted, however, ... [and] Smith came home a gallant second, chalking up his first six points towards the World's Championship.

The carburetted single cylinder Norton was ever-increasingly underpowered compared with, first, the Gilera 4 cylinder and later the fuel injected BMW flat twins and this meant that the outfit had to be geared 'short', i.e. run a slightly larger rear wheel sprocket, in order to avoid being out-accelerated and left behind on the exit of tight corners. However, this inevitably led to the engine 'running out of room' at the top end, as Wilson observed. That is, the high speeds attainable particularly with both the 1955 and 1956 streamliners meant that even with a new 5 speed gearbox, running the engine for extended periods in the red was simply inevitable. That is to say inevitable if he was to compete *as he wished*, and seriously 'mix it' with the BMWs, not just follow somewhat meekly along behind. A good example of this problem, along with Cyril's remarkable abilities as a sidecar driver as well as his determination, can be found in an analysis of the 1955 Belgian Grand Prix at Spa Francorchamps.

The official film of the 1955 Belgian GP race, held in July, focuses on Cyril and Stan pursuing and eventually overhauling the BMW opposition. Viewing this even today, the beauty of the outfit which looks resplendent in British Racing Green, and its sheer speed are still quite astonishing. An ultra-fast circuit, Spa is recognised in the shortened version used today as a place where only the very best stand out. This was even more so on the original nine-mile version used until the 1970s.

They had come second in the opening GP in Spain, but the immediate run up to the Belgian GP had been difficult. Ben Willets at Watsonian had re-made the all-tin fairing after Cyril had rolled the outfit driving back to the pits minus Stan at the TT in June. He had dropped his rider off at a first aid station after he had sustained facial injuries when the sidecar had clipped a bank, and decided to drive back to pits with an empty sidecar. This had all been caused by racing very close behind the works BMW of Walter Schneider and Hans Strauß; with their outfit on the opposite side, Cyril had been momentarily unsighted of the protruding verge whose profile had been changed by the local farmer in between practice and the race. Not winning the 1955 TT was one of Cyril's greatest disappointments. Having missed the German GP at the Nürburgring due to the injuries sustained at the TT, and where they had been favourites to win after success there at the May International, Cyril was determined to make up for it at Spa. There was a World Championship to be won!

He and Stan qualified on pole, with the reshaped sidecar fairing that offered improved streamlining proving a bonus, but the machine's streamlined tail cone had made it tricky for him to climb aboard at the start. They were fourth as they entered Eau Rouge but sixth by the end of the first lap, having lost a lot of ground in a very early dice with BMWs. It is probably fair to say that Willi Noll and Fritz Cron, Willi Faust and Karl Remmert, and Walter Schneider and Hans Strauß were so far ahead of the rest of the field by mid-race that they had likely gone in to a high-speed cruise, circulating at less than their maximum as Cyril and Stan rapidly caught them. But the Norton-Watsonian had been, literally, a mile behind them and even once it had been squeezed past the Oliver/Bliss outfit into fourth, they were still the length of the start/finish straight behind the third placed BMW as it entered Eau Rouge on the 5th lap. By the same place on the next lap they weren't just third but first.

To make up that amount of ground and overtake all three works BMW in a single lap at Spa is remarkable. Clearly, Cyril had left Eric far behind in his pursuit of the BMWs, no mean feat by itself, even if by 1955 Eric was not quite as fast as he had been the year before when he had won the race easily. Cyril had then slipstreamed past the third placed Schenider/Strauß BMW on the long flat out sections at the back of the circuit, and out-braked the second placed Faust/Remmert BMW on the approach to La Source, to be immediately behind Noll and Cron who were in first. Crucially, he lost no ground to Noll as they each accelerated out of the La Source hairpin, passed him over the start/finish line and was safely ahead by the entry to Eau Rouge. For the Norton a) not to be out-accelerated and then b) to actually overtake the BMW on the downhill start and finish straight, was made possible by a) short-gearing and then b) over-revving.

With the poor first lap, it had been a flat-out race to the finish for Cyril. So near the limit was he driving, that the outfit would be momentarily out of shape as it changed direction through the bottom of Eau Rouge – the fast left-right downhill-uphill sequence after the start. Once Cyril and Stan were in front on lap 5 the BMWs could not get past, despite their attempts at slipstreaming. But a flat-out race to the finish meant extended time in the red line for the engine. On the penultimate lap Cyril needed all the speed he could obtain up the Eau Rouge hill, to prevent being slipstreamed down the following long straight. With that in mind, he was at full throttle, the engine at maximum load as it climbed up the hill … Having fought their way up from sixth to the lead in just five laps, setting a new fastest lap in excess of 98 mph in the process, the Smith/Dibben Norton Watsonian dropped a valve in at the top of the hill and they coasted to a halt, leaving the BMWs to cruise to the finish. The sense of anticlimax even in the film is palpable.

Despite the retirement, this was one of Cyril's greatest drives, undoubtedly one of Cyril and Stan's greatest races. It was made all the more remarkable by the fact that Cyril had fractured his arm and Stan had required 15 stitches in his face only weeks earlier at the TT. Yet it was not a one-off, it was a regular occurrence. The record books and trophies in the family collection for 1955 and 1956 show many instances of 'Fastest Lap – C. Smith', but they are nowhere to be seen in the list of finishers. The 1956 Belgian GP was a repeat of 1955 with a new lap record of 5'18.0, 159.791 kmph (99.289 mph), two seconds quicker than the lap record they set there the year before. Another example is the 1955 Dutch TT where Smith/Dibben retired again while in the lead. This is not to say that Cyril and Stan did not enjoy any international race success – wins and podium finishes – during 1955 and 1956. They were particularly successful in France and Germany. For example, in France they won at Bergerac and Floreffe in 1955, despite having to negotiate members of the crowd standing in the road. At home, they won for example at Aintree, the then-home of the British Grand Prix for cars, and also the prestigious Huntchinson 100 Mellano Trophy that year at Silverstone, Cyril becoming the only sidecar driver to win it twice.

With Stan working full time at Perry Chains in 1956, Cyril had recruited the inexperienced Mick Woollet to ride with him. To Mick's credit, they had won at the opening international meeting at Mettet and again at the next one at Chimay, demonstrating the potential of Cyril's new and in its own way quite revolutionary outfit. The streamlining was a yet more integral part of the machine, and the engine had a heavily padded cover so that Cyril was effectively lying on the machine. This took all the weight off his arms and at the same time allowed the frontal area of the bike's streamlining to be significantly reduced.

The footpegs were set much farther back so that the bike was in effect a kneeler but one that allowed Cyril to move about a bit. As an 'open kneeler' so to say, it was therefore a remarkably similar position to that seen on solo racing machines today – a position that has only really come to the fore in the last few years. In addition, the sidecar streamlining was now the opposite to the way the 1955 outfit had been in its original configuration, with the flatter part now nearest the bike and the 'nose' fairing behind which the rider would be lying when on a straight nearest the sidecar wheel. This limited the windage effect of the rider as he worked his way out for left handers. The 1955 outfit had been modified after the accident at the TT to extend the sidecar nose all the way to the left to correct for the windage problem, but this inevitably increased the fairing's frontal area. The 1956 version thus achieved the best of both worlds.

Furthermore, the flatter part of the sidecar fairing on the 1956 machine, i.e. that nearest the bike, now extended all the way back to the rear edge of the sidecar platform, in line with the bike's rear tailcone, which was itself more faired in behind the rear wheel than on the previous year's machine. The petrol tank in both 1955 and 1956 outfits was of course, and as with Eric Oliver's kneelers, mounted beside the engine to reduce the height of the machine, but for 1956 Cyril worked out yet another innovation. A taller slimline 'engine pannier' tank was fitted with the engine padding encasing it and the fuel filler. This kept the weight of the fuel central to the outfit but crucially also, it kept the tank out of the sidecar itself which is where it had been in 1955 (as with Oliver's kneeler also). This in turn allowed the low sidecar streamlining of the 1956 outfit to carry through undisturbed from the front to the back of the platform. The Clypse Course on the Isle of Man was in fairness to Mick Woollett too big a place for anyone to learn quickly. Stan stepped back on board for the TT, and negotiated special leave from Perry to do all the 1956 internationals. Numerous cups from 1955–1956 in the family collection have the German word Ehrenpreis – 'special prize' – inscribed on them. They won internationals at Solitude and the Nürburgring in Germany, finished second at Saarland and won the cup for the fastest lap at Hockenheim, amongst numerous other successes on the Continent, including second place at the 1955 Spanish GP and 3rd place at the 1956 Dutch TT.

The Nürburgring in its longer Nordschleife form is another circuit renowned like Spa as a place where only the very best excel. They finished fourth there in 1954 and won the 28/29 May International in 1955, setting a new lap record. They were clear favourites to win the Grand Prix itself there in June, but missed it having had the incident at the TT. A large commemorative plaque shaped like the Nürburgring circuit was unveiled in the pits to commemorate the circuit's 70th anniversary, with the names of its most famous winners on two, three and four wheels inscribed within its circumference. Such was the esteem in which they were held as a result of their success at the Nürburgring, the names of C. Smith and S. Dibben were both to be found therein.

The 1954 season saw Smith/Dibben finish equal second in the World Championship standings on points totals but third on the 'four best results' system, as a result of the retirement at the TT. They finished second at the Ulster, Swiss and Italian GPs and third at the Belgian, and German GPs. Had they not retired but instead finished second behind Oliver/Nutt at the TT, they would have run Willi Noll and Fritz Cron a very close second in the championship. As we have seen, 1955 was also a very successful season, but as far as the Grand Prix were concerned it was marred by three engine failures, two as discussed while in the lead. In terms of the World Championship, therefore, this one was 'the one that got away'.

Cyril was offered a works Gilera four-cylinder engine. Indeed none other than Geoff Duke had implored Cyril to join him at Gilera. The speed and reliability of that engine was renowned. It had nearly won the 1951 sidecar World Championship in the hands of Ericole Frigerio/Ezio Ricotti and Albino Milani/Guiseppi Pizzocri, and Milani came out of retirement to win with it at the 1956 Italian GP at Monza. This was just to prove the point, and it must be said Pip Harris and Ray Campbell finished an excellent second on their Norton Watsonian that day, beating the BMWs. The engine also took Geoff Duke to three consecutive 500 cc solo World Championships 1953–1955 against quality Moto Guzzi and MV Agusta opposition, and with Umbreto Masseti it had won the 1952 World Championship as well; four in a row. In short, the Gilera 4 was *the* engine to have in the 1950s; had he used a Gilera engine in his streamliners, there is little doubt Cyril Smith would have been a multiple World Champion. His hard war experience fighting against the Italians and the Germans in the Desert of North Africa and in Sicily and Italy never left him however.

IX. Later Years

Cyril was a quietly, perhaps even secretly, religious man as a result of his Quaker upbringing. War experiences can also strengthen faith, and that can be seen clearly in the poem above. He had gone on a tour of and photographed all the religious sites in Jerusalem, including the tomb of Christ, during three days' leave from the North African front in November 1942. One of the few bad war stories he did speak of openly, and with disgust, was of being shot at by a sniper who was on a balcony in Italy, firing from beneath the cassock of a priest. Using a Gilera engine was simply never going to happen. Nor similarly a BMW for that matter. Perhaps by contrast, Geoff Duke had spent the war in the UK as a riding instructor at the Royal School of Signals. Although, with the hindsight of the many years that have passed between the 1950s and today, Cyril's attitude seems a short-sighted (and indeed given his eventual suicide, tragic) position to adopt, it is worth remembering that World War Two was barely a decade past. Eric Oliver, who had experienced all the traumas of Bomber Command where the survival rate was frighteningly low, remained loyal to Norton also – regardless of the fact he had an Italian sidecar rider. For those who experienced the worst of the fighting, memories were still very fresh, principles still equally firm.

Cyril's sense of loyalty to people, too, was such that he engendered much affection but he was easily taken advantage of. While Stan never saw him depressed, it seems his other great friend on the circuit, Bob Mitchell, did (Mitchell, 2012). There is no doubt he became quite disillusioned at what he saw and experienced, things that many would have simply dismissed and even expected by others – 'that's racing', 'that's business'. 1957 with Eric Bliss riding in the sidecar was again not without its competitiveness. A retirement late in the race while lying third having split the three works BMWs at the TT for example. Perhaps most notably, an excellent second place just pipping the Camathias/Cecco BMW at the final GP of the year, the Italian GP at Monza.

Ironically enough, they were over a minute behind the Milanis in what was (as per the year before) their only race of the year, demonstrating the speed of their Gilera 4. This second place had nonetheless buoyed Cyril and, despite a growing lack of money – his wife Irene long-since helped pay for the racing singing in a local Birmingham dance band two nights a week, he vowed to carry on. In 1958, he and Eric Bliss were fourth at both the Dutch TT and at Spa with an innovative oil-in-the-frame set up built by Ken Spreyson (Sprayson, 1998: 52–3). However, an engine failure in practice at the first race of the 1959 season the Isle of Man TT the following year prompted his immediate retirement. In an interview with Murray Walker, he explained he could not afford to continue knowing now for certain he could not make the Norton competitive.

Cyril quickly found a job as Service Manager at the Ford dealership in Redcar but his wife Irene was miserable there, missing her friends in Birmingham. Her daughter was by now living with her husband Stan at Stroud in the Cotswolds.

Kathleen had named the Stroud house Bethany, after the Biblical village home of Mary, Martha and Lazarus. Cyril and Irene had travelled from Birmingham to visit on four or five occasions but, although Stan and Kathleen travelled to Redcar to visit them, they only came South once – in the Summer of 1960. The house has kept its name to this day, a three-bedroomed cottage in about an acre of land overlooking the town. Irene had complained to Stan why it was he had taken her daughter so far away from Birmingham, and declared the house haunted. On the other hand, Cyril rather liked it and saw Stan was making a decent living for himself with Perry Chains, thus offering a possible future for his daughter other than the life of a secretarial assistant at Norton. But he could see little future for himself, with no work available in Birmingham where Irene vociferously and repeatedly made clear she wanted to move back to. Without the racing, he could not get away; doubtless he felt trapped. He was found dead by hotel staff on 24 November 1962, aged 43. The pain of 'knowing the pain of knowing' had grown too great.

X. Conclusion

In sum, Cyril's was a good example of how holding true to one's principles, being true to oneself and one's own sense of values, doing the right thing by others, can do one more harm than good in the cut and thrust of life. This is not to say Cyril was naïve in not always seeing what was likely to happen, for he did see the possibility. His view was 'Above all things, you have to be true to yourself. If you have to behave in a way that is not in line with that, who are you?.' This can be seen not only in his persistence with Norton despite their increasing lack of competitiveness, but in his difficult marriage to Irene.

It can be seen too in his approach to the business of racing, which is neatly summed up by his explanation to Stan of how any profit would be shared between them: 'A third for you, a third for me and a third for the bike.' Cyril saw Stan as a team mate, as an equal partner in the venture, and gave him the money he was due. Eric Oliver, on the hand, employed him. Stan was paid 10 pounds a week plus expenses and the use of a 500 cc Manx solo. Stan was perfectly happy with the arrangement, having been paid 7 pound a week by Norton the previous year, but it was a different business relationship to the one he was to have with Cyril. Cyril, too, provided Stan with a Manx solo to race, but whereas Eric kept the start-money from Stan's solo appearances as his employee in 1953, Stan kept his own solo start money when he was with Cyril during 1954–1956, on top of his share of the profits from the sidecar venture.

To consider M.G. Scott's arguments regarding entrepreneurship (1989) and the difference in approach between a small businessman and an entrepreneur, Eric's approach to the business of road racing is more akin to the entrepreneur, paying his employee but keeping money he feels should rightly be his for the opportunities he has created when under his employ, and negotiating additional payments from his sponsors such as Watsonian. By contrast, Cyril's is more akin to that of a small businessman, focused on the needs of the 'shop', the bike, and on absolute openness and fairness with his partner in the business as a point of principle. This is not to say Eric was dishonest, but his approach to the business, the starting premise of it, is quite different.

We have focused all but the last third of this chapter purposefully on Cyril Smith's military life and sought to provide some insight into what his experiences in the 50th Royal Tank Regiment would have been like. Not only has this period of his life never before received any attention, whereas there have been numerous – if short – renderings of his life as a sidecar racer, but to understand his later civilian life and death we are clear it is vital to view it *in the light* of his war experience. Cyril was remarkably self-disciplined in most aspects of his life and a lot of this discipline clearly came from his time in the Army. There is no doubt his success in the military as a young adult shaped much of what he did as a person thereafter.

Being a Quartermaster Sergeant at 23 is indicative of his organising and engineering abilities. In the Army he was clearly somebody, and we might only wonder at what he might have achieved had he stayed in and not had his service changed to 'Duration'. In comparison with Eric Oliver's, Cyril's race van was always very clean and tidy. 'Ollie' had spent a hard war as a very successful Flight Engineer in Lancasters, working in the aeroplane but living in the officer's quarters at the airfield. 'Smudge', on the other hand, had lived and worked in difficult conditions in the field for extended periods of his war service. In those circumstances, neatness in materiel is an essential aspect of a Quartermaster's military life, and Cyril's race van was arranged correspondingly with everything in its proper place. He adapted quickly to a racing life on the road, which necessarily entailed spending extended periods on the Continent away from home and repairing and rebuilding machinery 'on the move', because the whole thing was a straightforward replication of his time with 50 RTR. Unlike his wife, who hated the caravanning and very much preferred the comforts of home, he was perhaps more 'at home' there than when he was at home in Birmingham. For he *knew* that life, and so it is natural he would seek to replicate it. He was happiest there.

On the race circuit, Cyril always tried to win, his determination was such that second was second best. He would never be satisfied with it unless he had gone all out to come first, even if there was only the merest sniff of victory. His view was there is no point in racing unless you are at least challenging for the win. Why are you there otherwise? This explains his willingness to allow the engine to spend real time in the red. Yet to finish anywhere in the final points tally for a season, let alone first, first you must finish consistently. In the final analysis of an entire career as a racing motorcyclist, therefore, ironically enough perhaps his racing instinct was his greatest – and at the same time most endearing – flaw.

Underneath the tough public persona was a patient and even sensitive character. He was highly competitive as a racing motorcyclist at the international level for some nine years '51–8, years in which the British Norton marque to which he was unwaveringly loyal was increasingly outclassed. He won a great many international races from Sweden (he won the Swedish TT twice in 1952 and 1953) to Italy and all points in between, quite apart from the GPs. When he finished a race he was almost invariably the first Norton home, and in doing so frequently beat German and Italian machinery that was quicker than his. He was brilliant and determined, and it was his brilliance and determination that not only made him a World Champion but kept him competitive thereafter. Not least as a result of the values instilled in him as a young man in the British Army, and of his war experience, he saw life as a matter of success. Yet even more so for Cyril Smith, life was a matter of loyalties and of principles.

At whatever the cost.

Cyril Smith with his Ford V8 Pilot Van, c.1955. He was sponsored by Castrol Oils amongst other suppliers including Avon Tyres

8

INTO THE CHAIN INDUSTRY

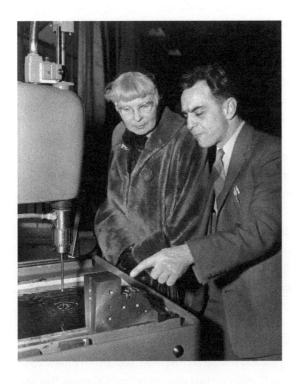

Stan Dibben with friend Andrew Mustard's mother Via, Fort Dunlop in Birmingham, 1963. Perry Chains, had by this time been taken over by Renold

1. Perry Chains

I joined the Perry Chain Company on 1 January 1956. How did I become a trade baron's assistant? The conversation during a visit to me by the Managing Director of Perry, while I was in a post-operative state in hospital recovering from a couple of crash repairs, went as follows:

'Stan, how are you?'

'Not so bad thanks'

'Don't you think it's about time you started acting your age and settled down to a job in industry. How do you feel about that?'

'Well, this sidecar activity has done more for my ego and reputation than it has for my bank balance. So I must confess that the idea of change had crossed my mind.'

'Good. Peter Tye our Competitions Manager is keen to have you join him as his Assistant, and I'd like you to do just that. You'll be paid 20 pounds a month plus expenses. Start in three weeks' time, on January 1st.'

I was punctual, and I had a new challenge, in giving product support at all major motorcycle events. Classic racing enthusiasts may remember the primary chain falling off the Norton ridden by Reg Armstrong as he crossed the finishing line to win the Senior TT in 1952. This failure resulted in the hand-made Perry race chain used successfully by the works Norton team in the 1953 race season, but race success can be a two-edged sword.

Perry were given an original fitment contract for the standard production machines on the Norton factory production line, but the standard production chain, which bore no resemblance to the hand-made race chain, although suitable for the more mundane industrial applications, was certainly not suitable for arduous motorcycle use in the hands of the general public. This resulted in many failures, embarrassing publicity, loss of the Norton contract and, more importantly, loss of much of the business resulting from the race successes. When given the standard production chain, now with the trade name 'Perry 53', it was easily demonstrated to the reluctant directors and their shop floor managers that their standard product was, in motorcycle terms, useless.

We needed to quickly develop and test innovative chain designs. To this end, a new 350 cc Manx Norton race machine was purchased, and with every other tooth removed from the engine sprocket to put extra load onto the experimental products, high speed testing started at MIRA, the test track I had been racing around when at Norton as their chief experimental tester. The test routine I devised was to lap at about 100 mph average, with a change to bottom gear every 1.86-mile lap for some 5 or 6 hours a day, inspect the product, replace or change it and back the next day to repeat the process. 10,000 miles were covered on the first test series, and similar mileages on the following series of programmes. MIRA testing was never monotonous or boring. How could it be, when circulating behind gull winged Mercedes, XK Jaguars driven by the factory chief tester and Le Mans 24-hour racer Norman Dewis, and not forgetting the warmth of riding behind the experimental Rover turbine car.

During this work, eleven major engine failures occurred, all the result of broken engine connecting rods. Under these test conditions, I became very aware of slight differences in engine performance and general feel, and became so in tune with the machine that I could detect an engine problem before total failure. Head man at Norton, Bert Hopwood, considered the failures to be the result of mis-treatment and was not the least bit interested to examine the failed components. To my mind, this was a golden opportunity missed to improve this fragile component.

During the Isle of Man TT in June '56, where I was giving product support on behalf of Perry Chains, friends and I were having a drink in the Castle Mona hotel in Douglas one evening, when the gathering was disturbed by the well-known voice of Norton's Managing Director, Gilbert Smith, castigating, in an alcohol-induced stentorian voice, the product that I was promoting. I was sober and not amused, and said in equally aggressive tones, 'Perry chain failure has never been responsible for the death of a rider on a race track. That is more than can be said for your wretched conrods.' His red-faced departure from the bar was immediate.

Failed conrods are serious and Gilbert Smith knew it of course. The connecting rod connects the crankshaft to the piston. When total failure occurs, engine seizure invariably results, often causing major breakage of the whole engine, depositing its oil all over the locked rear wheel. It doesn't take much imagination to visualise how difficult it then is to keep a solo motorcycle upright on an even keel, especially as failure usually occurs at maximum speed/horsepower, probably in excess of 100 miles an hour on a racing Norton. In the pre-war race years of the mid-1930s, conrod failures were quite common. So common in fact that riders spoke in euphemisms about it. Riders used to call horses 'hay motors' and broken conrods were thus described as 'the horse putting its foot out'. Serious accidents and fatalities were often the result; many riders have lost their lives or been badly injured when this failure occurred during races.

I used to visit the Dunlop factory for new tyres for the test programme quite often. On one occasion, I was told 'Sorry, we haven't got any.' 'Oh, come on!' I said. After much discussion it transpired that the batch of race tyres recently produced had not passed inspection. Since I was only circuiting MIRA I got my way but was warned 'watch it!' The MIRA high-speed track was triangular with three banked corners. My practice always, when fitting different or new tyres, was to circulate using all the banking and come down until the machine felt unstable and then move up a little. In this way I knew my safety margins and

I followed the same procedure with these new tyres that had failed inspection.

I rode around until I was able to circulate without recourse to the banking. Never had I experienced such good cornering ability. I phoned the man at Dunlop, Dennis Durbridge, at lunchtime, 300 miles later, and said, 'You had better come out and look'. After some discussion he did. 'You might have good grip', he said 'but we couldn't market them – look at the wear'. I pointed out that they had only been going anti-clockwise, no race circuit anywhere consists of all the same direction cornering. Besides, an Isle of Man TT was only 264 miles! Nothing more was said to me. I found out much later that these under cured, soft tyres were given to Bob McIntyre to try in 1958, at Mallory Park and he proclaimed them 'fantastic'. Andrew Mustard, who was at Fort Dunlop and racing solo motorcycles, and who I had helped when he first visited the Isle of Man, let me into a secret: 'A new soft rubber race tyre has been developed – and it's *absolutely incredible!*'

As for Perry, we now had a standard general application chain resulting from the MIRA test programme that was suitable both for motorcycles and industry, and that was equal to any other similar product on the market. After a further few thousand miles of testing at MIRA, we went about our chain business with confidence. My time now was taken up by attendance at all the forms of motorcycle competition, with a supply of chain to sell to riders, or give free of charge according to ability. Successes were noted, and we high-tailed it back to the office on Monday. Riders, successful at meetings not attended by us and enjoying gratis chain, were expected to – and invariably did – notify us of their success in time for us to insert right-up-to-the-minute success advertisements in the weekly motorcycle press.

As the Assistant Competitions Manager, I was given the task of drawing up a bonus schedule for presentation to the British Cycle and Motorcycle Industries Association approval, naturally I included sidecar riders (passengers). Imagine my annoyance when told by an apologetic Howard Gibbs, the Perry representative at the meeting that my request for their inclusion had been turned down by all the senior members like Norton's Gilbert Smith, AMC's Donald Heather and others, who held the view that if they paid riders they would have to pay mechanics too.

This organisation was all-powerful in the industry. It interested itself in the regulation of advertising, distribution of prizes and bonus payments awarded in competitions. It decreed that their wholesalers could only purchase from members. Retailers too were included in this decree. The increase in imported machines, together with the abolition in law of the manufacturers' retail price maintenance, destroyed the Association's dominance in the market place. Good riddance too. I came across its restrictive practice when marketing Perry chains.

The restrictive practice was so firmly entrenched in the industry that after the first couple of months out in the field selling, I reported back that none of the major outlets for motorcycle chain were really interested in buying the product. It was obvious that a new sales policy was needed where I could sell direct to the smaller outlets. I was told that was impossible and that as a member of the British Cycle and Motor Cycle Industries Association I could only sell to other members. So I ignored the instruction and came back with some sensible business and much argument, to the amusement of the Managing Director, Bill MacLeod, an American. Thankfully he supported me. Interestingly Bill told me that Gilbert Smith had said to him in the Isle of Man, 'If Stan Dibben had not left us he could have had a great future'. With hindsight, I wonder!

Trade support in the Isle of Man both for the prestigious June TT races and the September Manx Grand Prix events, was very important. All competitors were visited in the multitude of sheds and garages in and around Douglas during practice week and between race days, to check and where necessary, replace spring connecting links and rivet endless all the primary and rear chains. It was customary to be working well into the night and still be up at the start by 4 a.m. ready for the early morning practice sessions. On rare occasions, when not occupied with chain matters, riders would be given the opportunity for learning and familiarity drives round the course. This was all part of the trade support, and was happily and freely given.

Interestingly, at the Isle of Man TT race weigh in, riders had to declare the accessory and lubricants marques they were using in the race. After the race, machines were checked again, to ensure that the products declared had in fact been those used. Any infringement would have meant disqualification. Such was the honesty expected of race success advertisements. I was aware of many infringements where a superior product to that declared was used contrary to contract, but never to my knowledge did this result in a disqualification. There were times pre-World War Two when disqualifications did occur but by the 1950s money was a powerful incentive.

We also developed Perry felt pad primary chain lubricators. I haven't seen one for years, not even at shows with classic parts sales. I had many conversations with pre war stars like the great Stanley Woods, and others, and their advice about what was expected from trade barons was of real value. Many successes came and with them, good increases in general sales figures. Perry were very appreciative and good to me. Things looked good, but it didn't last.

2. Purgatory After Perry

After about two years Perry was taken over by the much bigger company Renold, who were our near-monopoly opposition. I was told my services on the racing side to the much admired and understood riders were no longer needed, as they had their own race service team. Things were never the same. And then, while I was mowing the lawn one Saturday morning in January 1964, came the phone call that changed everything.

'Hello Stan, Andrew Mustard here!'

'Hi. Andrew. Good to hear from you'.

'Stan, it's on! I need that assistant to help me manage the Bluebird Land Speed Record Project, who is happy to work, and I mean work, in bloody uncomfortable conditions, with temperatures in the 100 Degrees Fahrenheit area. I know you can do it. Can you really get a few weeks leave of absence?'

'Yes', I said … I was going to, come what may.

Andrew had written to me from Australia about this idea in November and December, and I had gently sounded the company and they'd only said that someone else would need to be 'making up my pay' – a leave of absence. I realised that leave of absence *for real* wouldn't be easy. My employer was a Donald Campbell sponsor with product, and there would be people in management who would stop me going in favour of themselves, regardless of what Andrew might have been able to say. I couldn't take the risk. On Monday, after a weekend to reflect, I phoned my old boss saying,

'You know there's that remote chance that I may be asked to go out to Australia for the Land Speed Record Attempt. If it happens, do you really think I could have that leave of absence please for about 8 weeks?'

'Oh, I'll need to think about it, but I expect it'll be alright if it happens.'

On the very next Friday morning the Qantas tickets arrived. On Friday afternoon I phoned Renold back.

'The Bluebird trip to Australia has come up. The unpaid leave of absence will be okay, won't it?'

The answer, clearly surprised, was 'Oh! Well yes, I suppose so. When do you go?'

'Tomorrow morning. Thanks a lot'. I hung up.

I did indeed catch the flight to Australia the next morning. I returned from Australia two months later. On return my leave of absence was honoured and I was grateful to the employer and said so on reporting back to my local Bristol office. Within a few days, however, I was instructed to report to the

Manchester office, nearly 200 miles away. Upon arrival I was told to find a house and move from my cottage in Gloucestershire. No relocation help was offered. On looking around, there was no way that I was going to find affordable, comparable accommodation.

So I commuted up and back to Manchester weekly for about four weeks, during which time a lot of snide remarks were made suggesting that I wasn't qualified to be in the Campbell Squad, and why had I been chosen to go? In fact all the reasons for me being a bit devious before I departed for Australia, were now seen to have been justified. Large organisations can be riddled with a bullying culture, both verbal and physically threatening, and frankly I'd had enough. The final straw in ending my association with Renold came when I was told that my house in the Cotswolds was 'above my station in life' and that I was no longer allowed to use the company car to travel to and from work. I handed in my resignation and the key to the company car and caught a train home to join the unemployed.

***

I. Solving Product Problems with Exhaustive Testing

Stan's experiences of being employed in the motor industry during the late 1950s and early 1960s obviously reveal the reality of the politics of industrial life. They also reveal the tendency for corporate perspectives to not only get in the way of innovation but act against those who are not seen to not be falling into line with the employer's view of their place in the corporation.

His old employer Norton was not interested in helping resolve the numerous engine failures that occurred during the MIRA tests because the MIRA tests were deemed unique and placed the engine outside its normal operation even as a race engine. Whether or not this was expedient or genuine, nonetheless the company saw no reason to expend money on solving a problem with a production engine that had benefited already from years of development. Bert Hopwood's view of the Manx racing project recognised the importance of it for maintaining domestic road racing on the one hand but, certainly by 1958, saw it as a complete misallocation of resources on the other hand. As he notes (2012: 159), the AMC group chief

> Donald Heather need only to have instructed me to cease the
> production of the Manx Norton which would have pleased me

greatly, and enabled me to concentrate important personnel on very urgent work in a more realistic field.

So Bill Stuart, a former colleague from Norton, did the rebuilds at his home, invoicing Perry privately. Once the production motorbike chain was properly developed and made similarly to the way the excellent racing chain was made, Stan spent a little time on the industrial application side. If an inquiry came in for a chain replacement, he would visit the factory and see what they wanted. Stan was the only representative at Perry involved in the chain business, the other two were focused on Bayliss Wiley and Co. and Perry cycle components.

While with Perry, Stan had a request to give a talk to the Coventry Motorcycle and Cycle club, to which he agreed. He was then warned by Bill MacLeod, to be careful what he said, because it was a set-up by the Coventry Chain Company, who had an association with Renold Chains, to have him disclose the work at MIRA. He got around this very easily. During his talk, when one or two members of the audience starting asking technical questions, he replied by suggesting there were plenty of people in the room better qualified to answer the questions.

II. James Perry & Co.

According to Grace's Guide to British Industrial History, James Perry & Co was founded in Manchester in 1824 as a manufacturer of pen nibs and later as Perry & Co, also of bicycle chains and hubs. In 1926 it acquired Bayliss, Wiley and Co Ltd, the premier cycle hub manufacturer, when J.W. Bayliss joined the Board. In 1945 'the company transferred its chain making and cycle coaster hub business to a subsidiary, Perry Chain Co Ltd. The pen business was continued by Perry and Co (Pens) Ltd, while Perry and Co (Holdings) Ltd became the main parent company, with financial control of the whole Perry Group' (Grace's Guide, Perry and Co, website). Graces Guide details the history of Perry & Co. (Holdings) Ltd (Grace's Guide, Perry and Co (Holdings), website) as follows:

> From 1948, there three overseas selling and distributing companies, in Belgium (Brussels), the U.S.A. (New York) and Canada (Ontario). The company had manufacturing works at Lancaster Street in Birmingham, Tyseley in Birmingham and Abercrave in Brecknockshire [Brecon, Wales].

1951 AGM told of the death of J W Bayliss who had been connected with the company for 50 years and a member of the board since 1926; he had been closely connected with establishing the cycle works at Tyseley. Subsidiaries included Perry Chain Co, Bayliss, Wiley and Co, both in the cycle trade, and Perry and Co (Pens) Ltd.

1954 58th Annual general meeting; chairman A.E. Wiley; J.B. Bayliss presided over the meeting. Subsidiary companies were the cycle component makers Perry Chain Co, Bayliss, Wiley and Co Ltd, as well as Perry and Co (Pens) Ltd. Lancaster St. site had been sold and a new factory in Tyseley was nearing completion.

1959 Following the merger with Renold Chains, the subsidiaries in Belgium and Canada were closed, although the subsidiary in America remained in existence, changing its name to Renold Perry Inc., in 1964.

The main Perry concerns were undertaken by a new company Perry Engineering Ltd., which went into voluntary liquidation in 1965, once these concerns were fully integrated with Renold Chains Ltd.

Perry and Co (Pens) Ltd remained in existence until its sale in 1960 to British Pens

The Tyseley and Abercrave factories were closed in 1962 and 1964, respectively, after the Renold Group decided to end its involvement in all aspects of the cycle fittings industry, other than chain.

Renold's own official timeline of the company's history shows a business strategy that was heavily focused on the merger and acquisition of smaller chain manufacturers, including Coventry Chain Co. Ltd 1932 and Arnold and Stolzenberg GmbH in 1963 as well as Whiney Chain and Manufacturing Co post-World War Two (Renold, website). The official timeline also states 'Perry Chain Chain Co, Ltd formed' in 1945. No other mention of Perry is made. Taken together, the chronologies available from Grace's Guide and Renold offer no insight into the merger.

Cecil Bayliss, the youngest son of J.W. Bayliss, became Chairman of Perry Chain Co. and W. (Bill) MacLeod, was brought over from North America having had great success for Perry there, and appointed Managing Director of

Perry Chain Co, based at Tysleley, c.1955. Perry's Tyesley site made not only chain but also pen nibs, although the writing was on the wall for the pen side as early as the mid 1950s. Conversations around the factory told of the Perry Pen Co. having previously turned the patent for the ball point pen down on the grounds the new technology did not allow character into one's writing.

III. Working at Perry and the Impact of the Renold 'Merger'

All the work Stan had done at MIRA on developing the Perry chain went to waste, however, because Renold had their own chain. Neither did they approve of Stan's solution to the problem of broken chain rollers, caused by the inner and outer plates of the chain binding. This resulted in tight links, which in turn put too much stress on the rollers. To cure the problem, Stan worked with the Perry Technical Director Nigel Blackstad. Their solution was to induction-soften the extreme ends of the bushes, and on assembly, these were then riveted over to stop inside plate movement. Renold did not like this, because in doing so, it raised two 'high spots' between the rivet and the bush, as a result of the pressures applied. If the chain was then disassembled, these two 'high spots' could be seen as two rings on the bushes. This resulted in increased bearing pressures within the chain. Stan had proven the reliability of the chain at MIRA through extreme testing in excess of 20,000 miles; removing every other tooth from the engine sprocket removed to increase roller loading.

Although the bearing pressure was higher, it was higher over a smaller area, and so the total pressure within the chain was less, and the mechanical efficiency greatly improved. Perry primary chain with this technology ran efficiently enough for it stay cool to the touch, and was still at the correct tension, even at the end of 6 laps racing around the Isle of Man. However, this solution was contrary to accepted chain technology. Along with Coventry Chain Co., Renold had themselves developed and patented notched bushes in 1933, which had by the 1950s evolved into industrial chain that had two notches. In the race chain, in order to avoid cracked end plates, they adopted a method of selective assembly to ensure the notches were set in the parallel plane relative to the direction of the chain's run. This reduced stress on the plates. In short, despite the evident success of the riveted bush chain Dibben and Blackstad developed, and the proven nature of the technology, Renold saw no need for it and rejected it.

A problem that had been experienced for many years by motorcycle racers whose machines, to save weight, routinely ran exposed primary chains rather than having them than enclosed in an oil-bath, was the total loss system employed to lubricate the primary chain by drip feed. This system was renowned for not only lubricating the chain but also the clutch, the rider's boot and the rear tyre to boot. Peter Tye, the Competitions Manager at Perry, had the idea of a felt pad oiler, where the pad was housed in a robust aluminium casting and placed above the bottom run of the chain as it comes off the engine sprocket and loops upwards slightly, allowing the chain to rub the felt pad. This successfully lubricated the chain while almost eliminating the extensive and dangerous oil loss. Stan tested these oilers at MIRA during the chain testing programme, without any indication of failure. The oil feed reservoir, that supplied the pad with oil by gravity, only needed very occasional topping up. In addition, the chain bushes were very accurately oiled by the pads. The product was made purely for the racing fraternity who, sadly, did not trust the system in terms of its inherent security; they feared it would break off, get jammed in the clutch and thereby lock the rear wheel. These fears were clearly unfounded but this remarkable innovation never went beyond the circa 100 units Perry's tool room staff made by hand.

Stan was not involved with the main shop floor to any great extent, working as he did with the experimental department and being based in the main office as Assistant Competitions Manager. Perry's culture was a person-centred 'family' atmosphere in which, unlike BSA, there was little interpersonal competition or cliques. Instead people were invariably helpful towards each other with no notion of 'aggressive' management practice. The works manager would speak with employees very much as equals and there was no internal fighting for jobs or promotions. People were valued for the skills and experience they brought to the company; Stan's World Championship and his use of Perry Chain with Cyril Smith, who had a long-standing relationship with Peter Tye and was 100% loyal to Perry Chain, was much valued and appreciated from top to bottom within the works.

When Stan was selling Perry Chain across the Midlands, on a company Triumph Cub motorcycle to prove the chain, there were no sales targets. He would take orders for the chain from retailers he visited and take these to local wholesalers to gradually build the business. As the business grew and he spent more time on the road, staying away overnight, Perry gave him a company car. One problem arose in that Stan was taking orders from retail businesses who were not members of the British Cycle and Motor Cycle Industry Association, and BCMCIA affiliated wholesalers criticised him for doing so. His response was to go to wholesalers who weren't members either. This was blatantly anti-monopololistic behaviour, and the Bayliss-Wyley Sales Manager Howard Gibbs told him to stop selling the company's products to non-members. Gibbs was a long-standing authority in the cycle industry, but there was a difference of opinion between Gibbs and Stan's boss Bill MacLeod, who told Stan to keep going, 'Thank goodness we've got someone actually doing some selling!'

Stan did numerous trade shows for Perry, including the Earls Court Motorcycle and Cycle Show. At one of these Earls Court shows, he met Serge Binn the owner of Mobyke Accessories Ltd, a wholesaler of motorcycle components, and discussed the possibilities of him selling Perry. This discussion was in the typical friendly gentlemanly Dibben style; no hard selling was done, he merely talked chain. At the end of the discussion, Binn said that he thought Stan would be 'better working for someone like me', as part of a small family business, than he would 'working at an organisation like Perry. If you ever want a job, give me a ring.' Stan thought nothing of it at the time. All the time he was selling for Perry, there was an unwritten understanding on his part that he needed to do the best he could, and a similar understanding on the company's part that he would do the best he could. There was no need for this to be made formal; trust was at the forefront of the employment relationship. The point was that Perry, though by no means a small business, had nonetheless retained a small family business culture.

Stan and Peter Tye heard of the merger between Perry and Renold one day in the office, with a certain amount of disgust and trepidation. Bill MacLeod told them officially the merger had occurred and McLeod was very disheartened by it. Peter Tye, who had been a Dunlop sales representative, left almost immediately and went self employed as a sales agent; one of the products he took on was NGK Spark Plugs. Within days, the Renold-Perry merger was called a takeover at Perry's Tyseldale works. The rumour was that the major shareholder, who was believed to be Cecil Bayliss, had died leaving the majority shareholding to his wife. She had simply offered the shares to Renold Chains. It was clear Renold had little or no interest in Perry as a separate concern; this was a heaven-sent opportunity to obviate an increasingly significant competitor. Irretrievably disconsolate, feeling his commitment to the company in his move from North America had been betrayed, McLeod committed suicide.[1]

Stan too was devastated. He was informed he was to move to Renold's Bristol office and report to the manager there. The Bristol Office Manager was

196

entirely sympathetic, and knew the work Stan had been doing but explained that as a result of the 'merger' there would be no further Perry race chain. The technical solutions were trumped by the company's own established views and policy. Stan found no challenge at Renold, and there was little for him to do within the Bristol area because there were already Renold representatives working the area. Every morning he would drive from his home in Stroud to the Bristol office, spend most of the day sitting around talking, occasionally visit some retailers, or other chain customers, and then go home.

Once, he was sent to a farm to solve a problem with a grain elevator. When he got there, the famer declared himself to be too busy to see the likes of someone with a collar and tie! When Stan asked what the matter was, he was told there was a herd of cows to be milked. To the amazement of the farmer, he proceeded to help milk them, and then fixed the grain elevator. By the time he got back to the office, the farmer had already phoned the office, declaring himself to be very impressed with the chap that had been sent out for helping him milk his cows. Stan, however, was immediately told off for wasting company time. He went to a Renold annual conference and was told his experience was totally motorcycle and of limited use to the company. It was at this point Stan received a phone call one Saturday from Andrew Mustard in Australia asking him for his services on the Bluebird World Land Speed Record project.

Fed up with Renold, and determined to go to Australia, Stan immediately said he would get leave of absence; the ticket was immediately put in the post. Knowing he would never be allowed to go if he told his superiors the offer was serious, since they were a sponsor of the project and would have vetoed it on the grounds there were others better qualified to represent the company, as they would have seen it, Stan told his bosses on the Monday there was only a remote chance but said he would take unpaid leave if it happened. They seemed happy to accept that given the apparently unlikely possibility. Having received the air-ticket in the post on the Friday morning, he phoned the office to say it was now certain he was required in Australia and that he was indeed leaving by air the following day from Heathrow. He put the phone down not waiting for a reply: End of conversation.

On his return from Australia, Stan reported back to his Bristol manager and was told off-hand to report to Manchester. The manager at Manchester was equally off-hand, and he was again told he was too exclusively motorcycle experienced and that there was no work for him on the motorcycle side since they had their own people. Stan replied that a chain drives a sprocket and chains and sprockets are still chains and sprockets. He was next told to find a house and after a month of house-hunting, it was obvious he was not going to buy a house equivalent to the cottage he had in the Cotswolds. The office manager told him 'We have seen the house you are living in, and it is above your station in life. And furthermore, you'll have to find accommodation up here because you won't be allowed to use the company car to go backwards and forwards to Stroud.' Stan's reply was 'If that's the case, perhaps the company is below my station in life.' The reply to that was 'Then you had better resign your position. That way you will keep your pension.' Stan dropped the company car keys on the desk and caught the train home.

By contrast Doug Crennel, who was a race service representative, had a very different experience of Renold. To Crennel (2017), Renold was a superb company to work for.

> They were so well organised. If you went out of the factory even for an hour you were on expenses. They gave me a car to go around all the dealers one winter. I remember one of the chaps was at a race meeting and fell ill with a stroke. The company looked after him and got him back to work. They paid for everything wherever we went in Europe without question, and left you alone to get on with your job. If you did your job they looked after you. In regards to planes and bookings to do, you just booked it, no problem at all. When you got back from the continent, there would be all your pay packets waiting for you. Perry was just a small company, part of the opposition. I mean we got on well with each other as people, but that's all I knew about them. I thoroughly enjoyed my time with Renold, they were absolutely marvellous.

How can the different experience of the company be explained? Two observations stand out. First, Crennel was directly employed by Renold, whereas Stan was 'acquired' rather than hired; there was no job for him to do. Second, Crennel's approach to his employer was rather more focused on doing what his employer told him. He towed the line and did the job. Stan's entrepreneurial independence, as witnessed by his decision to get orders in direct contravention of the restrictive practice demands of the British Cycle and Motor Cycle Industries Association was, as Serge Binn noticed during their conversation at Earls Court, not best suited to corporate life. For someone who had previously been in the Royal Navy and had worked for such a giant corporation as BSA, this might seem an odd conclusion. However, in both 'corporate' settings, for the Navy is in its own way a corporation replete with rules and hierarchies, he had found his niche in small units where he had a great deal of autonomy. The lack of any real job at Renold, coupled with their view that his experience was too narrow to be of use, meant that he could find no semi-autonomous niche. Any sign of entrepreneurial spirit, such as having the forethought and general decency to milk cows on a farm in order to win over a customer, was frowned upon as not what he was paid to do. As Stan explained to the Captain of the Electrical School on being sent back from the battleship HMS *Nelson* to re-qualify, he was not a 'big ship man.'

Notes

1. Of course it would be valuable to relate this account to the Directors Minute Books and other related materials. Access to the Renold Chains Archive held in Manchester Central Library is only possible with permission from the company. Permission was sought twice but we received no reply.

Stan Dibben astride the Manx Norton he rode some 20,000 miles testing Perry chains and Dunlop tyres. Fort Dunlop, 1957

9

THE BLUEBIRD PROJECT

Stan Dibben discussing the state of
the track with Donald Campbell,
Lake Eyre, 1964

1. Flying to a Different World at Mulloorina

Heathrow on a Saturday morning was busy. I went to the VIP lounge as
instructed in the itinerary, and there I met Tom Scrimshire who had done all
the main bodywork at Motor Panels in Coventry. Donald Campbell (just 4
years older than me) arrived and we introduced ourselves.

> DC   'You're Stan Dibben I presume. Welcome aboard.
> You 're going to help Andrew Mustard I understand'.

SD	'Yes, that's right. I'm quite excited and looking forward to the work. It sounds like quite a challenge'.
DC	'Oh I say, you do have a bit of a burr. A champion motorcycle man I believe' (in his public school accent with derogatory tone of voice).
SD	Somewhat surprised at his comment. 'Yes, that's right. I'm going out to work not to talk Donald.'
DC	(Equally surprised) 'Oh, yes of course. Who has Mr Mustard got you booked with?'
SD	'Qantas'.
DC	'Give me the tickets – I'll change those'.

He came back some fifteen minutes later with Pan Am tickets ... I wondered why ...

The flight out was on a Boeing 707, then a new jet. I'd not been on one before. All my previous flights had been on piston engine planes. Take off was fantastic. We landed at Frankurt, Beirut, and Karachi. There, a voluminous lady sat next to me sweating profusely. I would say 'glowing' but the stench was overpowering! It isn't often the smell gets better on arrival in Calcutte, but it did for me as that was where we got off. Thence to Singapore, Darwin, Sydney, arriving in Adelaide 36 hours after taking off somewhat jet lagged. Within thirty minutes I was airborne again in a twin-engined Cessna with Andrew Mustard and the Ampol Petrol man – BP by now replaced as the fuel supplier – bound for Mulloorina and Lake Eyre.

This flight over Port Augusta, the Flinders Range and all the small dried up salt pans were a real eye opener and I began to wonder what I'd let myself in for. After flying over the Lake Eyre area, where I was to be working, we landed at Mulloorina where I was introduced to Elliot Price, the homestead founder, a real old time founding father in his advancing years, his son-in-law Blue Hughes and family and other members of the Elliott Price Clan. My first impressions were right, they are a fine, tough family and would have little time for anyone not prepared to rough it as they had to. Now I could see why Andrew wanted me with him. First impressions of Andrew with his precise, almost Royal elocution, could give the wrong impression.

After a brief look around, cups of tea and general chat, I was happy. I knew I'd cope and we flew back to Adelaide where I died for 24 hours. The next few days were spent rushing around Adelaide. I was introduced to Cliff Brebner, Senior

Police Chief in South Australia who was organising matters related to the Army presence at the lake to control any general public that might appear. I learnt from him that the army was treating it as an outback exercise. Arrangements had to be made for the departure of the convoy which would include Bluebird, the car. Mulloorina is about 650 km north of Adelaide through rough tough uninhabited country and un-made roads. The implements for grading the salt had to be made three 6 ft lengths of railway line, welded together to form three scraping edges to be dragged at an angle behind Land Rovers.

With much to do at Lake Eyre, Andrew and I set off in a donated Humber Snipe to traverse the area over which I had flown just a few days before. First stop Port Augusta to fill up the car and drinking water cans. Late summer up here is hot. Then on to Hawker, Leigh Creek, over rough and un-made roads to Maree – a dot on the map – a rail head with a few houses a pub and some camels. There are thousands of camels in Australia, a left over from the days when the Afghans came to work on the Sydney to Perth railway across the desolate Nullaboor plain, the longest straight line on earth.

We stopped a few times en-route to avoid flash floods due to rain in the Flinders mountain range rushing down on to the plains. These can be very frightening, catching the unwary at tremendous speed and ferocity. Leaving the road at Maree, we headed roughly north east across the desert something like 40 miles to the Muloorina homestead, our base, passing the artesian bore bringing water up from the depths of this barren land at just under boiling point, to form a river to the homestead and beyond. 'You can't drink it, it'll give you crook guts,' said Andrew, the Australianism strangely emphasised when spoken by him.

Muloorina Station is about 600 miles north of Adelaide, and in the desert area of central Australia. Much has changed now I understand, but this is more or less how it was in the early days up to 1964. Muloorina homestead was owned and run by Elliot Price and his family. It was 1,500 square miles in area, with 870 square miles of the total 'developed' by virtue of a dingo (wild dog) fence all the way round, and further blessed in this arid land by Price engineered water holes. At this time, it is supporting 12,000 sheep and a few hundred cattle. No grass here, just a load of gibbers, what the Aussies call pebbles, and dust, where the animals feed on sparsely spread acacia and salt bush. Flocks of hundreds of white cockatoos flying in screeching circles.

The homestead consisted of six bungalows built by the early homesteaders. The first one by the founder Elliot Price in the 1930s, had a thatched roof and corrugated iron walls. Imagine that with daytime ambient temperatures in the late 20°C s in winter and 40°C in the summer. Prior to Elliot Price, it was originally the biggest camel breeding centre in Australia. There was also a chicken house, a big wool storing and shearing shed, an engineering workshop, the sheep shearer's quarters and an electricity generating house. The first electricity in 1940s, was a homemade wind driven 32-volt direct current to keep out the dingos, with a large battery house. In 1964, they built their own hydro power station using water from the Elliott Price drilled Artesian bore, a 460-volt ac system, with a step-down transformer to 230 volt and a 7-mile single overhead wire line to the homestead using earth return. It's a wonder nobody was electrocuted.

The total homestead area was about the size of Gloucestershire with enough fodder to feed one sheep every 20 acres. The main artesian bore produces 2 million gallons of water per day, coming up at 7 degrees under boiling, and forms a creek 10 miles in length. To get water to the 152,000 sheep and 7,000 cattle, they made a 40 mile 2 inch pipeline using a tractor to dig the trench, with a concrete water tank every 5 miles. These are tough people with the very positive and selfless attitude necessary to survive there.

I noticed on the old original house, holes in the walls. They were made by stray shot when killing snakes. It was normal in the early years on the homestead to kill at least 7 a day. I saw regularly one or two a day. The English people there were accommodated in the houses, whereas I was sleeping in the concrete floored contracted sheepshearers' quarters. Nearby was the Station's nearly new Cessna 172 single engine aircraft, some Land Rovers, the remains of a home-made helicopter and a BSA Bantam which gave me a lot of fun. The helicopter, which performed very well I was told, had to be scrapped by order of the Department of Aviation, much to the dismay of all concerned. Elliot Price had not been to school, could neither read nor write. An amazing farm this, and an amazing farmer!

The homestead and the surrounding area was not the 5-star accommodation most involved were expecting, and had been a source of discontent during the 1963 attempt. Staffed largely by the Price family, the children now had a regular school on site with one teacher. Prior to this, teaching was done over the radio. They were great kids who entertained themselves with ball games, picnics, hunting and spotting the wild life. I read in a wonderful book by Cindy Mitchell and Deb Churches *Looking Forward Looking Back*, that there are 117 varieties of bird life. Kangaroo pets are treated with great kindness and are not in the least fazed by snakes, spiders, cockroaches, scorpions, and any of the other 'nasties'.

On arrival back at the Station we were given more cups of tea and I was taken to my 'room', a bunk bed and a wardrobe in the quarters used by the travelling sheep shearers at wool gathering time. Someone said to me, 'How come you are mixed up with this bunch of poofy pommie bastards?' A comment no doubt resulting from the Hampshire burr in my accent, compared to some of the others attending from the UK whose dignity was sleighted by being expected to sleep in such modest accommodation. Things soon changed when we all, the team, got down to work. Clearly, accents can lead to initial misunderstandings, but the outback Aussies are wonderful people and soon set aside first impressions when one's actions demonstrate the opposite.

2. Building the Track

And so to work. Life here for me was tough, not exactly comfortable, but thoroughly enjoyable after driving around the UK selling chain. Most days started by my alarm clock going off at 4:30 a.m. Getting up in total darkness with a rude awakening when bare feet landed on the cold concrete floor. One morning I discovered a brown snake coiled up in my underpants that I'd thrown on the floor when going to bed. This was quickly removed by a well-aimed pillow thrown from a very safe distance. A quick cold wash with an outside temperature of about 4 degrees C, followed by the one-hour drive with Andrew Mustard in the Humber Snipe car, kindly loaned by the Australia Rootes agent, eating our sandwich breakfast en route.

After a 12 hour or more day working on preparing the track, in temperatures well into the late 30s early 40 degrees centigrade, we would return to the homestead and the shearers quarter's for a welcome break. There then usually followed a frantic search for a woollen jumper to stop the shivering and dispel the goose pimples with the evening temperatures still in the high 20s C. It's funny how the body acclimatises to different temperatures but the difference between maximum and minimum still matters! An enjoyable meal and evening with the Blue Hughes family, a few beers and then: tomorrow and tomorrow and yet again more tomorrows. Well, Andrew knew that I could cope without moaning!

The area consists of Lake Eyre North, Madigan Gulf through to Lake Eyre South. It was first discovered in 1840, followed by Lake Eyre North in

1858. The lake is 9,000 square kilometres, 10–15 meters below sea level. It contains an estimated 32,500,000 megalitres of water and is a repository of 500,000,000 tons of salt, mostly sodium chloride. Salt increases on the lake, by my experiment, approximately one inch per year. The drainage area is 1,300,000 square kilometers. That by estimation is roughly the combined size of France Italy and Spain. When there is serious rainfall on average about every 7 years, it takes 3 months to fill and about 8 years to dry out, forming a load bearing salt crust surface of approximately 400 m away from the shore.

Madigan Gulf, the area where we would be preparing the track, was about 30 miles each way from the homestead over rough, dry dusty track, then over the ½ mile causeway built by Andrew Mustard for a further 10 miles on to the load bearing salt. With a catchment area of 500,000 square miles, Lake Eyre is about 30 miles away from homstead, along a red talcum powder like bull dust track to be traversed every day. Overhead, endless blue sky, the lake is a full flat 360 degrees of bright dazzling white salt. Lake Eyre North is the lowest point on the Australian continent and 3,600 square miles in size. It joins with the 500-square mile Lake Eyre South through the Goyder channel via our destination Madigan Gulf.

Here just south of Brooks Island, where the Bluebird track was to be, the salt crust thickens to about 10 inches. With about 800 square miles to choose from it was adequate for our needs. At this point, we are approaching 46 feet below sea level. Under the salt crust, there was a highly concentrated brine solution of water and mud, the consistency of rice pudding. In all, something of the order of 400,000,000 tons of salt (Bonython, 1955). Actual annual salt growth was about half an inch a year, and was due to evaporation of the brine solution that rose up through the salt at a rate of rate of 80 to 90 inches a year.

We noted early on, and with some concern, that the Cooper creek discharges its water into the lake close to Madigan Gulf. We hoped it wouldn't rain there or anywhere else for that matter with its Europe-sized catchment area. The average daytime temperature was about 34 to 36 degrees centigrade. It was going to be hot in those Land Rovers. The moisture below the salt crust seeps up by capillary attraction to the surface, where it evaporates to leave salt crystals. Anything that gets onto the surface; a bird, rabbit, a piece of brushwood quickly becomes encrusted in salt and grows to become a salt island, sometimes 8–10 cm high and often many square metres in area, with the centre so compressed that it becomes rock salt.

Arriving at the lake shore we drove parallel to it for a mile or so along a track, until we reached a half mile long causeway, which had been made by Andrew Mustard using a Fordson tractor and front-end loader. He had filled the bucket with sand and rocks from the land and emptied it onto the salt, back and forth for days until the causeway was built, enabling him to get over the thin salt crust around the edges and onto the thicker crust farther in. In this sense, the salt on Lake Eyre was just like ice on a lake in the winter, thinner near the edge, thicker near the centre. The salt would not take the weight of vehicles until the thicker crust was reached.

Blue Hughes was the station manager as well as Elliot Price's son-in-law, and had only learnt to fly the previous year, 1963. But he flew the Station's Cessna with great gusto and supreme confidence. My first flight of many that I did with him was with the passenger's door off, flying up and down the Lake looking for the best 16 miles we could see, with the minimum of salt islands. When we found likely stretches, we dropped bags of red dye so that we could drive out and find it later. I found these trips all the more fascinating once Blue told me that we were flying all the time below sea level!

Lake Eyre was used in preference to Utah in the USA, because there, there was only a usable 11 miles, whereas Donald wanted 16. It was also chosen on the advice of Professor Bonython, the recognized Australian expert on salt lakes. With hindsight, Lake Gairdner some distance south would have been better. Mud flats used in the latest record successes had not been thought of at the time. Once we had located the bags of red dye we'd thrown from the aircraft earlier, the next step was to drill 2 cm boreholes to determine the salt thickness. Something strange emerged here. The water level in the holes seemed to vary in inches, when one would have thought it would have been the same – anyway, our marked area seemed a good stretch with minimum of salt islands and plenty of thickness.

The Aveling Barford grader, so kindly lent, was great for removing well-established salt Islands, bursting into beautiful shades of blues, pinks, and greens during the heavy cutting process. Then with the railway lines, scraping away day after endless day, week after week, stripped to the waist, mostly on my own, always with the radio ready to transmit to Muloorina in the event of problems, consuming huge amounts of water, stopping for a sandwich. Which was instantly covered in flies – where the hell did they come from? – and the odd fly catching bird. I became aware of the total silence – broken, just faintly, ever so faintly by a 'swish, swish, swish'. And then I saw them, miniature whirlwinds, called whispies, 8–12 inches high, scurrying their ghostly way, picking up salt as they went. It scared me stiff the first time I heard it. No wonder the Aborigines don't like the place.

After the break, back to work in the 130-degree Fahrenheit oven that was the Land Rover cab, engage a low ratio, bottom gear-up and down at 5 mph the full length of the 16 miles track until it was finally done. A shining white scar across dusted brown and white marble salt. Were we overdoing it for smoothness? Consider a depression of say, 12 inches over 200 yards. When travelling at 195 yards a second, 400 miles an hour, that is a pot hole! Those Land Rovers performed their arduous task so well. Not a break down, not a mechanical failure, sustained by a multitude of 50-gallon Ampol petrol drums.

The next job was the lines of dye (blue of course) by which to steer the car, three separate lines, equidistant from each other to give three separate tracks, 30 ft apart. That was not quite as easy as it sounds. We did it by knocking in hundreds of 2 ft iron stakes, lining them up to form a single black line when lying on one's stomach. Next a line on the Land Rover windscreen, a drum of water and soluble dye, line up the stakes with the line on the windscreen and off you go – don't stop or you'll leave a large blue spot! It worked. DC had rejected a green dye. I believe it came in useful years later for Roscoe McGlashen on Lake Gairdner, when he achieved a New Australian record of 580 mph.

Then we were back to grading again, this time to make a landing strip on the salt. The next day, Campbell arrived in the chartered twin-engined Aero Commander, and the following day took off with a few of us to fly over the lake for an aerial view. He was meticulous in his flight cockpit routine and obviously a very good pilot. I had to change my shorts, they were green, a colour forbidden in this congregation. I found a blue pair. Even the plane had to be blue and white. For someone who had raced many times on outfits painted in British Racing Green, and having used the number 13 regularly, I found his superstitions astonishing.

3. The Bluebird Car

The car itself, called Bluebird as were all of Donald's world speed record machines, was designed by Norris Bros Ltd., headed by Ken and Lewis Norris, and built by Motor Panels Coventry. The car had a length 30 ft width 8 ft. Wheel dia. 4 ft 9 in. The structure was aluminium honeycomb ¾ inches thick, faced with aluminium sheet. Most of the bodywork was done by Tom

Scrimshire and his team of half a dozen metal workers, including a 23-year-old lad who did the wheel arches. The panel tolerances they were working to were a few thousandths of an inch over the whole length! They were highly skilled and deserved more credit than they – or he – were given. The wheel track was 5 ft 6 in and wheel base 13 ft 6 in. The tyres and wheels were by Dunlop and designed by Andrew Mustard and the Dunlop design team. The special test plant alone cost £150,000: a lot of money in the late 1950s'. Tyre and tube weight was 52 lb with a rolling diameter of 52 in by 7.8 in, and inflated to 120 lb psi of nitrogen. The wheels were steel forged and weighed 195 lb with a total weight, excluding balance weights, of 247 lb. The wheel speed at 400 mph was about 3,500 rpm.

The car was extensively damaged when it crashed at Utah in the 1960 record attempt. It was rebuilt for the 1964 attempt and sponsored by Rubery Owen, the semi-trailer axle and running gear manufacturer. The World Land Speed Record rules at this time stipulated that the power had to be transferred through the wheels rather than pure jet propulsion. At the time, the only engine readily available in the UK to do this, that is to drive something else with sufficient power and itself be of a small enough size was the Bristol Proteus turbo prop jet engine, as used in Royal Navy patrol boats, aircraft like the Bristol Britannia, power stations and the like, suitably adapted. Modified with two output shafts rather than the usual one, it drove all four wheels via 2 gearboxes made by David Brown, each weighing 380 lb with a fixed reduction ratio of 3.6 to 1 with an input speed of 12,000 rpm. The maximum power of 5,000 shaft horsepower (with the uprated Proteus 755) used in Australia could only be applied at 400 mph otherwise wheelspin would occur. I am given to understand wheelspin induced by over-application of the throttle was part of the reason for the problems that ended the 1961 attempt (even though the engine only had a meagre 4,500 horsepower then!) and hampered the 1963 attempt also.

Brakes were by Girling disc with a peak temperature of 2,200 degrees F to dissipate 36 million ft-lb. To give some idea of the enormity of the problem, consider stopping 400 saloon cars at 40 mph. They were compressed air operated and assisted by air brakes and parachute. Steering, not power assisted, was of the re-circulating ball type through a bevel gear box and duplex chain, with a maximum 4 degrees either way. Independent suspension on all four wheels, with conventional wish bones. Vertical movement was 2 in only. The dampers were Girling and nitrogen filled. Fuel tank held 16 gallons.

4. The Prevaricating Donald

My task during the car's runs was to relay by radiophone to those controlling affairs, wind speed over the measured mile prior to runs. The ideal run time was the same as it had been at Utah, immediately after sunrise when the salt was hard and dry, and wind speed was virtually nil. On Lake Eyre, as the sun got up the temperature rose very quickly, so wind speed became unreliable and the surface wet as the brine solution evaporated through the salt. For some reason some people weren't early risers and so practise runs began invariably too late in the day and ruts appeared in the salt. I could never understand complaints of ruts on a return run affecting steering. Why not use one of the other two unused tracks?

More scraping, more repairs, and then it rained. It was said that the rainwater would evaporate quickly thus fill in the ruts. There's not much in the way of salt crystals when fresh rainwater evaporates. So it went on with everyone getting more and more frustrated. The original track was deemed by DC to be unsuitable and unrepairable, especially in the measured mile area, this part being most affected by water. DC said he would go off in a car and look for somewhere better. He was advised by me and the others to beware of thin salt and off they went after lunch with no indication of which direction they would take. He had flown on to the Lake as usual, so in order to fly back to Muloorina he would have to be back at least 45 minutes before sunset.

We waited, and by now it was dark. Off we went into this vast expanse of salt. There, in the distance we saw headlights pointed skyward. The story was that a 360-degree turn had been attempted when the front wheels began to sink in, the back wheels went in too. Everyone got out in haste and waited for rescue. From experience I knew that when the front wheels begin to sink in, it's best to back off into the original tracks and return safely. The plane remained on the salt all night and everyone went back by car. In the morning we went back to find the car, hopefully at least some of it still on the surface. We dragged it out with a front power winch fitted to a Land Rover.

DC still wasn't entirely happy with the new track, saying it was wet in places. I remember saying to myself, 'Of course it is, it's practically mid afternoon!'. It still seemed to me that from further bore hole observation the water was subjected to flow between Lake Eyre North, through the Goyder into Madigan Gulf. At the time I was convinced it was tidal, since it seemed to happen twice a day, but I was told some years later that it had been worked out the area was not tidal. Instead, the water beneath the salt was being affected by wind blowing on those parts of the Lake, the Gulf and the Goyder, all connected, where there was surface water. Of course in the whole area, there was a lot of open water with no trees or shrubs to act as wind-breaks, and since the wind would increase and decrease with the changes in temperature, so the water beneath the salt would rise and fall as a consequence. The measured mile was at the point of the track where it crossed the exit from Lake Eyre North into Madigan Gulf, so this would explain it. It was just unfortunate the measured mile, necessarily positioned roughly half-way along the track to allow for sufficient acceleration and deceleration periods, was at this very point. As such, it was subject to the most rise and fall in the water level as the water was pushed one way and then the other. Still very odd to me I must confess!

A run was planned for the next day. Andrew and I had been on the salt since about 5:30 a.m. All seemed fine after some more test runs in the Elfin Catalina, a single seater Formula 2 car built by Elfin Sports Cars in Edwardston, South Australia. It had special wheels, shod with scale Bluebird tyres and was also fitted with a g-meter that would 'stick' at the highest recorded reading until re-set. Andrew used the car to check how grippy the salt was at high speed by driving flat out and putting the little car into a 360-degree spin. By using the g-meter reading, he could calculate the co-efficient of adhesion and then Ken Norris would use this information to adjust Bluebird's power settings to make sure DC stayed on the edge of grip rather than go beyond it as had happened at Utah four years previously. After Lake Eyre, Andrew broke a string of land speed records. The Elfin officially fell into Class F and took the flying mile record at 136.77 mph, the standing mile at 105.9 mph, the flying kilometre at 138.00 mph and the standing kilometre at 88.78 mph. It is now on display at the Birdwood Mill Museum near Adelaide in South Australia. DC wouldn't get in the Elfin, declaring firmly 'I wouldn't drive that nasty, dangerous little thing!' He and his entourage arrived some time later – too much later for me. Hold On! – couldn't these people get up in the morning? A run was made at 250 mph. More complaints about salt. Another run at about 300 mph – that's better, but no more. DC wanted four or five days for the track repairs and for the salt to harden off. By now it was mid-May. My leave of absence was running out.

I had a long chat with Andrew. DC had complained about serious vibrations at 300 mph plus, which turned out to be salt build-up on the wheel rims. Once cleaned everything was fine. 'Don't go just yet old geezer' he implored, and so I stayed on and the new track was graded to about 12 miles. After weeks of intensive work in such extreme physical conditions, tensions were high. There were DC health concerns flying about. Apparently the official International Automobile Federation (FIA) Timekeepers were not too happy. There were concerns about stress-related over-breathing (on the part of the driver, not the timekeepers!), which could result in loss of concentration – which some thought is what had happened at Utah. Accusations of disloyalty were being bandied about as a result. Stirling Moss had been heard to say it needed a racing driver to drive the car, and he wasn't the only one.

The press in Adelaide was now very hostile, and much of the reporting was becoming negative. A lot of journalistic licence was used in the reporting I seem to remember. There was one article in the August 1964 issue of *Modern Motor*, an Australian motoring magazine, that said DC lost a tooth from the vibrations of getting the wheels caught in a rut on a run one morning. Cobblers! He broke it on a piece of toast before he went out.

Certainly none of the Mustard team was involved, although we were all – me included – rapidly losing patience. In spite of all the doubts and recriminations, or perhaps because of them, Campbell managed to dig up enough guts from somewhere. Probably his determination to emulate his father was his real driving force. He most certainly was more at home enjoying the night club environment and detested the 'minus 5-star' scene at Lake Eyre and Muloorina; Although full of the wonderful hospitality of Lorna and Blue Hughes and owner Elliott Price, his grandchildren and all, it was certainly a tough, rough place to be. The wealthy lifestyle DC and his wife Tonia, a well-known singer and entertainer, obviously had in the UK was very different! That desert 'outback' Australia was hard to endure.

It was rumoured that Lex Davidson, a wealthy well-known Australian racing man had been promised a drive when he and DC met in Sydney. He arrived on the lake to take up the promise. It was kept. The throttle was fixed for a good deal less than maximum power and a frustrated Lex was heard shouting over the radio 'The throttle's stuck!' He damaged the mechanism in his frustration I was told, which took some time to fix.

Came the end of May, about 6 weeks before the successful 17 July run, and I had no choice but to go home. Andrew saw me off at Adelaide, and Cliff Brebner the Chief of Police too was there with his flattering parting, 'You're the sort of man we want out here. If you're not back in a couple of months I'll be applying for an extradition order!' How nice. At least *they* both said thank you. Of course I didn't go back out in a couple of months and the extradition order never came. It took 30 years before I came back to see my old friend; in all that time, Andrew and I never lost touch.

5. The Record and the Aftermath

The speed achieved on 17 July 1964 was 403.1 and was the World Land Speed Record. According to Appendix 4 of Richard Noble's book *Thrust*, Craig Breedlove had done 407.5 mph at Bonneville Salt Flats in August 1963, but 'Spirit of America' was a pure jet car and it wasn't recognised. But the writing was on the wall; designed basically in the early 1950s, Bluebird was out of date. Even Campbell's wheel driven record only lasted a year. Bob Summers took it up to 409.277 mph in 'Goldenrod', again at Bonneville, in November 1965.

Bluebird was designed to go far faster than it did. There was a great deal of speculation as to the reason for its poor performance when compared with its design speed of 500 mph. Was it Campbell simply not capable of going faster? More likely, if indeed there was a driver factor, was the idea of raising it bit by bit over the years. Other world speed record holders such as Craig Breedlove and Art Arfons were out of a different mould and, according to Andrew Mustard, could just as likely be found on a racing motorcycle, something which could never have been said of DC. And unlike the current World Land Speed Record holder, Andy Green, DC was certainly no fighter pilot.

He was, though, a very determined and, in his own way, a very courageous man. He was also a fantastic publicist, capable of garnering the best technical support from British industry. By comparison with Richard Noble, who had to fight extremely hard to get the support he needed for both the Thrust 1 and Thrust SSC projects, Campbell could conjure funding from industry very easily indeed. I knew Richard as a customer briefly, when he had an aircraft manufacturing business on the Isle of Wight in the time between his two land speed record projects. He is a remarkable man, very plain speaking and down to earth. Campbell, by contrast, operated in the upper stratosphere of British society. To me this shows, as much as anything, the fact that in the traditions of British industry it isn't what you know, what you can do, or even who you know that counts. The only thing that counts is what who you know thinks of you, right or not.

Are there any other possible reasons for the discrepancy between the design speed of Bluebird and the speed Campbell achieved? Both the rolling resistance of the car on the salt and the mechanical losses involved in transmitting the power through the wheels ended up being greater than originally anticipated. Different wheel and tyre designs, a different surface other than salt, and more power – all things the designers of Thrust SSC recognised in designing their twin-engined car to break the sound barrier in the Black Rock Desert 37 years later.

After the car record, Donald set a World Water Speed Record in Australia also. He was really a boat man, and brilliant at it; no-one questioned his authority in that. He was killed attempting the World Water Speed Record some years later on Lake Coniston, and his sad demise has been well recorded. The Coroner's report stated that the ripples on the water from a previous run were instrumental in part to the fatal instability of the boat. Practice runs had been going on for weeks. On previous runs he had waited until the previous run ripples had subsided. Why did he not wait on this occasion, Jan 4th? This was the day of the London International Boat Show – a premier event in the world boating calendar – opened. I wonder whether his actions that fateful day were influenced by any expectation of official recognition, had he achieved the coveted record that fateful day. I suspect, but of course do not know, that he wanted to achieve the honour of a Knighthood for his efforts. His father, the famous speed king of the 1930s, had been knighted for his exploits in capturing the World Land Speed Record for King and Country. What is certain is that Donald was a very complex character, a social success, the possessor of guts of a different type to my racing compatriots, but a man certainly not devoid of courage over fear and superstition.

***

I. Introduction: A cook's eye view

Ian Goldfinch was another member of Andrew Mustard track crew and his wife Richenda, whom he met on the Bluebird project, has written her account of the project. It is a useful introduction that provides us with another perspective by way of introduction to the discussion (pers. comm. Richenda Goldfinch with Mark Dibben, May 2018):

> Lake Eyre and Muloorina Station were an adventure for my friend Christl and me. After sailing from Southampton in January 1964, we had been in Australia for less than two months when we received a telephone call from Donald Campbell. 'Can you cook,' he asked. 'Yes,' I lied. 'If you can be on Lake Eyre in 48 hours you've got the job.' 'There are two of us,' I said. 'You

can share the £6 a week.' We stayed in the main homestead of the station, with the owners, Elliott and Minna Price, Donald Campbell and his wife, Tonia, Leo Villa (the Campbell family auto-engineer) and his wife, Evan Green (PR), Ken Norrish (Girling Brakes) and ten others who suffered camp beds on the wide verandahs – we were cooking for twenty.

On our first night a party was held to welcome us – and I met the man who later became my husband, so that added another dimension to the project. Ian graded the 16 km track for Bluebird with a length of railway iron towed behind a Land Rover. He was employed by Andrew Mustard the Project Manager, and was part of the Dunlop team which handled the wheel changes on Bluebird. On our second night we were gathered around the kitchen table, Christl and I wide eyed and twenty, listening to the stories being told and songs being sung by Tonia, a talented and funny Belgian cabaret singer. There was a loud bang, the heavens opened and rain deluged on the corrugated iron roof. We could tell by the shocked silence and the tortured look on everyone's faces, that this was a disaster.

Donald's worst enemy was rain which softened the salt – his second was fear. His father, Sir Malcolm Campbell, had set a family precedent. He broke nine land speed records and three water speed records. His son grew up in his shadow, with the belief he must continue to uphold the family honour and to retain the records for his country. [So it was that] over the next three months Christl and I witnessed a drama set in outback Australia, involving a team of men, specialists in their field, plucked from their comfortable British homes, dealing with uncomfortable conditions of both the environment and human emotions. Tensions built up as test runs were undertaken, wet salt cruelled speed and critical public outcry increased pressure on some kind of outcome.

Donald Campbell fought public opinion that his record attempt was out-dated. In America and in England the land speed record was being challenged in a jet-propelled car. The technical import of Bluebird being propelled solely by her wheels, was not recognised by the general public as an achievement.

The Australian Government were spending taxpayer's money on providing Army support to the project. The Army had [re] built [the] causeway from land to lake [Andrew Mustard had built it originally the year before], Military Police manned a check point at the entry to the lake, and a camp and mess was provided for personnel working on the project. ... And nothing much was happening ...

On Friday 17 July (exactly the same day and date on which Donald had crashed at Utah) we all left for the lake before sunrise. Christl and I had already prepared the sandwiches for lunch and with picnic boxes and thermos' packed we drove out to the lake for the last time. Out on the salt everything was black as we waited for the sun to come up. As the sky turned red all eyes were on the flags which indicated the state of the wind. Dark figures moved about, silhouetted against the dawn sky. The Dunlop flag was blowing too high. We just managed to lower it before Donald landed in the Aero Commander. Detailed wind checks were being made at the north, south and middle of the track.

The atmosphere was different from former runs. There was half the manpower and nobody seemed to know what was happening [...] It was a last-ditch attempt and pretty chaotic [...] The south end didn't know when Donald was on his way. At 7.17 am the great car streaked away in a roar of power. We somehow knew there was something special about this run. Chritsl and I followed down the track, making notes on the conditions and ruts. The ruts were there but not too deep. At the southern end there was pandemonium. Donald was white and trembling. He had pre-arranged a code with the timekeepers so that they could tell him the speed before everyone else, but he couldn't remember the code. When he saw the state of the tyres he panicked. Rubber had been torn off them by sharp salt crystals. The tyre change team worked frantically and checked every possible bit of the car. The sweat poured off them. Finally, Bluebird was turned and ready to go. The radio from the timekeepers coughed into action. Donald had averaged 403.1 mph over the measured mile. The record he had to beat was 394 mph. He had to make a second run within the hour, to secure the record.

8.10 am: The service engine purred, the Rolls Royce wined, there was a boom as black smoke and flames burst from the exhaust pipes, and she was away … none of us had ever seen her go like that. As we followed behind we were shattered to see pieces of black rubber all over the track in the measured mile. It seemed an eternity until, at Base Camp, we could see Bluebird in one piece and Donald being carried on the shoulders of the team with tears pouring down his face. He had averaged 403.1 mph over the measured mile within an hour. It took Bluebird 8.9 seconds to cover the all-important mile. Donald Campbell had broken his own World Land Speed Record.

All I can remember was a feeling of intense relief, being crushed by the embraces of everyone in turn. In the hubbub that followed Tonia instructed Christl and I to hurry back to the homestead and put champagne on ice. The euphoria was short lived and was soon followed by a massive anti-climax which had to be broken quickly. I do remember (and so does Ian) that the first run was slower than the second [and] Donald had been hoping to reach 450 mph, but [according to the timekeeping] had broken his previous record by only 9 mph. He knew Bluebird could go faster, but the dampness of the track made it impossible. Nobody quite knew what to do next. Two sheep were killed for a barbecue. Christl and I scrubbed and wrapped 160 potatoes and somehow managed to fit them all in the ovens to bake. The party took place in the Army Mess tent. The sense of relief and camaraderie was intense. One of the shearers brought his guitar and sang rock 'n roll standing on the mess table. Then four of the station children sang 'Click Go the Shears', shouting the words of the shearers' song, their faces upturned to the strumming shearer. Tonia sang and danced. The night was a fitting end to an historic day.

Bluebird was rolled onto a massive low-loader and hauled from the lake to stand passive but magnificent in the yard near the homestead. Many people left the next day, farewells were continuous and tender. There are questions that can be asked about the validity of such a project, the benefit to science, the waste, the expense. But in the face of so many difficulties, the burning desire to live up to the family reputation, the sense of adventure, the superstitions and fears and finally the weather and the condition of the salt, it was truly a great achievement. We were privileged to witness the last World Land Speed Record by a friction driven car and what a magnificent car she was.

It had also been a life changing experience for two girls from Europe, observing a human drama set in one of nature's harshest environments. We were welcomed into station life, taught how to whistle up dingoes and find water in the roots of plants. We became comfortably familiar with the red earth and sandy tracks, the shining white lake. We marvelled at the all-enveloping sky, at dawn, at noon, sunset and at night, when the canopy of stars reached down to touch us.

II. What Speed Was Achieved?

The Bluebird World Land Speed Record (WLSR) story is well known from the perspective of the difficulties encountered with the weather at Lake Eyre and its impact on the surface salt, and the growing acrimony between the various 'camps' – particularly during the 1964 attempt as it dragged on to its underwhelming conclusion (Feldman, 1964 and Pearson, 2002). What is perhaps less well known is the business aspect. There is some dispute as to the design speed of the car. Donald Stevens was of the view that 'the design speed was 450 mph … but CN7 [the official name of the vehicle] was well capable of going to over 500 mph given the right salt conditions' (pers. comm. with Stan Dibben, Feb. 2012). Lew Norris, one of the car's two main designers (the other being his brother Ken) maintained 'We designed that car for 600 mph. We had gears for 400 and gears for 600. [Campbell] had the gears for 400 in it, at the time of the [Utah 1960] crash' (in de Lara, 2016: 132). Leo Villa, Campbell's right hand man, was clear (in de Lara, 2016: 125) that

> Donald continued his record breaking activities for two reasons: he had to keep himself in the public eye while the car was being planned and constructed, and indeed, the amount of sponsorship he could expect would very largely depend on the

success of his interim record attempts and how much press they got. The other reason Donald had to keep breaking records was that it offered him a source of revenue.'

Although Villa is here speaking of the water speed records Campbell attained in the 1950s, nonetheless having a car designed to be capable of far higher speeds than it was driven at either at Utah in 1960 or at Lake Eyre in 1963 and 1964, with different gearing made for the purpose, is strongly suggestive of a similar scheme. A study of the speed-time curves from the graphic recorder film, the data recorder on the car, during the record breaking Southeast–Northwest and Northwest–Southeast runs is also instructive in this respect. Campbell had a speedometer in the car, so he should have known the speed he was travelling at.

Bluebird had quite sophisticated telemetry built in for data analysis. As Donald Stevens notes, 'The speed/distance graph shows the actual speeds recorded by telemetry on the record runs. Because of reception problems they are unfortunately not complete, but do show CN7's capability given the right conditions' (2012). Studying this data (see Stevens, 2010: 116) is instructive. The first run, the Southeast–Northwest run, indicates Bluebird accelerated linearly reaching 200 mph in 20 seconds (the same time as a Porsche 918 hybrid) and on to 320 mph. This speed was reached thirty seconds after the run commenced (of course far exceeding modern hypercar performance). The speed then levels off with only gentle acceleration over the next 45 seconds to 350 mph, and at 75 seconds the car then accelerated rapidly again, entering the measured mile 79 seconds after the run commenced at 370 mph and continued its acceleration. It exited the measured mile at 87 seconds and 420 mph, continuing to accelerate for another 3 seconds, reaching a maximum speed of 440 mph before the car then started to decelerate. The recording stops at 93 seconds with the car travelling at 430 mph. The Northwest–Southeast run's data recording is unfortunately incomplete, however, commencing at 23 seconds from the start of the run with the car already travelling at 300 mph, and continuing a linear acceleration to 37 seconds and 420 mph. Extrapolating backwards gives a 0–190 mph time of 15 seconds (1.5 seconds slower than the current Bugatti Chiron). The rate of acceleration then lessens so that by 41 seconds the car is travelling at 440 mph, the same maximum speed it reached at the end of its first run, and it continues at this speed to 44 seconds at which point the recording stops.

In the first run Campbell elected to accelerate through the measured mile, rather than accelerating to the measured mile and holding a constant speed through it. The average speed through the measured mile on the first run was 403.1 mph. The Northwest–Southeast run that followed it was recorded as exactly the same speed (Tremayne, 2004: 321), resulting in a World Land Speed Record of 403.1 mph. This is puzzling since the graphed data for the second run suggests the car's speed at the point the acceleration phase concluded was 440 mph. Lew Norris notes (in de Lara, 2016: 158), Campbell's target speed for the record was 450 mph and this is close to it. If he had maintained 440 mph through the measured mile, rather than accelerating at the point of entry as he did on the first run, then this should have resulted in an average speed for the two runs of around 420.65 mph. Had he adopted the same technique as the first run, of accelerating through the measured mile, he should have exited the measured mile at around 490 mph assuming the same rate of acceleration through the measured mile as on the first run. This would have resulted in an average speed for the two runs of over 445 mph. This would have been satisfyingly close to the 450-mph target.

If both Southeast–Northwest and Northwest–Southeast runs are extrapolated using the same level of acceleration from standstill, this is even more revelatory. That is, extrapolating the acceleration at the same rate beyond 30 seconds and 37 seconds respectively, which the telemetry clearly demonstrates was possible, and then gradually levelling off as the car approached the measured mile, so allowing for the increased wind resistance at these speeds and also taking into account the increasing power levels required to maintain them. This modelling clearly suggests the car should have been capable, theoretically, of entering the measured mile at 525 mph and 535 mph respectively that day. This would have resulted in an average speed for the two runs of 530 mph. If nothing else, it seems the car had the gearing for 600 mph fitted in Australia. As Donald Stevens (2012; see also 2010), Lew Norris (in de Lara, 2016) and Andrew Mustard (anecdotally) have each argued, this was the car's real performance potential.

Without much doubt, therefore, the World Land Speed Record set by Bluebird on Lake Eyre should have been set at or over 500 mph. Why was it not? Clearly, the salt conditions were far from ideal. But, set in the light of these figures, extrapolated from the real data on the car during its record breaking runs, 403.1 mph still represents a remarkably poor performance. Traction was clearly a grave problem, particularly on those parts of the track that were less stable and led to tyre rubber being ripped off in chunks as the salt tore at the tyres while they scrabbled for traction under acceleration. The worst section of track was on the South – North entry/North – South exit to the measured mile (de Lara, 2016; Tremayne, 2004; Pearson, 2002 and Feldman, 1964), due to the water level changes under the salt in that area.

It seems even more odd, then, that Campbell would look to accelerate out of the measured mile on the second run, when he knew this was the area of poorest surface quality – and had experienced it earlier running in the opposite direction on the first run. It would have been far more prudent to adopt the standard practice for the second run of achieving a set speed before the measured mile and then travel through the measured mile at the set speed, reducing the chance of any accelerative forces further damaging the track or the tyres, or upsetting the car's balance. It seems from what is available of the telemetry for the Northwest– Southeast run that this may have been what Campbell was intending. On this second run, he accelerated from the start more rapidly, reaching 100 mph in only 9 seconds, maintained that rate of acceleration, and reached the maximum speed he had attained on the first run (440 mph) some 30 seconds *before* he entered the measured mile, instead of (as in the first run) after he had exited it.

It seems strange, too, that on the first run Campbell settled the car at 350 mph prior to entering the measured mile when the target speed was 450 mph. On the second run from the telemetry available he had the car settled at 440 mph very early on, 40 seconds from its start. If he had followed the same pattern in the first run, there would have been a gentle acceleration to the target speed of 450 mph prior to the measured mile. Then, in contrast to the first run but as is standard speed record practice, a 'roll-through' the measured mile with only sufficient throttle to maintain the sustained target speed. Two points are worth noting here, first of course Campbell would have known that maintaining the target speed of 450 mph on the second run should, despite the poor first run, still have resulted in a sizeable lift in the record into the 420s. This would have sufficed, for the time being. Second, given the state of the measure mile track, it was imperative not to attempt to accelerate through it, as this would have been, he knew on the evidence of the first run, most unwise.

Campbell's acceleration through the measured mile in the first run also remains highly unusual. The state of the tyres after the run was indicative of the rate of acceleration; they had lost their rubber and were down to the canvass beneath, with chunks having been torn off them (de Lara, 2016; Feldman, 1964 and Pearson, 2002) as the shards of salt crystals cut into the tyres (Tremayne,

2004). That experience, according to Richenda Goldfinch above, had left him 'white and trembling.' Campbell himself admitted, 'I nearly killed myself on that first run I was so close to going out of control it was funny' (in de Lara, 2016: 159). Little wonder, since he achieved a rolling acceleration from 350 mph to 440 mph, a 90 mph increase in speed *at those velocities*, in just 17 seconds, in a car with a turbine engine whose characteristics meant that the 'spooling up' of the jet engine lagged slightly behind the throttle application, and this can be seen in the speed graph. We can only conclude Campbell accelerated hard.

And yet the rate of acceleration is not as high as witnessed at the same speeds in the second run. This can only be because the acceleration through those speeds on the second run occurred far earlier in the run, on a part of the track that was stable. The slower rate of acceleration at those speeds on the first run through the measured mile can be explained by the poor track and the consequent lack of adhesion. Indeed, right at the entry to the measured mile on the first run, the speed graph dips very slightly, perhaps indicative of Campbell having his 'I nearly killed myself' 'moment'. That the car continued in a straight line perhaps says much for the enhanced directional stability, particularly in low adhesion conditions, by the addition of the tailfin fitted in the light of the 1960 Utah crash (and despite the fact it 'added a considerable amount of drag'; Stevens, 2010: 107). That Campbell continued to accelerate hard shows considerable courage.

It also suggests he realised he had made a mistake in allowing the car to settle at 350 mph. Donald Stevens suggest this was perhaps because Campbell may have 'omitted to press the power-limiting override switch that had been fitted to the steering wheel' (2010: 116). The staged throttle system had been fitted in order to help prevent the problem that occurred at Utah. Otherwise it may be that Campbell misread his instruments, and mistook 350 mph for 450 mph. Either way, he knew he had to accelerate hard from the moment he realised he had made a mistake, up to and through the measured mile if he was to stand any chance of breaking the record. He made no such mistake for the second run where it is clear he was setting the car to be at 450 mph by the time he entered the measured mile. Stevens again notes that this may have been because the car's maximum speed was pre-set (2010: 116).

The second run, too, perhaps suggests yet more courage, for it seems as Chendra and Ian Goldfinch remember, it was faster. This time he knew the poor rutted state of the track; a tyre blow-out at 450 mph, for example, would have been at best uncontrollable and at worst utterly catastrophic, far more so than the 370-mph crash at Utah in 1960. Worse, the car was 'tobogganing' through the measured mile as it bottomed out in the ruts from the previous run (Tremayne, 2004: 321). If it entered the measured mile on the second run at around 450 mph, which is what the limited telemetry reasonably suggests, and yet achieved a return run exactly the same as the first run of 403.1 mph, a 'remarkable coincidence' (Tremayne, 2004: 321), then this implies the car slowed dramatically as it progressed through the measured mile. For this to be the case, it would require an almost precise inverse of the first run. The precise inverse would be decelerating from 440 mph, entering the measured mile at 420 mph and continuing to decelerate linearly through the measured mile to reach 370 mph on exit from it. Tobogganing, the car's entire underside length bearing the weight of the car with the wheels through the upper surface of the salt exerting little or no forward moment on the car as it bounced along, would indeed have a significant frictional braking effect. This is particularly if combined with an almost precise inverse throttle application also, that is a complete 'lift' of the throttle so that when the wheels are in contact with the surface they too are exerting a braking moment through adhesion, coupled of course with aerodynamic drag of the car body travelling through the air surrounding it. The tail, which was arguably unnecessary so long as the wheels maintained traction but 'would keep the car from slewing *if airborne*' (Steven, 2010: 107; original emphasis), would perhaps have contributed to the car's directionally stability while it was 'tobogganing' and thus out of control. The speed decrease at the very end of the first run where the car decelerates 10 mph in 2 seconds, presumably as the throttle is 'lifted' and power is reduced after the car has left the measured mile, suggests that a speed decrease the inverse of the previous speed increase through the measured mile was indeed possible.

On the other hand, perhaps it is the case that from the speed of 440 mph recorded on the speed graph at 40 seconds, Campbell then slowed the car significantly back to around 350 mph and then re-accelerated through the measured mile, ruts notwithstanding, in exactly the same way he had done on the first run. It has to be said, something like this approach would appear to be borne out by Tremayne's account (2004: 309–27). He states that Campbell accelerated through the measured mile on both runs, and on the second run 'seared out of the measured distance, peaking again at 440 mph' (Tremayne, 2004: 321), to achieve *precisely* the same average speed – to a decimal point – for the measured mile on both runs.

Campbell was the consummate professional speed record breaker. He would know the safest approach would be a constant speed 'roll-through' the measured mile. This approach, compared with hard acceleration through the measured mile, is safest in terms of guaranteeing a pre-determined speed, safest in terms of limiting the risk of a mechanical failure, and safest in terms of limiting the risks of an accident. This is because in all respects the car is a 'stable platform'; to use an aviation term, it is 'established in the cruise'. The telemetry bears this approach out. There is no doubt that Campbell accelerates the car to a given speed early, 320 mph on the first run and 440 mph on the second run and then reduces the rate of acceleration well before the measured mile. Thereafter, with the main acceleration phase of the run complete, he appears to have gently accelerated the car towards the measured mile to ensure he maintained his target speed. That is, first, apparently either mistakenly not pressing the speed limiter override switch or misreading his speedometer, 350 mph, in the first run. And, second, on the basis of the speed reached on the partial telemetry reading of 440 mph, coupled with the acceleration pattern of the first run up to the point of entry to the measured mile, the target speed according to Lew Norris noted earlier of 450 mph, in the second run. For the sake of completeness, Donald Campbell himself appeared to intimate after the second run that the target speed was 440 mph, when he said after the record had been set that 'the track took 40 mph off what the machine would achieve on a surface that was hard and firm' (Tremayne, 2004: 324). As we have discussed, the telemetry for the second run shows an easing of the throttle to level the car's speed out at 440 mph very early in that run, indicating the conclusion of the acceleration phase. This may have been either because Campbell eased off the throttle at that point or that speed was pre-set as the maximum as Stevens argues (2010: 116) but, again, this approach, namely an acceleration phase followed by a more constant speed phase, is the approach of the consummate professional speed record breaker.

In short, the 403.1 mph record average speed seems far too low not only for what we know of the man but also for the available data and the Goldfinch's memories of it. It is reasonable to conclude the Campbell broke the World Land Speed Record by rather more than the official figure suggests.

III. The Business of Breaking Records

If the car was capable of setting a record considerably higher than 500 mph, and was even designed for 600 mph, why did Campbell have a target speed of only 450 mph? Donald Stevens (2012) suggest some explanations:

CN7 was well capable of going to over 500 mph given the right salt conditions. Yes we would have liked solid alloy wheel/tyres, but Dunlop did not do them and they were major sponsors. A 'mud' surface that [Richard Noble's successful] Thrust used would have been ideal, but such places were not known then!

More than this, though, Campbell was in the *business* of breaking world speed records to earn a living. He needed to be able to keep breaking records, and in theory the car Bluebird CN7 gave him that ability just as the boat Bluebird K7 had done. He did not need to break the world land speed record by a 'shattering' amount, indeed this would have been counterproductive. He needed to break it by a sufficient amount to build reputation and at the same time leave room for more, to be attained at a later date. In this regard, the target 450 mph was healthy and 420 mph would have been respectable. Unfortunately 403.1 mph, the published official record speed, was only a relief to all concerned and he openly admitted his disappointment (de Lara, 2016; Tremayne, 2004).

Worse still, it seems from the point of view of the motor industry 403.1 mph was emphatically not acceptable. In July 1965, Campbell presented plans for a Mach 1 car Bluebird CN8. 'A mock-up was made and presented at a sponsorship day … in 1966, with K7 and CN7 on display. But Donald got no interest at all' (de Lara, 2016: 179). Campbell was no longer able to conjure funding from the motor industry. Although he had, officially, broken the world land speed record on Lake Eyre, unlike his water speed record breaking he had failed to deliver a sustainable business prospect in land speed record breaking. Was this failure solely connected with the comparatively low speed recorded? An established record breaker with a direct connection to the history of the 'Best of British' record breaking tradition from his father and a great brand in 'Bluebird', proffering the opportunity to capture the record back from the Americans again, harnessing the best of British industry in the process, should have been sufficient to garner the necessary support. It has been since, for Richard Noble in developing Thrust SSC on the back of his Thrust WLSR success, and again for Bloodhound SSC. It was not so for Donald Campbell, who had a far greater track record than Richard Noble – at least ostensibly so.

Campbell's track-record had been severely damaged by the difficulties of the abandoned 1963 attempt and the 'only just' 1964 success. This was despite the fact he achieved what nobody else had ever achieved, including his father, of breaking both land and water world speed records in the same year. Even before the 1964 attempt, signs of industry dissatisfaction were very evident. Sir Alfred Owen, owner of the metal pressing, bolt and wheel manufacturing business Rubery Owen, that largely underpinned much of the British motor manufacturing industry, had built the Utah car and then built it again for Lake Eyre but, to put it mildly, had lost patience. This was particularly after the aborted 1963 attempt on the Lake (Tremayne, 2004, Stevens, 2010 and de Lara, 2016). The serious difference of opinion was resolved sufficiently for Campbell to have the car for 1964, Owen having initially claimed he could not, but a number of sponsors pulled out and Ampol, the Australian oil company had even replaced BP once he had arrived on the island continent. Such were the problems that some, like David Wynne-Morgan one of Campbell's managers, formed the view that 'his [Campbell's] business relationships almost always ended in tears' (in Tremayne, 2004: 333).

Some dispute even Campbell's ability to attract sponsors, let alone keep them. As far as the man who was in charge of the drawing office at Motor Panels where the car was built, Donald Stevens, was concerned (2012), 'the 100 firms [that sponsored CN7] were nothing to do with DMC's business acumen. It was hard work by me to find people that could supply and were willing to!' The seeds of these sorts of business difficulties and at least the decline in his business reputation can perhaps be traced back to the time in-between the Utah crash and the first Lake Eyre attempt in 1963. That is, while the car was being rebuilt and there was therefore a lull in the project's activity.

A steering committee meeting was held on 7 December 1960 at the Embassy Club, Berkley St, London W1, commencing 6 p.m. and concluding at 9:30 p.m. at which very senior representatives from the major sponsors were present (Campbell, 1960a). That is, Bristol Siddeley (engine), Accles and Pollock (chassis-related metal tubing), Smith Accessories (cockpit instruments and telemetry), Norris Bros (car designers), Ferodo (brakes), BP (fuel and oil), Joseph Lucas (electrics), Dunlop (wheels and tyres) and Motor Panels (car construction). This was the first meeting of the committee since the Utah crash three months earlier in September. Campbell (1960a) explained that from his perspective that

> Although the short narrow course, poor surface, and cross wind effects were contributory causes, he was convinced that the primary reason for the accident was human failure, resulting from oxygen poisoning or hyper-ventilation.

Sir Arnold Hall (Managing Director of Bristol Siddeley) concurred that the symptoms Campbell described were similar to those reported by fighter pilots. The two Norris brothers responsible for the design of the car agreed with Sir Arnold's next suggestion, 'that one of his Company's Engineers discuss the design of the vehicle with them in more detail.' Campbell then declared

> It was vital that a new car should be built and a further attempt be made on the World Land Speed Record next year [1961]. Such a course of action would enhance the prestige of the British motor industry particularly in the light of the present recession in this field.

Mr Phillips of Motor Panels was confident the car could be 'completed by July 1961' but, despite his positive assessment, the financial realities of the project and the wider industry immediately made themselves. Campbell next declared he had £40,000 of overheads to be paid, including designers' fees and other administrative costs, for the car to be completed. The meeting was then evidently surprised to learn that a further £70,000 was owed 'to cover the cost of the operations in America.' Although Campbell was confident he could find that 'from other sources', he was keen that those around the table contribute pro rata to the £40,000 needed between January and July 1961. Such was the puzzlement around the room that Campbell was asked to supply more information on both sums before monies would be forthcoming. Sir Arnold Hall sought a compromise of an initial £2,500 to be paid by each of the companies represented with a further sum of the same amount to be paid upon satisfactory explanation of the two sums. This was agreed to by all but the Dunlop representative 'who wished first to discuss it with his company.'

This meant that, with the help of Hall, Campbell had £17,500 to tide him over with the likelihood of a further £22,500 forthcoming if he could convince them of his budget. He set to work immediately and three days later sent off to each of the eight major sponsors who had been at the meeting a 'private and confidential estimated overhead expenditure for the land speed record project – 1961' on 10 December. In it, he itemised a whole range of expenses, totalling £41,550 (Campbell, 1961b; £889,170 at 2017 values, Historical UK inflation, website), but evidence of the difficulties he was already encountering are immediately apparent in the preliminary discussion prior to the financial detail. He was having an argument with the gearbox manufacturer, David Brown, who was asking for £1,100 – this being the difference between the in-kind agreed sponsorship amount of £2,500 and the final cost of the gearboxes. Campbell was having to use his personal relationship with the owner of the company to try to resolve the matter but had yet to hear back. He also noted that due to the accident and the expiry of the previous contract with the government for a loan of two engines, he was most likely going to have to purchase them at £2,000 each. Further, he stated that all the administration for the project was being done from his home, including the entertaining of 550 guests in the first eight months of 1960, and that

> No allowance has been made [in the estimated expenditure] for the cost involved in the operation of a private aircraft, which forms part of Donald Campbell's remuneration in activities unconnected with the endeavour. Between May and August this year 96 hours were flown in execution of the project. This equally applies to a Bentley, occasionally used in connection with the project and which is not included under the heading of Transport. What was included under transport were the following vehicles:

1 Healey Sprite	Peter Carr
1 T.R.3.	Leo Villa
1 Herald	General use and standby
1 Morris Oxford	Tech-Co-ordinator
1 Land Rover	Towing and material
1 Kenex Atlas Van	Personnel transport, material and component transport.

> Maintenance, wear and tear and depreciation. Calculated on 1960 total mileage of all vehicles in connection with the project – 97,000 miles £1,500

In addition, there was e.g.: £950 for telephone calls; £250 for transporting Bluebird around the UK; £5,000 for operational insurance for Bluebird and the engines; other general insurance including health insurance of £700; sundry purchases of £750; maintenance of four offices and associated consumables at Campbell's home Roundwood of £1,750; and £5,500 general entertainment expenses, press and promotional receptions and the steering committee meetings. There were also salaries:

Project Director – Peter W. Carr
Chief Operational Engineer – Leo Villa
2 Secretaries
1 Technical Co-ordinator/Material and Component Chaser
3 Mechanics
1 Driver/2nd Class Mechanic
£11, 750

A very conservative rendering of all the above figures in current values can be obtained by doubling the figure and then multiplying by ten. Thus, the salary item alone amounts to well over £235,000 (£251,450, Historical UK inflation, website) for the year. Each of these claims seems preposterous today, but indicate that Campbell was in the record breaking business as a way of earning a living. That each of the sponsoring companies with the exception of Dunlop agreed at the end of the three-and-a-half-hour meeting to provide over £50,000 each in today's values, sight unseen of these figures, is remarkable. How Campbell intended to find the additional £70,000 (£1.5 m) owed for the unsuccessful American adventure is unclear. What is clear is his approach to the whole affair raised eyebrows at the time. Donald Stevens notes (pers. comm. with Mark Dibben, Jan. 2017):

As far as DMC's spending goes, I can only relate my experiences as the Tech. man when visiting companies that were supplying parts. Most were in the Midlands so his PA would set up a tour of 2–4 days. After 2 days, even if we had finished calls, we would drive back to London in the evening, book into a decent 4-star West End hotel, go to Rules for dinner then on to the Embassy Club where we met 'a niece' then back to the hotel for a 'comfort session'; all paid for by him!!

The process of deciding which companies to approach was entirely up to Norris Brothers design team. I would advise his manager Peter Barker of the details and he would write asking for their co-operation. After that it was my job to do the technical liaison, and organise the delivery of parts to their site of need (mainly Bristol-Siddeley, David Brown and Motor Panels). When construction started I moved up to Coventry to work with Maurice Britton (of Motor Panels) to get CN7 built.

I put the blame for the Utah crash squarely on DMC's and Leo's shoulders. Leo should not have allowed the car to start so close to the central marker line (OIL!) and DMC should not have had the head up Acceleration/Speed Indicator instrument removed because 'it had green indicators', and he should not have gone over 300 mph ... [...] Leo [Villa was known for his] inability to understand the technicalities of CN7, despite sounding as if he did! Both DMC and Leo tended to make it seem that they were much more involved in the design and construction than they actually were. DMC always referred to 'his team' rather than Norris Bros. Even the car was originally the Campbell-Norris 7, but, in his first Press Release, DMC called it the Bluebird CN7 [i.e. similar to his record-breaking boat N7]. When I pointed this out he said that it could not be changed because it would confuse the Press! Later on he called it the Proteus Bluebird. (sod Norris Bros!)

At the end of Norris Bros work on CN7 in 1960, their costs were over £8,000 more than they had been paid by DMC and it was only a small private company! [...] I have a list 'in DMC's hand' of the latter days' sponsorship which, from memory, included £5000 pa from BP (plus £2000 for any attempt and £3000 for a record), Billy Butlin, Dunlop, British Aluminium, and lesser from other companies.

Certainly, at the committee meeting held at the Dorchester Hotel on Thursday 23 November 1961, all questions of money seem to have been settled, for the attention had turned entirely to the decision to run on Lake Eyre and to the logistics of transporting the car and equipment there (Campbell, 1961). Throughout the following year, 1962, however, 'sponsors ... had been dragging their heels' (Tremayne, 2004: 269), and this was delaying the project start. Campbell's January 1963 estimates of the project costs for running the record attempt in Australia were, perhaps understandably, even greater than his estimates for remaining in the UK in 1961, at £52,878 (£1,131,589), and some were no less preposterous than the 1961 estimate. They include 'U.K. based twin engine Apache [aircraft], including outward ferry charges, insurance, ferry pilot's fees and expenses [of] £2,800', and 'Management, Press and Public Relations fees at Base in Melbourne and London, including office expenses [of] £7,000' (Campbell, 1963). Little wonder the sponsors were united 'in the hope that he would give up' (Tremayne, 2004: 269) and that Sir Alfred Owen formed the view that 'Campbell's [1963] record attempt at Lake Eyre was not pushed with sufficient urgency' (in Tremayne, 2004: 267).

IV. Comparisons with the Flying Kiwi Project

There is no denying that CN7 was a highly sophisticated machine built with no expense spared and, innovatively for a motorsport vehicle at the time, to aircraft principles. Indeed, even at its insured value in today's figures of £2.14 m, it can only be regarded as extraordinarily good value for money. It is therefore clear from the foregoing costings that a great deal of the remarkable expense of the Bluebird project came from aspects other than the car itself. A real sense of the enormous and arguably unjustifiable costs associated with the Bluebird land speed record project *as a whole* can be gained by considering another Australasian land speed record project at the other end of the business scale, that of Phil Garrett's Flying Kiwi Project that successfully broke the world record for sidecars in New Zealand in 2005. This is pertinent comparison because, in contrast with Campbell's projects which benefited from being at the heart of British industry, as will be seen Garrett's existed very much on the edge of the motor industry in New Zealand (Dibben and Garrett, 2006; Dibben and Dolles, 2013).

Unlike Campbell who had a wealthy family history of land speed record breaking, Phil Garrett was very much a working-class Englishman who had emigrated to New Zealand and was a stores manager for a local D.I.Y. shop in Christchurch. The project had its genesis in a drink-fuelled realisation with a friend that, as a result of a rule change, the sidecar land speed record was still only 260 kmph. That had been set by Bob Burns, a New Zealander, not far from Christchurch in 1955. Immediately he set himself a target of 320 kmph or 200 mph. Rather than have millions of pounds in sponsorship and businesses building the vehicle for him, Garrett resorted to grass-roots merchandising and a '320 Club' where individuals could purchase 'involvement' in the project. This was classic awareness-raising marketing and it raised funds sufficient to get the project started with materials and volunteers to start building the machine in his own garage. He did secure in-kind sponsorship from Suzuki who provided some performance parts so that the engine would be powerful enough, and from Wynns the oil company.

As Dibben and Garrett note (2006), one problem

> rapidly became apparent when Garrett did try and procure materials, even to furnish the workshop. The New Zealand motor parts industry had been supportive of previous 'mad ideas dreamt up in pubs.' Businesses claimed time and again they had been 'stung' by others in the past, giving them materials for which they said they had never been paid. Garrett didn't know whether this was true or not, but the fact was everyone was wary of getting caught out. With no reputation of his own to work from, Garrett was both up against other forms of motor sport in the competition for resources, and also ghosts who seemed to be rattling chains of bad credit and spooking the very businesses whose help he so desperately needed.
>
> The only way around this was to pay for everything before he took delivery. The 320 Club monies, plus some of his own savings helped start this process. He had a catch phrase: 'I haven't got the cash just now. When I do I'll come and pick it up.' While this was very demanding on the business's limited funds, his reputation as not only a prompt payer but one who paid before delivery, grew to the extent that businesses eventually recognised Flying Kiwi as legitimate and became quite relaxed about him taking materials that he had not paid for. However, even when offered usual business terms such as 30 days credit he refused, insisting wherever possible on paying for things in cash and up-front. The more this positive reputation grew, the more a variety of companies offered their support, most often by giving products for free to the project on a 'break the record and keep it' basis.
>
> Six months out from the scheduled attempt, Garrett had written over 200 sponsorship proposals to different companies. Each proposal was specifically tailored, often having visited the company first to discuss the project, and he grew more skilled at writing them; they became shorter and more to the point. He

emphasised the only thing he could, the kudos that this was to be a world land speed record that would reach 200 mph. Some proposals sought cash support but most, such as the successful approach to American tools supplier Powerbuilt, suggested the company sponsor in materials – all the tool equipment for the project.

The differences between the Bluebird project and Flying Kiwi are stark in almost every respect. The New Zealand industry had been caught out by its support of the iconic Britten project but, in many respects, Garrett's project was much more in keeping with the history and ethos of the Bonneville speed record breaking festivals. That is, of amateurs bringing their own home-built machines to see how fast they will go over, rather than the professional world land speed record project that was Campbell's or indeed Richard Noble's Thrust SSC and Bloodhound projects. Perhaps the most significant difference between Bluebird and Flying Kiwi, however, was Garrett's down-to-earth honesty and warmth, coupled with a perpetually demonstrated business integrity that increasingly inspired people to donate their own time – unlike the Campbell project, no-one was paid a salary – and businesses to give materials to him on a 'break the record and keep the toys' arrangement. Also, of course, the New Zealand industry is far less structured on the basis of class; there are no 'upper echelons' or 'higher circles' to break into as such. Indeed, the more working class, to use the British term, the better; in this respect it bears greater resemblance to the motorcycle road racing fraternity in the UK and Ireland – perhaps as one might expect.

Despite being on the opposite side of the world to the wealth of motorsport and speed record-breaking expertise most particularly found in the UK, Christchurch New Zealand does have two universities and even aeronautical engineering expertise; Pratt & Witney have an engine service centre at the airport. Engineering advice found its way into the team from there, Christchurch University donated time in their wind tunnel to perfect the fairing (which was the only part of the vehicle that was paid for and cost $10,000), and Lincoln University staff (including Mark Dibben) did much of the event management planning for the days of the attempt. In its own way, and like the Bluebird and the Thrust projects, Flying Kiwi brought all the diverse and otherwise unconnected expertise available together around its aim to be world record breakers. The kudos of being on the world stage remains ever-alluring, and especially so when the people and business involved are geographically so far from the 'centre of gravity'; the achievement is correspondingly all the more impressive.

Like Campbell, Garrett experienced difficulties that nearly scuppered the project during its two years existence. Unlike Campbell, however, this was not a sizeable lack of funds requiring industry bail-out, although Garrett existed on a shoestring and sometimes even on a day-to-day basis. Nor was it a problem with the track per se, although being a public road – and the only road in New Zealand that met the FIM's requirements for minimal change in elevation – it proved to be a little too short to allow the necessarily long acceleration phase; the machine was accelerating all the way through the measured kilometre. Nor was it with the vehicle, which ran faultlessly, although it turned out that more power was required than was available not to break the record, which was set at 272 kmph, but to break the hoped-for 320 kmph/200 mph barrier. Rather, the most serious problem was with the timing gear.

The timing gear was the only part of the project that Garrett subcontracted out to a third party. Like Richard Noble's projects which are also almost entirely in-house, this stands in contrast to Campbell, who effectively retained only project promotion and general project oversight, subcontracting every other aspect of the project, the vehicle design and build, and track preparation (to Andrew Mustard's company), as well as timing (to Longines). In the case of Flying Kiwi, there was only one set of timing gear in New Zealand officially certified for accuracy by the FIM and it was owned by an individual who had not used it for many years. On the first day of the attempt it did not work and this meant the runs, which were timed unofficially by the FIM delegate on his own stopwatch and which, from his point of view, were faster than the existing record, did not count. The copper wire connecting the two timing devices placed at the entry and the exit to the measured kilometre, was not one piece but was multiple pieces, joined at various places to make up the kilometre. Clearly somewhere along its length it was broken and this had not been checked beforehand. Although he had had no choice but to subcontract the timing, Garrett took full responsibility himself for the failure. He drove into Christchurch that afternoon to buy personally a single piece of kilometre-long new insulated copper wire at a cost of $400. But as Dibben and Garrett note (2006), the failure of the timing on the first day would cost Garrett more than the price of the wire. He had made a gentleman's agreement that Glenn Hayward, who had led the build of the machine and supplied the engine, and who was the second driver, would do the first run if the attempts ran to a second day:

Tuesday 12 July 2005, and the morning's weather forecast wasn't as good as Monday's. It was going to be tight. Thankfully, everyone knew what they were about having 'practiced' the set-up procedures the day before; the whole crew had gone from collectively having little or no experience of organising a motor sport event to being seasoned pros in 24 hours, and the transformation was remarkable. They set up in half the time and were ready to run by 7 am. The two drivers had agreed they would take it turn and turn about each day. Day two meant it was Hayward's turn to go first. Hayward had said he would do his run as a test first, and then hand the bike over to Garrett, but the weather was closing in; you could see the front approaching that would bring un-drivable wind. Garrett was happy with his decision to let his friend do the first 'high speed evaluation.' He had the option of taking that first run; as Project Director, he could justifiably turn the bike around and go for it. But they were really close friends, after having got the project this far together. After all, he reasoned, it was Glenn who had built the bike and had as much of a right to the record as he did.

Garrett was happy with his decision – and the justice of it. Hayward got in and, after a moment's hesitation, went for it. Ten minutes later, the return run completed, he was the holder of the new world land speed record, at 272 kmph. The bike was prepared again, and Garrett set off, knowing that with record already in the bag, this was [most likely] the last time the bike would ever be used. The weather 'window' was almost closed and they wouldn't be coming back; apart from risking somebody getting hurt or damaging the bike, they couldn't afford to. Garrett's average speed was 264 kmph, a New Zealand record.

Some weeks later, Garrett closed a sports bar in Christchurch and held an evening's celebration for the volunteers and sponsors. Much of the equipment used in Chertsey, such as the wind meters and the signs that were used to close the roads, were auctioned off. He calculated it had taken 15,000 hours of unpaid labour to make Flying Kiwi a success, and thanked everyone for the time they had put into 'not my dream, our dream – our success.'

A contrast with Bluebird is immediately apparent, namely that Garrett held to his agreement to allow Hayward to inevitably be the one to break the record. Campbell on the other hand was adamant that only he would drive the car at speed. That both men were entirely comfortable with their respective decisions says much for their approaches to their projects in general.

From the business standpoint which of the two men, Garrett or Hayward, actually broke the sidecar record turned out to be of little consequence, since Garrett was – and is – synonymous with it. As Dibben and Garrett further note (2006), he had been

> confident he would break the record on the very first morning with his so-called 'high speed evaluation.' More than that, he had needed to. Every day of the attempt was costing $5,000 in the hire of the emergency vehicles from the council, the chase car from the local race circuit and the fuel for it, the bus to transport the volunteers backwards and forwards, plus catering. He had raised $212,518 of sponsorship. Some of this was in cash from the 320 club and from a fund-raising evening at Christchurch casino a month before the run. The 320 club had been invaluable, especially at the beginning when he had had to buy things cash up front, and also for paying the US$10,000 to the F.I.M to formally apply to attempt the record. But most of the sponsorship was in materials, components, workshop machinery and the like donated by companies; they all had their company logo somewhere on the bike. He had thereby broken even, more or less, getting the project to the starting line. But every day spent trying to break the record was costing him personally. This was getting serious. The opportunity cost of two years' lost wages was $150,000 and, although he had set up Flying Kiwi Promotions Ltd to protect 'the family' from 'the project,' those 'lost wages' had meant using personal savings to supplement his wife's income to live day-to-day.

These figures again stand in stark contrast to the cost of the Bluebird project, even when setting the cost of the car aside. According to Campbell's own estimates (Campbell, 1956) the car itself was budgeted to cost £50,000 (£1.2 m today) and, after the rebuild which left Norris Bros significantly out of pocket (Stevens, 2012), was valued by Campbell for insurance purposes at £100,000 (Campbell, 1960b; £2.14 m today). While the project undoubtedly also cost Campbell personally, as we have seen it was largely paid for by industry rather than as with Flying Kiwi, volunteerism. The volunteer aspect of Flying Kiwi and the strong team spirit this fostered meant that, unlike the Lake Eyre attempts in particular, there was no acrimony. Indeed, 'the F.I.M delegate declared Flying Kiwi to be the best organised record attempt he had ever attended' (Dibben and Garrett, 2006).

V. Conclusions: Taken for a Ride?

Undoubtedly the Bluebird project's most equal comparison, in terms of technical advancement, speeds attained and overall sophistication, is Richard Noble's Thrust projects (Noble, 2012). However, in the language of E.F Schumacher ([1973, 2011, 1980], the Flying Kiwi story shows what is possible using a genuinely entrepreneurial spirit where, unlike Campbell, the emphasis is not on a presence and significance maintained through corporatisation via the 'idolatry of giantism' to achieve a close connectedness to major industry players. Instead, the focus was on establishing a small group of volunteers with flexibility in roles to deliver the land speed record and an immediate person-centred relationship with suppliers and even the general public. The official tag-line of Flying Kiwi was of being a 'Good Bastard', which captured Garrett's emphasis on integrity while at the same time making use of the Antipodean light-heartedness and down-to-earth respect inherent in the way the word 'bastard' has translated into the New Zealand language. Another way of summing up the project without doubt is that it demonstrates Schumacher's adage that 'small is beautiful' and that 'good work' is inherently successful. Which is to say E.F. Schumacher's arguments regarding the efficiency of and reward for small groups of people working in collaboration on a cause beneficial to society (viz, the high levels of public support for it set in stark contrast to the bank manager's profit focus) are paramount in the Flying Kiwi project. The corporatisation of the Bluebird project stands in some contrast to it.

This corporatisation came close to being the Bluebird Project's undoing. It is clear that the British motor industry grew to feel it was 'taken for a ride' by Campbell and found itself compelled to support the Lake Eyre attempts almost on the basis of sunk cost bias. That is, having contributed so much to it and having become so intimately associated with it, they could see little way out of their involvement in the project (Tremayne, 2004). In contrast, the New Zealand motorsport industry grew to feel a genuine pride in being associated with Flying Kiwi, and wanted to support it and see it succeed not for commercial reasons but for human, personal reasons. This is perhaps because whereas Campbell was focused on using industry connections to make a living from water speed and – he hoped – land speed record breaking, Garrett was focused *solely* on delivering the record for New Zealand. He was not interested in making money from land speed record breaking and he gave no thought to the aftermath. The idea of 'sport as business', understanding in this case motorsport and particularly land speed record breaking projects in business terms, allows us to see the immediate connection between the personalities and the projects. Indeed, by way of conclusion, the question of the aftermath presents itself as a final instructive comparison between Bluebird and Flying Kiwi.

On repatriation from Lake Eyre, Bluebird CN7 languished unused and eventually was housed at a scrap metal business in Hounslow, before being donated to the National Motor Museum at Beaulieu (de Lara, 2016), where it has remained ever since. By contrast, Garrett refused substantial offers from museums for Flying Kiwi, instead accepting a lesser sum from an American amputee who wanted to use the machine at Bonneville. Flying Kiwi's controls were all hand-operated, there were no foot controls unlike an ordinary motorcycle, and as such it was perfect for the new owner's wishes. Garrett was delighted to know that his machine would not only achieve his own dreams but also those of someone else whose own circumstances meant that they would most likely otherwise remain unfulfilled. Flying Kiwi did indeed break the American Land Speed record the following year at Bonneville. For Garrett this was not about money, which was wholly secondary in the greater scheme of human achievement.

In short Garrett was, like E.F. Schumacher, concerned more than anything with the question of human value, i.e. the record and the associated feel-good factor associated with it as the underpinning purpose of the people who came together to enable it – as the lynch-pin for meaningful business. Indeed, Garrett's 'good bastard' ethos stands close comparison with Schumacher's argument that people be allowed to do 'good work' (1980), that emphasises community and relationships, by maintaining the purpose of work at the human scale. That is, rather than the more remote multinational scale as characterised by Campbell's Bluebird project and the benefits he argued would accrue to British industry from its association with him. In other words, and in contrast to a purely utilitarian view, the real satisfaction from motorsport as business lies in the achievement of meaningful and mutually sustaining relationships with and for other people. The evidence from this chapter, and indeed perhaps from the preceding chapters also, is that this seems more easily achieved by and with people who, either by force of circumstance or by choice, find themselves having to act entrepreneurially on the very edge of the industry they work within.

The team at work servicing Bluebird prior to a run, Lake Eyre, 1964

10

ANDREW MUSTARD (PLURAL)

Andrew Mustard (right) with a colleague at Fort Dunlop, with a quarter scale Bluebird tyre, 1957

1. Andrew Mustard – Bluebird and Beyond

Andrew Mustard was my loyal friend for nearly 50 years, played a great part in my life, and my story would not be complete without paying tribute to him. No person involved with Donald Campbell's World Land Speed Record Attempt projects both at Utah in the USA in 1960, and Lake Eyre in Australia 1964, was more dedicated to the task or more enthusiastic. This tall lean red-bearded man with a precise, almost Royal elocution inherited from his aristocratic parentage, had the air and confidence of early British explorers, Andrew was in my opinion frequently misunderstood and certainly never given the credit deserved.

For more than 5 years he was involved in the development of the wheels and tyres at the Dunlop main works at Fort Dunlop in Birmingham. He and I spent many hours discussing his work, and it was obvious that this ex Southampton University man had an astute engineering brain. A member of the University Air Squadron, he told me many stories of his flying experiences in the piston-engined aircraft of the time. Racing motorcycles both solo and sidecar as a 'passenger,' he rode in many European and UK events in the 1950s and won a bronze replica in the Isle of Man TT races.

His father was awarded the Military Cross in the First World War, probably the first ever to a member of a tank regiment, and was taken prisoner by the Japanese in Singapore during World War Two.

On behalf of Dunlop, many months were spent searching the world for a suitable venue for the Bluebird World Land Speed Record attempts. Months driving around the Australian desert areas, unaccompanied with only a radio for communication. Much of this land unexplored and inhospitable. Finally, after consultation with sponsors at the time, British Petroleum, and the Australian Professor Warren Bonython, at the time considered the salt lake expert, Lake Eyre was chosen. It must be said, with some misgivings by Andrew, who thought Lake Gairdner the more reliable and nearer to habitation. (This venue was chosen with success by Australian Roscoe McGlashen.)

After the 403 mph record by DC was achieved, Andrew decided to stay in Australia and moved to Adelaide with his family. His three sons are all quite brilliant in their fields. Peter a computer programmer, Harry and Dr Roger expert geologists.

Andrew's design for a water jet unit, marketed under 'Aquajet' for small boats, gave his sons much fun and racing success, and was some 5 years ahead of Jet Skis. He is next to be found in Sydney working the American mining giant Kennecot, who sent him to Papua New Guinea as their feasibility engineer to look for the best route for a road up to the remote Ok Tedi copper mine. He was one of the first white men ever to walk in the Star Mountain Range, and told me many stories, some quite hair raising, of his encounters with the local head-hunters!

In geological terms, the young terrain was extremely difficult for road making. Roads made into the mountain would disappear under landslides as the earth slipped away. The project, as far as he was concerned, was abandoned and he returned to his family in Sidney.

In typical style, we find him next working in North Queensland, on the alluvial gold deposits on the South Palmer river some 140 km north west of Cairns and 100 km south of Cooktown about 8 miles across the great west desert west of the Mulligan dirt road highway. This is arid land of sandstone and scrub, snakes and scorpions, dingoes and kangaroos, suitable only for four-wheel drive vehicles driven by experienced bushmen who can use a compass, are experienced enough never to venture without copious amounts of water and a radio. At the camp, a caravan, a Fordson tractor with front-end bucket, a tipper truck, a soil washing plant using water from a Mustard made dam, soil graders and a workshop.

This was man's work and certainly no holiday. I was lucky enough to spend some time with him, learning where to look and pan for this elusive metal. It is rare indeed to find nuggets now.

In the 1870s, this whole area was worked by Chinese and a few Europeans, and one could still find artefacts like cooking pots and pans, and the remains of ovens abandoned when the gold rush ran out. In 1875, some 7,750,000 grams (Frank Demsy, 1930) of gold were recovered. Imagine the work involved then when the only transport was horse and cart or packhorse or merely horseback riding, not forgetting the discomfort in the searing heat of the day.

Work here in the 1980s with mechanical aids, was producing something like 125 grams from 150 cubic metres of riverbed soil. The alluvial gold, having been shaken out, is put into a crucible of mercury where it amalgamates with it. Heat is then applied, the mercury evaporated, leaving the gold. A highly toxic operation which eventually, coupled with the extremely arduous conditions, ruined Andrew's health and he returned full time to his family now residing in Townsville.

Not one to do nothing, he began to work on outboard motors and soon discovered that spare parts for the discontinued range of popular Volvo and Seagull units were no longer available. He quickly became the Volvo and Seagull man in Australia. Parts not found he made, and his expertise in renovating those long idle but loved motors was legion.

Andrew died in July 2002, my loyal friend of so many years, after bravely enduring much pain. He was a man of great integrity, in no way devious, with no time for aggressive arrogance or for those acquaintances whose standards were a good deal less. He was sorely missed by his loyal – and now late – wife, his family and friends and in particular, me.

***

I. Mustard – Father and Son

Andrew Harry Mustard embodied many of the traits we might identify in an 'English gentleman'. That is, patience, honesty (in every sense of the word), gentleness, sobriety, loyalty, and sagacity. He also had an impish sense of humour. He once painted footsteps as a guide in his house, from the backdoor through the kitchen to the living room door, that went up the wall across the ceiling and down again. He dealt with a nosey neighbour, who would spy on the garden through a hole in the fence, by gluing a picture of an eye cut out from a magazine over it and then ran upstairs, giggling, to watch the recoil effect! The postman was successfully kept to the path and off the garden with a sign 'Beware of the reptile', that referred to the resident tortoise.

Andrew Mustard's birth was announced in The Strait Times of Malaya on 10 November 1930 (p. 10) as follows: 'A son was born to Mr and Mrs Andrew Mustard, of Burlescombe, Devon, and Petalang, F.M.S., at Ellendan, Sandhurst, on Oct. 5.' In this simple statement lies a host of interesting facts. First, he was born at Sandhurst, because his father had been a decorated officer in the Royal Tank Corps in the First World War and, through the patronage links that still held sway in the inter-war years for former officers, was able to organise it such that his wife could be cared for there. Second, Andrew's mother, Viola Speer, was related to the aristocracy on her mother's side and all her children inherited the same bright sparkling blue eyes that have come to be associated with Queen Elizabeth the Queen Mother and her children. Third, Andrew's father was at the time of his birth living – as he had done much of his adult life – in the British colony of Malaya, now Malaysia, as a tea planter; he was one of the founders of the rubber industry there. That is, he and his wife led almost entirely separate lives, for Via only once left England to visit Malaya and soon returned home. They were, though, an inseparable couple and lived together happily for many years after the Second World War in Wiltshire. They had married in December 1916, in the middle of the First World War, when Andrew was home on leave from the front.

Andrew Mustard Sr was the sixth of ten children of the Rector of Hackford, a parish in Norfolk. He served in the 8th Battalion of the Tank Corps and won a Military Cross for conspicuous gallantry during the Battle of Cambrai, 20–23 November 1917. This was the first major battle in which British tanks played a significant part; at the earlier Battle of Passchendaele they had largely been rendered useless due to the boggy ground. According to the official history (Mallpress and Mallpress, 1999), on the evening of 23 November a composite company of 12 tanks was ordered to support the clearing of Bourlon Wood. Having ensured the infantry were well-established in the wood, they then proceeded to Fontaine Village itself, where the fighting

> was of the severest nature. The [German] garrison was in great strength and offered a most spirited resistance, refusing to evacuate their positions even when the tanks were on the point of overrunning them. With hand grenades and machine guns firing armour piercing ammunition. they made a desperate and most courageous effort to put the machines out of action. During the fighting in the village, Second Lieut. A. MUSTARD had an exciting experience, during which the normal roles of tank and infantry were reversed. Becoming separated from the rest of the company, his tank stopped through engine trouble in one of the streets and was surrounded by large numbers of the enemy, who employed every possible artifice and stratagem to disable the crew inside the machine. Bundles of hand grenades were used in attempts to break through the armour, while several enterprising Germans climbed on the roof in search of vulnerable spots. Three of the gunners were wounded and the Tank Commander was summoned to surrender by a German officer, who, it is hoped, was able to appreciate the sentiments of the reply he received to his invitation. At length, after a defence lasting for three quarters of an hour, the engine was persuaded to function once more, and the tank got safely away after inflicting heavy losses upon its assailants.

The citation for the MC further notes that at this point in proceedings 'none of the infantry were in Fontaine' (Tank Corps, 1917: 37) and that

> ordering his gunners to keep up Lewis gun fire he himself worked at the engine … and succeeded in starting it. It was entirely due to his Gallantry and devotion to duty that the tanks was saved from falling into the hands of the enemy and the crew becoming prisoners.

Mustard was 31 when this action occurred and was shortly promoted to Captain. From the foregoing, there is no doubt that he was remarkably brave and resourceful, capable of inspiring the men who served under him in some of the most deadly circumstances imaginable. While the future son had his mother's sense of humour, there is little doubt either that much of Andrew Mustard Jr's character, outlook and demeanour came from his father. Yet this was as much an inverse influence, for he came to disagree profoundly with his father's colonial attitudes even if he inherited not only his accent but his love of adventure and exploration. His father in turn felt his youngest child and only son to be a bit of a let-down, having failed to live up to his own expectations of a successful military career such as his own had been; nothing could have been farther from Andrew Jr's aspirations than that!

The story of the son necessarily commences, therefore, with the story of the father whose life in Malaya sheds a light on the time of colonies and on the transition from colonialism enforced by the surrender of that colony to the Japanese. That light is shone by the man himself, through his personal account of the period, for his attitudes and values are woven quietly through it. Just as a greater understanding of Stan Dibben's approach to life can be gleaned from a study of his own father's life and death so, too, a greater understanding of Andrew Mustard's approach to Donald Campbell, his work on the Bluebird Project and his decision to remain in Australia afterwards, can be gleaned from a study of his father's personal story.

II. Mustard Senior and the Japanese Occupation of Malaya

As such, this chapter focuses first on Andrew Mustard Senior's experiences in Malaya immediately prior to the invasion of Malaya by the Japanese in December 1941. The account continues in the Appendix, culminating in the horrors of internment in Changi Jail on Singapore Island. His grandson Harry has given us permission to publish it for the first time, not only because it offers an insight into his own father's relationship with his father, but also because it offers an almost unique glimpse into the events it records. One broad-sweeping account of a fellow businessman caught up in the invasion and occupation has been published by Grey (2009a) and occasional references to the rubber and tin businesses and the horrors of the civilian internees' experiences and the brutality of the Japanese military towards the expat population during the occupation of Singapore appear in Thompson (2005), Turnbull (2009), and Warren (2002).

Peter Thompson's account of the Battle of Singapore relies explicitly on the diary of one of the military PoWs but a detailed eye-witness civilian account such as Mustard Sr's is rare. In this respect, Harry Mustard's wishes are the same as his grandfather's, that the account contributes to the written history of those events and our knowledge of them. The author's wish was that the account might also contribute in some small way to a continual striving for peace, from which we can hardly demur. As originally introduced by the author, the account creates the impression that he is writing up a tale told to him 'by a man who for three and a half years suffered the horrors and privations of a Japanese Prisoners of War camp in Singapore.' Andrew is remarkably close to his source, however, for of course he is speaking of himself. He was a leading figure in the expat business community in Malaya, helping to shape the development of the rubber plantation industry there after the First World War.

Indeed, on the strength of his work and reputation in the industry, on 10 September 1935, Mustard was elected to the board of Amalgamated Malay Estates, Ltd, a subsidiary of J.A. Russell & Co., the leading tea and rubber company in Malaya. Having spent almost his entire adult life in Malaya, he had become inspector of the company's estates and (as his own account below notes) personally responsible for two of them. The nineteenth annual general meeting of shareholders was held at the registered office of the company, No. 1 Embankment, Kuala Lumpur. Mr R.C. Russell presided over the meeting, which proceeded as follows (Grey, 2009b).

Messrs Weston and Mustard

> After notice convening the meeting was read by a representative of the secretaries, Messrs. Boustead and Co., Ltd., the chairman addressed the meeting as follows: 'I presume the directors' report and accounts having been in your hands for the prescribed period, you will allow them to be taken as read. Before proceeding with the business before the meeting, I must refer to the very serious loss the company and your board has sustained by the death of Mr J.S. Weston. Mr Weston was a member of your board for 12 years and also acted as visiting agent and I can state that during that period his advice as a practical planter was of the greatest assistance to the board, his keenness in the matter of the efficient and economic working of the company

was unbounded and is sadly missed. Our sympathy is extended to his widow in her bereavement and I would ask the secretaries to convey the same to her. We have been fortunate enough to persuade Mr Andrew Mustard to fill the vacant seat on the board and also to be the company's visiting agent and later on you will be asked to confirm his appointment as director.

Divided Distribution and Capital Disbursement

Turning to the accounts you will see that the profit for the year under review amounted to $82, 316,03, an interim dividend of 5 per cent was paid and your directors recommend a final dividend of 6 per cent, making 11 per cent for the year, a result, I think, you will agree is very gratifying. It may strike you as shareholders that our investment account standing at $122,634 and cash with bankers at $75,327.19, a total of $197,961.19 is far and away in excess of the requirements of the company and should be properly be distributed among you. These investments have accumulated in the main from the revenue derived from mining on the Jinjang Estate and I may say that, as soon as the area is worked out, (probably in about 3 months time), it is the board's intention to recommend that these receipts be distributed by way of a reduction of capital.

Until we finally know the sum total we will receive from this area it is hard to know to what extent the capital of the company will be reduced, but your board have a scheme which will be submitted to you in due course for your consideration and approval whereby not only will the capital be reduced but the new shares be of $1 nominal value instead of the present $2 shares, the number of the new $1 shares to the existing $2 shares and the cash distribution can, as I said before, be only determined when the mining area is worked out.

The Condition of the Company's Estates

Mr Andrew Mustard visited the company's properties on August 2nd and 3rd and his report is to the effect that the two estates are in perfect condition. Tapping ceased on Jinjang last October, the company's standard of production being easily obtained from the Serdand Division, tapping there has been on the A.B.C. system and Mr Mustard has suggested – a suggestion which is being carried out – a re-orientation of the fields so that the various fields comprising the blocks A.B. and C. be more contiguous than they are at present, thereby effecting better supervision and cheaper working. I cannot do better than to quote from Mr Mustard's report under general. With regard to Serdang Estate he writes, 'the Estate is, I consider, in excellent order and one of the best estates I have had the pleasure of inspecting' and he made a similar reference to the condition of Jinjang Estate. The high yields on Serdang estate referred to by the Chairman at the last annual meeting continue to be maintained and the labour situation at Serdang is eminently satisfactory. 'I do not think I have anything further to say and therefore, I propose the directors' report and accounts for the year ended 30 June 1935 as presented, be adopted and passed and I will ask Mr Chisholm to second the proposal, but before putting it to the meeting I shall be happy to answer to the best of my ability any questions shareholders may care to ask.'

No questions were asked and the proposal to adopt the report and accounts was carried unanimously. A final dividend of 6 per cent in respect of the past year was declared. The retiring director Mr C.J. Chisholm, was re-elected and Mr A. Mustard's appointment to the board in succession to the late J.S. Watson was confirmed. Messrs. Neill and Bell were re-appointed the company's auditors for the ensuing year. There being no other business the meeting terminated with a vote of thanks to the chair.

By the time of his appointment to the Amalgamated Malay board, Andrew Mustard was the father of three children, two daughters and the youngest, son Andrew Harry. All three children, and his wife, were in England where they were brought up by their nanny Gea. She remained close to the family all her life, and was looked after in her old age by the middle daughter Denise; family loyalties were strong in their own way. Throughout the 1930s, it is clear from the foregoing that Andrew Sr was continuing to live the life of a successful colonial expat with, as shall be seen, the servants to match. We have included the foregoing account of the 1935 Annual General Meeting of Amalgamated Malay Estates Ltd not only because it demonstrates the operations of British colonial enterprise in the inter-war years, and not simply because it demonstrates Mustard Sr's position in that enterprise on the edge of Empire. Our main purpose of including it is because it provides a valuable background in readiness for the account that follows, an account that recalls in vivid detail how Andrew Sr's peaceful and carefree time as an influential operator in the colonial rubber industry came to an abrupt end.

A 1935 sum of $197,961.19 is equivalent to approximately £3.2 m today. Being a director and shareholder of the company, Andrew's financial future in retirement after he returned home following the war and the re-establishment of British rule and plantation ownership in Malaya was reasonably secure as the motor industry boomed and the demand for rubber grew exponentially. Nonetheless, it took five years of constant care by his wife to nurse him back to something approaching his former strength, but he remained in poor health for the rest of his life. What photographs exist of him show a thin, diminished gentleman, older than his years. A man who held on to his class by being very careful about the company he kept, more so at home than ever he did in Malaya, and whose expectations for his son were conspicuous in being largely unmet. (His daughters, by contrast, were the apples of their father's eye and, as expected, married dashing young men.)

III. A First-Hand Account of War Games on the Edge of War

We have only amended the following account as presented here and in the Appendix very simply, and in three ways. First, the original contained numerous small chapters and we have instead inserted appropriate (and fewer) subheadings so that its layout remains in concert with the rest of the book. Second, we have removed occasional uses of what would now be regarded as highly derogatory pronouns for the Japanese, notwithstanding their common use among the Allies at the time and immediately after the war by the generation that encountered the Japanese Army during the Second World War. Third, we have redacted one paragraph, because it tells a story not witnessed by Andrew himself but rather retold from the story of a friend. Given the events described in what follows, we felt it important to ensure the published account is genuinely and solely a first-hand account in all respects. It is, Andrew Mustard Sr assures us:

a true story and without exaggeration. To history it is but an incident which occurred at a period in the World's history when human passions became uncontrolled, and when enlightened, civilised man sank to depths of degradation and bestiality which will shame him for evermore. Should such a blot on the history of the human race be hidden away and forgotten? It were better not a thousand times; rather that generations to come should have full knowledge of the disgrace in their past without stint of detail however lurid, and remember that disgrace as a warning to the future. This [account] therefore is dedicated to the future peace and happiness of mankind, and to all those whose indomitable courage and cheerfulness brought them through hell to live again.

It was over twenty years since I had, with intense relief and thankfulness discarded army uniform for what I hoped and trusted would be the last time in my life. Here on an isolated rubber plantation in the heart of the Malay Peninsular the Second World War, which was eventually to stretch its cruel fingers to every corner of the earth, seemed so far away. Perhaps I may be excused for thinking at that time that it was for the younger men to offer their services to their country, rather than the older men of my generation. Yet one day in December 1940, a Government document arrived at the Estate office appointing me a Lance Corporal in the Local Defence Force. The instructions in this document were brief and left much to one's own imagination and initiative. The total number of men under my command would be seven, all volunteers. Parades would start on a date given, and would be held at the Parit Police Station. No more, no less.

I laughed! At that time the very idea of the Japanese getting into this country was laughable. They hadn't the gumption to try, and not a hope in hell of succeeding even if they did try. The front door was the strongest in Asia; Singapore, an impenetrable fortress, with its fifteen-inch Naval guns, its aerodromes, and a harbour to form a base for the most powerful battleships in the world. The back door was impenetrable jungle with a few easily defended roads and waterways. A handful of men could hold an aggressor there with ease. Internally, the most cosmopolitan population of any country of its size was content in its prosperity under the benign British administration. No trouble there. Why worry? To hell with the Japanese!

So I thought at this time, rather welcoming the diversion from the somewhat humdrum existence of a rubber planter tucked away by himself in the back reaches, little dreaming of the days of horror and privation which lay ahead. On the day appointed for the first parade I arrived at Parit Police Station to take over my seven charges. The Police Station was a wooden hut sparsely furnished with a few wooden benches, a desk, and, most prominent, a large board on which hung a number of pairs of shining handcuffs. At the back of the hut were three cells each with stout wooden bars. Outside was a compound with a few tall coconut palms, a mangostene tree laden with its delicious fruit, and a number of banana plants. All this presided over by a smart Malay sergeant of police, resplendent in Khaki uniform and an immaculate 'Sankoh' (hat).

Although in actual fact a rank lower, I was greeted with a magnificent salute by this village potentate. Behind him were the seven volunteers; a Malay of high rank stood a little apart from the others, and three other Malays squatted under the mangostene tree, splitting the skins of the ripe fruit with their fingers and cramming the sweet delicately flavoured white flesh into their mouths. A Chinese, a Tamil, and a Sikh completed the party. I recognized them all. The Malay of high rank was a youngster from the Kuala Kangsar Government, now studying for an appointment in the Land office, and temporarily attached to the Parit branch. The the other Malays included the postman of a downriver village 'Kampong' which I had frequently visited on expeditions to shoot snipe, and two local peasants who peacefully and happily cultivated their rice fields, and tended a few rubber trees on a small holding in the village. The Chinese and the Tamil were both interpreters in the local police court, and the Sikh a watchman on a nearby plantation. Each of them knew me and welcomed me with friendly smiles.

I laughed again: If the Japanese came in, here were seven stalwarts with which to repel them: Anyway the young student

250

would be useful, he could help a lot licking them into shape. When finally marshalled into some semblance of order they made a comic picture; the Sikh towered above his fellows while the Chinese, intensely eager, and rather owl-like in his spectacles looked pathetically miniature at the end of the line. An attempt was first made to march the section but this was doomed to failure from the start. With the Sikh setting the step his comparatively miniature fellows appeared ludicrous in their efforts to take sufficiently long strides. With the Chinese leading, the antics of the Sikh were reminiscent of a woman with an over-tight skirt attempting to hurry. The leading file found their calves being kicked mercilessly by the rear file and in turn their own heels frequently came in contact with the shins of those in the rear. The result was chaos, the lanquage unrestrained, and in a short time I was reduced to uncontrollable laughter. Not a good start, but who cared about marching drill anyway?

Parade followed parade without any appreciable improvement except that the young Malay student developed a vocabulary akin to a British drill sergeant. The next step was to study the mysteries of a service rifle, and to find out how to fire it at a target. Efforts here met with greater success until the time came to acquire the art of aiming. Each of the recruits was handicap at the start by finding it almost impossible to keep one eye closed for any length of time. It was eventually decided' to improvise a rifle range on the estate tennis court which had at one end a convenient bank about seven or eight feet high. A .22 rifle, some ammunition and targets were obtained and the fun started. The house lay at the top of the bank overlooking the tennis court. It was hastily evacuated when the section arrived for their first shoot. Targets were put up against the bank and, having distributed ammunition I hurriedly retired behind the firing line to watch the fun.

The postman was the worst; concentrating upon every lesson he had learnt he succeeded in keeping one eye shut until a split second before pressing the trigger, at that point however his powers of endurance were exhausted, the second eye closed in sympathy with the other. Sometimes a window was shattered, or the bullet phutted into the trunk of a rubber tree far behind the house. Occasionally a frightened squawk would be heard from the chicken run several degrees off the line of fire, or a broken slate slid down the roof of the house to shatter on the path below. Never was the allotted target anything but clean at the end of the session. When the time came for reports to be sent to Headquarters the targets of one Ahrnat bin Udin, postman, Kampong Bota, were inadvertently missing.

Who cared? The Japanese were still a long way away.

So the weeks passed into months and still there was no immediate threat. True, in Europe a series of disasters had followed one another at a breathtaking and alarming speed, but Britain although battered and scarred by the furious onslaught of German bombers was gloriously intact and would remain intact. The small wealthy Protectorate of Malaya with its British Colonies continued in peace and prosperity. British, Australian, and Indian troops were in abundant evidence, and from time to time visited even the little village of Parit on reconnaissance or manoeuvre. This only tended to increase a general sense of security. It was now three years since I had enjoyed any leave, and it needed little persuasion from a friend to decide on a trip to Australia. Arrangements were made for the seven stalwarts of Parit to be placed under the care of a neighbouring plantation manager, and in mid-September I boarded a plane at Singapore little thinking that before the end of the year I would be caught up in a tide of hopeless confusion and devastation leading finally to the most agonizing degrading years of my life.

Startling developments and rumours reaching me in Australia caused me to hurry back to Singapore, arriving there the first day of December. There was little outward change here. More uniform in the streets perhaps, and a greater proportion of khaki in the Raffles hotel, but still an atmosphere of optimism pervaded, and there was no noticeable change in the way of life of that wealthy city. The Japanese were certainly closer; they had occupied Indo-China. The French, poor devils, had little say in the matter. There was the possibility of an attack down that narrow neck of land joining the peninsular with Siam, but that hellish piece of country gave every advantage to the defence, and Siam lay between Malaya and the aggressors. Siam was barking like a frightened dog, threatening un-named aggressors, but who cared about that?

Approach by sea from the east was another possibility but there was said to be a strong naval force at Singapore waiting to deal with such an emergency. It was with a feeling still of optimism that I arrived back on the estate next day. I was greeted by the man who had taken over from me and looked after the estate in my absence. He was his usual cheerful self and reported that everything was running smoothly. Sitting on the veranda in the cool of the evening we discussed everything except the war. Visiting the Tamil and Malayalee tappers at their tasks next morning however, I noticed a feeling of uneasiness amongst them. The Chinese cook and house boy too appeared restive, and there was an unusual amount of chatter from the servants' quarters. The syce, I could see was almost frightened. He told me that he wanted to bring his family down from Penang, and asked if I could help him to make the necessary arrangements. I could do nothing to dispel this uneasiness and fear; it were better not to attempt it.

One of the aspects of the foregoing that perhaps strikes one most is the all-pervading sense of status and rank inherent in it. Herein lies a clue to the post-war differences in the perspectives of father and son. The author's call-up was part of an attempt by the British military in Malaya to prepare for war, but his account speaks powerfully to the inadequacy of the British military position in Malaya. It is widely understood (Turnbull, 2009; Thompson 2005 and Warren, 2002) that the peninsula was woefully unprepared militarily for war with Japan, even although the top brass of the military on the peninsula understood the threat and even understood the most likely direction from which it would come. The view expressed by Andrew of the security of the peninsula was the general view held by expats at the time, whose knowledge was gleaned from the expat papers such as the Strait Times, which were supportive of the British Government. They were thus keen to continue to maintain a 'business as usual' atmosphere, providing rubber to the allies and economic wealth to the British Government, uninterrupted (so far) by World War Two; there is little doubt London needed the money.

The locals by contrast were rather more aware of the potential threat. Many of them were Chinese immigrants, and as such they knew the true capabilities of the Japanese military, their relatives in China having by now witnessed it first-hand. The Malays themselves were far more aware of the geographical realities of the country and that a successful invasion from the North of the peninsula through the jungle was more than possible. They knew this from local knowledge, the top brass in the British military in Malaya knew it from a training operation in 1935 that had rehearsed just such an invasion (Thompson, 2005). This knowledge was not acted on, however, for a variety of reasons both political and military, not least because the UK was first pre-occupied with its own survival and then with supporting Russia against Nazi Germany.

As such, sufficient military strengthening of the peninsula that was understood as necessary never took place (Warren, 2002); neither the airbases nor the ports, nor Singapore itself, had sufficient Army personnel or materiel for their defence. All that was left was for the plantation owners, such as Andrew, to be called-up and 'prepare' the local population using the police stations as local barracks. Andrew's account both here and as it continues in the Appendix is all the more poignant in the reading, then, for we know what is coming. When Mustard Sr finally returned to England in September 1949 he was, according to both his daughter Denise and son Andrew, doubtless recalling their mother's perception of their father, never the same as a result of his experiences as an internee in Changi Jail; he remained a shadow of his former self until his death in 1963 (pers. comm. Denise Bompas and Andrew Mustard with Mark Dibben, 30 Aug 1991; and Harry Mustard to Mark Dibben, 25 Mar. 2018).

IV. Mustard Jr – Insights into the Bluebird Enigma

Of Andrew Mustard Jr's childhood, i.e. the time when his father was in Malaya 1930–1946, little is known except that he was quite frequently laid low by illness and never attained the strength his father had once possessed. As a boy, he was fascinated by aeroplanes and rockets and was forever building them, even from an early age. He built some that he intended to launch from a bicycle at a rival 'bunch of kids' and only managed to get in his words 'rocket propelled up the next hill, while burning his legs', as they never launched (pers. comm. Harry Mustard to Mark Dibben, 25 Mar. 2018). Rocket building particularly impressed his future wife Brownie. When they met he had just blown up a neighbour's fireplace with a rocket intended to go up the chimney; Brownie thought this was marvellous! Andrew's love of all aircraft is why he preferred the air corps over the army alternative that was preferred by his father.

After an apprenticeship at the Bristol Aeroplane Company, he went to Southampton University to read Engineering but dropped out after a year. They were certainly memorable times, as according to his son Harry, 'he always spoke of them' (pers. comm. Harry Mustard to Mark Dibben, 25 Mar. 2018), and

> [m]ainly of his dastardly deeds that he and his mates conjoured up, such as white washing bobbies, placing helium filled balloons in shopping centres (which Dad reckoned one time caused an employee to fall through a glass show case he was standing on). He once let off a balloon in the middle of town at night when locals were all filing out of the movie theatres, and so they saw something that looked like a UFO. It made the papers as it ripped on take-off and Dad said it looked like it had some flapping propulsion mechanism. One story Dad loved to mention was a night out with 2 friends David Smelley and Peter Wurms (a Dutch guy). While driving home drunk in an MG they were pulled over and had their papers checked. During the discussion Mr Wurms, who was in the small back compartment of the car, popped up and announced 'Smelley, Wurms and Mustard at your service!' The Police obviously didn't believe their names – too much like 'smelly worms and mustard'. They spent a night in the lock up until their land-lady came and bailed them out with ID.

Clearly, Andrew's time at university was spent rather more in having fun with his friends than ever it was in studying his subject.

Having dropped out of university, Andrew returned to full time employment at the Bristol Aeroplane Company, and particularly the car and commercial vehicles divisions, for he was involved in designing Bristol coaches. The emphasis at the time he was working on the coaches was a stable 100 mph (pers. comm. Andrew Mustard with Mark Dibben, July 1989); this was before speed limits in the UK. The focus on aerodynamic stability and tyres inherent in this work provoked a move to Dunlop's experimental division. His involvement with the Bluebird project began in 1956. As he explained in an interview at the National Motor Museum Beaulieu (Beaulieu, 1991):

I was instructed to drag out the designs of the tyres used by John Cobb in 1949, and see where they could be improved on in the light of newer materials and with the basic outline of the Bluebird car design. I didn't meet Donald Campbell for a couple of years after that, by which time we had created the 700/41 tyres and checked them for their tyre handling characteristics and speed characteristics up to 550 mph. [This was done] with some very sophisticated equipment at Fort Dunlop … The tyre handling characteristics were determined on a very sophisticated machine which measured forces with all sorts of gadgets. The high-speed tyre test machine was a complete two-million-pound installation built underground, with the dual purpose of testing aircraft tyres and high-speed tyres under extraordinarily accurate conditions … The tyre size [was] seven inches wide, forty-one-inch rim size. The original tyres intended for Utah in 1960 had a vestigial tread because the potassium salts of the Bonneville Salt Flats have a very low abrasion characteristic. It was as smooth as a baby's bottom but very very thin, about 0.4 of a millimetre.

The Bluebird project gave him a significant distaste of corporations. He did not approve of Campbell's switch from BP to Ampol and from Land Rover to Toyota. This was not on patriotic grounds but on ethical grounds, since the British companies were the sponsors of the project. Of Campbell obtaining £1 m for logistics and then arranging for the Australian military to do it for free, he said 'I like to think I wouldn't have done it' (Beaulieu, 1991). Despite being a product of it, Andrew despised the class system and the business behaviour it begat; Campbell came in his eyes to represent the very worst of it. This is evident in a letter he wrote on 29 November 1963 from South Australia, asking Stan Dibben to join the project (Mustard, 1963a):

> My dear old Stan,
>   I am very much afraid this is going to have to do in lieu of a Christmas card – it's shock value will probably be greater anyway – you will be amused to know if the press have not already told you, that friend Campbell turned up in Australia, spent three days in Adelaide and buggered off, leaving the

welfare of the entire Bluebird operation in our sticky little paws.
I may add that Mustard is fast becoming a politician, and had
spent the preceding few days haunting Ministries. I believe that
Donald and I have parted with a pretty fair opinion of each
others' fencing abilities.

Stan, I am now completely satisfied with my contract [with
Campbell's Bluebird Project, employing him through his own
company; see below], and am also first in line for co-driver. On
this point Donald has asked me to contact everyone I feel might
be valuable to the new team. Frankly there has been so much
mucking about over the last few years I welcome the proposal
to get some fresh blood. You have always wanted to carry the
bags – how about an expense paid two months trip to Australia
next Spring? [...]

To say the least, this letter does not represent a positive character assessment
by its author of the main protagonist! At least Andrew's understanding of the
way in which class and status operated meant he knew what he was dealing with
in Campbell. He was also well aware of the project costs that had been covered
by British industry over the past few years (see Ch. 9), took a very dim view of it,
and understood very clearly the position that British industry was consequently
adopting. He set this out in a second letter written under the 'Andrew Mustard
& Co. Pty. Ltd. Engineering Consultants and Engineers.' letterhead of his own
firm, on 26 December 1963 (Mustard, 1963b):

My dear old Stan,

Thank you very much for your letter [... noting Renold
Chains' had not blocked Stan's initial soundings to take leave of
absence to join the project ...].

Stan, I certainly can justify bringing you out. I'm just
beginning to realise what it is to have a 2½ million-pound
British project on my shoulders, particularly in that Breedlove
[who had just broken the World Land Speed Record in a car
which, being pure jet-powered rather than powered through
the wheels, did not then officially qualify] is now morally the
fastest man on wheels. A hell of a lot of people are looking to the
Bluebird project to justify itself on this, its last chance. I have

quite a responsibility on my shoulders apart from the prestige aspect. As General Manager of the Project, I may well be stand-in driver, Dunlop technician, public relations dogsbody, the Lot. I have to deal with the Army, the Police, the State authorities, the various contributing firms' personnel, provide reasonable amenities in one of the most desolate places on earth, and generally keep everybody happy. I know, probably, as much or more as any single person about all these aspects but I've got to delegate a hell of a lot of authority on this particular job. The responsibility for the track alone is a big one. I'm therefore trying to pick my men. I want this to be *my* team rather than Donald's, so that he knows damn well, if he doesn't get in and drive the bloody car when it needs to go, someone else will hop in pretty quick.

Right. Do you see the set-up? Stanley, I need a Number Two, and of the people I know, you're the boy, because I trust your judgement in many things absolutely implicitly, and you have a thing which the Bluebird team has sadly lacked, a lot of practical experience of racing and record breaking. This is quite important. At a pinch you could do quite a range of the jobs I have had to do. Quite apart from this you're an adaptable person, which many of the Europeans who come out to this neck of the woods are not.

Right. I'm not going to go into attributes any further – if you'd like to come I'd like to have you, and I'll have to set about seeing how this should be done. As far as your Company is concerned, and your directors, you might perhaps draft a letter such as you would like to have them receive, and I'll embroider it somewhat.

Time-wise, I can't quite get down to tacks yet, until I know the full set-up. You would, I think, be employed by Andrew Mustard & Co. rather than the Bluebird Project as such. The period would probably be March, April, May.

You'd better let me know your terms, because I find it rather difficult to interpret what perhaps Renolds means by 'making up your pay'. I'd better in fact check up whether they are contributors, or this might perhaps complicate the issue.

Anyway Stan, let me know your second thoughts, and in about three or four weeks time, when I get back to town, I'll write you again.

Sincere regards to all and sundry, and a woof to Cindy.

[signed]

Andrew

To take aspects of this letter in reverse order, the letter was written in Adelaide just before Andrew headed up to Lake Eyre once more. On his return he decided to telephone rather than write, in order to expedite matters, for he had by then worked out that Reynolds were indeed one of the sponsors and realised that this might cause problems – as had Stan. The question of pay was resolved by an agreement that Andrew would cover Stan's expenses during the trip and repay at a minimum the £500 that Stan would withdraw from his pension fund to cover his wife's needs in running their house in Stroud etc, while he was away. The two men agreed during the call that the best way forwards was now to act swiftly in organising the tickets so that there was little opportunity for the directors at Reynolds to step in and prevent the arrangement.

The two main paragraphs of the letter reveal more of the difficulties the project had already encountered in 1963, and would encounter further in 1964. First, that there was in fact little motorsport experience within the team. Second, a good number (but by no means all) of the 'Europeans' who had gone out at their companies' behest to support the project were not exactly happy with the conditions they found; there were no air-conditioned hotels in Lake Eyre! There weren't even any hotels. Andrew needed people who could get on without complaint, otherwise there was little chance of success. Equally too, he was not convinced he had too many people up there who could be relied upon to step in and deliver outside of their narrow company brief. It is the main paragraph in particular, however, that is most revealing, not for the amount of work involved but for the realisation not only of what was at stake but also of what might happen.

As early as December 1963, therefore, Mustard is already sure that there would be delays. He saw these as not imposed by the weather which, interestingly, is completely missing in his analysis for it was unheard of to get two bad seasons of weather at Lake Eyre – as was eventually to transpire. Rather, he sees the delays as potentially being imposed by Campbell's reluctance to drive the car at speed. It is clear Andrew felt an immense obligation to his former employers Bristol and Dunlop, who were sponsors, to deliver the project and – on these grounds – was determined to drive the car if he had to. These former employers, coupled with Castrol who had sponsored Andrew when he was racing motorcycles in the 1950s, 'had got together and inflicted [him] on Donald' (Mustard, 1991) as reserve driver precisely because they knew too what was likely to happen. Yes, there was a certain amount of youthful eagerness in him saying to Ken Norris that he would have 'given his left ball to drive the car' (Norris, in Tremayne 2004: 267), as he himself later admitted; 'I was young and dying to have a go myself' (Mustard, 1991). But there was, underneath this and as the letter reveals, a genuine comprehension of the issues and of the expectations from industry, who were making it clear, as Andrew noted, that 'the Bluebird project [had] to justify itself on this, its last chance.'

In addition, the letter uncovers the source of a fundamental misunderstanding that arose among the senior members of the Bluebird Project, as to just precisely who Andrew worked for. Because he continued to oversee the tyre side of the project, there was an assumption he was still directly employed by Dunlop, as he had been at Utah and in 1963. However, by 1964 this was not the case for he had his own company, as he notes in his letter above. Further he had by this stage emigrated to Australia and, as he further noted to Stan Dibben (Mustard, 1963a), 'we have not the slightest intention of going back to poor old England. We have got a nice little house [9 Lynmouth Avenue, Brighton, South Australia], somewhat scruffy at present, but the garden is full of fruit trees, which are laden.' So, for example, Ken Norris was not correct to say that Dunlop 'pulled [Andrew] back' from his role as Project Manager (Tremayne, 2004: 298). In point of fact, contrary to Norris' presumption, it was Campbell who employed Mustard. A 'Big Row' with Campbell on 1 June saw 'Andrew sacked & reinstated' (Dibben, 1964). He was reinstated immediately because at that point (although not in July when he was again removed from his position, by which stage all the track work was finished), Campbell needed Andrew and his team to work on the rebuilding the track. Why did Campbell fire Andrew twice? Because he had realised that he was intending to use Lake Eyre to set his own Class F land speed records in the Elfin (pers. comm. Andrew Mustard with Mark Dibben, Aug. 1991).

Why did Andrew set out to do this? There were three simple reasons. First, youthful exuberance and, at least initially, not a little naivety as to the politics of the situation. It was never going to be acceptable to Campbell to have other class records set around the edges of his own project, using as he would perhaps understandably see it, the track that had been paid for by the Bluebird Project and in any case taking advantage of the circumstances that made it such that the Elfin and Mustard were there at all. From Andrew's point of view, however, further record breaking should have been welcomed as more success. That Campbell's reaction was annoyance to the point of fury only served to cement Mustard's disdain, which had grown to amusement (pers. comm. Andrew Mustard with Mark Dibben, Aug. 1991). As Andrew chuckled in his interview at Beaulieu 'there was even a book written about the rows I had with Donald!' [by which he meant Pearson's 'Bluebird and the Dead Lake'.] The three main sponsors Bristol, Dunlop and Castrol 'got together in London and inflicted me on Donald as stand-in driver after the unsuccessful 1963 attempt, so he had every reason to resent me' (Mustard, 1991).

Second, the Elfin car was perfectly capable of setting class records, so why not? Third, as he reasoned, his own company and employees had built the track and he indeed owned the Elfin racing car (Andrew was a fine in-the-field engineer and innovator in his own right). In any case, Campbell had declared 'there's no way I'm going to drive that dangerous little thing!' (pers. comm. Andrew Mustard with Mark Dibben, Aug. 1991). Further, Andrew had the correct tyres to run the car on Lake Eyre, that is, in the scale replicas that he had used to measure the drag coefficient of the salt. So it was a perfect opportunity – again, why not? Campbell's refusal to allow the record attempt on Lake Eye only delayed matters, fortunately, for Andrew set new Australian Class F records with the car at the Weapons Research Establishment, Salisbury, in South Australia on 11 October 1964 (CAMS, 1979).

V. Andrew Mustard After Bluebird

Andrew's view of the Bluebird project was that, since 'we only put the record up by three or four miles an hour when it should have been a hundred', it was 'something of a failure really' (Mustard, 1991). When the Bluebird project finished in 1964, as he had suggested to Stan in his November 1963 letter, Andrew indeed decided against returning to England and re-joining Dunlop to continue his career. He believed his young family would have a far better quality of life in 'the lucky country' than in the UK. Staying in Australia meant he could be his own person, cut free from the expectations of society in England, in a country where what one did was more important than how one spoke – or so he thought. In fact, his first five years' experience in Australia were not good; a number of initiatives failed, such as Stanley Self-steering Trailers.

These were well-proven in trans-Australian bush haulage experience as reducing tyre wear and fuel consumption, but came up against fierce opposition in the more lucrative inter-city haulage markets from traditional semi-trailer manufacturers, who were developing their own ideas for self-steering. It cost the inventor Geoff Stanley and Andrew a lot of money; Andrew was simply not accustomed to the cut-throat realities of business life, shielded from it as he had been in the UK (ironically enough). Stan put in a great deal of effort as Andrew's representative in the UK, attempting to secure UK interest, but also came up against fierce opposition from other more established trailer manufacturers who had their own versions under development. Perhaps most notable, however, was Andrew's own invention of the compact Aquajet unit (now seen on many marine applications, including personal water craft). It failed along with the associated Foamcraft small boat and regardless of Stan putting a lot of work in exploring the UK market. Such is the way with original ideas brought to market too soon, because at that time people did not like the idea of having to cut a hole in the bottom of their boats to draw water into the jet unit. In addition the engine that Andrew decided to use, for all the right engineering reasons, was itself too new, being a Sachs rotary engine. In both cases, new ideas were resisted because their simplicity went against established thinking, and in the case of the semi-trailers (as well as Norton and the McAndless' Featherbed frame) of course patented ideas can get a lukewarm reception from industry players reluctant to pay royalty fees.

These failures meant that by 1968, Andrew had to find work, which proved more difficult than he had at first supposed, at least in South Australia. He wrote to Stan in early July of that year, that the State, 'has gone completely to pot since you were here. [...] Progress is in the North and North West and how, with all the opportunities in the world' (Mustard, 1968). His mother Via, 'Granny Mustard' to her grandchildren and thus to everyone in and around the family, spent July–August–September of that year with them and noted 'Andy is trying for a suitable job in and around Adelaide or in the Northern Territories – Darwin or Alice – but hopes not to have to go to Sydney or Melbourne. [...] He is finding it difficult' (Mustard, V., 1968a). By October, she wrote 'A. is now hoping for a job in Darwin – but it's all rather dicey – and he is doing a lot of work with insurance companies in hand with the Police over accidents on the roads and faulty tires' (Mustard, V., 1968b). This work, too, proved taxing, because the legal system worked in such a way that the focus often fell upon the 'expert opinion' being questioned. This was not, however, through an analysis of the facts but rather through the attempted character assassination of the witness himself; the accent was an easy target (pers. comm. Andrew Mustard with Mark Dibben, May 1989).

In the end, Andrew did have to go to Sydney, at least for the purpose of Head Office location, for he joined the Australian subsidiary of Kennecott Utah Copper (now Rio Tinto Kennecott) as Feasibility Engineer. In this role, he was the company's exploration geologist responsible for evaluating the feasibility of possible mine sites, and discovered deposits of opal in the Northern Territory and copper in Papua New Guinea. Both were mined successfully, although the latter copper mine at Ok Tedi has become something of an environmental nightmare. Even at the time of its discovery, Andrew foresaw the environmental problems as a possibility, due to the potential for contamination of the local waterway (pers.com. Andrew Mustard with Mark Dibben, May 1989). According to Harry Mustard, (pers. comm. to Mark Dibben, Dec. 2016), Andrew

> was based on the Fly River which was a sea route for barges to bring supplies up to a river side village (Kiunga), from which the cargo was taken to the mine site 140 km away … As part of the exploration of the area, Dad was one of the first white people to walk over the Star Mountains … The river is still a thorn in the side for the mine owner (BHP) nowadays, as the locals are suing them for contamination of the environment.

Andrew got on well with his original American bosses of the company but when these were replaced with Australians, who seemingly could not see past 'what' they were looking at in this tall thin bearded man, or indeed what they were 'hearing', he was soon without a job. Throughout all his time in Australia, he had had to overcome where it was possible, through hard work and delivering on objectives, a first impression that he was the archetypal 'Pommie Poofter.' Where it was possible, undying respect and affection was invariably the result, but it was not always possible. Undeterred, Andrew set himself up in a freelance geologist capacity. As one example, he established an alluvial mining operation on the Palmer River in Northeast Queensland on behalf of a consortium of investors that required 9 miles of roads to be constructed or upgraded and a dam built holding 20 million gallons of water; the mine was valued as capable of delivering over 4 million dollars profit at contemporary gold prices (Mustard, 1983). In the 1970s he was also a main dealer and service agent for Volvo Penta in Townsville, where he had settled with the family on account of the children's needs, and ran a successful car garage there as well. Unfortunately, Andrew's share of the proceeds from the sale of the mine were lost by one of the other members of the consortium when his own investment company to which the money had been entrusted went bankrupt in 1989.

VI. Retirement

In his retirement, Andrew grew his beard long and delighted in using his pipe to shower sparks in all directions to produce amazed hilarity in any children, be they friends of his own children or children of friends, who happened to call by the house in Pallarenda. Imagine Ian McKellen's Gandalf in *The Lord of the Rings* film (except with a bald pate) in a polo shirt, shorts, socks and suede desert boots. There is no doubt that, perhaps inevitably, 23 Dyer St. was a small outpost of the best elements of British expat society, on the very edge of the old colony. There were endless supplies of tea, cake and sandwiches available, and the first experience of snorkelling and diving many of the local children had was on Andrew and Brownie's boat. Even the boat itself was an example of the best of immediate post-war British engineering for it was a De Havilland, built of aluminium on aircraft principles. It was easily rendered unsinkable by Andrew, 'just-in-case'; there were dozens of empty plastic two litre milk and juice bottles, crammed beneath the deck boards.

Andrew became renowned for keeping old Volvo Penta and Seagull outboard engines serviceable. He used a venerable Volvo Penta as his standby engine on the De Havilland and as far as he was concerned, there was 'no reason why these engines should not be serviceable; they were built to last a lifetime and there's absolutely nothing wrong with them' (pers. comm. Andrew Mustard with Stan Dibben, July 1994). Engines would often arrive at his home in Pallarenda on the back of pickups entirely unannounced, delivered in many cases by people he had never met, yet who had heard on the grapevine that he was the man to fix them. He would regularly receive phone calls seeking advice from across Australia and New Guinea, where these engines were still relied upon. He once received a similar call out of the blue from America, from a man who had been put on to him by Volvo Penta in Sweden, as being the only person from their network who still had working knowledge of their old engines. Andrew was both amused at the realisation he might well be 'Oh sh*t, The-Last-Man!' (pers. comm. Andrew Mustard with Mark Dibben, Apr. 1988), and at the same time quietly proud to have still received Volvo's recommendation almost twenty years after he had ceased being one of their main agents.

Apart from regular servicing, at which time he would make suitable improvements such as adding grease nipples to the control cables to prevent them seizing or failing due to salt corrosion and excessive wear, the most common problem was old electrics whose insulation had broken down. He used the low voltage from the primary winding of the standard flywheel magneto, whose secondary winding high voltage capacity had failed, to energise a modern two stroke ignition system. In so doing he was able to get old but otherwise perfectly reliable Seagull and Volvo outboards, built at a time when designed – in obsolescence was un-thought of, running again – to the delight of their owners.

Despite not having much in the way of disposable income in retirement as a result of the lost money from the mine venture, Andrew did this for no pecuniary benefit. He would rarely charge more than the cost of the replacement components and would regularly accept in-kind payment, even mangos, from people with less than himself. The barter economy was well established among the local community in and around Pallarenda, where profit came a distant second to doing good deeds for people. It was far more important to Andrew to keep the engines working, doing the job they were designed for, and in so doing help the people, than ever it was to make money from them. This was despite the fact he knew, and had even been told by his wealthier customers, that he could charge more than the market rate; people genuinely valued both the engines and the quality of his work. To Mustard, however, this was about doing something more significant. Making money out of his reputation was irrelevant. To suggest such a thing was, as he said, 'to miss the point *entirely*.' E.F. Schumacher would have heartily approved, for this was an excellent example of his 'good work' (1980) and a demonstration of 'economics at the most micro level, where "people mattered"' ([1973] 2011). It is, as he said, the 'height of folly to make material so that it would wear out quickly [when one is concerned with] how to attain given ends with the minimum means (Schumacher, [1973] 2011: 42). That is to say, it 'misses the point entirely' when the focus becomes not the making of money but meeting the needs of the people in community, and in the immediate example the use value of the engines themselves built to last a lifetime and therefore without the marketeer's concern for a product's 'commercially acceptable life'.

VI. Conclusion: Enterprise on the Edges of Australia

In sum, the Mustard trait of exploring new country had left Via to bring up three children with the help of nanny Gia in the 1930s, and it had left Brownie to bring up three children in the late 1950s/early 1960s. That said, from Andrew Jr's letters to Stan and knowing the man particularly as Stan did, that adventuresome urge invoked too a painful sacrifice, for he adored his children and spent most of his time thinking about their needs. As an example, the move to Pallarenda was purposefully one aimed at ensuring the boys were: a) able to get the university education in geology they wanted from a department at James Cooke University renowned in the field; and b) at the same time ensuring they had access to the water sports and nature that both Andrew and Brownie viewed as an essential element of a well-rounded childhood and early adulthood.

Just as was the case with Andrew Sr and Via, so Andrew Jr and Brownie were inseparable. The same is true of their son Harry and his wife Kim, and indeed the 'adventure trait' seems to have carried on at least into the third generation as well, for Harry has spent much time abroad, for example in China and the United States as an exploration geologist, while his three children have been growing up. Perhaps the most striking aspect of this, then, is not the exploring, nor even the fact that these three generations of Mustards have each brought up three children. It is, rather, the remarkable strength and loyalty of the three women.

No doubt like his namesake father, as an adult Andrew Mustard was tall and straight-backed with an air of constant quiet authority, an effortless supervenience. This was all added to by the piercing bright blue eyes he inherited from his mother, and by his trademark red beard. As has been noted, unfortunately he could easily be misread. He never denied, for example, he would have loved to drive Bluebird but this was simply the eagerness of youth. He was in fact fiercely loyal to the project and to the companies concerned, for as we have already noted he had of course worked for two of them, Bristol the engine supplier and Dunlop the tyre manufacturer, and in his own motorsport activities was sponsored by the third, the oil company Castrol. His main aim was simply to see the project succeed; he wouldn't do anything to jeopardise it.

That the project raised the record by such a small amount was, for him, not only a disappointment but indeed an embarrassment. The people who built Bluebird deserved far better, and the car itself deserved far better. But for Campbell's speed record professionalism, perfectly reasonably focused on the business of breaking records to earn a living, it would have achieved far more. It is clear enough in the interview he gave at Beaulieu in August 1991, that this knowledge pained Andrew. Far from being difficult to get on with he was, in fact, remarkably personable and caring, both for his fellow man and for other living creatures, and there were few who met him who were not in at least some small way affected by him. With a tireless almost mischievous curiosity and hard-working inventiveness, Andrew was an exciting person to be with.

The authority and supervenience only seemed to become more profound, but more gentle also, as the years passed and the beard grew ever more white: You *felt* Andrew's presence before you saw him; you were in the room with a Victorian explorer. When he spoke, that room would be filled with the voice of royalty from a bygone age. As we have seen, this accent meant his character was all too frequently misunderstood. We have come to associate his accent now with aloofness but, unlike his namesake father who not only was the product of the class system but was always very careful about the company he kept, there was nothing aloof about Andrew. Regardless of creed, colour or background, he focused all his attention on the person he was speaking to and the topics at hand, and with an intense immediacy: You *knew* you were talking with him!

Andrew Mustard's approach to life and work – and the undeniable place of Nature within that, is illustrative of many Schumacher principles. To take but one example, Schumacher argued strongly, contrary to the standard view that uneconomic activity should be stopped, the value of human activity to society transcends a mere use value. As such, 'society, or a group or an individual within society, [should] decide to hang on to an activity or an asset for non-economic reasons – social, aesthetic, moral or political [, or one that] preserves the environment ([1973] 2011: 28–19). Further, Andrew's approach to life was founded in an 'understanding of one of the basic truths of human existence, namely that work and leisure are complementary parts of the same living process. [They] cannot be separated without destroying the joy of work ([so long as that work is intentionally something other than] meaningless, boring, stultifying or nerve-wracking) [...] and the bliss of nature' (Schumacher, [1973] 2011: 40–1). It was this perpetually lived appreciation that made him just precisely exciting to be around. Mustard's influence continues not only through his children, but in and through those others who took the time and trouble to look beyond the accent and genuinely get to know him, and thereby upon whom he – *inevitably* – made a strong impression. Like Schumacher's influence, although of course in a far more localised way, it extends rather beyond his time.

After Bluebird, Andrew set Australian speed records in his Elfin car at Salisbury in South Australia. This is the family celebrating the new records with what else but a flask of tea! Source: Harry Mustard

11

THE EARLY YEARS OF
SELF EMPLOYMENT

Stan Dibben, sales engineer

1. Happy, Fulfilling Times

Two days after leaving Renold I was in possession of an agency for Mobyke, selling
motorcycle parts and accessories, and joined the ranks of the self-employed at 40
years old. I was selling on a straight commission of 5½%. If I didn't sell, I didn't
eat! Kind Mrs Mustard, when hearing the story, lent me £500 to buy a car, an

269

Austin A40. She was a character and kindness itself. She had been all England Junior Tennis Champion in 1913 I think it was, Miss V Speer.

This was the beginning of many happy and challenging years, earning enough to pay back Mrs Mustard, eat out occasionally (never done as an employee), pay the mortgage and take a holiday. At the end of the first year I was told to get an accountant to satisfy the Inland Revenue. On doing so the accountancy accompany told me that I was insolvent and should find employment. My reply in no uncertain language was, 'If the lifestyle enjoyed during the first year of self employment, without debt, was anything to go by, I was going to stay with it'. To put it mildly, I was not amused. The same evening Basil Moore, the manager of the firm of accountants, phoned me to say how sorry he was that I had been told I was insolvent, he said, 'Don't worry, I'll do your accounts for you in the future'. And he did, for the next 25 years.

Another central figure for me was Freddie Hawken, ex TT rider, whom I had met in 1956. He had a motorcycle and car retail business in Newton Abbott in Devon. Dear Rene and Freddie were wonderful, never to be forgotten friends. Freddie introduced me to many in the trade and his help went a long way to the success of my sales agencies. They even made sure I had a holiday and took me down to Rapallo in Italy with them by road. Both sadly no longer with us.

The agency for Fosdrive, which smelt like Wintergreen Oil, quickly fell a commercial victim to WD40 but it worked and earned me some cash for a while. Much fun was had driving into garage forecourts, spraying the engine with water until it stopped, watched by incredulous proprietors, spraying the product over the engine and starting it up without a hitch. Charles Owen and Co. with full-face helmets first in the market, earned me some much-needed cash. It is interesting to note that those full-face helmets were not approved by any of the motoring authorities or government departments, yet are now the standard wear. Ironic too that the safety helmets for cyclists, so insisted upon today, were laughed at by the cycle trade when I tried to sell them this safety helmet. 'Do you honestly think that my customers would wear that cissy product!'

My agency for Mobyke Accessories, a wholesaler of a host of motorcycle and scooter accessories was good. This was at the height of the scooter boom when the 'flower power' crowd were ascendant, and earned me a good regular income. I was introduced to Lester Simms, the NGK Spark plug importer, by my old colleague at Perry Chains, Peter Tye – father of BSA works motocross rider David and his younger trials riding brother Jonathon who later became a Vulcan Pilot. Things then began to happen with a very large market potential.

The business became a major challenge and interest, along with a German chain manufacturer, Ruberg, who had a whole range of motor and industrial chains. It gave me great pleasure to sell industrial chains to some of my old chain customers who were very loyal to me, and from these sales I managed to pay off my mortgage, buy a new house and a new car.

After a couple of years, the chain concession was lost due to a sell out or takeover or call-it-what-you-will, and NGK Spark Plugs really became my major work/hobby and life. Lester Simms was a good entrepreneur and he knew how to market. He was ahead of his time in particular with promotional clothing and decals, and the product soon became my major earner. I was attending motorcycle competition events of all types, boat racing events, car rallies and so on, giving technical support and very few free plugs. The product was technically so far ahead at this time it was not too difficult to demonstrate improved performance and speed and to record many successes. Poor lamented, dear old friend from my Norton days, Laurie Hands, of Champion Spark Plugs, castigated me for selling a Japanese product, as did many others. At this time, as an agent, I spent some of the money from other commissions earned on local paper advertisements. Even customers would ask 'Why are you selling that Jap crap?' They had been brainwashed into the idea that original equipment is always best, and Champion's sales policy of cheap or free replacements. So far as I could work out, Champion had largely bought their monopoly. For example, they had a deal with BSA of 1 p per plug on the understanding that they only approved Champion. The plugs they sold to BSA had fixed terminal nuts while the standard plugs had detachable terminal nuts which ensured that the plugs sold to BSA at 1 p per plug did not reach the retail market.

2. Pioneer Selling NGK

Pioneer selling is tough, especially on a commission only basis. Every day is a gamble where the wager is the cost of getting around the territory. A normal day was up and away in time to make the first call as soon after 9 a.m. as possible, often more than 100 miles away, sometimes more. My first month's pioneering with the NGK spark plug products was 10 sets of 4 plugs to try! Visits to active wholesale accounts were made after cold calls to possible new outlets for the unheard-of marque, especially visits to outlets where the product opposition was entrenched. These cold calls eventually led to sales and I would take the orders to active wholesale stockists. Keep going all day, often making 15 to 20 calls with perhaps success only at 2 or 3. Frustrating, challenging, worrying and certainly not the work for the faint hearted or easy riders looking to take the maximum number of 'sickies.'

I had learnt much about spark plug operation and application during my active racing. A similar promotional approach was needed but with the advances in engines in the twenty years since, there were different technical problems. With a product so much more advanced than the opposition these were fun. It became a teaching job as well as a marketing one. How surprising it was to discover how little spark plug knowledge had been passed on to both racers and all aspects of the motor trade, by the existing barons and how many misfire problems existed.

In no time, practically all the racing sidecar brigade were using NGK and many solo racers as well. Almost without exception, there was no longer the need to warm up on hot running plugs and the ensuing finger burning operation of fitting cold race plugs after the pre-race warm up. Firing end spark plug readings was a skill learnt when at Norton and during my sidecar and solo racing. It was invaluable in determining plug choice, not only to suit the machine, but also the way it was ridden. This art, incredibly, was considered by one of the senior sales staff as mere mystique. He was an ex cigarette salesman.

My knowledge of the multitude of the back-street garages and workshops used by racers in the Isle of Man amazed Lester Simms who wasn't at all keen on putting in these sorts of visits. For him, it was better the rider come to him than be visited; his real strength was marketing. Japanese directors over for their first TT race experience, were delighted at the mass of daffodil yellow NGK caps lighting up the grandstand in the summer sunshine. This was in the very early 1970s and for Lester too, it was a first with promotional clothing in the form of waterproof and lightweight summer jackets, suitably emblazoned with the appropriate logo. The customary rain showers on the Isle of Man during the TT meant the jackets were *everywhere* that year.

***

I. 1964–1970

When Stan got home from having dropped his Renold company car keys on the desk in Manchester, he phoned his old boss from Perry, Peter Tye, and told him what had happened. Peter said he was so sorry to hear what had happened and asked, 'what are you going to do?' At that time, the Friday evening, Stan didn't know. By the Saturday morning, Stan had remembered the conversation he had had with Serge Binn of Mobyke. He phoned Binn, explained all that had happened and asked, 'that job you offered me, can I have it?' Binn's answer was immediate. 'Yes, fine. Do you want to sell for me as a paid representative or as a commission agent? I think you'd do better selling on commission.' Stan's reply was 'Right, when do I start?' Binn said 'Okay, you'll be on 5.5% invoice value commission and I'll put a catalogue and price list in the post. You can start as soon as you get it. I'll organise the area for you based from where you are living now'. This turned out to be Hampshire, Oxfordshire, Warwickshire and all points West. A huge area with great potential. This transpired to be the best business decision Stan ever made. The date was October 1964.

Before he could get out on the road, Stan had to get a car. He went to the local Austin dealer and got an A40 on lowest deposit hire-purchase. One of his first trips in the little car was to Lambourn in Berkshire, to see Andrew Mustard's mother Via (Viola), to tell her about the land speed record project, for Andrew had by now decided to stay in Australia permanently. He explained what had happened at Renold. Her immediate reaction was she should tell her son off for dragging Stan away and endangering his job. Stan explained he had effectively made the decision by agreeing to go. Nonetheless, when she found out the car had had to be bought on hire-purchase she declared 'We can't have that', and lent him the money. This was a godsend as he was by this stage very short of funds, having been on unpaid leave while in Australia and having not been paid anything other than expenses while he was there. Stan paid Via back after two years as a lump sum without interest; Granny Mustard wasn't interested in interest.

Mobyke had been set up in November 1954 by Serge Binn, a German Jew who had escaped from Nazi Germany. He was a good businessman who anticipated general market demand and was totally trustworthy in respect of (e.g.) paying commission for sales with absolute honesty. As a wholesaler, Mobyke was selling direct to motorcycle retail outlets who were interested in products they could sell relatively quickly to motorcycle and scooter owners. Thus the requirement was for regular visits that were timed to coincide with anticipated stock depletion, and visits purposefully took advantage of any advertising being undertaken by the manufacturers of the products to the end user, that were in the Mobyke catalogue of sale. Mobyke had a very comprehensive product range of over 200 different items, ranging from motorcycle clothing, bike accessories such as mirrors, brake shoes and top boxes, helmets, boots, gloves and even badges. Nonetheless, the range was restricted by the fact Mobyke was not a member of the BCMCIA and so it was not able to carry manufacturer approved Original Equipment Manufacturer (OEM) replacement products.

Stan spent his time calling at motorcycle dealers at a time when there were a lot of scooters on the road, as a result of the 'flower-power era' of the early 1960s. The accessories that sold most well were for scooters, such as the archetypal chrome mirrors and other fancy goodies. As far as the motorcycle retail trade were concerned, the staples of the business were the consumable items such as brake shoes, clutch plates, footrest rubbers, handlebar grips and exhaust pipes. Stan never found himself talking about his racing, because he sensed it was not of any real interest; the focus was on the sidecar driver. Stan used to travel up to the Mobyke office in London once a month and discussed possible new products with Binn, as well as looking at new samples Binn had received from manufacturers. He never saw any of the other agents at the office. Binn always paid Stan his sales commission monthly exactly as agreed. At the start, this was around 70 pounds a month (1,200 in today's prices, Historic inflation calculator, website), about 10 pounds a month less than he had been earning at Perry and Renold, out of which he had to pay travelling expenses.

There were four major wholesalers in the area selling similar products to those offered by Mobyke. Among these were W.E. Wassle and Motorcylcle Equipment and they were all centred in and around the Midlands, the home of the British motorcycle industry. This gave them access to the manufacturers of genuine OEM products. In comparison Mobyke was small and, being located in London, had no such immediate access. Neither, being small, were they able to purchase on the scale and thus on the financial terms of the major wholesalers. In this highly competitive marketplace, Stan therefore needed a strategy that would allow him to build the business that was not focused on products, since they were similar and not always price competitive, but rather on service. He made certain that his visits to his retailers were reliable and predictable. He would always call at least once every six weeks. In addition, Binn had established a superb back-office system that meant deliveries from Mobyke as the wholesaler, too, were absolutely reliable and if an item was out of stock, he would send it as soon as it arrived, rather than wait to include it in the next regular order. Taken together, the regular visits and the promptness of deliveries meant that retailers could reduce their inventory to no more than two months' stock, reducing money tied up on the shelves and thus easing cash flow.

At this time, retailers much preferred to give the orders face to face to representatives and agents. Over quite a short period of time, as the reputation for reliability of visits and delivery, grew, so customers gave Stan more and more of the important regular consumable business, in addition to the occasional fancy accessory item, safe in the knowledge that goods would arrive on time and before they went out of stock on the shelves.

Being told by his accountant at the end of his first year self-employed that he was insolvent was indicative of the times. Self-employment was still regarded with some disdain by many in the financial industry, who saw the risk of irregular income as being too great for personal wealth protection. From Stan's point of view, however, there were only positives coming from being self-employed. These could be summed up as the psychological wealth of strong personal, humane, business relationships that could be relied upon. Such was the strength of this agent-customer-wholesaler relationship, Stan never had a Mobyke account 'go bad'; all accounts were paid and usually within one month. Serge Binn knew for himself, too, the lesson Stan had learnt as a youth at Hardings the grocers, namely that in order to build a business, customer needs come first and foremost. Further, the strength of the relationship between the two men was crucial. Binn knew that Stan would never take on an agency that sold products in direct competition with Mobyke. In return, Stan was paid with absolute regularity, and never was his commission cheque queried, his percentage commission cut or his territory reduced. There was absolute loyalty between the two men, between the wholesaler and his sales agent.

This was not to say that Stan was not looking for more agency opportunities, just that he was resolute in ignoring opportunities that were in opposition to Mobyke. He had seen another agency opportunity arise from his knowledge of a group of old Perry chain customers. The old Perry firm made cycle parts and Stan had sold chain and other parts to bicycle retailers. Seeing an Owen helmet on a bicycle retailer's stand at the Motorcycle and Cycle Show at Earls Court in 1965, Stan realised the importance of the product and contacted them. He was invited to the office in London and came away with an agency to sell them in his area. The bicycle trade's view at the time was that children, who were of course at that time the main riders of bicycles, would not want to be seen as sissies and so wouldn't be willing to wear them. It took Stan a couple of years to get sensible orders.

Owen was one of the first to make a motorcycle helmet in the UK, in 1928. They were also the first to do a full faced motorcycle helmet in the UK.

The first time Stan saw one was in the office of Owen's owner Mr Burek; it was on the desk. He was impressed and declared he could sell them, so was allowed to do so. When he first started selling them, the full-face motorcycle helmets were not then approved by either the Auto Cycle Union (ACU; the UK governing body for motorcycle sport) or the Royal Automobile Club (RAC). It was very difficult to get them off the ground to start with, because of the considered dangers regarding removing them in the event of an accident, and they were often regarded as too heavy. It was not possible to patent the idea of a full-face helmet because it was established through the space programme in the United States. Once the idea of a full-face motorcycle helmet became established, all the major manufacturers starting manufacturing them and, with his ever-deepening involvement with NGK, with some reluctance Stan let the Owen agency go. He would later use a Charles Owen helmet, specifically a white open face Mastergarde Deluxe, for the 1978 vintage races. Owen too abandoned the motorcycle and cycle helmet business and instead focused on equestrian helmets; they still do (www.charlesowen.com).

II. NGK 1965–1976

One evening in early 1965, Stan received a call from his old colleague at Perry, Peter Tye. Having left Renold, Tye was operating as an agent himself, selling a newly imported sparking plug from Japan, called NGK. He had heard that Stan had left Renold and phoned to say that NGK was far ahead of anything else in the marketplace and he could introduce him to the importer. Knowing something about sparking plugs, and the technical problems with the established manufacturers such as KLG, Champion and Lodge from his racing days, Stan was happy for Tye to make the introduction. Tye's attitudes to business were the same as his, loyalty and customer-first; Cyril Smith had been one of Tye's customers and it had been Tye who had got Stan into Perry. There was a sound trust between the two men. A few days later, as they had agreed, Stan phoned the owner of the company Lester Simms, and went to see him in London.

NGK Spark Plugs is now the world's bestselling spark plug and is the leading OEM spark plug manufacturer. Lester Simms was a London entrepreneur, who in 1963 received a box of NGK spark plugs from a friend in the Netherlands who knew that these spark plugs worked very well in American made cars and that Lester owned one. After trying them himself, he realised the technical excellence of the product and, despite it being 20% more expensive than other plugs on the market, saw a potential market opportunity to sell NGK plugs to his friends in London who also owned American cars such as big flashy V-8 powered Buicks and Fords. He quickly sold the plugs he had acquired from the Netherlands and contacted the factory in Japan.

An agreement was reached where a purchase of 5,000 plugs gave him the wherewithal, with NGK Japan's permission, to sell them in the UK. His was not the only business in the UK to have distributed NGK plugs but it became the biggest, not least because he chose to call the company 'NGK (GB)' and in order to cover the entire country, Simms took on a number of self-employed sales agents. These two decisions were very entrepreneurial moves. The use of sales agents gave rapid 'reach' country wide. In addition, no distributer of NGK either in Japan or indeed *anywhere* in the world has ever had permission to use the name (pers. comm. Noboru Torii to Mark Dibben, Dec. 2017). Nonetheless, the use of the name 'NGK (GB)' no doubt gave the impression of being not just a distributer but of being the officially recognised importer; there is a fine line between honest enterprise and ingenious deceit. Certainly, Stan was never aware that he was not selling for the official importer. There was no officially recognised *importer* in the UK before the establishment of NGK (UK) by NGK Japan themselves in 1976.

Stan's first impression of Simms was that he would in fact be straightforward in business terms, and that he would appreciate his efforts in selling spark plugs. Simms explained the advantage of the product over others on the market, the greater thermal flexibility which meant that one NGK plug would cover three Champion plugs, which gave greater benefits in a vehicle running in a wide range of conditions from high speed motorway through to low speed urban traffic. It was less likely that a plug would overheat on the motorway or foul in town. This made a great deal of sense to Stan, having experienced both these problems while testing for Norton and Perry. Stan knew he could expand on these arguments in the marketplace to sell the product. Simms made it clear he was not interested in building a corporate presence, he was only interested in selling the product. He would expand the office staff in line with the sales growth. Stan felt reasonably sure he would pay the commission agreed – 5.5% on invoice value. He left the meeting with an agreed territory of Hampshire, Oxfordshire, Warwickshire and all points West, the same as with Mobyke. He took some catalogues and price lists home with him on the understanding more would be sent through by carrier.

There was great resistance in the market place among Stan's Mobyke customers, on the basis that NGK were not original equipment in British cars and motorcycles. NGK were original equipment in the Japanese cars and motorcycles that were just beginning to come onto the market, such as the Yamaha FS1E, the Honda C100 step-thru moped, as well as the Honda N360, N600 and S800 cars as well as the early Datsun (Nissan) cars. However, such was the all-encompassing presence of Champion in particular that, combined with their marketing policy of denigrating the OE fitment plugs, dealers were removing the NGKs that the vehicles came with and replacing them with Champion. They immediately began getting into trouble, with customers complaining of misfires, poor starting and many holed pistons. The response was to blame the vehicles, rather than the plugs the dealers had fitted. The almost universal view of the trade was that Champion were the supreme product and any problems were to do with the vehicle design rather than the spark plug.

Stan was able to persuade some of his existing customers to try NGK, on the strength of the personal relationships that had been built up. These trial fitments were invariably successful. This gave Stan great confidence in the product and he was emboldened to explore opportunities to solve technical problems with a range of vehicles. There were many problems occurring with the advent of high speed motorways (before the 70-mph limit), where the continued high speed running of the engines was beyond the thermal capacities of the standard plugs fitted. He started calling on garages that were dealing in cars he had heard were persistently getting into trouble with in-traffic misfires, for example the two-stroke Saabs and the early Peugeots, such as the 504. The dealers were sufficiently frustrated and concerned at the damage to their own reputation and their capability to sell the vehicles, that they were willing to try even a Japanese plug whose retail price was 20% more expensive than the opposition. The product proved itself when genuinely tried. Cars and motorcycles that ran flawlessly were, inevitably, more important to the dealers than what plugs were fitted. The success with Saab led to the company adopting NGK as original equipment.

Being an ex-racer, Stan went to race meetings and listened to conversations among the mechanics that clearly indicated there were problems that could easily be solved. The engine modifications meant that the original grade of OEM plug was undoubtedly no longer suitable but where the next grade of plug was often causing problems by being too cold to be used, for example, to warm the machines up, or on low speed circuits. He called in on the car racing and engine tuning businesses where there was an immediate willingness to try anything that might offer solutions and give a greater chance of race success. Here, with people who were interested in the technical aspect of the product, Stan began to have serious technical conversations and, with his own background in racing alongside his technical knowledge, was able to enter into what were in effect partnerships of trust with them, to explore how to develop the engines to take advantage of the plugs' strengths. Some long-standing relationships were built on this, such as with Jan Oder at JanSpeed who were famous for tuning Mini cars for rallying. Stan was not able to pay sponsorship monies, but the opportunity to have NGK associated with cars that they were not usually associated with justified a special price for the plugs in return for stickers displayed on the cars; this was affordable sponsorship.

The early pioneer selling meant that Stan was talking to the garage trade directly. He largely ignored the car accessory shops in the early days since they were only interested in stocking OEM products and, without vehicles to demonstrate the advantages were not open to much positive discussion. This was in contrast to Lester Simms in London who, with a background in that business, was focussed mostly on selling to them. Despite the different approach, he was using his own connections to develop the market as best he could.

As with Mobyke previously, Stan was not only introducing the product into the market place, he was introducing the business; the trade needed convincing of the quality and reliability of the supply as well as of the product itself. Just as Serge Binn fully understood the needs and expectations of customers in regards to total reliability of supply and delivery, so too did Lester Simms. A key component of this was a stable price structure. Simms and Dibben were of the same mind with regards to the need to maintain the hard-won reputation of the product, and understood that this would quickly be eroded with any market place price wars. Simms was adamant that the 20% retail price difference was maintained by the retail trade selling NGK, and held rigidly to a clear and explicit price structure that in effect made it impossible for retailers to discount. As sales of the product grew a distribution network had to be established but here, too, they were equally determined that a clear and rigid price structure would be maintained thus exhibiting the quality of the product and ensuring all customers from wholesalers through to end users knew the price they would be paying. NGK was sold solely on the basis of its quality. This was in stark contrast to the way in which other manufacturers, particularly Champion, were sold.

Two Acts are relevant to this discussion, the Resale Prices Act 1964 (RPA), which abolished resale price maintenance, and The Restrictive Practices Court

Act 1976 (RPCA). The RPCA was excellent in that it provided a means of arbitration against restrictive practices witnessed in the marketplace and thereby strengthened the provisions of the Restrictive Trade Practices Act 1956 and the Fair Trading Act 1973, allowing small players not associated with either the Society of Motor Manufacturers and Traders and the British Motorcycle and Cycle Industries Association to sell into the UK market. That said, the RPCA 1973 was often circumvented by manufacturers and major suppliers through the stipulation that only recommended original equipment products could be used without invalidating the manufacturers' warranties. The RPA 1964 was problematic for small traders in that it prevented the development of a stable market place. Increasingly the only factor of note was price, service became very much a secondary factor. It meant, too, that large players could discount retail prices to below cost for a time, thus driving small businesses out of the market, at which point the resulting oligopolistic players could control the retail price to their own ends. In this sense, while the end-customer may benefit from low prices for a time, the wider interests of the customer and community took second place in the longer term.

Worse, taken together, the two initiatives allowed the entry into the retail market of large discount oligopolies that were able to sell products at prices far below what the small independent retailer could even buy for. This hastened the end of the motor parts high street shop, and in many cases high street shops more generally. In this respect, the Acts also meant that the long-practiced requirement for a change of use for a retail shop application to be approved by the local council meant that local markets were no longer able to be protected from large multiple-shop retailers. Of course, there are differing points of view in this regard, but from the point of view of pioneer selling into the marketplace, maintaining market stability through price stability and the careful development of wholesale customers and retail outlets is key to ensuring long-term stable growth, not the other way around. While quality product is also key, and not allowing it to be denigrated or devalued by the offering of free replacements, this is the conclusion to be drawn from the introduction of NGK into the UK market from 1964. It is also pertinent to the pioneering of Perry Chains from 1956. The coincidence in the dates of the original acts is indicative of the problems faced by people engaged in such work. In a pioneering situation, Stan found selective area distribution gave individual businesses throughout the supply chain incentives to sell, which they would not have had if the product were generally available. Further, resale price maintenance enabled sustainable business not only for the manufacturer, but for the importer, the wholesaler and the retailer as well. It also ensured genuine customer choice of product was maintained and placed the focus on service quality rather than basic price.

III. Serge Binn Industrial Components

Serge Binn Industrial Components was established in the early 1970s to distribute the German chain manufacturer Ruberg's motorcycle chain in the UK, to which rights Binn had acquired. He had seen a market for chain that he could not buy as OEM replacement and used his contacts in Germany to come to an agreement with Ruberg for the purpose. Having seen a Ruberg catalogue on Binn's desk, the potential for industrial chain sales became apparent in the light of Stan's experience with Perry. Much to Stan's delight, he was able to approach and sell to his old Perry customers for general replacement and even OEM fitment. This was selling that took business directly away from Renold, who had a dominant position in the marketplace. Stan's attitude to Perry customers had been the same as that which he had to Mobyke customers, i.e. absolute reliability. Since leaving Renold, his old customers had experienced a loss of service, with the result that they were happy to give Stan the business he had had before.

Of particular note, OEM proved lucrative in the grain elevator business, especially through Perry of Oakley near Basingstoke (now in Honiton, Devon; www.perryofoakley.co.uk), whose products were and are used (amongst other things) for loading grain onto ships. In this case Renold were supplying 3 in pitch girder chain with pusher attachments, a special chain manufactured by Renold and others for the grain elevator industry. Stan changed the application to a standard inch and a half pitch industrial chain that would do the same job without any major engineering or structural alterations to the elevators. This chain was also cheaper to manufacture. In addition to a lower price, it saved the customer significant sums because there was an additional benefit to running inch and a half pitch: the conveyor speed could be increased, leading to greater volume throughput – again without structural changes to the conveyor. Stan had first seen the opportunity while at Renold, but such a move was not welcomed by Renold because it reduced their income, and Stan had been ordered to stop selling standard chain for this application. With Ruberg chain now available to him, Stan was able to deliver what his old customers wanted, and they were delighted. So too was Serge Binn.

Stan also secured OEM for Ruberg from Archie Kidd, now Kidd Machinery (www.kiddfarmmachinery.com), manufacturer of a range of farm machinery. Archie Kidd had been an engineer in the railway industry. In the drawing office in 1970 they were initiating a change from imperial to metric, and were re-working sprocket diameters to centimetres. Confusion reigned until Stan noticed the decimal point was in the wrong palace. One batch of 50 chains for the muck-spreaders came into Mobyke having been made to the wrong length, and Stan had to go up to the warehouse one Saturday morning and shorten them all, ready for them to be delivery by lorry 48 hr later on the following Monday. Of further interest was Stan's experience in approaching large manufacturers who, in contrast to the small manufacturers such as Archie Kidd and Perry of Oakley, refused to buy through an agent. The common reply was 'we wouldn't buy from an import agent, we'd only buy direct from the manufacturer.' This itself is indicative of a different set of values, attitudes and beliefs. Sadly, Ruberg were acquired by an American chain company who set up an office in the UK and proceeded to take over the OEM accounts. Inexplicably, Serge Binn gave the Americans the details of all Stan's major accounts. Disgusted at how he had been treated, and left with nothing but the small replacement business, Stan ceased his involvement in chain altogether.

IV. 'Teaching, to Sell' NGK

By 1967, once Stan had got NGK established in his territory, he realised that building on this early success and significantly growing the business would require establishing a network of small, loyal and enthusiastic wholesalers. At this stage, the large multiple outlet wholesaler/retailers were not interested in NGK as it was not a big enough selling brand, and they refused to be taught product knowledge. Their view was that they did not need product knowledge, as they were simply selling to OEM catalogue recommendations. Technical knowledge was unnecessary. Stan's main selling task was to focus increasingly on small wholesalers who were open to being taught. He began taking orders into wholesalers from new retail customers, to convince the wholesale businesses there was sufficient demand for them to invest in the product. He also spent large amounts of time doing work-outs with the wholesaler's own representatives, teaching them about the product and giving them the knowledge to solve any technical problems that arose.

The reason for this was threefold. First it, gave the wholesaler greater confidence in the product, minimising the risk of him taking back 'faulty?' plugs from retailers. Second, it built a trusting relationship between Stan and the wholesalers, who saw the benefit in their own representatives gaining greater knowledge of the products they sold, and how to sell them; this Stan called 'Teach, to Sell' as the principles he imparted were useful for selling other technically oriented motor parts products. Third, it created the correct impression that Stan's primary focus was on ensuring the wholesalers did well out of selling NGK. He took steps and gave advice to ensure that over-stocking did not occur, minimising the exposure of the wholesaler to the risk of having bought product they could not sell in a reasonable time, and in so doing also avoiding the risk of the product being 'dumped' on the market at a cut price. This would have undermined the unremitting focus on selling NGK for its quality; Stan was of the view that selling a product by cutting its price denigrated that product. So successful was he in this that many wholesalers allowed him to place orders for them on the basis of stock-takes that he did when he visited. Stan knew that, in order for the plugs to sell, his primary loyalty had to be with those who were doing the selling in the field, rather than the supplier. This was entirely different to a corporate approach whose focus was on sales volume and immediate profit.

Stan focused on educating the regional distributors who sold the plugs to the local retailers. He found that to make these sales required a great deal of teaching about the product to overcome long-established and heavily entrenched preconceptions regarding the veracity of OEM brands, both at the distributor and retailer levels. He spent a large proportion of his time working to educate the retailers on the benefits of NGK spark plugs and how selling them could help the retailer create strong end user customer relationships, and then providing these orders to the regional wholesaler to service. By educating his customers, both retail and wholesale, Stan found that he was able to much more effectively sell by creating mutually beneficial, and profitable, long-term relationships.

The challenge faced was attempting to enter into an established market with an oligopolistic market structure that was bordering on monopolistic. That is, Champion were dominant brand leaders in the UK with Lodge and KLG almost non-existent, and with Bosch holding a strong market position due to its German manufacture leading to it being specified as OEM in most German vehicles. In addition, Ford and General Motors were each using their own branded plugs, Autolite and AC respectively. The effect of this on the wholesale and retail customer, and also the end-user public motorist, was that whatever Champion, in particular said about their product was taken as the gospel truth for *all* spark plugs, regardless of the manufacturer. In this respect Khaneman's (2011) observation that people in dominant market positions 'seem to suffer from an acute sense of competitor neglect … [and t]his is a case of over-confidence [in that they] seem to believe they know more than they actually do know …' accurately describes the opportunity Stan realised in pioneering NGK. In Champion's defense, their approach to marketplace dominance was not uncommon in the UK motor industry; the ties that bound manufacturers and OEM suppliers to each other were understandably very strong (see also e.g. Hopwood, 2007 and Todd 2012).

A further problem was the discounting that Champion gave motor and motorcycle manufacturers to retain OEM supply as this led, in part, to the development of an argument that only OEM equipment was satisfactory, and that anything other than OEM equipment would invalidate warranties. This is a practice still common today in the motor industry more generally, and Stan considered this 'scare selling'. More interestingly still, he also knew that failure to teach honest facts to customers and end-users, can also be a deliberate and expedient policy employed by dominant market players, in order to maintain preconceptions and monopoly retention, leading to poor customer service and consideration. Stan realised that this common monopolistic policy made the selling of a new pioneering product, especially one of better quality and service, much easier. In short, a great deal of pre-conceptions and misconceptions about spark plug technology was thoroughly embedded in the 'mind' of the market at the time of the introduction of NGK as a new product into that established market, which Stan worked to overcome.

A further problem was the creation of a customer base. While it was possible for Stan to use his reputation selling motorcycle parts, coupled with the introduction of Japanese motorcycles, to establish a foothold in the motorcycle after-sales market, that market – like the motorcycle market in general at the time – was dwindling. Thus while 'warm-calling' customers was possible in the motorcycle trade, entering the motor car parts market – which he knew was essential to increase sales and general market presence – required 'cold-calling' from the start. Stan's adage here was that a no-order cold-call is a warm-call next time.

He also realised that to establish any foothold in the market required him to, as he put it, learn, think, and teach. By learn, he meant having knowledge and absolute respect for the opposition's product to be a credible source of knowledge in the sales discussion. By think, he meant anticipating questions from potential business to business (B2B; i.e. not selling direct to the general public, but to other businesses who themselves as retailers sold either direct to the general public, or as wholesalers sold to retailers) customers and having honest answers. By teach, he meant educating the customers on the comparative technical realities of the products and having the marketing perspective of always working for customer, and their best interests. In taking this view, he was relying on the maxim taught him by his friend and business supporter Freddie Hawken, that making money for oneself requires that one makes money for other people. Taken together, these steps developed very firm trusting relationships, in the vast majority of cases spanning two and even occasionally three decades, which yielded long term and continuous sales growth.

Stan realised that often the 'learn' aspect meant that before going out to try to sell the product, a great deal of research was required to be able to both anticipate potential customer questions and formulate honest answers. This research concerned not only the product he was selling but also the oppositions' products, notably Champion due to its almost monopolistic position in the marketplace. This was in terms not only of its marketing and sales tactics but perhaps more importantly the technical aspects of their products. To be able to sell into a market dominated by oligopolistic players in particular, he realised that expert knowledge not only of one's own product but also – and perhaps more importantly – of the oppositions' products, created an impression of competence in the minds of the customers to whom he was trying to sell – and again more importantly – who sold the oppositions' products.

He found that only having demonstrated mastery of the oppositions' products was it possible to be listened to by the trade about a new competing product they had usually never heard of, or that at best they had considerable misconceptions about. Stan leant it is also paramount to know and understand the needs of the marketplace, and particularly any technical problems the trade and the end-users were encountering with the oppositions' products. Knowing how, when, where and why the oppositions' products failed was key to understanding how the new competing product could be sold. This extended to finding out what it was that buyers and end users liked and disliked about these products, their problems, technicalities, presentation, price structures, marketing policies and sales tactics.

Having this wealth of information, however, could be misused if one attempted to denigrate the various opposition, and in particular the established opposition. Stan understood that doing so would only denigrate by association the product being pioneered, and in every sense. It was, he decided, in thoroughly bad taste, and was just plain bad sales practice. The wealth of information needed to be used properly, by allowing him to teach customers how – objectively – the problems they were encountering could be overcome. In some instances, this included offering technical solutions that could actually be found in the oppositions' own product catalogues, and even pointing this out. The effect was to build credibility and an appreciation that Stan understood his customers' needs were most important; he wasn't there simply to sell at all costs, to (as the term was) 'flog' NGK.

An example from the pioneering of NGK Spark plugs in the UK is Stan's discovery, when looking for opposition problems, that Saab had serious difficulties with the OEM spark plugs in their two stroke models. Visiting and speaking with the dealers revealed the reason, which allowed NGK to be successfully demonstrated in every Saab dealer he could find. Teaching about the product and overcoming dealer reluctance to disbelieve the preconceived, resulted in dealer pressure on the manufacturer, culminating in the whole original fitment business, at a time when the product was 25% more expensive at trade level than the opposition. A similar case occurred with Peugeot which resulted in product approval as a replacement part.

With this approach, and having built the confidence of the customer, it was possible then to encourage the customer positively, to help them work out and understand for themselves the objective solutions to the technical problems being encountered. In essence this was about encouraging the customer to engage in a genuinely inquisitive approach, to think about what they were being offered, for example in the asking of 'Why-questions: Why does it work, why is it the price it is, why is it doing this instead of doing that, etc. This was about teaching customers to think for themselves, as opposed to accepting the taken-for-granted pre-conceptions established by the oligopolly through (e.g.) the accepted wisdom of the sales catalogues. Stan argued that the thinking should not stop with the catalogue's full stop; there are no 'thinking' full stops in a manufacturer's sales catalogue or product technical manual.

One aspect of sales policy that followed from Stan's 'Teach, to Sell' principle concerned free-of-charge (FOC) replacement policy. He was clear that to protect the integrity of the product being pioneered, FOC replacement should only occur where there was a genuine product failure. Using FOC replacement to pacify a customer when product failure was due to misuse only denigrated the product and the service. This was where product and marketing teaching was again paramount in order to overcome preconception, especially when dealing with long standing and established near monopoly product market penetration, such as was the case with NGK. On one occasion Stan was given an order on the assumption that a box of plugs supplied previously was entirely 'faulty' and would be replaced FOC. The order was torn up in front of the customer, and it was explained that his preconception of FOC policy was not applicable to NGK.

Further, although the (correct) technical explanation for the 'faulty plugs' lay not in the plugs but in the mis-application of the plugs to the vehicles into which they had been fitted was not immediately understood, it was understood in the fullness of time. In spite of the immediate disagreement, a mutual respect was retained. Taken together, this led to a very good long-term relationship with the customer, as a result of the customer learning about product application. That lesson would not have been learned, if FOC replacements had been given as the easy way out of a difficult sales moment. Further, the market monopoly holder rarely taught technical facts in any avenue of the trade, in the way necessary to give the customer and end user real value, since their policy was aimed at selling (unnecessary) new replacements, with ad lib FOC replacements regarded as 'no argument generosity.'

The nature of the B2B relationships required in pioneering new products can be seen in the following example. In the initial stages of NGK's market penetration, a last call was made one winter's day to a Toyota dealer over 120 miles away from home, at 4:30 p.m. on a Friday. Stan had refused to give this dealer a direct account some months before, telling him to buy from the local wholesaler. This had impressed the owner of the dealership because of the loyalty it demonstrated to the wholesaler. Yet, in addition, Stan had always advised the Toyota dealer that he was ordering from the wholesaler too many plugs and too many types. 'You don't need half as much or half as many.' It had got to the point where the owner of the dealership allowed Stan to do the stock-takes himself. Having done the stock-take that day, the owner said to him:

'Where are you staying tonight Stan?'

'I'm not, I'm heading home.'

'What?! In that little old Austin A40?'

'Yes.'

'You can't drive that worn out thing three and half hours up the road in the dark after the day you've put in.'

'Well I've got no choice.'

'No, no. I'm not having that. You need a better car than that.'

'I can't afford one!'

'Sure you can. Have my demonstrator Toyota Corona. I'll take that rubbish old Austin and you give me 200 pounds.'

'But I haven't got 200 pounds!'

'You will have by the time I see you again. When will that be?'

'Well, about six weeks.'

'Jolly good. And I suppose I need to organise insurance for you too?'

'Umm, well yes. Because I can't do it now – it's gone 5 p.m. and it's a Friday.'

'No, that's fine too. Come into the office and we'll do that. Oh, and here's the keys!'

Clearly, the Toyota dealer knew there was a benefit to his business for it would mean a Toyota, in the early stages of the brand's penetration into the UK market, would be seen all across the South-West and Midlands of the country, and with his business' name on the number plate. But even allowing for this, working in every sense for his customer meant that Stan's customer was willing to work for him too. In short, he sought to build very special B2B relationships, using a clear step-by-step approach to pioneer selling.

VI. Conclusion: Some Initial Insights from 'Teach, to Sell'

In sum, 'Teach, to Sell' built customer, personal, product and end-user confidence. However, the teaching needed to be based on matters of fact, not opinion, and above all needed to be absolutely honest. Those B2B customers who are willing to learn invariably made the best customers, since they were the ones in whom Stan could trust the future development NGK's position in the local marketplace. This was because these customers needed to be able to think for themselves and explain technical issues with their customers, have the confidence to do so and provide the correct technical advice. If B2B customers were unable or unwilling to do this, then they most likely would not be able to sell the new product (NGK) and would fall back on selling the established one (Champion). Stan quickly found they could not be relied upon to build a product presence for NGK, since it is always far easier to sell an established product with established pre-conceptions. Whereas it was crucial in pioneering NGK as a new product to break down preconceptions, otherwise B2B (and retail) customers jumped to (often erroneous) conclusions, led to do so by the views of the end-user and the car engine manufacturers.

To help build both product and personal customer confidence, adopting a policy of area exclusive territory allows the B2B customer to develop the business. This also requires regular visit frequency, with on time visits to suit the customer's own work schedule. In the early days of NGK's market penetration, Stan racked up very high mileages in order to meet his self-imposed 14–16 calls a day, often 6 days a week. Helping to develop the customers' business not only required ensuring rapid fulfilment of orders and rapid response to queries and complaints, it also required careful calculation of trade/wholesale/retail price structures, to protect customers' exclusive markets. Extracting the maximum from the customer by selling a higher priced product than necessary, for short term gain, was, Stan reasoned, the very best way to lose them. Saving customer expense was the best way to keep them.

In this respect, it became clear that in pioneering the product, he was also in effect pioneering the customers, who needed to be worked *for* and whose requirements need to be thought about. This was not least because once the product was better established, he knew enough of the competition that they would likely – and did – use price discounting and other forms of 'loyalty buying', such as entertaining customers to lunch and other events. Stan realised this usually meant that the biggest entertainer would get the business, if the loyalty of his customers was not built on firm long-term business principles. He obviously could never compete with corporate business on the entertainment front, so he never tried. He sought to obviate that as a relevant sales strategy. Perhaps most tellingly, therefore, in forty years of selling to the motor trade, Stan only once entertained a customer to a meal. He was, however, regularly invited to Christmas lunch by his customers, and this would occur right up until his retirement. This was not because he could be bought, rather it was because they trusted him to look after their interests and they viewed his contribution to their businesses as significant enough to be considered a part of them. Stan always looked upon this as a tremendous honour.

NGK Spark Plug Co. Ltd Headquarters in Nagoya, Japan. Source: Noboru Torii.

12

SELF-EMPLOYMENT AND NGK (UK)

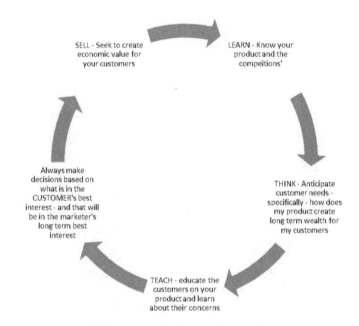

SELL - Seek to create economic value for your customers

LEARN - Know your product and the compeitions'

THINK - Anticipate customer needs - specifically - how does my product create long term wealth for my customers

TEACH - educate the customers on your product and learn about their concerns

Always make decisions based on what is in the CUSTOMER's best interest - and that will be in the marketer's long term best interest

The principles of 'Teach, to Sell' rendered as a virtuous circle. Source: Morgan Miles

1. NGK – from (GB) to (UK)

The time came when Lester Simms had grown to become NGK Spark Plugs GB and then in 1976, became the Japanese owned NGK Spark Plugs UK Ltd, under the command of Mr N Torii. I was told by him that my territory, which was made up of rural counties, was producing 40% of the turnover at the time of the takeover, and Lester had reduced my commission back to 5% by then because he said he couldn't afford it. I was also surprised to discover that whereas most of the turnover from my territory came from wholesalers selling to a wide range of retailers, cars, motorbikes and also horticultural businesses selling chainsaws and lawnmowers and the like, the turnover from other territories came from motorbike retail sales. One of my earliest customers had in fact been a horticultural business, owned by Terry Bass. And he was happy for his orders to go through a wholesaler. Under Mr Torii, I was gratefully paid a retainer and commission on sales, and began a wonderful and rewarding relationship with this Japanese company.

The Japanese directors were over to see the Isle of Man TT races on one occasion, and I had been asked to accompany them to a suitable place on the circuit for photographs. I took them to Doran's bend about 8 miles from the start, and they chose a spot to watch from. This was on the outside of the corner, directly beyond its apex, and they chose it to get the best view through the corner and back up to the hill from where the bikes would appear. My insistence that they move from this highly dangerous area was reluctantly agreed to, and they settled down just a few yards away. A few laps into the race, world class racer Mick Grant collided with a slower rider and both machines hit the bank, one of them bursting into flames, precisely where my group had initially wanted to sit. It was a serious collision. Fortunately, none of my group of Japanese visitors were harmed. One English member took a panic backward leap into a blackberry bush and suffered a few scratches. Talking about it later in the day, one of the Japanese party said, pointing skywards 'You must have a telephone line with Him up there.' I'm not too sure how the photographs turned out!

2. The Effect of 'Corporatisation' at NGK (UK)

When success comes after sustained long time effort, jealousy is often its colleague, especially when the pioneer's income exceeds that of the employed directors and personnel who enjoy salary, company car and expenses.

The last five years or six years, by which time the product had become dominant in the market place, were not as exciting as those early years. By this time, Mr Torii and his successor Mr Arai had both returned to Japan, replaced by Jim Hughes, an Englishman who had come from Champion. Before he left, I took Mr Arai to the TT Riders Association luncheon, and introduced him to a number of the star racers of the era. During the general conversation, Mr Arai confided in me, saying 'there is much jealousy in high places, Stan, over your self-employed position in the company.' Those 'in high places' at NGK UK that

Mr Arai was referring to had either forgotten, or simply did not know, that I had worked many years subsidising the product in the early days, spending many nights away from home at my own expense to get as many calls in as possible the next day. Many were the times I had been confronted by ignorant garage trade and told to 'Eff off! You ought to be ashamed of yourself selling that Jap crap!!" The jealousy was itself born of ignorance. My policy had always been based on many small loyal customers being better than one or two big ones, whose loyalty could maybe only be bought by helicopter trips to race meetings, meals out, overseas trips etc., as seemed to be the general and normal business practice among large British firms. It was soon indicated to me that giving and receiving customer loyalty was regarded as an apathetic attitude to finding and opening new accounts. I was now regarded as lazy. To my mind, 10 accounts worth £1,000 each were better than one worth £10,000. One account could be lost at the drop of a hat. I had many loyal customers right up to retirement. One or two still contact me from time to time and I say a big 'Thank you' to them. My aimed for 6-week customer visit frequency resulted in mileage in excess of 50,000 miles a year with only a few minor incidents and one parking ticket. This would be impossible today with the traffic density, speed cameras and parking restrictions as they now exist.

I consider myself to be very fortunate to have served NGK for 25 years. Mr Torii has never once failed to send me a Christmas Card since the day he left the UK company to return to Japan around 1981/2. Mr Arai, has never failed to send me a birthday and a Christmas card. They had and still have my absolute loyalty and deservedly so. They were fabulous people to work with and I owe them so much. They had me visit the factory in Nagoya on a couple of occasions, booking me en route into the premier hotel in Tokyo, the New Otani, where UK Prime Ministers stay when on official visits. The incredible trips on the high-speed train, the Shinkansen, from Tokyo to Nagoya were another highlight. Such was their appreciation of my efforts. I find it interesting that Lester Simms never once contacted me after he sold his business to NGK, not even a phone call.

The 25 years of selling on a commission on sales only basis, has had a great influence on my attitude to monopolistic supermarkets and the giants of retailing, who do nothing to assist in pioneering new products, and whose directors would never consider doing business with a mere agent. One once said to me 'You can take your commission off my buying price', and my reply was 'You must be joking'. He wasn't and neither was I. There were plenty more customers out there.

3. An Unwanted Retirement

With my 64th birthday came notification from NGK (UK) Ltd that my services would no longer be required one year later on my 65th. By this time the UK organisation had been subsumed as a subsidiary into NGK Europe. In 1990 I was summoned to meet the European supremo, in the company of the English UK director to agree a termination of agency payment. It proved to be a take it or leave it meeting and I departed reasonably happy with the result but not too pleased with the way the meeting had been conducted, since I was told to leave the room when the remuneration decision was made. There was no negotiation after 25 years of loyal and honest service.

I was sorry to leave NGK, but what had been a 'family' fighting the opposition had become a 'team' fighting each other for the biggest monthly sales, and for promotion. Not my scene.

Even after only two months of it, I was fed up with retirement. It was so boring and unrewarding. At least the finances were okay. Basil Moore, Peter to me, had done me proud for the 26 years of my self-employment. He told me when to change the car, where to invest money, pension provision etc. After such a long and faultless association, I trusted him implicitly. I received £400 a month plus the pensions he had arranged. Then he departed this life suddenly, leaving behind a £1,000,000 scam! The £400 a month was lost, along with most of my savings. He was a member of the Association of Chartered Accountants, but they did not accept any responsibility for his actions as far as his business with me was concerned. Fortunately all my eggs were not in the one basket, the pensions were secure, so all was not lost.

***

I. The Principles of Pioneer Selling

The previous chapter examined the period of Stan Dibben's time as a self-employed sales agent from its beginnings in 1964 with Serge Binn through to the early 1970s and the zenith of NGK (GB) under Lester Simms, by which time he had developed the 'Teach, to Sell' approach. This had its origins in his time at Harding's the grocers in Ropley as a teenager, developed in the 1960s with Mobyke and thoroughly to pioneering NGK in the UK market. Immediately, therefore, we can usefully derive some of the broader principles from that approach, as follows:

1. Before selling the product: Anticipation of questions and having honest answers

    a. Research and Learn all about the product.

    b. Research and Learn all about the opposition's products.

    c. Research and Learn from the marketplace all about the oppositions technical problems – what is it that buyers like, and don't like.

    d. Research and Learn all about the oppositions marketing tactics.

2. In selling the product: New product selling requires absolute respect for the opposition's product, to be credible in the sales discussion. The principles apply to selling the product to an individual, but for pioneering a product in a marketplace, it is important to develop a 'business-to-business (B2B; see all Chapter 11) network of other business who on-sell to individual members of the public

    a. Never denigrate the oppositions' product or tactics.

    b. Find B2B customers who are willing to question established in-market generic product preconceptions, and explain the advantages of the product, ie. how it overcomes existing problems, so that they have inherent confidence in the product and its people.

    c. Ask and answer 'Why' questions. E.g. Why does it work, why is it the price it is, why is it doing this, etc. Dozens of Why questions!!

3. Work for the Customer in all respects

    a. Teach your B2B customers – who must be willing to learn – about the product to allow them to build end user confidence in both the product and the people representing it.

    b. With these B2B customers, build area exclusivity wherever possible, to allow them to grow the market for themselves and support them in doing so.

    c. Avoid over-stocking by customers (over-selling).

    d. Ensure rapid response to customer orders.

    e. Ensure regular, on time, customer visits. Establish with

the customer a visit frequency they can rely upon which is based upon frequency of customer product use and frequency of sales.

f. Ensure mutual respect in the event of disagreement, be this technical or marketing.

g. Never give free-of-charge product replacement unless the product is genuinely faulty, ie. not when it has been misused. To do otherwise is to devalue the product and play to established technical and sales preconceptions.

h. Never discount a product to ensure first sales as this takes the focus away from the product and onto the price and encourages bully-buying.

i. Work tirelessly – and honestly – to break down preconceptions by teaching the new, which must – through research – be matters of fact, not opinion.

j. Never 'manage' your customers, grow and develop them; if there is any 'management' going on then it must be collaborative mutual management in that each manages the other for the benefit of both.

In this way, product teaching *evolves* markets rather than directly grows sales, and is much more sustainable. Much of it goes against established marketing principles. For example, clearly this approach also requires that customers are treated as one's employer; Stan's adage given to him by Freddie Hawken was 'in order to make money for yourself you have to make it for other people'. This sort of pioneer selling is genuine sales *engineering*. It is both Education in the creation of value that is owned by the customer through thorough comprehension of the product and its proper application, and Entrepreneurship (not management) in the extraction of value for reliable, sustained and sustainable sales growth. It creates a virtuous circle.

Pioneer selling such as Stan Dibben employed with NGK requires teaching to be the foundation of customer relationships and business growth, since it establishes in the customer base a genuinely objective loyalty. At the same time, pioneering a product requires personal loyalty to one's customers and developing market policies that meet their needs; the customer comes before the profit and sales targets are a negative influence by placing the focus on the product rather than the needs of the customer. In this respect profitability is of course essential but is not in and of itself the key to long term success. Pioneer selling, then, involves both entrepreneurship in the creation of value in new customer bases, education in the creation of value owned by the customer, through thorough comprehension of the product and its proper application and, from this in sum, a genuinely sales engineered extraction of value in reliable, sustained and sustainable sales growth.

II. NGK 1975–1990

It did not take Stan long to realise that there were other markets, such as lawnmowers, chainsaws and marine engines that must have been experiencing similar problems, so he began cold-calling on stockists in an exploratory way. Stan discussed the market potential with Simms who, seeing the potential and having similar confidence in the product to Stan, happily ordered the appropriate plugs in from NGK, thus increasing his stock product range substantially. Stan then started selling them successfully. The potential for the growth of the business increased markedly and, using the same approach of regular and reliable calling on his customers as he employed with Mobyke, commission from NGK began to overtake that which he was receiving from Mobyke. The demand for NGK and the work involved in developing a wholesale network meant that Stan was devoting more and more time on the road selling NGK and less time with Mobyke.

One of the big differences between selling Mobyke and NGK was that, while the regular repeat business was there with the latter, it had to be brought in by visiting the businesses concerned with the former. NGK orders from wholesalers were regular and they were willing to phone them in to Stan at home, or to NGK directly. The difference between the two became starkly apparent when Stan contracted a bad dose of flu in January 1970 and was unable to get out into the territory for a month. During that month, the Mobyke sales virtually ceased whereas NGK business continued coming in. The difference between the two agencies was that Mobyke was a wholesaler selling a range of products in direct competition with other wholesalers, often selling the same brands, whereas NGK was effectively the sole importer of a single product. In addition, the British motorbike sales that Mobyke largely relied upon were sharply declining. Stan realised the potential for growth with Mobyke was increasingly limited, and put as much of his focus as possible into developing NGK, eventually relinquishing the Mobyke agency in 1982 when S. Binn Industrial Components sold Ruberg (see above).

At about the same time as relinquishing the Mobyke agency, Stan saw an advert in a trade newspaper inviting people to apply for agencies with a wholesale distributer of imported parts for Japanese cars, KJ Motorparts in Leicester. Seeing the growth of Japanese cars, and with an increasing number of older Japanese cars on the roads, Stan recognised the potential, contacted them and paid them a visit. He was immediately offered the agency for his NGK territory. This agency, Stan reasoned, would provide a range of products that complemented NGK for his own wholesalers and retailers. He quickly discovered, however that KJ had plans to sell into the UK market genuine NGK spark plugs, reconditioned and imported from China. This was disclosed at the first sales meeting Stan attended with other agents from around the country.

When Stan raised an objection, questioning whether they were to be sold as if they were brand new, and indeed at all, other agents saw nothing wrong in the practice arguing 'a sale is a sale, a plug is a plug'. Stan then questioned whether, if any were faulty, they would be sent to NGK in London. The answer was 'yes, I suppose. Why not?' Stan immediately resigned his agency, left the meeting, and informed NGK in London what was happening. It was unlikely that they would have ever found out otherwise. The matter was eventually dealt with through the Head Office in Nagoya. Stan warned his own wholesalers of the possibility, and Stan never encountered any of the Chinese sourced plugs in the marketplace.

NGK Japan recognised the network established by Lester Simms' company and made an agreement with Simms to the effect that he sold the assets of NGK (GB), stock, customer list and building infrastructure, to NGK in Nagoya in 1976. This was to ensure the distribution rights of Simms' company were held in perpetuity by NGK Japan. The agreement also contained a 10% profit share for the next five years. NGK (UK) Ltd thus became a wholly owned subsidiary of the Japanese company. In this way, their direct investment in the UK differed from their approach in the rest of Europe and the USA, where the importing businesses were established without any agreements with local companies; joint ventures were only used to establish manufacturing facilities (pers. comm. Noboru Torii to Mark Dibben, Dec. 2017).

At the time of the takeover, Stan's sales made up around 40% of the total turnover of the business, something the incoming Managing Director Noboru Torii was both impressed with and concerned by. Torii now had the job of taking the business forward and growing it further. It is therefore apposite, at this juncture, to consider perspectives other than Stan Dibben's, on the growth of NGK in the UK post-1975. Two are noteworthy, that of Noboru Torii the first Japanese Managing Director of the company and that of Jim Hughes, the person who joined NGK from Champion first as Sales Director when Mr Torii returned home and then later (when Mr Arai, Mr Torii's successor, too returned home) as Managing Director.

III. Jim Hughes

To take the latter first, Jim Hughes' view on his time with NGK and of the company at that time is in the public record. He is clear about what he had experienced at Champion, what he found by contrast at NGK, what he tried to do and what his focus was, as follows (quoted in Harnet, 2014).

> Champion was a world leader. It was strong, aggressive, very professional and very profitable. In the UK it was run by Hubert Starley, CBE, who was a very strong leader and made a big impression on me. He was a massive disciplinarian and the company was run in a military style which, with my background in the Army, suited me. [...] I loved working at Champion and had fought so hard for the company over the years, but there was a wind of change blowing through Champion and I knew it was the right time to leave. [...] I was very surprised to find a culture of individualism and a lack of teamwork amongst some of the English-speaking staff [at NGK]. Knowledge was something that was not shared as it was seen by some individuals as power over others. Office doors were literally closed and not open. My first priority was to create teamwork and team spirit. Certainly, there was a need at NGK Spark Plugs (UK) Ltd for the people to be held together as a working team, a need to achieve the common task and the need that each individual had a virtue of being human.
>
> I had a board made for our small conference room which carried the message 'Teamwork = Success'. Some years later this message was replaced by 'Teamwork and Togetherness = Success'. It can still be found today in the large conference room at NGK's offices at Hemel Hempstead. Before writing a strategic plan for the company, I decided as a next step to work with each salesman on his territory. This enabled me to obtain all the information

I would need. There were only ten salesmen which included three agents. I have always been a good listener and I listened carefully to what the salesmen and their customers said about the company. It took me nearly two months to complete the exercise. As the sales force had no pre-set standards to measure their performance against, no single salesmen could tell you what represented a good day's work for the company.

My next task was to visit with Brian Childs [Sales Manager and later, after Hughes retired, Chariman] every existing NGK direct account in England, Wales and Scotland. The conclusion was that if NGK Spark Plugs (UK) Ltd was to have any chance of increasing market share in the automotive sector of the market the priority had to be the appointment of new distribution within a short timescale of two to three years maximum. This would ensure availability of NGK Spark Plugs at point of purchase. So began the creation of a strategic plan for the company. My dream was to make NGK Spark Plugs the brand leader in the UK market. By working with the OEMs at the early stages of engine development, NGK engineering provided us with another vital sales tool. As time progressed, the industry began to identify NGK Spark Plugs (UK) Ltd more and more as the spark plug engineering specialist. [...]

I was always concerned for the development of [people in the company] as businessmen and as human beings. Building respect for each other is essential in a Japanese company as is joint decision making. I cannot remember having had any loud arguments with Japanese colleagues. The key to success is working together in a mature, respectful fashion. In Europe I inherited the proud title of 'Grandad'. I am delighted to say that over the years, I have kept in touch with most of the Japanese colleagues it was my privilege to work with. I have enjoyed watching their progress, with a feeling of pride and satisfaction that perhaps in some small way my contribution helped them to achieve their personal ambitions.

Early in my working life I was told, leadership from within is more valuable than leadership from above. Some of my best creative thinking has come from what I call 'walking the job', talking to people at their work station, encouraging them to talk about themselves by showing genuine interest in what they are doing and not being afraid to ask, 'Is there a better way?' It is important to seize natural opportunities to lead people in face-to-face interviews; perhaps I am old-fashioned but e-mailing does not communicate and in my humble opinion, never will. The spirit of leadership that I wish to convey depended always on my presence. You can influence others by thinking deeply, speaking gently, laughing often, working hard, giving freely and being kind.

Even admitting that the sales of oxygen sensors assumed ever-greater importance as time went on (it now – 2018 – accounts for 60% of NGK (UK)'s sales), there is no question Jim Hughes' approach was highly successful. After all, NGK's sales grew linearly to become UK market leader under his astute stewardship. Yet there was no relationship between Jim Hughes and Stan Dibben. Neither did Stan experience personally much, if any, of Hughes' undoubtedly laudable approach to leadership (with which he agrees; see also Chapter 14 for the serendipitous application of a very similar approach in academia). It is worthwhile, therefore, to consider the foregoing quote in more detail to discern why this might be the case. As a matter of fact, Hughes never joined Stan for a work out and, almost from the beginning of Hughes' time with the company as Sales Manager, there was a breach of trust when he discovered that Hughes had visited his customers without informing him he was going to do so. To Stan this was a basic common courtesy. He only found out at all, because his customers told him they'd had 'some blokes in here from NGK asking about you.' This behaviour was not something the Japanese, in Stan's experience, would ever have engaged in.

The difference between the two men, though, perhaps begins in their military background and formative work experiences in the motor industry. Stan did not like 'big ships' when in the Navy, preferring the informality and fluidity inherent in being one's own person able to get on without being subject to authority as one can in small ships. In contrast, Hughes' military experience in Malaya where he served two years on an active tour of duty during the Malayan Emergency with the Royal Army Veterinary Corps and the Kings Own Scottish Borderers (Harnett, 2014), was quite the opposite. This was added to during his time at Champion, where his military background was in concert with the culture he found. So too, Stan had been able to find cultures on the edge of the motor industry, at BSA, Norton and Perry which were more informal and less structured but still highly successful. That both men thrived in the environments they found themselves in is clear, that the environments were almost the precise inverse of each other is also clear.

What can we discern constructively beyond the very different personalities of the two men? Stan's sense of the culture in NGK among the English employees was much the same as Hughes' conclusion; it was not a place he wanted to work. The difference is that he perceived the culture getting worse as time went on, the competition among the group becoming more fierce, Hughes felt he was building a strong team. It is clear enough from the foregoing that Hughes was not particularly comfortable with agents, and this perhaps explains part of how Stan felt he was treated. There is no doubt that under Mr Torii, Stan felt himself to be a part of the family, whereas under Jim Hughes he felt very much on the outside, as the 'team' inside was built. It might be natural to conclude that Stan was not a team player, but the success he had in building a strong and loyal network of wholesalers whom he supported and developed suggests he was. Indeed, both men were good at building teams to do the job they each required of them.

It seems from the foregoing that Jim Hughes was most focused on two things. First, on building a team inside NGK to work together to grow the sales of the business through sales targets. Second, on establishing technical engineering relationships with car manufacturers to develop wider OEM adoption by helping to improve the engines they manufactured and put into their vehicles. Stan too was focused on two things. First, on building a group of wholesalers and motor parts factors and retailers with whom he worked to grow the sales of NGK through *their* businesses in concert with market demand. Second, educating them about the technical advantages of the product and how to use that knowledge to solve vehicle problems they encountered with their own customers. Whereas Hughes needed to build a sales team inside NGK, it seems under his close supervision, Stan needed to make use of the wholesalers' sales teams obviously not under his supervision but nonetheless who always felt closely supported. As a matter of principle, he always believed in people being left alone to get on.

Hughes it seems was concerned primarily with the needs of the people who were his employees, and since Stan was self-employed he was not considered a member of the sales team and therefore not a member of the company; this was most likely the basis for the lack of relationship between the two men. Further, Hughes saw his major customers ultimately as the car makers who bought the product. This would guarantee OEM supply (as it did, during the period of this chapter's historical focus, with e.g. Bentley, and eventually BMW), from which there should be no divergence from the agreed plug type, and from which aftermarket sales would naturally follow. Whereas Stan was concerned primarily with the needs of the people who were his customers, namely the wholesalers, and retailers, who bought the product. OEM work would naturally follow (as it had e.g. with SAAB and eventually Peugeot) from strong demand from the authorised dealers who saw the technical advantages in customer cars on the ground. These technical advantages arose from demonstration that OEM was not necessarily the optimal solution depending on the way the vehicle was driven. In short, Stan saw his needs and those of NGK as a company naturally flowing directly from meeting the needs of his customers.

In sum, there are real similarities between the perspectives of the two men, both are very focused on the development of people and expounding the qualities of the product, but clear differences are apparent. For Hughes, the people development was for those inside NGK and he expounded the quality to OEM manufacturers, whereas for Stan the people development was for those outside NGK and he expounded the quality to retailers and later wholesalers. The two approached the very same matters, people and quality, in almost the exact opposite way!

An illustration of this fundamental difference in approach may be seen from a discussion at the NGK office in London, during which Stan was told that an employed sales representative had just had one account go bankrupt owing NGK £7,000. Stan voiced his surprise and explained it was possible with care to discern when customers were likely to go bankrupt and take steps to prevent the loss of money and product, to the benefit of both NGK and the customer. Hughes' response was that this simply demonstrated Stan was not taking enough risk in growing sales. We might ponder the total number of bad accounts! In all his 25 years selling NGK, Stan only had something in the order of £5000 of bad debt. Of that, £2000 came from a single order telephoned in to the office in London by a company in Frome that Stan would not deal with because, having done his research, he knew of its poor reputation in the area. The office opened the account, having done a credit check, unilaterally and unbeknown to Stan, simply on the strength of the number of plugs being ordered. For Stan, there is always more to opening accounts than pure finance. The character of the people involved needs to be considered; financial status reports can appear healthy but mask underlying problems. Discernment in the selection and support of customers remains, for Stan, the signature test of a sales engineer's professionalism.

An example of Stan's focus on customer above all things can be shown through his visit to a wholesaler in the Isle of Wight, whose shop layout was such that Stan discovered NGK were hardly visible. This was not because the product was not displayed or because there was not enough presence, but rather because the entire layout of the shop was disordered and poorly arranged, so that in effect *nothing* was visible. Stan spent three hours helping his wholesaler to re-arrange the shop, giving every product display more coherence and generally arriving at a better shop layout. So preoccupied was he in this that he forgot that his ten-year-old son, who had come out for a work day during his summer holidays, was sat in the car outside – and had grown thoroughly bored of listening to the same 'Glen Campbell Live' tape over and over!

The effect, however, was threefold. First, it cemented the relationship between Stan and his wholesaler on a personal level. Second, it demonstrated Stan's commitment to the success of his wholesaler's business. Third, it ensured NGK was properly displayed and visible. The wholesaler, as a thank you for the work done, allowed NGK to take the best spot but, importantly, this was not at Stan's request; it was the wholesaler's decision. There was nothing pre-planned or ulterior in Stan's decision to spend the morning helping to re-arrange the shop, simply that the effect was the building of real trust founded in what was clearly a genuine concern for the wholesaler's business success. When he returned six weeks later, Stan found the shop unaltered with NGK still in pride of place, and he was allowed to do the stock-take himself. This was a repeat of the customer focus that led him to help milk a farmer's cows when at Renold, for which he was castigated by head office. The outcome at the level of the customer was the same in both cases, a personal relationship, gratefulness and respect.

IV. Noboru Torii

Whereas the relationship between Stan Dibben and Jim Hughes, such as it was, was merely contractual, the one that preceded it with Noboru Torii, NGK (UK) Ltd's first Managing Director, grew to become a close and enduring friendship that transcended work. For example, when Mr Torii returned home his son Kan remained for a short time at boarding school and he spent a Christmas with the Dibben family. The first trip overseas Stan's son did on his own, aged 12, was a fortnight spent with the Torii family in Japan. It is therefore worthwhile now exploring Noboru Torii's family and business background with a view to examining his approach to NGK (UK) Ltd in the context of both his earlier and later work for the parent NGK Spark Plug Co. Ltd company. This is so as to explore both the reasons for this difference in personal relationship, and also the approach Mr Torii adopted to leading and developing NGK (UK) Ltd. This is in itself noteworthy, since it was at the time of the pivotal transition from NGK (GB) owned by Lester Simms to NGK (UK), NGK Spark Plug Co., Ltd's only wholly owned sales distributor. As such, it represented a very considerable foreign direct investment commitment for the parent company in Japan; Mr Torii's approach would not only determine the success or otherwise of the UK business, but would serve to determine the guiding principles for any future European FDI strategy.

Noboru Torii graduated from Nagoya University in 1958. His mother, Kiyo, was from the village of Togo on the outskirts of Nagoya and was born to a famous wealthy landlord and local governor dynasty. Her grandfather, Nizaemon Kato VIII resisted the confiscation of the village common and was imprisoned in Nagoya by the new regime of the Meiji Emperor (i.e c.1868–1869; the Meiji Restoration of Emperor rule in Japan occurred with the fall of Edo, the seat of the samurai Tokugagwa Shogunate in 1868). However, such was the esteem in which he was held by the local population that the villagers took good care of him, visiting him in jail three times a day with lunch boxes. He was freed after half a year as a result of a concerted campaign to have him released, and the common too was released untouched by the government and allocated among the villagers. As a result, there were no tenant farmers in the village; they were all farm owners. The dynastic importance of the family in Japanese life was such that, in 1927, a member of the Japanese royal family stayed at Noboru Torii's grandparents' house when his mother was 19 years old; she 'was always boastful of having rubbed shoulders with him' (pers. comm. Noboru Torii to Mark Dibben, Apr. 2018).

Noboru Torii's father, Seiichi, was (like Stan Dibben) left fatherless at the age of three. Seiichi's father, Noboru's grandfather Seitaro, was killed by a stray bullet in the Russo-Japanese war in Liaoning, China in 1904. He had been the proprietor of a sake (liquor) store in Lower Chaya-machi in Nagoya, but the store was closed when he died. Seiichi was brought up by his mother, Yone in her native town, Narumi, on the outskirts of Nagoya city and entered a pharmaceutical college (now Nagoya City University) in 1931 (pers. comm.

Noboru Torii to Mark Dibben, Apr. 2018).

After graduating from the college, he operated a pharmacy in Kyoto, but he was brought back to Narumi half forcibly to get married to a lady, Kiyo Kato, by his mother's arrangement. He at first opened a pharmacy in Narumi again, under the store name 'Kagetsu-do' (Flower & Moon Store in English), but soon started to work for the local government as a clerk, leaving the storekeeping to his mother, who changed the store to sell cosmetics and haberdashery. He enjoyed performing local Kabuki as a hobby with his associates in Narumi and was used to seeing authentic Kabuki all through his life. He worked for the local government until the town was merged into Nagoya city. A day after the celebration of the merger, he was hospitalized and passed away within half a year in 1957. At his funeral, Mayor Mr Saburo Nomura, a famous archaeologist, made a farewell speech to praise him as a living dictionary of the town.

One of my father's uncles, Mr Kakugoro Aoyama, and his family lived in Liaoning as a wealthy merchant, because the territory had been captured from Russia after the Russo–Japanese War. But the Russian army invaded the region and reoccupied it at the end of the World War II. 600,000 adult Japanese males were captured as prisoners of war and 10% of them died in 5 to 10 years of slavery in Siberia or Russian occupied area. Mr Aoyama's family were, however, exceptionally lucky for they escaped from the capture and returned safely to Japan. My father had met his family in Liaoning, when he went there accompanying a government officer to be assigned there.

I was extremely fascinated by Mr Aoyama's success before the war and wanted to join the international trading company. But, I eventually found a job in NGK Spark Plug Company, one of the progressive groups of the Morimura zaibatsu [large Japanese business conglomerate] for which four relatives of mine worked and two of them, Seiji Tsuda and Tadashi Kato, became vice president. Two others, Kaoru Kato and Nobuya

Kato became senior managing director before I was assigned as senior managing director at NGK Spark Plug Co., Ltd [NGK] which was the newest member of the group established in 1936. Five relatives including me were listed in the Japanese contemporary social register [the Japanese equivalent of the 'Who's Who' directory]. Four members of the group are now centenerians.

When I joined NGK I was at first assigned to the research and engineering department for a year and then moved to the accounting department for two years and finally to the overseas department. I was engaged in overseas correspondence in English, German, Spanish, and French as well, for no one other than me could do it at that time. I typically worked until 10 or 11 o'clock at night together with a lady typist particularly in the latter half of the month, during when most of the shipment of goods were made for the convenience of ocean vessels available in the port of Nagoya, Japan. Around the time I got married, it became customary for me to make overseas travel once a year for a month to Asia, Africa, the Middle East, North or South America. I happened to encounter riots of young soldiers who entered my room to search for president Anastasio Somoza Debayle in Managua of Nicaragua. The Hotel Intercontinental, where I stayed, collapsed a week after I left. Howard Hughes, a movie producer and founder of Hughes Aircraft, was staying there as his temporary house at that time. When I was in Uganda, I noticed a threatening atmosphere in town, and soon after I left there, Idi Amin carried out a coup d'etat while the country's President Milton Obote was abroad in England for a conference of the British Commonwealth. When I stayed in Teheran, Iran, I noticed many citizens and even police women looking fearful of riots and a few years later, Shah Pahlavi sought refuge in the U.S.A. (pers. comm. Noboru Torii to Mark Dibben, Apr. 2018)

From almost the beginning of his career with NGK, therefore, Torii had a focus on international business development through a specific focus on the technical aspects of the company's spark plugs. Torii's international trips for

NGK in Australia were the source of some tension but also led to him meeting his wife (pers. comm. Noboru Torii to Mark Dibben, May 2018):

> In World War II, the Japanese army bombed Darwin and attacked Sydney Harbor from underwater, and the relationship between Japan and Australia was terrible for a long time after the war. There was also a case when a young Japanese man who was hitchhiking was murdered for raising the flag of the Hinomaru [i.e. the Nisshōki, the national flag of Japan]. When I went to Australia a few years later, I was deeply moved by the unexpected hospitality there. While I was visiting the University of Sydney, a student threw a bible at the table spitting 'That's why the Japanese started the war', when one of the [panellists] answered that he didn't have a religion. But other than that, the Australians were generally modest and very kind. This prompted me to create the Japan–Australia Friendship Association [https://jafa.asn.au/], and that is where I met my wife Machiko, who took on the accounting responsibilities there.

For any student of Japan, Machiko Torii's family history is just as fascinating as that of her husband and is similarly rooted in trade. Her father was a landlord and antique dealer, and her mother is the descendant of the head of a village in Gifu Prefecture. Just as Noboru's family has dynastic connections, being descended from the Seiwa emperor who ruled Japan from 850–878, and from samurai at the end of the Edo period (i.e. c.1868; the cherished family *Katana* swords dating from this time were confiscated in 1943 by the government, for their metal to be used in munitions), so too does Machiko's. In 1183, they were given the surname Ogiso in recognition of their service to the imperial family. At this time, the general public did not have surnames; only those with nobility acknowledged by the emperor were allowed to have them.

As a further interesting aside, the Morimura zaibatsu, of which NGK was a part, has its origins in the Morimura family who established a company 'in Tokyo and another in New York as early as in 1877 and 1878 respectively. They were successful traders [of luxury leather and other goods] like the American 'Coach', 'Hartmann' and the European 'Cartier', 'Hermes' and 'Dunhill' brands. Torii explained the origins and research and development focus of NGK in a speech given on 11 January 1995, when he was NGK's Senior Managing Director, to welcome the U.S. Senator, the Honourable Mr J.D. Rockefeller IV and his Project Harvest Trade Mission to the company (Torii, 1995):

> Two brothers of the 6th generation of the Morimura's changed their minds [about foreign luxury goods] and started selling things Japanese, most original [jewellery that took advantage of the] gold which was abundantly produced those days in Japan, [and exported] to the U.S.A. in exchange for silver. NGK's 'grandmother' company, Noritake Chinaware, was incorporated in 1904 to manufacture porcelain dishes to export to the U.S.A. This was the same year as Rolls Royce was established. Our 'mother' company, NGK [the acronym literally translates into English as JIC; Japanese Insulator Company] was set up in 1917.
>
> Our own company [NGK Spark Plugs] was formed in 1936 and now is specializing in highly advanced technical ceramics. Previously ceramics were used for their static properties such as thermal or electrical resistance. We are now developing their dynamic properties. As you may be surprised to know, the ceramics produced here are breathing. An amount of oxygen inhaled through these ceramics can be detected electronically and are used as oxygen sensors. We also have ceramics which perspire passively so to speak, and are used as humidity sensors. Some ceramics can transform sounds or mechanical shocks into electricity and are used [in] cellular phones.

In 1972, Torii compiled the first English language set of cassette tape and colour slides and used these to conduct technical seminars in Sydney, Melbourne, Adelaide and Canberra to illustrate and discuss the wide heat range performance of the copper-cored spark plugs with which NGK has become synonymous. Such was the success of these talks to the motor parts wholesale and retail industry, that 'it awoke a veritable sensation among them' (pers. comm. Noboru Torii to Mark Dibben, Apr. 2018).

Returning from Australia, he then made a more comprehensive technical film with a leading movie production company, TOEI, again the first time this had been done in English. The challenge was to ensure that, even though a native English speaker was hired from the NHK broadcasting company (the Japanese equivalent of the BBC] to narrate the film, TOEI asked that Torii supervise the narration to ensure it matched the corresponding pictures perfectly. The film was a great success and 'was shown to foreign visitors to NGK for a long time' (pers. comm. Noboru Torii to Mark Dibben, Apr. 2018). At this time, Torii and others at NGK developed the famous 'Spark Boy' cartoon character, a figure dressed in dungaree overalls with a hat shaped like the body of a spark plug. The hexagon formed the brim and the ceramic body of the plug and the terminal cap made it the spark plug equivalent of a top hat. With this cartoon, the way in which heat range affected the performance of the plug was cleverly illustrated, 'Spark Boy' being shown as having a fever if the plug chosen was too hot, or freezing if the plug chosen was too cold. A thousand copies of the cartoons were turned into display mobiles, painted on cardboard in a folding paper frame, to be distributed among gasoline stations for the purpose of technical education of customers throughout Japan. Spark Boy was used by the company for many years as the main technical information 'medium' to help illustrate the company's technical superiority in a light-hearted but illuminating way. In 1976 Torii left the overseas department to become the inaugural chairman of NGK Spark Plugs (UK) Ltd, becoming President in 1980.

He explains his approach to the UK marketplace and the question of oligopolies at that time, and on his return to Japan, as follows (pers. comm. Noboru Torii to Mark Dibben, May 2018):

> You're not free to do *anything* [you like; emphasis added] in a free economy. The developed countries with liberal economies, the US included, have learned that unrestricted liberalism is liable to monopoly and vice. The Japanese merchants [in ancient times] were too consumed in calculation and were indifferent to fairness, which is equivalent to justice in [Japanese culture].
>
> When I went to the UK, Japan was underrating the competitiveness of the UK, because of the 'British disease'. Certainly, at the time, many of the British had lost motivation for work. I felt [it would be] bad to introduce excessive competition, so I sold our products for luxury cars like Lotus, Rolls Royce and Aston Martin, but not for popular cars such as British Leyland or British Ford. I went to a technical briefing at a Jaguar factory, but only supplied spark plugs for racing. I

did cooperate in the improvement of Jaguar's engines, after I returned home. This was because spark plugs can also be used for the [R&D] measurement of heat resistance, and contribute to structural analysis.

The British automobile and automotive parts industries were in danger of decline. I was afraid that it would be a vandalism of the British industry, if we set up factories like Sony and Matsushita did. [...]

What can immediately be gleaned from all the foregoing is that Torii's focus as a human being is evidently on others. For example, he was clearly concerned that a rapid expansion of exports would become a real political problem. Further, during Torii's tenure at NGK (UK) no one left the company for anything other than private family reasons (pers. comm. Noboru Torii to Mark Dibben, Dec. 2017); his was a very harmonious period in the company's development. In complete contrast to Hughes, Torii was happy to have agents selling and, as we have already noted, he even paid Stan a retainer to keep him on that basis and give him a modicum of security while he continued to build the product in his own territory. In stark contrast to Hughes again, Torii was very reluctant to become involved with the major mass market car manufacturers and was clearly arguing very early on for a more nuanced approach to product export from Japan. Like Stan, Torii was not a fan of rapid growth through large price discounted orders from major wholesalers with multiple branches; the product needed to be built progressively rather than quickly (pers. comm. Noboru Torii, Dec. 2017). It is interesting to note, then, that under Torii's leadership the sales of the company grew exponentially (NGK, 2017) as its reputation for technical excellence and also price stability became ever more strongly established. This was because there was a thoroughgoing and positive impression of reliability inherent in the company's products and the way it went about meeting demand for them.

Noboru Torii and Stan Dibben evidently shared a very similar view with regard to the dangers of expanding too quickly, and that the way to develop the sales of the company's products was to focus on 'technical education as marketing'. Torii had of course developed this technical approach originally with Spark Boy, while Stan relied on his electrical and racing engine performance knowledge to engage in technical discussions in the field, using the Spark Boy campaign as a jovial but important element of it. In recognition of their shared philosophy of enabling customers to make informed decisions about spark plug selection, and cognisant of his electrical knowledge, Torii appointed Dibben as a Technical Adviser. This gave him formal titular support over and above the purely verbal agency agreement they had made together when NGK (UK) had been established following the closure of Lester Simms' NGK (GB). It is worth noting that almost immediately Jim Hughes took over at NGK (UK) on Torii's departure, the Technical Adviser title was revoked. The company adopted the mantra that individuals should be told to fit only what was in the catalogue with no discretion or exceptions and with technical advice only to be offered from head office. The technical selling inherent in Stan's 'Teach to Sell' approach was no longer deemed apposite; it was, perhaps, seen only as an insurance risk in the event of a mis-application.

Prior to Torii's return to Japan in 1981, there was a 7th anniversary celebration held at the Churchill Hotel in London, with the

> announcement of a sales campaign for the promotion of the copper-cored NGK spark plugs. Representatives of Rolls Royce, Aston Martin, Lotus Cars, British Ford and automotive parts distributors were invited. A Honda Cub motorcycle painted in copper was demonstrated as the prize for the competition [...]. Some donations were presented to Hendon Hospital, a guide dog association, and so on. (ibid.)

In many ways, this event was a signal that NGK (UK) was now firmly established in the market and Torii left NGK (UK) to be assigned as Advertising and Public Relations Manager at NGK in Japan. In 1984 he was made Manager of the company's Tokyo Office and then Chief Financial Officer in 1986. His approach to selling NGK in Japan at first appears to have been different to the position he adopted in the UK, but he was persuaded otherwise and this was evidently in line with his core beliefs (pers. comm. Noboru Torii to Mark Dibben, May 2018):

> when I served as the branch manager of the Tokyo branch office, I was unsatisfied that NGK spark plugs were not used as original equipment on the Prince Skyline, Nissan's sports car for the general consumer. I made thorough proposals to have dealers sell the plugs as spare parts. We made an aggressive move

when the Prince Skyline started using ceramic fins for their turbo rotors [since NGK was of course a ceramics company]. This time, [my] supervisor, Mr T. Niwa, told me not to sell spark plugs for the car. If we kicked out the competitors from the market, it would be suicidal as the market would become oligopolistic, competition intensified, and the coexisting and prosperous market would be lost. I didn't have any doubts about this, but [even so] a few years later, a competitor, Hitachi, withdrew from the business [i.e. stopped selling sparking plugs].

In the latter role as Chief Financial Officer of the worldwide company, the 'total reliability' mantra Torii had established at NGK (UK) became part of his broader approach to the challenge of business growth. Both when in the UK and when CFO, he simply would not countenance the prospect of taking over companies with inferior products. This was because of the difficulties of re-tool large numbers of old production facilities, and the costs associated with such takeovers would therefore eat into capital reserves even beyond accrued profit. That is, his policy was not to engage in investments that were larger than the combined average annual profit of the past three years and the projected three years to come. He would allow additional strategic investment within twenty percent of the annual standardized investment, and this criterion was applied as a general standard to all investments made by NGK when he became CFO (pers. comm. Noboru Torii to Mark Dibben, Feb. 2018).

This was not to say that investment *per se* was discouraged by Torii; the opposite was the case. Every divisional general manager was invited to discuss their proposals with him as CFO for investments by their division on a monthly basis. The only exception to the investment rule of no loans was where research and development was concerned, and then medium-term government loans were countenanced. In sum, Torii's approach to investment was incremental, prudent and highly effective; it prevented unstable rapid growth and allowed the company (both the UK subsidiary and later the main company in Japan) to focus its attentions where there would be medium-term R&D returns, and other affordable investments (ibid.). In respect of FDI the decision to open a plug factory in France, for example, was made for two clear reasons. First, to ease pressure on the factories located in Japan, and second to create some balance in Europe with regards to Japanese motor industry investment, rather than having it all in the UK; it was always the intension to ensure a local person head the operation up, which is what happened (pers. comm. Noboru Torii to Mark Dibben, Aug. 1991). In short, Torii's approach to investment not only shaped the development of NGK but, by default, it in fact largely shaped the development of the wider spark plug industry.

In 1992, Torii was appointed Managing Director and then later President of NGK Spark Plugs (USA) Inc. This was the largest of the wholly owned subsidiary companies and he again was careful in the way he dealt with the question of competition, as follows (pers. comm. Noboru Torii to Mark Dibben, May 2018):

When I was president of the US subsidiary, a plug, called Twin Spark, that imitated the structure of our plugs was being sold, and a sales manager argued that they should file a complaint. So, I went to their head office and met with the president. He was really keen on explaining spark performance. He gave me the impression that this product would not inflict damage on us, but would be good publicity for us to prosper together. We didn't request a termination of the product. The theory behind the Twin Spark was to split the end of the central electrode and let off sparks from both ends. The sparks don't happen simultaneously, but only separately, as each end is corroded differently. It was one of the three ideas I proposed in 1958 when I joined the company [i.e. NGK]. It was not in agreement with the intent of the [NGK] designer of later years, Mr K. Dejima, but we advertised my hypothesis of the improvement in fuel efficiency because of the reliability in ignition and the speed of spark propagation. This hypothesis was proven by Professor Michikata Kono of Tokyo University, using a transparent engine made with fused quartz, while I was still in the UK.

[... This was 'V-Groove' technology but, more generally,] the secret of [NGK's] success [...] lies in the combination of a copper center electrode and a high alumina insulator both of high heat dissipation. Nevertheless, the optimal temperature is kept by craftsmanship based on a differential equation of heat dissipation per micro second, formulated by Mr. Y. Watanabe at NGK. Based on this doctrine, Dr K. Nishio of NGK carried on improvements of spark plugs. In fact, he received his doctorate at Tokyo University, one of the best if not the best Japanese universities, for this work; it is a first in our spark plug industry.

Again it can be seen (apparently in contrast to Jim Hughes) that Torii's starting point for sales and wider development was always technical knowledge and advancement, and the benefits this can bring in the marketplace. Building from the UK experience in racing, he involved the US subsidiary formally in sponsorship of the Indy Car Racing series in 1994, through an association with Rahal-Hogan Racing and Honda Motor Co. He explained the reason for the decision as follows (Torii, 1994):

> At NGK, we do not consider our racing activities as propaganda. All we want to do is to fully devote ourselves to help our drivers perform at their very best, to the expectation, enjoyment and excitement of the spectators. [Our focus is on] loyalty and honesty. I hope that we can all work well together.

This statement, made at the NGK-Indy Car Press Meeting on 21 January 1994 in Newport Beach California, powerfully sums up Noboru Torii's approach to business. It seems to stand in stark contrast (again) with Jim Hughes' decision to have NGK (UK) sponsor horse racing (the NGK Spark Plugs Handicap at Newmarket). On the other hand, and as should by now be clear, Torii's approach bears close comparison with Stan Dibben's. Torii's decision to sponsor IndyCar in 1994 was around the time of the earthquakes and wildfires in California. In a signal of his all-encompassing focus on people, he announced too that NGK would 'support the American Red Cross Earthquake Relief as well as three other charitable organizations'; he had in fact made an emergency donation to the Red Cross immediately following the earthquake (ibid.). The three other charities were the Mission Hospital, the Make-A-Wish Foundation and Guide Dogs of America. Here, too, Torii was going against the traditional UK business approach (ibid.):

> When I was working in London twelve years ago, I was told by our company's auditor not to make donations on my personal taste or hobbies but to make donations on the company's business interest. I am not sure if a similar advice applies in the

United States. The reasons why we have selected the recipients of our donations are simple.

That same year, at the invitation of Senator John D. Rockeffeller IV and the State of West Virginia, Torii also helped establish a separate company to manufacture ceramic sensors in West Virginia, USA which was later incorporated into NGK Spark Plugs (USA) Inc. His central role in that project was recognised after he had returned from the USA to become Senior Managing Director in 1995, when Rockefeller and a trade mission from the state of West Virginia visited NGK's Komaki factory in Japan, where Torii was then located.

Noboru Torii's business philosophy has, he says (pers. comm. Noboru Torii to Mark Dibben, May 2018), been influenced by the family's close association with Buddhist temples; two family relations 'each created a new temple in True Pure Land Buddhism (Shinshu). This is quite rare in modern times.' As such, his philosophy has an emphasis on doing 'good deeds for others,' and is also rooted in 'the spiritual structure of the Japanese samurai (Samurai or Japanese knight)' as rendered by Inazo Nitobe (1969). According to Torii (pers. comm. Noboru Torii to Mark Dibben, May 2018),

> In 1876, the founder of Hinode Shoukai [the original business that went on to become the Morimura conglomerate, of which NGK is a part] once scolded a clerk who sold a pair of umbrella stands [at its New York shop] for $5, even though the price was $2.50, and ran after the customer to give him the refund. [… While] Bushido (Japanese chivalry) is a moral cultivated under the feudal system, [I] pay attention to Royalty and Mercy, Honesty and Sincerity, Shame and Honour.

He retired from NGK in 1997 but Torii's association with NGK was extended in 2003 when he became Chairman of Tokuyukai, the retirees club of NGK Spark Plug Co., Ltd; he held that post until 2007 and then became an honorary member. In addition, from 2003 to 2008, Torii was a Councillor of Soyukai, the Ex-Directors Association of the Morimura zaibatsu. At present, he is a Life Member and Fellow of the Directors Association in London and a Life Member of Gakushikai, the alumni association of the seven state universities of Japan. His wife Machiko, meanwhile, is licensed to teach *Chadō* (the Japanese tea ceremony) and *Ikebana* (Japanese flower arrangement), and has sung Beethoven's Symphony No.9 'Choral' at Carnegie Hall in New York in 2002 and at the Musikverein in Vienna in 2003. Importantly, then, deep connectedness to traditional culture and the Arts is a fundamental aspect of the Torii way of life.

V. Conclusion – 'Small is Beautiful'

We hope to have shown in the foregoing that Noboru Torii's approach to investment, growth and, crucially the development of people, stands up well to interrogation through E.F. Schumacher's economic principles of 'small is beautiful', 'economics as if people mattered' and a 'resistance of the urge to giantism.' Had NGK (UK) and indeed subsequently NGK Spark Plug Co. Ltd each attempted to grow rapidly through acquisition, the outcome would have been rather less certain than it was. Torii's model for sustained growth, and his clear appreciation that financial over-stretch would have serious problems not just for NGK but the wider industry and indeed even the countries concerned such as the UK in relation to Continental Europe in the context of the European Economic Area as it then was, is clearly explained by Schumacher's arguments regarding genuine sustainability of industrial production ([1973] 2011: 22),

> The upper limit for the average amount of capital investment per workplace is probably given by the annual earnings of an able and ambitious industrial worker … If the cost is significantly higher, the society in question is likely to run into serious troubles, such as an undue concentration of wealth and power among the privileged few; an increasing problem of dropouts who cannot be integrated into society and constitute an ever-growing threat; structural unemployment; mal-distribution of the population due to excessive urbanisation; and general frustration and alienation, with soaring crime rates and so forth.

In short, Torii's reliable, affordable, incremental approach stands in stark contrast to what is (as Schumacher predicted) commonly seen today. As a direct result, he ensured NGK's future dominance of the spark plug and oxygen sensor industries.

We hope to have shown too that there are, however ironic the judgement may seem, notable similarities between Jim Hughes' approach to growing his (i.e. NGK's) business and Stan Dibben's approach to growing his (i.e his wholesalers' and retailers') business. More importantly, however, the close study of Mr Torii's business career and family background in small business, as well as the presence in it of paternal loss and the consequent hard work involved in making a living, goes a long way to explaining why it is that Noboru Torii and Stan Dibben gelled so very well. Torii was always remarkably impressed by the realisation of the amount of real trusting teamwork involved in racing a sidecar outfit, for it resonated strongly with his own values and person-centred focus; 'you need to know your sidecar team mate better than your own wife, for even more than with your own wife you place your life in his hands!' (pers. comm. Noboru Torii to Mark Dibben, June 1992).

Stan's loyalty to Mr Torii, and also Mr Arai who succeeded him at NGK before Jim Hughes took over, stems directly from the way he was treated by them. When he retired from his NGK agency on his 65th birthday, not only was he forced to retire but he never received compensation for loss of territory. Rather, the final ex gratia payment was based on the idea that he was a retiring employee, whereas of course he had made a substantial personal investment in the business as an agent. Stan has always felt his final treatment by NGK (UK) was poor and it is difficult to conclude otherwise. What is certain is that it directly informed the business decisions he would make in retirement with regards to Brisk Spark Plugs and the development of his idea for self-steering castors.

Finally, his 'Teach, to Sell' approach to the introduction of NGK into the UK market and its subsequent development in that market, was founded on a family-oriented customer focus that might be easily dismissed as irrelevant in today's corporate big-business internet-reliant world, especially in the light of the theories of today's established sales and marketing textbooks. Such easy dismissal would be to ignore the fundamental person-centredness of its success, not to mention the success itself. NGK (UK) is undoubtedly a very different business to the one Stan Dibben and Noboru Torii knew. Without doubt this is in no small part due to the remarkable contribution Jim Hughes made to growing the sales of what was, by the time he joined, a product that was established in the market. However, in short, without the foundations laid by the sound groundwork that Stan Dibben and others put in, without his (and in his own inimitable way, Noboru Torii's) absolute focus on (loyalty to, development of, and honesty with) customers for the sake of the development of their businesses, it is unlikely that the corporate approach taken by NGK (UK) following Torii's return to Japan could ever have succeeded in the way that it did. The irony is that it was Noboru Torii who appointed Jim Hughes, on the strength of his vast knowledge of the UK motor industry, but advised him not to grow the business too quickly (pers. comm. Noboru Torii to Mark Dibben, Dec. 2017); evidently, Hughes ignored the advice.

In noting this, however, we don't seek to deny Jim Hughes' achievements at NGK (UK) are anything short of remarkable in and of themselves. We have, however, sought to demonstrate that if Jim Hughes is rightly thought of as its 'Grandad', then there is little doubt whatsoever that Noboru Torii is the founder and 'Great Grandfather' of the company. Furthermore, the principles he developed and applied to the UK marketplace were the same ones he was to use in Japan as CFO and later in the United States. Taken together, Noboru Torii's achievements over a forty-year career with NGK are such that he remains one of the key architects of today's world-wide spark plug industry.

Stan Dibben's approach to selling can be traced right the way back to his experience of selling bread and groceries at Hardings village shop in Ropley as a teenager. It was there that he leant true customer focus, where quite simply the people on the outer reaches of the village who were without transport were almost totally dependent on Hardings for their survival; if they were not supplied with food their lives were at stake. In return, Stan learnt to be totally dependent on his customers, both direct and indirect. This customer-centred approach was honed through Stan's time at Perry, brought into sharp relief by the painful corporate experience of Renold, polished once more through his time as an agent of Serge Binn's and finally given full voice in the pioneering and development of NGK in his territories in the South-Southwest of England.

In a letter to Mark, written in Japanese when he was an undergraduate studying the language at Stirling University, Noboru Torii described Stan's contribution to NGK (UK) as 'worth his weight in gold' (pers. comm. Noboru Torii to Mark Dibben, Aug. 1991). The vast majority of the other agents and representatives in the early days stuck, by and large, to the simple OEM motorcycle replacement plug market. Had they done as Stan did and, instead, focused on the development through technical teaching of their customers' businesses across the entirety of the plug market, there is little doubt that NGK (GB) and even perhaps NGK (UK) during Torii's tenure would possibly have been yet more successful. We have taken the trouble to explore 'Teach, to Sell' and render it in some considerable depth here and in the previous chapter, therefore, because we believe it still has relevance. It is not possible to pioneer a product using sales techniques founded upon a presumption of established market presence but, we argue, it is possible to sell an established product using 'Teach, to Sell' principles.

By way of a conclusion, E.F. Schumacher spoke powerfully to the problem of individualistic behaviour in the marketplace. In business, he said ([1973] 2011: 30),

> 'to be relieved of all responsibility except to oneself', means of course an enormous simplification of business. We can recognise that it is practical and need not be surprised that it is highly popular among businessmen. What may cause surprise is that it is also considered virtuous to make the maximum use of this freedom from responsibility. If a buyer refused a good bargain because he suspected that the cheapness of the goods in question stemmed from exploitation or other despicable practices (except theft), he would be open to criticism of behaving 'uneconomically', which is nothing less than a fall from grace. Economists and others are wont to treat such eccentric behaviour with derision if not indignation ... In the market place, for practical reasons, innumerable qualitative distinctions which are of vital importance for man and society are suppressed; they are not allowed to surface. Thus the reign of quantity celebrates its greatest triumphs in 'The Market'.

In sum Stan's 'Teach, to Sell' principles may well be regarded by marketers as 'eccentric', but they speak directly to Schumacher's implicit argument here. Namely that qualitative distinctions are absolutely of vital importance in the marketplace, and can (indeed must) be emphasised. Stan's early pioneering of NGK in 'The Market' demonstrates, too, that if people and not numbers, if others and not oneself, are the focus of one's attention, then the people who are the customers that comprise the market will, in fact, respond in a humane way – with their firm loyalty. His is a supreme example of successful enterprise on the edge of industry, where (to the incredulity of the big business mindsets Stan encountered both at NGK (UK) post Torii, and at major wholesalers) something other than absolute profit, or even absolute market penetration, is *significantly* more important.

Machiko and Noboru Torii with their Son Kan at Narita airport, 1983

13

OF MARRIAGE, RETIREMENT, SHEEPSKINS AND SHOPPING TROLLEYS

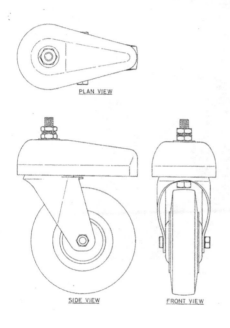

PLAN VIEW

SIDE VIEW   FRONT VIEW

A drawing by Stan Dibben's friend Derek Lewis, one of his former chain customers, of Stan's self-centring trolley castor. Jeremy Clarkson tested it, and declared they made a shopping trolley 'steer like a Ferrari'

1. Family Life

Marriage came in 1959 to Cyril Smith's daughter Kathleen, a beautiful girl with long auburn hair and dark brown eyes, who had in her own way inherited her father's gritty determination. We had been such good friends ever since I started racing sidecars. After her father's death, she found life very hard. She needed some activity aside from being a secretary to me – which was in itself an enormous help and without which I'm certain neither Mobyke nor NGK would have been as successful as they were. So Kathleen bred German Shepherd dogs for a few years, with some success. They are superb animals and, properly bred and properly trained, which is as much about training the owner as it is about training the dog, absolutely loyal and utterly reliable and dependable.

When our son Mark was a baby, one of our dogs, Rusty – so-called because of his deep reddish colouring – would sit for hours by the side of his cot. You could almost see pride in the dog's face, guarding his new charge. Indoors or out and about, no child was more safe than Mark was, on Rusty's watch. Kathleen was also a trained Cordon Bleu cook and I remember a very pleasant gastronomic week in France when she did the course, but she never wanted to go into the restaurant business. Many years later, though, she did have a little shop selling sheepskin coats and other clothing and country wares, and in many ways she made a very great success of it. It was meant to be something for us in our retirement but in the end she was undone in that enterprise by thieves. Everything she turned her hand to she was good at but our marriage ended after 7 years of separation, with divorce in 2002. It had been unrewarding in many ways to both parties who had less and less in common as the years went on.

The marriage wasn't a failure though. We had a son and it was fun and very rewarding bringing him up. Teaching him to swim, not on the bed like I was, but in the local sports centre. He was proficient at 5 years of age and very good at 9 when he got his mile medal. Snorkelling at about 7, day after day in Malta when on holiday, fascinated by the under-water vegetation and fishes, while floating above the seemingly bottomless warm blue ocean. Walks in the country eating blackberries picked fresh from the hedgerow while looking at birds and insects. Peeling back the bark of trees and turning over stones looking for all sorts of creepy crawlies. Pointing out the beauty of clouds: the black nimbus that brings the rain, the big fluffy cumulus and the lovely pink cirrus high in the summer sunset sky. At home, playing with his Scalectric racing cars laughing at the monumental crashes.

Playing with words was always a giggle. 'What do you want for breakfast? Those snip popple and crap-pip crapple and snop.' 'Oh! Dad – snap crackle and pop. Rice crispies!' Bedtime stories invented about Fred and his mate, the dustbin lorry drivers." Tell me about the day they picked up that smelly load. Phew, what a stink. He even wanted to be a dustbin lorry driver when he grew up. And spoonerised nursery rhymes – 'Hey diddle diddle the fat and the kiddle, the mow jumped over the coon. The little log daft to see such sport and the spish ran away with the doon', was always good for a giggle, at a time when the racial connotations of that particular 'c'- word were unknown to me. Not forgetting 'Old mother cupboard went the hupbourd to fetch her door boggy a pone, when she got bare the hupboard was care and so the door boggy had pone.' So many laughs: and then school.

Now that was a real problem. The village school was a shocker still catering for the local kids on the presumption that they would never want to leave the village, but just become far hands. The only way Mark was going to maintain any educational growth was to get him into a local prep boarding school, run by the Christian Brothers. He was reading at 5 years of age and the boarding school head, a very warm-hearted man who was kindness personified, was happy to take him. It took some persuasion, though, to get him accepted as a dayboy, the first ever at the school, but it would inevitably lead to full time boarding. The thought of that obviously upset Kathleen tremendously, and horrified me remembering my experience, but a compromise was reached, and he finished his 'O' levels as a weekly boarder – again to my knowledge the first at the senior school – home every weekend.

On his school holidays in his pre-teens, Mark would come out with me in the car on my workdays. He was regularly changing gear for me by the age ten. He could barely see over the top of the dashboard, but would listen to the engine and watch my feet, knowing exactly what was required and when. His favourite trip was to the Isle of Wight and I remember one trip all the way to Lymington, a two-hour drive across country to where we used to catch the ferry over to Yarmouth, without touching the gear lever once. Doubtless this sort of activity would be frowned on in today's motoring environment, but properly done, absolutely safe. His first trip overseas on his own was to Japan at the suggestion of NGK's Mr Torii, who had him at home in Japan for a few weeks. A wonderful experience for him, and typical of the generosity of all the Japanese people at NGK that it was my honour to receive.

One of my old customers, Peter Tolputt, had owned a SAAB and Mitsubishi dealership in Bath but sold up when he realised he was paying his employees more than he was paying himself – 'What's the point in that!' He got a Yachtmaster Instructor qualification and set up a sailing school, with his wife running a B&B in support. He suggested we come down to spend a day on the water. We turned up at the yacht haven, in Lymington as it happens, to be greeted by a gruff, burley, moustachioed man who soon had the little eight-year-old hoisting a mizzen sail. 'Go on lad,' he rumbled. 'And stop panting – put some lead in your pencil!' It had been a long time since I was last on board a boat with the expectation of being anything other than live cargo, but rope handling came back pretty quickly and I remembered something from the dinghy sailing I had done in the Navy. Soon we were making our way up the Solent to Portsmouth, short-tacking as we went. The usual 'Ready about – Lee oh!' was replaced by a strident young voice commanding 'Ready about – Tally ho!' from behind the wheel. Peter and I, dutifully pulling and winching sheets to shape the sails to the other side of the yacht, did our best to remain serious by trying not to look at each other, but finally collapsed into peals of laughter.

Peter had been in the Special Air Service briefly, but had given up after being ordered to parachute over jungle in the Far East – 'Done it once, and that was enough. Still don't like the idea of jumping into trees. Bloody dangerous.' He had a habit of tunefully humming a laugh in-between sentences, 'hmm-hmm-hmm.' Sat in the cockpit of his 36-foot Westerly Conway, with his feet braced against the lee-side seat, he would peer around the windscreen, slurping tea noisily and ducking the spray. Once he mistimed and was drenched by a face-full of icy water. Looking around at the young boy who was still at the helm, he winked and roared 'Argh, got the bloody lot!' He wiped his moustache, slurped more tea and belched for the effect 'Hmm-hmm-hmm. Burrrp – MY boat!! Hmm-hmm-hmm.' He looked back at Mark, giggling at the helm. 'You enjoying yourself? Good – fun isn't it!'

One of my favourite tricks however bizarre it may seem – is the extermination of wasps. It's a good conversation stopper and has often come in handy as Mark had once got stung very badly on the ear lobe at a grass track meeting (where we had been supporting another customer of mine, the grass track sidecar ace Pete Robson); he lived in great fear of them. Back in Lymington we were in deep conversation with some others who had come on board for a brew when the little insects, smelling jam, came buzzing down the companionway hatch into the saloon, sending people ducking and waving their arms. The way to kill a wasp is to wait until it has settled on a window pane and starts walking up it. Too busy trying to work out why it can't get through, it will fail to notice the looming shadow of a large thumb aimed at its head. They can't lift their tail to sting you. So long as you are quick and administer a decisive blow …

The discussion halted temporarily while I briefly concentrated on the immediate job at hand. 'What do you think about that, Stan?' 'I don't know, Peter. It might' – THUMP – 'be an idea. We could come down in the evening, head out first' – THUMP – 'thing in the morning and spend a couple of days.

Go all the way around the Island. Maybe get as' – THUMP – 'far as Poole.' The dead wasps were picked up by their wings and tossed over the side to the astonishment of all on board, and the considerable relief of our youngest crewmember. I have never to this day convinced him to try the trick!

Besides whatever influence I was on him as a young boy, Mark had a great and long-lasting relationship with his step-Grandfather. Cyril's wife Irene re-married in the very early seventies to Ron Barrett, a remarkable man with a rich sense of humour. Shortly after they had married, Ron suffered a massive heart attack, from which Irene and Kathleen nursed him back to full health over many months. The Accident and Emergency ward overlooked the Blue Cross animal sanctuary in Birmingham and he would often joke 'When I woke up, the first thing I saw was that cross and I thought 'Good – I made it.' Then I saw all the wires and thought 'Oh. Sod it!'' The episode brought the two families together and Ron adopted our little boy as his own grandson.

He was a very gentle man who stood well over six feet tall, with a soft Birmingham accent and a military moustache which, like Cyril, he had first grown to make himself appear older to the troops he commanded. Apart from having steely-blue eyes, he looked not unlike Sean Connery's General Urquhart from 'A Bridge Too Far' and was in the Corps of Military Police (CMP) during the war, having deserted from the mines. Strictly speaking you weren't meant to desert from the mines and he should have been sent back, but when he explained that he had been sent there as a sixteen-year-old, and had been made to work on a foot-tall seam all day every day, the Army recruiting Sergeant took pity on him and swiftly stamped all his papers, tut-tutting sympathetically as he did so. 'Once I was in the Army, I was in the Army. They can't get you when you're in the Army!' Ron was in India for the duration of his war service, and he told wonderful stories of his time there. His first job, at eighteen, was to guard Delhi railway station. He would step over the lepers, the beggars and the women in labour on the station platform. 'The stench – Gad above! The rats were tall enough to knock the lids off the dustbins. And they did!'

All MPs were taught Judo for self defense (Ganarpathi, 1982: 56–57) and Ron had been an unarmed combat instructor. As with most who, unlike me, had seen real conflict, was very reluctant to speak of the nasty side of things. When pushed on the matter of the enemy by his wide-eyed grandson, he would briefly admit that he had 'only killed one or two.' 'But,' he would emphasise quietly, 'I never shot anyone.' Then he would quickly shift the conversation to the time he was guarding a troop train across the continent and had pinned down a soldier while a medic removed a carbuncle from his backside – without anaesthetic 'Coz he didn't have any and we were to be on that train for a week.' Or to the time when a panther had wandered into the centre of their jungle camp one evening and leapt onto the top of an army truck. 'It sat there blinking, all night. And so did we,' he laughed. 'All night!' He seemed to derive some genuine comfort from the fact he had never pulled the trigger, as if that was a dirty way of killing someone.

When he had returned from the war Ron had married but his wife had run off with somebody else, leaving him with a son to bring up as a single father. This he did with great pride. He was a plumber by trade, but ended up working for Lucas Industries as a buyer. And a very good one – he was a customer of mine for a while and was fair, honest, and knew precisely what he was up to. In fact, Ron was one of the most intelligent men I have ever met, whose father I believe had been British chess champion. I often felt his enormous talent was wasted. But he was entirely satisfied living a quiet life and spent almost all of his spare time gardening, growing the most spectacular roses. He had an old-fashioned stand-up electric roller cylinder mower that he would use to manicure his lawn, often with his young grandson perched on the front of it.

A republican, one of his favourite quips was 'Ask yourself who you could live without, the bin man or one of them lot? The answer's obvious. And I mean: Obvious!' He was a staunch union man and 'old' Labour supporter, and our political views were poles apart. But it was he, not I, who made money on the stock market; he would finance his cars by shares trading. Ron died of a second heart attack in 2002, shortly after the wife who he had long-cared for had finally succumbed to the horrors of Alzheimer's. His grandson adored him, and learned a tremendous amount from him. I'm pretty sure the feeling was mutual, and I remain indebted to Ron's great warmth and kindness.

His grandson was an easy boy to raise. He once asked me, as a 13-year-old, 'Dad, what would I do if you and Mum were killed in a car crash?' I still don't know where he got that idea from. Probably some silly television show! 'What, tomorrow? Well, I am sure your Nan and Grandad would look after you. You'd be alright, you'd cope. I wouldn't have done my job properly if you couldn't. Just remember, never say 'no' to anything. Otherwise that door will be shut forever. Say 'yes, but let me think about it.' You can always say no after you've thought about it.' 'But what if I made the wrong decision?' he replied. 'Oh, don't be worried about making mistakes. I've made loads! Just try your best to correct them, or at least learn from them. However old you are, always try and learn from them. As long as you can go to bed every night and say honestly that you did your best under the circumstances that's fine. That doesn't mean hide behind the circumstances, use them as an excuse. It means be realistic about what the circumstances allow you to achieve, and be honest with yourself about that.'

Came 'A' level time and it was felt that, again from my own experience, the single sex education thus far was no longer the way to go, and he went into a state Sixth Form College. A good, good move. He had a two-stroke Honda single to go to school on – often far too quickly! – and he was home every night. A very lucky lad I admit. He was spoilt rotten, like many only children, but he got over it. I meanwhile could never properly get to grips with that bike or the four stroke Kawasaki twin that followed it. Quite apart from the fact that the gear change was completely the wrong way around – left foot and up for up, down for down – they both produced their power at what seemed to me to be mind-boggling revolutions. The Kawasaki for example produced the same power as my old 350 cc Manx Norton, but at 14,000 rpm. Double the revs! This, coupled with a tiny stroke, seemed to me almost diaphragm territory. Surely no pistons on a production machine could stay reliably attached to their conrods at those dizzy numbers? How little I knew! Mark would grow impatient with me. Pointing to the rev counter, he said 'Look, Dad, just divide by two if that makes you feel better.' Well, sort of. When I complained it needed a slower acting throttle he was amazed, saying he was wondering how to get a faster acting one. Either I was getting too old or he should have gone racing.

In fact, I fell off the Kawasaki shortly after we took delivery of it – the only time I ever 'dropped' a road going motorcycle. Apparently, the bike came from Japan in a crate and the dealer had to assemble the front end. In doing so, the plastic front mudguard had not been secured properly and it dropped onto the front wheel. The plastic melted onto the tyre due to the friction and when it reached the cold air at the leading edge of the mudguard it then rapidly re-set, sticking the tyre to the mudguard as surely as if it had all been super-glued. It felt at the time as if the bike had run out of fuel and so I grappled with the reserve tap, but to no effect. The front wheel eventually locked solid and the bike slid along, upright, with me trying to keep it straight for about 60 yards. Finally it ground to a halt and, trying to steady it on tip-toe (I am, remember a shorty!), I could hold on to it no longer. Puzzled, and nursing a very sore leg, I limped home. When we got the bike back, I managed to work out what had happened.

We went to see the dealer, another old customer of mine, and told him the story. He was visibly shaken – I felt sorry for him. He sacked the fitter and repaired the damage free of charge. Apparently his insurer told him that one or two people, who wouldn't be named, had been killed at the TT as a result of very similar circumstances and I'm not surprised. What I couldn't understand was why nobody fitted a metal plate on the inside of the mudguard, and wrote to a number of manufacturers asking this very question. They all wrote back saying the same thing: If mudguards are fitted correctly it cannot happen. But it seemed to me that was hardly the point.

After eight years at university in Scotland and three degrees, the boy was a young man and he began a career in academia. It seemed unjust to me that youths at 18 or 19, have achieved nothing at school, can be paid by the state to go back to school to learn what they failed to do – for whatever reason – the first time around and so be made employable. Meanwhile young, self-disciplined, diligent young men and women with the highest academic qualifications, find it difficult getting a credit card and a mortgage because of their indebtedness resulting from student loans, incurred out of necessity to survive during their university years. Speaking from his experience, graduates don't always earn higher salaries once they have graduated.

Mark lived for seventeen odd years in the Antipodes and is married to Rebecca, a delightful girl from Liverpool. She too has a PhD, in anti-terrorism law, and now works as a disaster relief manager having spent a number of years as a Police Officer, patrolling the streets in the North of England. A 'community beat manager' who once briefed the then-Prime Minister Tony Blair in Downing Street, she was responsible for some of the large housing estates in one of the towns in that not-very-well-off part of the country. The stories she recounted made the blood run cold; it's like a never-ending war! Without doubt, Rebecca had seen more of the harsh, relentless realities of life in her first three decades than I have in my nine, and it certainly puts things in perspective. However, life does occasionally indeed deal its blows, as we all know; Mark now has Multiple Sclerosis, which has meant that he has recently had to return home to the UK. Apparently, people with MS do not tolerate heat well and he was increasingly finding it a struggle over there. Thankfully, he was able to retire early on a medical pension so I am grateful for small mercies. His in-laws are, just as Ron was, avid gardeners with tremendous sense of humour and great dignity. And a manicured lawn! He's been very lucky but you often make your own luck, and they have been very supportive too in their own way. He's a fine chap who made a career out of his passion, which is a tremendous thing to be able to do. I'm proud of him.

2. Retirement Boredom Alleviation!

When I retired, I felt for months as if I was on an extended holiday and then I just grew bored. Bored. There's only so much swimming and dog walking you can do. One day, my friend had her car damaged by a recalcitrant shopping trolley and another had serious bruising to her legs. I thought 'It's crazy we can't make a controllable shopping trolley.' So, I went out and tried one. Ridiculous! It had no directional stability at all, especially when loaded and with infants having a ride, a recipe for disaster. 'What about airport trolleys?' The same, worse if anything. Obviously, I'd used trolleys for years and hadn't given it a thought, but it's amazing what you see when only you look for it. The need to glide in all directions was the problem. But then, those industrial ones I looked at were fine, but they wouldn't go sideways. What was needed was two fully rotating casters that lock when going forwards and automatically unlock for sideways movement. Easy!

My simple original home-made effort, although impractical from a mass production point of view, proved the principle precisely. I applied for a patent. Then I had another one of those life changing phone calls. It was from the ex Managing Director of a one-time major UK spark plug manufacturer, whose product we had used when racing sidecars to the World Championship, and that I had always used on my solo racing motorcycles.

'Oh! Stan, now that you have retired from NGK Spark Plugs what are you doing?'

'Playing with my trolley'

'Would you be interested in marketing an East European made spark plug my old colleague and me are involved with?'

'No, no thank you'

'What's this trolley you are talking about?' After a rough explanation of what I had in mind, 'Oh! My colleague would be interested in that. Can I come up and have a look?'

He did, and after nearly ending up in my fishpond, he was impressed and said, 'You've cracked it, I'll get on to my colleague who lives in Majorca'

We met in the Overseas Visitor's Club in London a week or so later, signed confidentiality agreements, agreed that I would help with the spark plugs and that they would finance, develop and market the caster. With me to get a percentage of profits before tax, and a percentage on the sales invoices of the spark plugs. I wasn't too happy about the involvement with the spark plugs. NGK had been very good to me, but the caster potential was enormous, and in view of what had happened to my planned retirement finances, I needed an income. The idea was developed. My patent application had failed, I was informed, because a similar idea had been patented in the USA in 1943, some 48 years earlier. However, the promise was given that our caster agreement was not in jeopardy. Just under a year later, having set up a team of agents to sell the spark plugs, things were beginning to move when I was informed that plug sales growth was too slow and the plug business would be wound up! It had taken 5 years to get NGK off the ground.

All interest was now centred on the casters. New patents had been taken out in the names of the directors of Variguide Ltd (the name of the company and of its protagonists have been changed to protect those concerned), the company formed to develop and market the product. I continued to make regular visits to the factory unit, and with enthusiasm discussed the now marketable product that was being purchased in volume by a major trolley manufacturer as original equipment. I saw it demonstrated on the news one evening by Jeremy Clarkson of TV fame, who declared it to 'steer like a Ferrari'. A deal was then made to retrofit all the trolleys of a major supermarket with, as I understand it, a time penalty clause for the completion of the retrofit. My suggestions regarding spring rates were ignored; my own feelings on pushing a trolley around with the new improvement in directional stability, were that there could be nothing like it. By this time, I had grave doubts about my association with these two people and although nothing was ever said, it was obvious that I was not going to be involved in the company in any way, despite promises. It was equally obvious that these people were not interested in long term business. Their interest lay in a quick company sale.

The only way to meet the time penalty was by an alteration from a positive lock attachment to the use of a shake proof washer, which when fitted by inadequately trained, sub-contracted retro-fit teams, who had little or no understanding of the major points of operation of the product, resulted in a high percentage failure rate and poor operation.

Had I been consulted, I would never have agreed to go to a supermarket direct. A few trolley manufacturers make a much better customer base than one large monopolistic supermarket. The supermarket concerned, rightly so, threatened legal action and withholding of payment, and Variguide Ltd went into voluntary liquidation with a £1.854 million turnover. I had never received a single penny piece. The liquidators honoured my part in the idea and asked me to sell the patent. My efforts to do so were met with promises and deliberate prevarication for over 12 months by one of the major caster makers. The patent then lapsed. The caster manufacturer concerned was involved in a merger or take-over or some rearrangement and so ended a disappointing and frustrating attempt to cure what is still a major handling problem affecting the vast majority of shoppers and giving work in some measure to physiotherapists sorting out pulled muscles world-wide.

The trolley problem, directional stability, and its cure are still there.

What is needed? Most industrial trolleys have rotating front casters and fixed rear ones, as do almost all airport ones and shopping too in many countries. The problem here in the UK is the public demand for fully floating ones that will go effortlessly in all directions. It therefore needs rotating front casters and rear ones that are locked in the straight-line direction but automatically release to full rotation when pushed or pulled sideways. My trolley caster 'plaything', although as already said, not practical from a production point of view, certainly proved the operational requirement and resulted in the cam and spring design manufactured and sold in large volume at low cost by Variguide Ltd. I can imagine other practical ways of achieving this directional stability at low cost. It is such simple engineering.

One major lesson to all would-be inventors, never agree to a percentage of company profit by a manufacturer of your idea. The nature of big business is that it will be years before a profit is declared by reason of development and marketing costs. Always insist on payment based on units produced before sale, the selling price will then include your unit payment. Seek out young entrepreneurs who are interested in building a business rather than a couple of ageing not very healthy characters whose prime interest is making the fastest possible buck on which to retire. Experience makes us what we are, but come what may, life is there to be enjoyed; this is not a practice run.

Enjoy it now with loyal friends.

***

I. Variguide

To take the foregoing in reverse order and consider the shopping trolley affair, Richard Right the owner of Variguide (all names have been changed to protect those involved) apparently saw the trolley castor business as a straightforward way of making money. The focus was on delivering to contract with the supermarkets, not on serving the needs of the end user per se. It seems that as soon as it became clear this was all going to be less than straightforward, he wound the company up. Customers had complained that there was free-play, the castors wobbled slightly when they were pushed forwards. When this was passed on to the company, Stan found himself the subject of criticism. Yet, for the system to work, just as with the steering wheel of a car, there needed to be some free-play. Timothy Truth the Managing Director, as an engineer, knew this but his focus at this stage was on fulfilling the contract, not selling the product through educating the customers.

Timothy Truth sent Stan a £10 note in the post once, to cover his expenses in making a trip down to the factory in Hampshire. Stan knew, at that point, there was no prospect of any further involvement with the business; he had been cut out. This was plain when Stan saw his castors on trolleys at his local supermarket. The retrofit team had visited, but no one had told him. He saw this as a missed opportunity to sell the product to the public, 'easily done but you need to be there'.

In the *Guardian* newspaper obituary for Trevor Bayliss CBE, inventor of the wind-up radio and thousands of other useful things he was quoted as explaining his experience as follows (Barker, 2018):

> He held in contempt what he called 'spivs, crooks and vulture capitalists.' [...] He went to the city [to fund a host of earlier inventions]. It was a fateful error. 'Within 18 months they had relieved me of my inventions and changed the name of my products, all without any financial reward. They had done me up like the proverbial kipper, eaten me for breakfast and spat me out, bones and all.'
>
> He learned his lesson, and as a consequence, the wind-up radio was produced by a firm in which he had a secure interest, ensuring that the inventor benefited along with the management and the customers. [...] He admitted that his chief defect was a distrust of people. 'Anyone in possession of a good idea is at the mercy of jackals wanting a piece of the action,' said the ebullient inventor. 'In business, basic decency has no cash value.'

The shopping trolley affair taught Stan a very similar set of lessons and gave him a similar level of distrust to Bayliss'. It was a distrust instilled though the experience of working with people whose approach to business originated in the British motor industry, and that was in complete contradiction to his experience as a sales agent operating on the edges of that same industry. That this experience occurred in retirement was probably a blessing as little harm came from it, other than immense disappointment.

Variguide's focus on shopping trolleys was obvious since it was, to use a phrase common in business these days, 'low-hanging fruit'. It was, however, also very constraining because the application of auto release castor technology extends far beyond supermarkets, from children's buggies at one end of the spectrum to port shipping container cranes at the other. Further, the castor and the shopping trolley manufacturers were all keen to retain their dominant oligopolistic position in the market while eliminating as far as possible any additional costs. On the face of it, this is sound business practice, if one is focussed on one's own profits.

The 'solution' to the handling problem commonly seen today is fixed rear castors and this is no doubt the cheapest way of achieving some basic improvement in handling. In reality, however, the real end-user focused solution Stan had developed was simple – and the problem undoubtedly still exists. In hindsight, Stan should have gone to Noboru Torii at NGK with the castor idea in the first place, but the treatment he felt he had received by NGK (UK) at the time of his retirement ruled that out.

II. The Sheepskin Shop

The Woollen and Sheepskin Country Shop (WSCS) was located on the grounds of a garden centre, sold a wide variety of country-type clothes, shirts, socks, slippers, rugs, and sheepskin coats. It was made of 50 mm tongue-and-grooved Swedish timber, which created a warm and inviting ambiance. It also smelt beautiful, too, with the rich aroma of the wood perfectly in concert with the type of products being sold. Stan's wife had been working part time there for a year when the owner mentioned he was thinking of selling. This was an opportunity for her to run a business for herself. After a short negotiation, Stan bought the business and widened the range of products to include not just woollen products but other quality items such as shirts and even embroidered handkerchiefs made by his niece.

One day, a customer came in and said WSCS was charging too much for the shirts it was selling, and told Stan what the price of them was in Cirencester, the town half an hour's drive away. This was less than Stan could buy them for from the manufacturer! The next time the representative called, he was told to collect up all the shirts that were on the shelves and not to come back. He couldn't understand what the problem was and argued that since the shop was only a single outlet and not selling many shirts, in comparison with the larger retail multiples in the towns, he was charging Stan a fair price. His sale price was based on quantity, which made it impossible for the small retailer to compete with the big corporations. The implications were not only that people would increasingly not buy from WSCS, but that the shop's reputation, built up over five years, was being damaged. Stan was being accused of being a rip-off merchant and there was nothing he could do about it, other than stop stocking the shirts. The buying power of the larger businesses was killing off any reasonable opportunity for customers to have any choice about where they were able to buy their products from.

Notwithstanding this problem, the shop was garnering a strong reputation for selling quality coats. This was partly because of the range that was stocked, going from one end of the shop to the other along the back wall. It was also because the coats were made by Fenland, the UK's top sheepskin manufacturer. Now no longer in existence, they were based in Bridgewater, Somerset, and were keen to support the shop as much as possible. They agreed to allow Stan to have coats on a sale-or-return basis. This meant that the range that was able to be kept was disproportionate to the turnover, because coats were only paid for by WSCS once they were sold to the customer. Such an arrangement would never normally be entered into with a single retail shop, but the two families got on very well; Stan's niece made a beautiful gown, hand embroidered with forget-me-nots, for the owner's son's christening. This was a personal arrangement based on shared business values. In return, Stan kept the margins low, and he could afford to because he did not have large amounts of money tied up in stock. The result was that Fenland revealed the WSCS quickly sold more Fenland coats than any other single retail shop in the country, and was one of their very best performing customers.

At this point, one of NGK's senior employees complained that NGK was subsidising the shop. Stan countered that he was reinvesting the commission – his own pay – in the shop and what he did with his own pay was his business. They were his earnings, his 'salary'; it was nothing to do with NGK what he did with his salary. It could not be said that he was using his commission to sell a competing product, but this was an example of the corporate attitude that had by this time begun to thoroughly pervade

NGK (UK): Involvement in other things even unrelated to NGK was read as disloyalty to NGK.

Since Fenland were being very supportive of WSCS, it was important to Stan to support the company as much as possible. Stan's view of retail clothing sales was based not on the potential margin available within the item being sold, but on the cost of the time taken to sell it. The time taken to sell a coat was not very much more than the time taken to sell a shirt. Neither did they take up that much more room in the shop. So there was no justification for putting a large mark-up on the coats. This served only to enhance the relationship between Fenland and WSCS. The shop became known as an unofficial factory outlet, and Fenland happily endorsed and enhanced this; they would send prototype styles and colours to WSCS to test the market.

This strong reputation brought with it some unwelcome attention. One Saturday, with the shop full of people, the exit alarm went off and a man slipped out of the door with two coats under his arm, the security tags still in place, and was seen sprinting across car the park. The prospect of criminals targeting the shop forced Stan to wire all the coats up to the rail along the back wall. This was annoying as it limited peoples' ability to try the coats on. Nonetheless, they were sympathetic to the issue, and patient with the inconvenience. All seemed well, and the police were supportive; the shop's infrared alarm system was linked directly to the local police station. However, one Saturday morning Stan came in to open the shop up, only to discover a large hole had been cut into the back wall of the building. And yet the alarm wasn't going off. He got into the shop, to discover dozens of coats missing. The security wire that ran up the arm of every coat linking them together with padlocks had been cut and the coats pulled off their hangers. The hole had been cut at coat railing height, was approximately six feet long and two tongue and groove boards wide. A drill had evidently been used to cut a small hole and a jig saw then used to cut the boards out. Police inquiries turned up no clues, other than one coat had been dropped in a nearby field, but there were no fingerprints on it or on the shop. No-one in the local houses had heard anything suspicious.

Clearly, Stan was told, the perpetrators had properly 'cased the joint', knowing what height to cut the hole, knowing they needed strong cutters to cut the security wire, and knowing not to park near the shop to avoid being seen. The police estimated it had been the work of at least three people, but local inquiries turned up no leads as to where the coats had been 'offloaded'. The conclusion they drew was that this was a criminal gang that had come down from far afield, possibly the Midlands or the North East. That was as far as the Police investigations went and, despite Stan saying he had been told there was someone trying to sell sheepskin coats around the local pubs, he was told there was nothing they could do. They finished by saying 'You have insurance, so there's nothing to worry about.' Stan was disappointed and annoyed at that, but thankfully Fenland were very supportive and did not charge for the coats that were stolen. The building was quickly repaired, but the joy had gone out of the business. Psychologically, it had been sullied.

In addition, there was little support from the garden centre owner, who received a monthly ground rent for the building's footprint. The popularity of the shop, however, was such that it was attracting visitors to the garden centre who came just to visit WSCS. For the garden centre owner, this was the opposite of what he wanted; the WSCS was meant to be an addition to the portfolio of 'offerings' not the main attraction. He refused Stan permission to put up a sign advertising the shop at the entrance to the car park, and changed the layout of the car park and garden centre building entrances so that, to get to the WSCS, visitors had to go through the garden centre first. Immediately, the number of people coming to the shop fell.

With no prospect of being able to protect the coats, short of installing an eighty by ten feet piece of sheet steel which would have been prohibitively expensive, and with the prospect of the shop being able to maintain its current sales severely curtailed by the garden centre owner to suit his own needs and expectations, the decision was taken to sell up. The stock was sold off at cost, and the building was sold to the garden centre to be turned into their office space. Five years after Stan had bought the business, it was all over in three weeks. The accountant later calculated that the business had lost around £4,000, and all of that in the final eighteen months, i.e. once the burglaries started to happen and stock had had to be wired up, and the losses worsened with the change to the garden centre entrance layout. It was a sad end to a good little business that had given Kathleen real purpose and pleasure – pleasure that had been snuffed out by theft on the one hand and strategic self-centredness on the other.

Stan Dibben signing copies of *Hold On!* at the Stafford Classic Bike Show, April 2009

14

MARK'S STORY: BUSINESS ON THE EDGE OF UNIVERSITIES

Mark in Malta, aged 9, concentrating with characteristic intensity on the job in hand – reading an Asterix comic book!

I. Of Sheltered Beginnings

Well now, I was born in 1970; I enjoyed a naively care-free childhood and was always close to the man I knew as my Grandad, Ron Barrett. My maternal Grandmother had remarried some years after the death of Cyril Smith, and Ron was a tremendously kind and gentle man who would often be found in his garden at their home, 6 Boulton Walk in Erdington. That part of Birmingham was a secluded little spot on the edge of the frenetic busy-ness of the city, so secluded that even the taxi drivers didn't know where it was – which was just as he liked it! In many ways, as very much more of a 'home bird' than Cyril, Ron was the perfect match for my grandmother. His time as a military policeman shaped his sense of duty and propriety, and stature; whenever he walked into a pub the place would often go quiet for a moment, for he had the air of a policeman. He served in India right at the very end of World War Two, returning home in October 1946. That time in India was one of some unrest and disquiet presaging the later Indian Independence, and the CMP in India were inevitably called upon to 'handle' it, as well as arms and other smuggling of war materials; India appears to have been a gateway to the theatres farther East (e.g. Crozier, [1951] 2014). Not to mention a serious problem of VD among the troops that required strong action to be taken against the prostitution networks (see e.g. Ganapathi, 1982). Ron would only say they got 'very, very tough' with it; he would never say what 'very, very tough' meant. He also spoke of 'dealing with the "dacoity"', a form of violent gang robbery particular to the Indian Subcontinent subculture , and which was 'an ever present menace' for British troops (Crozier, [1951] 2014: 182). All this, along with the usual day-to-day work of policing an occupied country. There were just four and a half thousand British nationality Military Police in India, and seven and a half thousand Indians, for an Army strength of 2.5 million men across the Subcontinent (Sheffield, 1994:127-30). It cannot have been fun, especially for an 18 year old. Whenever I asked Ron if he would like to visit India again he always replied with a flat 'No.' Sometimes he would pause and add simply, 'Not after what I saw there.' He cared for me deeply and I was very fortunate, for example when we went on holiday, in that it was like having two fathers in some respects. I remember eating paella with him aged six, on Majorca – 'Oh this is good, I think you'll enjoy this, but don't eat too much rice. It's the seafood that makes this dish fabulous. Now, the way you open a shell is like this ... Okay?' He ate 90% of it, naturally, but that wasn't the point of the exercise so far as he was concerned; it was about giving me a shared experience. All when Majorca was still a secluded island of course.

I remember, too, the next year snorkelling in the aptly named Blue Grotto in Malta, Dad on one side and Grandad on the other, peering down into the Mediterranean through carpets of brightly coloured fish. I was absolutely fascinated by the depth of it. I remember being a bit nervous about it beforehand, as we got ready to jump off the charter boat that had taken us and two dozen or so other tourists out there, but I knew both of them were very strong swimmers. After all, whenever Ron swam front crawl there was a bow wave! There was no one else my age in the water, the reason for which though obvious now I didn't appreciate then. Once in the water I felt safe. We were away from the boat for a good two hours, snorkelling for what seemed like miles in open water; the Blue Grotto is not secluded inlet swimming. Of course, a lot of that time was spent simply floating about but, nonetheless, even with mask and snorkel and fins I realise now that was a mighty big swim for a seven-year-old! It was a *good* experience for a young boy to have.

Even in my teens I was blissfully ignorant, only focused on enjoying riding my motorcycles. There too I was very lucky, as my father bought me a brand new two stroke NS125 Honda to ride about on. I had started to ride on a TS50X Suzuki trail bike moped, and on it I learned I didn't like riding on mud. Like Dad, I found it to be nowhere near precise enough. The Honda was much more my scene, and I rode the wheels off it. Going from the Suzuki to that was like jumping on a superbike. I often asked my Dad what the Isle of Man was like in terms of the roads I was riding on and he said, 'very much like here', here being the roads around Kempsford, the village in Gloucestershire where I grew up. I was never convinced of my ability on a bike and spent the two years I had the Honda, as well as the fabulous but much maligned-by-the-press ZZR250 Kawasaki four stroke that came after it, convincing myself I wasn't.

It was good fun though. I worked out that Kempsford, Hannington, Highworth, Shrivenham, Ashbury, Lambourn, and back, was 38.2 miles. Not far away from the length of the TT circuit's 37 & ¾ miles. All C & B roads, narrow and quiet. I have ridden all over the world now, on all sorts of machinery and enjoyed myself tremendously, but the B4000 from Highworth to Lambourn is still the best small bike (and small car) road I have ever ridden. It's useless for big bikes because you simply can't see far enough for anything much beyond the national limit to be safe, using one side of the road. (The road fund licence only pays for one side of the road, namely the only side of the road you have a legal right to be on.) Importantly, too, being able to stop within the distance of your vision. Even the 250 was a bit too quick for that road to remain safe, by which I mean you couldn't do so and at the same time really *use* the bike, but by contrast the 12 hp 125 was perfect.

I could reliably get out to Lambourn in 20 minutes but could never get back in under 21 and it used to annoy me. It wouldn't be possible to do this now as the roads aren't as well maintained as they were then, too many potholes to be able to reliably commit to an apex, and the speed limits are probably rightly more extensive. Anyway, I decided I wasn't good enough – although some years later my Dad told me I probably would have been. Unlike the Dunlop brothers who have achieved so much, I was never prepared to risk the family reputation – on both sides of the family of course – by possibly only being able to trundle around at the back. So I looked for something else to succeed at.

II. 'Feel the Fear and Do It Anyway'?

I became an academic because of the need to know, and the enjoyment I got in discovering knowledge, but my life has been shaped by the feeling of fear above all things. At least anxiety, but fear really. Fear of school, that is of being bullied in the playground and of not knowing in the classroom. Fear of getting the slipper at school, although I never did. Fear of not obtaining the grades to get into the University I wanted, although I never didn't. Fear, let's face it, of being a potential embarrassment racing motorbikes. A perpetual fear of inadequacy. As a colleague of mine says in the signature line of his e-mails, 'normal is a failure of potential'. This may very well be a learnt response to the high-achievers in my family, certainly the men in my family and others of influence such as Andrew Mustard.

I was very fortunate to spend three months as part of a gap year between A Levels and University with Andrew and Brownie Mustard in Pallarenda. Other than my father, I was influenced more by him than anyone else. It will already be clear from the previous chapters that it was almost impossible not to be. We spent a good deal of time on the Palmer River and much of that was spent in discussion. By this stage, I was very aware that my parent's marriage was not in good shape, and questioned much as a result. He was a real steadying, guiding influence. What impressed me most about Andrew and Brownie was the deep connectedness they had, which until I witnessed it I had never seen before in two people. So she and Andrew together, as well as the time I spent with Andrew not only in the bush but also working on outboard engines with him, were incredibly influential in giving me a sense of selfhood that I would not otherwise have had aged 18. Of course, the reason my father sent me over there was to achieve precisely that purpose; unbeknown to me he and Andrew had spoken about all this before I went out. Andrew's sister Denise Bompas, too, was very supportive all through my subsequent university years. She funded my Master's degree, and it was from her I understood that all this high-achieving malarkey was well and good up to a point, but *actually* it was perfectly okay just to 'be'.

I should say it was never suggested for a moment that I was inadequate, quite the opposite. It was rather self-installed. It may have also been the result of being a motherless child. Which is not to say my mother was not there in the way my father's father was simply not there, but it is to say she was physically-affectionately, and indeed just plain affectionately, absent. This itself was probably due to the fact that her mother Irene was, if I reflect on my grandmother and how she was, the same with her I'm sure. And this was in my grandmother's case, due I'm equally sure to the fact that her boyfriend had got her pregnant when she was 19. However much she loved Cyril and had supported him in his battles with his own father, she was then trapped in a marital relationship that was manufactured for the reality; my father only ever recalls Irene being dissatisfied, unhappy. So too was my Mother, who was herself ever-changed by her father's suicide; as with many daughters and fathers, there was a special bond. As my father has said, she always claimed vociferously it had been a 'cry for help gone wrong'. Certainly by the time of his death Cyril, too, was desperately unhappy.

And so I was the only child of an only child.

I remember as if it were yesterday, being driven to a kindergarten at RAF Fairford near where we lived, aged 5. It was the time of Concorde's flight testing there and so, it stands to reason, they must have needed a nursery for the children of the people working there. Ian Heaton who lived next door to us at the time worked on the programme and I presume had arranged a place. It was cold and raining, and Mrs Heaton was driving; my mother did not have a car then. I did not know where we were going until we got there. Then I realised, burst into tears and did not stop. I was totally overwhelmed by feelings of abandonment, betrayal, fear of the unknown and of all those imminent strangers. I remember my mother saying to her friend with an air of dismissal and resignation. 'Go home!' 'Are you sure? He might be alright if you can get him in.' Howls from me. 'No point. He's never going *in there* is he.' They drove back in total silence, while I peered out through the fogged back windows at the grey sky, wracked by a deep fear that I had done the wrong thing and, having upset her, was alone again. That memory is pure and crystal clear in its vividness and the feelings persist, fundamentally unchanged even if they are understood, as an adult.

The casualties of a war extend far beyond the generation directly touched by it.

The feelings of fear persisted, too, as an academic – even as a member of the professoriate. One of the light-hearted things you can have fun with is collecting letters after your name. I got to 25 and stopped counting – the game had long-since ceased to have meaning – and besides the feelings still persisted. First it was as a student, when I simply could not understand how my undergraduate peers could know so much to have so much self-confidence. It was only when

I started to mark students' work myself when doing my PhD that I realised their self-confidence was born of ignorance. As the saying goes, 'the ignorance of youth', but I was troubled by the knowledge that I knew nothing. They seemingly were not. I shared my father's feelings as a young man, too, about women. They were impossibly beautiful intellectually as well as physically, powerful in ways I could not fathom let alone grapple with. Whenever I tried, I made a complete Horlicks of it. I'm sure my wife Rebecca would say I still do! Second, as a paid academic rather than a paying one, the nature of the system is such that one is always left feeling inadequate, that what one does is never good enough, that one is incapable. It generates what psychologists call 'imposter syndrome', a fear that one will soon be found out as not knowing, as not good enough. The feeling comes from knowing enough to know gaps exist in one's knowledge which, of course, means the fear is unfounded.

Fear also persists in Multiple Sclerosis, though that is a fear of incapacity. Sometimes fear even of today, what it will bring. I should say immediately that I have been looked after by some brilliant people first at the Menzies Centre in Hobart and now at University College London and am very lucky indeed with it, so far. All it seems to be at the moment is an indicator of stress, poor sleep, lack of food, too much heat, or some combination of the four. Long may it stay that way. Still, when it's there, the symptoms for me are weakness in the legs and arms, and pain. Either occasional electric stabbing through the bones of the fingers or, when it's particularly manifest, of badly pulled muscles. Imagine you've pulled your stomach muscle or your calf. Except with MS you feel you have pulled almost all of your muscles. That isn't a relapse, that's just symptomatic of the disease. A relapse feels as if you have torn those muscles. I don't recommend MS.

MS has a small secondary hereditary component as it has been linked to being more prevalent than average in those with other conditions, but it's best avoided by getting rid of all stress both work and family – I think stress is a major factor – and maintaining your Vitamin D levels. My physician in Tasmania when I lived there, a leading Professor in the field of MS research, said to me the first time I saw him after I had been diagnosed that 'I know there is a link between MS and stress. I *know* it, but I don't have the evidence to publish it yet. I thought I was going to, because I had a PhD student studying the link between stress and MS, but then she gave up because she got too stressed!' He recommends everyone take Vitamin D supplements because of our indoors lives. I take 5,000 IU of Vitamin D a day.

A colleague of mine when I was a junior lecturer at St Andrews, who I used to work with on trust in the public sector, would invite me over to his house for dinner occasionally. He was most supportive and taught me much about what being a successful academic involves in the current era, in his words 'Delivery, delivery, delivery!' The 'midwifery model' of academe. He and his wife had three wonderful young boys. Once they had gone to bed we used to chat about life, the universe and everything, as wine occasioned us to do. Their lives as students were quite carefree and thus different to mine. They grew up, they said, when they realised their first child was on the way.

I grew up when my parents separated. My mother, for reasons best known to herself, was firmly of the view that as the 'one and only', I was responsible for keeping my parents together. When you are a child going through your parents' divorce, I imagine you are a ping pong ball, bouncing from one to the other and back again. My experience of going through it as a young adult is that you are a ping pong ball with a conscience. Not only did I now realise for certain that all I had thought was the case in my upbringing wasn't the case at all, I was made (by my mother) to feel responsible for it. My mother's powers of psychological blackmail were formidable. *Formidable.* (I have in hindsight realised, much to my chagrin, that I inherited just something of that capability, but thankfully it has been ironed out of me by events – and by the remarkable Rebecca.) I buried myself in my studies.

III. Academia – Life on the Edge of Society?

I fashioned a way of life from those studies and, in this sense, I am an old-fashioned academic of the Victorian era. I even have a Victorian beard. It's not a job and it's not a career, it's a vocation, a life's work: retirement makes it possible now to do it as a Victorian professor, as opposed to an industrial knowledge-factory worker, which is what academia has mostly become. My life is not one of physical exploration, the adventure of new places. Physical limitations prevent that. It is instead a rather monastic one of mental exploration; the adventure of new ideas. I find such adventures to be warmer and dryer, and they're usually less uncomfortable. But all the while there is an intellectual disquiet, a fear of sorts. Thickets to somehow be pushed beyond, out of the known and into the unknown.

These adventures are personal in the first instance. To be an academic, you have to be a self-starter. You cannot rely on others, it's up to you. If you don't come up with good ideas you don't have anything. Just as it was with my father that if he didn't sell he didn't eat, so it was with me that if I didn't come up with ideas that 'sell', I didn't get paid. By 'sell', I mean ideas that people found in some way resonated with them such that students pronounce themselves satisfied with what I taught, PhD candidates wanted to study with me as their supervisor, and academic journal and book editors wanted to publish my work. I should say we usually aren't paid by the publisher, we're paid by the university that employs us, and it's isn't quite as immediate as it was with my father because we're not on commission. Nonetheless, in the era of 'publish or perish' sooner or later universities will, if the results don't happen and don't keep happening, turn around and say 'be gone!' With the way universities are funded these days (i.e. on the basis of student tuition fees, PhD completions and publications) the reality, increasingly, is this all happens sooner rather than later.

We were at the Bristol Classic Motorcycle Show a couple of years ago and there was a stand there displaying the work of Roy Barrett, a now-retired artist who painted beautiful pictures of vintage cars and motorcycles in various backdrops. One was of the interior of a workshop with a chap stood behind a bench fettling something to go on one of the two motorbikes in the foreground, a fairly complete Triumph and a partially restored Brough Superior. I bought it immediately, for it was the perfect metaphor for how I tend to write papers and books. For workshop read study, bench read desk, Triumph read ordinary sort of paper, Brough read special sort of paper or book.

Some people churn papers out as if they are on a production line, taking the same topic and slicing and dicing to produce differently-the-same papers sent off to various academic journals for review, 'cold'. Of course you sell a lot of product that way, but I've never been able to do it. It leaves *me* cold! Everything I write is one-off, bespoke, commissioned to do a particular job for an editor-customer. Be this as a chapter in a book on a particular topic or to be part of a journal special issue. The similarities with motorcycles don't stop there. Papers have front ends, back ends, engines that do the real work of the piece, gearboxes that translate the power of the argument to deliver it to its destination, and so on. They have a 'suspension' built into them too, in the shape of their narrative and approach to their topic that hopefully provides the reader with a comfortable ride/read. Paragraphs are crafted, fitted together, re-jigged, partially built, disassembled, re-made, offered up to the rest of the piece to ensure they do the job for which they're intended, re-assembled, screwed up together tight, and finally the whole piece is polished before being sent off. If I'm writing with a colleague, then papers leave the workshop 'etherially' in various states of assembly to be worked on further and then arrive back for more work and so on. Thankfully, I'm not hampered in collaborative work by snail mail or the cost of parcel post.

Nonetheless, you live on the quality of your work. Even when working with multiple other authors in teams, if your work doesn't come up to scratch people soon stop working with you. Even although you may work in a university of 3,000 other employees and 40,000+ students, ultimately you're on your own. You're judged by the quality of the work you do, be this teaching, writing or even in committees. You're always being judged somehow. Looking good or sounding good won't get you very far for very long. To adopt another metaphor, if you're a professional racing motorcyclist, you alone ride the machine and you're paid by the factory to do it. You'd better deliver results on the race circuit or you'll find yourself out of a job.

Of course with racing teams there are other ways to find yourself out of a job. If you don't get on with people in the team, you would need to be an exceptional rider not to find yourself disposed of. The same is true in universities. Politics in universities are rife, because the performance one is being judged about is deeply personal, founded in the quality of your ideas. No-one likes their ideas criticised to the point they may lose their job as a result of them. But university politics extend beyond that sphere to a much wider one that can affect the future of the university itself, namely how they are funded.

IV. Living on the Edge – My Experience of University Funding and Its Impact

Although I have most recently worked in the Business School at the University of Tasmania, I have spent my entire career in Higher Education not only in Australia but also New Zealand and the United Kingdom. I have also held numerous visiting positions in the United States, the UK and on the Continent. What follows is written on the basis of that whole twenty-year experience; it is not aimed at one particular university but at revealing some fundamental issues that the parents of any university student, let alone students themselves, might find useful. Those not interested can skip to the conclusion!

It doesn't require access to confidential reports at the Government or University level to realize that the Higher Education industry in English speaking countries needs rethinking. One only has to take the population and divide that into the number of universities and then compare that per capita figure with other countries to understand that it cannot be afforded without greater commitment of funds. Or a radical rethink of the role of 'universities' in the tertiary education sector, in relation to other providers and the nature and extent of the latter's continued existence. This problem is even coming to the fore in the United States, which has long been held as the model for contemporary university industry in – at least English speaking – countries. The reality of the US system is that it only works to the extent it does because of the strong culture of philanthropy that exists there, whereby former students give a lot of money in endowments. This, however, only masks the same underlying challenges, and many universities there are not as financially well off as one might imagine, although some (a minority) are of course.

Apart from somehow changing what univerrsities do and where they do it, policies of deregulation ask the market to do the countries' work for them. Worse, asking young people to pay in the way they do forces them to saddle themselves with a lifetime of debt that will mean they will never be able to use their higher education to create *genuine* wealth for themselves; only the banks will benefit. Worse even than this, it seems governments are expecting students from other countries, particularly those from Asia, to suffer the same fate. That is a brass neck all round! To heap despair upon misery, quality in my experience is falling to accommodate for the plain fact that very many 'English as a Second Language' students do not have the English language ability to grasp the complexities of the topics being discussed. This is not their fault, but the fact they are paying such high fees means they must, in the hard market reality, be passed and not failed. Deregulation means a race to the bottom, a quality postcode lottery. This damages the education of current students, and the reputation of the degrees obtained of previously graduated students.

Worse still, universities have become places where the external accountability measures put in place by governments to ostensibly control quality mean that narrow-mindedness in teaching and research is what succeeds. You can only research what will be published in journals acceptable to your Department, and you can only teach what the students will give high evaluation scores for. The notion that academics have freedom to think, teach and research is just that, a mere notion. It no longer exists. In the larger universities, even among the so-called elite universities, there is tremendous pressure. The problem is particularly acute in business schools which are now simply cash cows for universities.

It is not very uncommon in English speaking countries of the Commonwealth for as much as 90% of a postgraduate business course to be made up of students from Asia, and they are increasingly being taught by part-time staff. Full professors are sometimes spread across upwards of 8 courses a year. Although in an environment of ever-increasing funding pressure, business schools are not the only cash cows, they have been viewed in this way for about thirty years, and so they are perhaps worth speaking about. This is quite apart from the fact that all my academic life has been spent in them and even on occasion managing in them, so I have some knowledge to speak through.

The first point to mention here is that the concern a lowering of standards coupled with ever-increasing class sizes – particularly of internationals – tends to be rebutted by politicians with a line that can be summed up as 'it is excellent to have campuses that have a wide range of nationalities to broaden student experience.' This is a fine liberal principle. It is not the fact that there are international students on campus that is the problem. It is the fact that there are just so very many and from a particular part of the world. There is no balance. Unregulated student demand is dictating terms insofar as the most students who have most access to the most money these days are Asian students, particularly Chinese from its ever-burgeoning middle class. Of course universities, whose funding from governments has been steadily cut – there is no denying it – in real terms for thirty years, are being forced to take those students who can afford to come in order to stay open.

Students witness the phenomenon directly in the business school classroom, in classes where the majority of their peers have trouble with the English language and the pace of learning in slowed. They also observe that their peers studying the sciences both do not have large numbers of international students and at the same time are being given an educative experience that plainly costs a great deal more. Why, the business student asks, are we paying the same as our peers studying Physics when we get nowhere near the amount or quality of education? The answer they get from vice chancellors and politicians is usually something like 'we are committed to the principle of equal fees regardless of course, so that any student can take any course they wish.' This too is a fine liberal principle but how this is achieved is worth exploring, for it masks a deep-seated immorality.

Although the details and actual balances of the arrangements vary by country, English speaking countries fund universities through a mix of payments for research undertaken after the fact, and payments for teaching to be carried out up front. In principle this is meant to ensure that the freedom to research is maintained and at the same time universities can prepare to teach students safe in the knowledge they will have enough money to deliver the course. As governments have reduced the amount of funding they are prepared to pay, particularly for the teaching, so universities have had to increase their fees to the students themselves in order to cover the shortfall. Some of the shortfall has been met through genuine efficiency savings. But a lot of the shortfall, and it is a growing shortfall, has been met by cross-subsidising certain subjects with the student fees accrued from students studying other subjects. It genuinely does cost more to teach a hard science (engineering, physics, chemistry etc) student, because of the cost of the laboratory equipment, than it does a student in the liberal arts (languages, history, business etc).

The cross-subsidisation occurs through the establishment of what are commonly called 'contribution margins', targets for the amount of money that each school or faculty must deliver to the university's central budget at the end of the year, so that it can 'balance the books'. Most business schools I am aware of are asked to deliver a contribution margin of between 50% and 70% of their total income. That is to say, if a student is paying – let us call it in round figures – £9,000 per annum, as much as £6,300 may well be going straight from the business school to the central university to cover central costs, such as the library fair enough, and also to offset the costs of students in the sciences. As well as pay the administrative staff in the centre of the university, and the senior academic staff in overall charge, the pro-vice chancellors, deputy vice-chancellors and the vice chancellor.

Again politicians and vice chancellors come up with lines such as, 'the exact proportioning of overall income from a business school or any part of the university is greater than just the student fees and so such black-and-white arguments regarding student fees in particular, and from a business school in particular, are not reflective of the reality of university funding models.' Of course they would say that wouldn't they and up to a point there is some truth in the statement, because business school income is not just student fees. But it is a very large component of that income, and that income forms a very large component relative to other schools of a university's income. In fact, bear with me here, the whole thing is done the other way around. By which I mean the schools and faculties are given a working budget to deliver their responsibilities for the year, and this is set in the case of our example and according to the wider needs of the university in question, at between 50% and 30% of the total expected income to be generated by them.

V. Business Schools as 'Businesses' on the Edge of Universities?

I said earlier that 'universities … are being forced to take students who can afford to come in order to stay open.' What I should have said was 'in order to stay in business', because this is what they have become. In point of fact business schools are research and teaching entities just in the same way as those that teach physics or history, but it might be argued that of all those parts of a university which should be able to be thought of as businesses it should be business schools. On the grounds they should practice what they preach. There are some real moral questions here, too, which will become apparent as we proceed, but let us run with the idea that universities and in particular business schools can be thought of as businesses. So what sort of business is a business school?

Obviously it is in the education business, but this implies the focus of an educational establishment should be the making of money, not the teaching of future generations. It implies that the purpose of teaching the country's future generations is the making of money. Whatever the rights or wrongs of this as a principle, it does mean in practice that private higher education providers can teach business students and legitimately make money. More than this, because they do not have to cross-subsidise the teaching or research of other disciplines, they can put more of their money into the actual teaching of the business students, to give students a better educative experience. So universities are at a competitive disadvantage in the teaching of business. At the same time, they are reliant on the income business schools provide as the aforementioned strategic 'cash cows'; they are milked for the money they earn. Again, in my experience it is not uncommon for this to be between 50% and 70% of their revenue nowadays.

Let us return to the question 'What sort of business is it?' How does it compare with other businesses? Is it a manufacturing business, a service business, a wholesale business, or a retail business? It is easier to answer this question by first of all pointing out what it is not. That is, with few exceptions, it is not a wholesale business. It is not buying in products from someone else and on-selling them to another business who then sells the products to an end-user. In terms of the development of patents and other products from the sciences, some parts of universities are in the business of manufacture in a very specialist way, but by and large business schools in any case do not manufacture a tangible feel-in-the-palm-of-your-hand product. In a peculiar way, however, they are indeed in the business of developing products, that is courses, packaging them into degrees and selling them direct to the student-as-consumer and then offering service support, i.e. face-to-face and/or on-line teaching, alongside that product to ensure the consumer gets the most out of the product s/he has bought.

So a business school is both a service product producer and retailer, to use business language. In retail terms, a 60–70% contribution margin amounts to around-about a 2.3 price mark-up. Well that's boutique fashion, supercar or superyacht territory today; not too many 17-year-olds, even Chinese 17-year-olds' parents, can afford a supercar or superyacht anything. And that's before one starts thinking about the relative quality of the product being bought. Cartier or Bugatti or Nicholson vs the average undergraduate business degree or even MBA? Which is not to say the degrees are worthless, quite the opposite. But a legitimate question to ask, when young people are getting into serious debt for their degrees, is can this sort of mark-up be justified? Is it fair for students in one part of a university to heavily subsidise students in another part of the university when, in so doing, they are getting into a level of debt that is out of proportion to the experience they have?

It could be argued that now the higher education sector, particularly in English speaking countries, has been opened up to the market, we can allow the market to determine prices and people will vote with their feet. Unfortunately, even although in some countries (such as the UK) business degrees are almost if not entirely paid for by the student as consumer rather than in some part by the government, the prices of degrees are established not by the market but by the universities in the light of the challenge of cross-subsidisation. The industrial structure, to use another strategy term, determines the price; the market cannot set the price because there is nowhere else for the market to *go* because there is, by and large, no substitute product apart from employment of some sort, or apprenticeships – which are not infrequently exploitative, as we saw with my father at MSUCo. Even in simple terms, some students do *go* abroad but as a proportion of the total it is a tiny minority, and almost all English-speaking universities in the Commonwealth, and many in America too, are struggling for funding to some greater or lesser extent. Students in business and other liberal arts fields are getting into debt, more than the cost of the delivery of their own degrees can justifiably warrant, to fund the delivery of courses for other students. Student A in the business school is, in no small part, paying for the studies of Student B in Physics. In what ways can this be justified, particularly when governments are reducing their own subsidisation of Student A's degree to minimal amounts?

If these were not significant enough moral quandaries in themselves, there is yet another challenge, namely the funding of research, and particularly that in the sciences. Since science research in universities is largely funded via government research councils with a remit to get the most outcome for each dollar or pound they award, they rarely tend to award funding to projects in their entirety. Universities often have to cover the shortfall. This is all the more so since some types of employment and travel necessary for research to be carried out often cannot be claimed against research grants. These have to be paid for by the university. Further, as a general although not universal rule, the less money you ask for the more likely it is that you will get what you ask for. The result is that almost all research, and particularly that in the sciences, ends up costing the university money.

In science the sums can be significant, in the order of millions of pounds. Where do they find the shortfall from? Already we know the answer, namely from teaching cross-subsidisation. Since the liberal arts, and within that business, is called upon to cross-subsidise most then we can rest assured that it is the students in these courses that are allowing universities to do research. Indeed, since universities are often providing internal grants to kick-start research projects in their early stages, these students are paying to *enable their own university to actually compete with other universities* for research income from research councils both at home and abroad.

Why do universities do research? The sciences do it genuinely to advance human understanding and well-being, and increasingly for the betterment of other species in the light of the realities of climate change. But there are two other purposes. First the enhancement of the reputation of the university on the grounds that the better the reputation, the more students will come and the more money there will be. Second, governments want universities to do research because it allows a country to compete with other countries for scientific discoveries. There is a growing trend towards collaborative research among international research teams but there is 'coop-etition', i.e. co-operation and competition at the same time, down to the level of the individual academics on the teams, as I have explained above. You live and die as an academic by your individual contribution to collaborative research. Science research is thus a global 'coop-etition' among and between countries, through the 'mechanism' of universities. It is funded in no small part by the cross-subsidisation of liberal arts students' fees, and within this most particularly business school students' fees.

In the liberal arts, research is both less immediately practical and certainly not 'blue-sky', rather it is of interest in the development of understanding of human culture and country history. In business, one of the great challenges is to conduct research into the nature and practice of business that reflects the realities or ideals of work but in such a way that it is not done at the behest of particular businesses, to further their aims. For this would mean otherwise that the research would have a bias built in. Obviously when money is an increasing issue, it becomes more difficult to resist businesses who seek to influence public opinion through the medium of sponsored research. Much less resist the temptation to actively engage with businesses as potential funders.

In fairness, this problem can also be seen in the medical sciences and even in the sciences where research grants from major industry players can be used to influence public opinion through the results obtained at the behest of the funder. Equally, too, research that is done in business schools is often dismissed by industry as irrelevant – precisely because it is not aimed at furthering the interests of individual businesses. Business schools increasingly find themselves not only doing research for the purpose of further knowledge but also at the same time doing additional research paid for by individual businesses. As a result, the latter is often unusable except insofar as it might change the behaviour of that business in its own interests. A leading professor of entrepreneurship once pointed out to me that 'business schools cease to be legitimate as university entities when they become the handmaidens of business. The role of a business school is to be the insightful critic of businesses, not its handmaiden.' Funding realities are making business schools illegitimate.

V. The Challenges of the International Student Dollar

These, then, are the realities and within them yet another moral question arises in respect of students. Is it right that universities and indeed nations should compete with each other for and in research using the money young people have borrowed to obtain an education? It is true to say that indirectly they benefit from the research because it is taught to them, but the plain fact remains that in no small part through the cross-subsidies in place, it is student fees that are allowing universities and countries to compete with each other. Should universities and countries be asking their young people to get into a lifetime's worth of debt to allow them to play research games? Is it right that international students from, for example China, should be cross-subsidising our countries' efforts to compete with their mother country in research?

Of course the repost is 'Don't you think it is important that our universities and our countries are competitive?' Of course the answer to this question is yes, if we wish to retain our sovereignty. The question is, should the youth of today be requested, expected and required to pay for today's research costs? They have their lives to build and might reasonably be asked to contribute when they can afford to from their earnings as adults, for the research being undertaken when they are adults. Not before they have barely started out! Particularly so when their student fees that they go into debt for are so directly being used to cross-subsidise other students and other fields of research.

In one of the university roles I have had, I was given the opportunity to ask a leading student recruiter with many years of experience this question: If you took all the international students out of the Australian higher education sector such that there were only Australians being educated through it, how many universities could the domestic student load support? The answer was 'between ten and twelve, depending on the year.' By this, he meant depending on the number of students leaving secondary school with university entrance qualifications, which fluctuates perfectly naturally year on year. Australia has 44 universities at present. That is, it has 4 times as many universities as can be paid for by the domestic student load. Australia has for many years now relied on full fee-paying internationals to sustain its higher education sector. Indeed, the current mantra from government and vice chancellors there is that international students are a major 'export earner' for the country. So the argument goes, the students are imported, value-added to, and then re-exported. So far awry have things got!

Australia is perhaps an extreme case, but it is probably safe to suggest at least half of the universities in other English-speaking countries remain in existence because of the presence of international students, and the vast majority of those students leave their home countries to study business. A wider question needs to be asked: Surely it is the responsibility of a country's own universities to educate its own people. So what is it about the higher education institutions of their own countries that means these students are looking to be educated overseas?

In any event, they do so in the oft-mistaken belief that obtaining a business degree from an English-speaking country will make them employable in that country, not in their home country. They remain unemployable even after three years' study, because their language skills are not high enough to allow them to be employable in the country in which they have chosen to study. And it does not make them very much more employable at home either. I have lost count of the times I have taken taxis driven by former international students I have taught who are unable to obtain a job for which their degrees (postgraduate taught course as well as undergraduate) have ostensibly made them qualified.

One solution to this challenge would be to raise the English language standards of entrants. To do that would be to cut off a funding source, because fewer students would be admitted. The next solution would then be to fail them if they do not make the grade. The answer is the same and in spades, since a failed student can have a significant word-of-mouth negative reputational effect. There might then follow the suggestion that universities should invest time improving their English language skills. The answer is that the regulations governing universities often make it difficult for them to offer degree-contributing courses whose topic is the very language in which the degree is taught. In other words, if the degree is taught in the English language, English language courses often cannot form part of the degree.

This principle stands on the assumption – a false assumption – that language acquisition occurs in the classroom while the student is being taught the subject of their degree. While there are always individual exceptions, by and large it does not. I know this from my own experience of learning Japanese and then studying in Japan. International students often form cliques to feel psychologically safe, and understandably so, both inside and outside the classroom. English language ability tends to fall as an international student progresses through their degree. Recognition of this fact can be seen in the number of English as second language people increasingly being hired into junior and senior lecturer positions, whose origins are the same countries as the students. So, for example, Chinese, Indians and Africans. Since these people are often on short stay visas or on permanent residency track, they are very willing to do whatever they are asked to do, for comparatively little money and even on occasion fixed term rather than permanent positions. This damages their prospects as academics because they have little chance of developing the research careers they need for promotion. At the same time, however, it makes the job of managing the teaching workforce easier. The Professors who manage are increasingly (and they were to an extent always) a very separate elite.

There is therefore the real risk of what can perhaps most pithily be described as a quasi-colonialistic indentured servitude. This is similar indeed to the circumstances experiencecd by Leo Kuzmicki, the Polish engineering genius who was paid a salary by Norton in the 1950s that was in no way relative to his engineering knowledge or experience, because they knew he couldn't go anywhere else until he had his permanent residency; as soon as he got it, he left and joined the Roots Group. It is indentured, of course, because the employee is indebted to the employer who has sponsored her work visa. Only once the terms of the visa are met (usually by a time period) is the employee 'released' from the bonds that allow her exploitation. She does all she is told to and dare not raise her voice for fear of being punished by dismissal. She is, to use the political phrase, 'whipped' into line, and remains there by force of circumstance. People deserve far better.

It also affects the culture of the organisation as well as, perhaps more importantly, risking inevitably a poorer service to students – despite or indeed because of the fact that they are able to speak with the lecturer in their own language. While this may improve their comprehension of the material in an immediate sense, it renders them less employable, again because their English language ability is not being developed. Universities are between a rock and a hard place here. They know the problem of English language ability, but must maintain comprehension levels as far as they can to ensure good student ratings, which impact on their own rankings. The next suggestion might be that it is incumbent on the student to find part-time work and/or the university to find work placements for students. International students do find part time work where there are opportunities, and these opportunities exist mostly within their own culture, for example Chinese restaurants. They don't improve their English language ability in that setting.

Besides, it is extremely difficult for a university to ask industry to take on a student if their English language is not sufficiently fluent for them to be able to interact, thrive and thus make a meaningful contribution to the business. Why should they? They are not a charity after all, and charities themselves are even more up against it, often having no slack whatsoever to devote to supporting a student as they learn their role. Very few students can 'hit the ground running', nor should they be expected to for they are not being employed. Many small businesses, I am sorry to say in my experience, tend to exploit work experience students as a source of free labour and put them under tremendous pressure all in the expedient name of 'understanding the real world'.

This has been my experience as an academic for 20 years, an experience that has only become more pointed and more poignant as the years have gone on, as the reliance on business schools for cross-subsidisation, and within business schools on international full-fee paying students, has increased. To whom should we turn to solve these systemic problems? Universities are unable to do much about it, because they are trying to survive and make the most of a dwindling public funding stream. All English-speaking universities are to a greater or lesser extent grappling with these funding challenges. The quick answer is to bridge the gap year-on-year with more and more full-fee paying international students, and attempt to lure funding from industry both for research and for teaching. With thought, long term philanthropy is possible.

Business schools are increasingly doing this by creating the impression that as a field of inquiry business is more like engineering, i.e. a science rather than a liberal art. This is nonsense, but it is a convenient nonsense. Business management is a fine art because at the end of the day it is about people not things. However, if one can draw an allusion with engineering it allows one to argue for more funding. It also forces upon the staff the argument that only the perspective of science and the carrying out of science-type research, the sort of research that is easily and often quickly done and is more straightforwardly published, is legitimate. This too is nonsense; it is force-fitting. I am known in academe as an applied process philosopher, and have been fortunate to learn from the American Philosopher and Theologian John B. Cobb, Jr. Taking my cue from him, I try to be someone who *carefully* uses the work of (mostly) the Cambridge Mathematician and Harvard Philosopher Alfred North Whitehead's process metaphysics to understand the genuinely and unremittingly changeful nature of all things, to understand topics in (e.g.) management. He once said (1941: 700), purposefully in two paragraphs,

> My point is that the final outlook of Philosophic thought cannot be based upon the exact statements that form the basis of the special sciences.
>
> The exactness is a fake.

When professional academics find something that is inherently interesting to them, that alone makes it worthy of study in the way they want to study it, not necessarily in a force-fitted way. More generally still, not only are business schools increasingly trying to be like their science counterparts, in no small part because they feel it gives them more credibility with their colleagues elsewhere in the university but, at the very same time, universities are creating their structures to look and even sound like businesses. This is on the premise that this will give them greater credibility, i.e. that businesses can only recognise as valid those structures and organisational titles that are the same as their own. This does business a disservice; in my experience, business leaders are far more intelligent than that!

VI. Managing Excellent, Highly Committed People in Difficult Times

My experience has been of operating on the edge of the university sector, for business schools are very much on the edge of universities. They are often viewed from within the university with barely disguised disdain for being insufficiently scholarly, very 'vanilla' is the in-vogue term, with little intellectual depth or research rigor. Whether this is true or not in each case, or in many cases, it is a general reputation that takes much hard work within the university from a Head of School to overcome. And even then, where a reputation is improved, it comes with the caveat 'well under him/her, it was better, but ...' In fact, business schools are increasingly seeking to marginalise themselves, in order to defend themselves against the heavy cross-subsidisation, by forming themselves into externally accredited associations that are separate from the universities they are a part of.

It is only unfortunate they feel the need to do this because in my experience of heading up a School of Management they are indeed special; they are made up of incredibly passionate people who devote far more than 37.5 hours a week to the task of teaching, research and, increasingly, wider community engagement. Do they need to become more efficient, if they can't do the necessary in 37.5 hours a week? A vice chancellor once said to me that if one wanted to get ahead in academia one needed to understand it would take at least 50 hours per week. He was absolutely correct.

We went through an efficiency drive during my tenure as a Head of School, where we reduced the total number of annual unit deliveries by 80 (a unit is a 13-week discrete topic of study, often delivered on multiple occasions in the year), to address a serious work overload issue. And still there was no question that, due to the rise in student numbers, particularly international students, coupled with increasing research and industry engagement demands, it was perfectly possible to spend every day of the week working. Like most of the people I worked for in the School when I was its Head, I very frequently had to. Even although, as Rebecca wryly noted, it wasn't as if I was the on-call neurosurgeon!

Managing a group of academics whose expertise is management is one of the most intriguing jobs, because they can see straight through what you are doing and right out the other side. They are masters at analysing management decisions, so everything you do will be viewed as a case study to interpret. This has its plus points as you know when you're getting it right and when you do get it right there is absolute support – even when the decisions you make may not, by necessity, be in the best interests of certain individuals. They too can see the picture objectively. It does require a great deal of open honest communication and ensuring you tell the same thing to everyone. This builds trust. We all have a propensity to a particular management style. Mine was and is open and consensual. To use leadership jargon, I am a 'collaborative leader.' I have always operated on the principle that leadership is about enablement, supporting people to flourish. If you look after the people, the people look after everything else. If you don't look after the people, you have to look after everything else – because the people are too busy looking after themselves – and you, simply put, can't.

I tended to 'manage by walking about', solving problems for people that they themselves found intractable, to free them up to get on. On the rare occasion I couldn't solve a problem I would explain precisely why, and people would be buoyed even by the procedural justice and the knowledge you had genuinely tried to get a solution for them. Of course I was always working with intelligent, thoughtful people who had a deep maturity which quickly saw them through the natural knee-jerk response, to a considered view. Management, then, is truly about creating the circumstances for people to grow and develop as human beings. If you can do that, people will almost invariably rise to that genuine challenge (and it has to be genuine), because by and large people do want to grow and develop. It's just that, often, work ceases to be the place to do that. So if you can make work the place where that is possible, people 'turn up' so to speak.

Managerialism on the other hand is the precise opposite. It is the use of management techniques to render the objectives of management itself – and managers too – as the be all and end all of the organisation. It is about controlling, limiting and enforcing. It is often described by its practitioners as 'good management', indeed it was described as such to me once upon a time by an immediate supervisor. 'It's just good management', she said. Balderdash! Of course I didn't say that to her because I was concerned I would lose my job … Managerialism is in reality the very worst kind of managerial practice because it is not interested in people but in targets. In managerialism, people are there to be used as a commodity. They are, to use E.F. Schumacher's thinking, de-humanised ([1973] 2011, 1980). They are there only to deliver the goals of management. Managerialism is dangerous then, and doubly so because it can be made to look like excellence by those skilled in its dark art. It will be clear I abhor managerialism and I abhor managerialists!

To return to my sort of management, a former manager of mine used the phrase 'show 'em the rabbit' to describe the approach – which was his approach too I might add and one used by many of the best academic leaders I have been fortunate enough to encounter. Having shown 'em the rabbit, all you have to do then is figure out why some people won't chase the rabbit, and usually there is a good reason. It's rarely laziness. You just have to figure out the rabbit they will chase and present it to them. This leaves only a very small number of folk who will not chase anything, and then you can deal with them as appropriate, frankly. The next thing then is to show people how to find their own rabbits to chase, within the bounds of what is possible (and most is), which leaves you with the best problem of all: people presenting you with all the wonderful things they've done and wanting more.

However, the one thing this does all require is a senior management team above you, and systems and processes, an 'atmosphere' that is in tune with this approach. This is because you are not working for senior management per se, you're working for your people; my approach to leadership is the same as my father's. An approach that is supportive of people will always work *so long as* the organisational systems are also seen by the people to support them. If they are seen to be there to critique and, worse, punish people, then very quickly a leader will lose all credibility. Not respect, because the respect for the person and their vision will remain. But what the person says will increasingly be seen as being flatly contradicted by the organisation's 'atmosphere'. Since the person is not working for their immediate line manager but for their people, they can then quickly become isolated.

This is especially if there is, or there develops, a 'them–us' culture where senior management see the leader in question, who we shall call Jane for the purpose, as part of 'them'. Obviously 'they' are not to be trusted (even if those more senior folk would not go quite as far as to say 'they' are to be in some way despised …). In any case, there is a change of thinking and a change of mindset. Jane can be saying and doing the same thing they were saying and doing a month ago but the response that was positive becomes negative, to her puzzlement.

The power of an organisation's growth-with-efficiency imperative will change the culture from 'small and personal' to 'large and impersonal', despite Jane's best efforts to retain the good of the small and to continue to support people *as individuals*. What once worked, however, works no more; Jane's way of managing is no longer seen as credible, even by the people she manages themselves, because it is no longer seen to be true for the organisation's approach to them. At this point, Jane becomes irrelevant. This is painful to be a witness of.

In universities, at least, the 'managing for' approach also requires a budget. Without a budget, the irrelevance is doubled. You know a leader by their followers. If a designated leader has no followers, s/he isn't a leader in the eyes of the people s/he is responsible for. It is often the case in universities, which are invariably running very tight if not impossibly tight budgets, that what works on the ground is money, plain and simple. And people know this. In other words, they will go to the person with the purse-strings. Because that is what works, what they have learnt works. Their view is: what happens is solely in the gift of the person with the money. And let's face it, are they wrong? Organisations use money to incentivise because it is the easiest way to incentivise. That does not make it the best way.

Another colleague of mine responsible for delivering a workplace change project was criticised by his line manager for using a consensus building approach, on the grounds that 'these academics just need to do what they're told'. The person who expressed that view is a remarkably successful academic administrative manager, but this represents a complete failure to understand management. If all you have in your toolbox is managerialistic orders, you have nothing. You cannot tell an academic what to do, for management by decree does not work. Not really. People will revert to a grudging behaviour that is the bare minimum, a contractual relationship. More interestingly still, they switch off in a very clever way – they are very clever people – that makes them look to their managers *as if* they are engaged. It is an active, passive resistance. They are telling that manager to Eff Off, but many managers (even if they recognise what is going on) don't care one way or the other because, when this happens, it's easy to set managerialist targets that make them look good to their own bosses. As in many organisations, the gatekeepers hold the real power in the universities, far more so than the executive cadre, because they determine what the executives know. That's not developing people, it's delivering minima. People are better than this, even if robots may not be. They certainly deserve better.

VII. Coping with Some of the Unwarranted Effects of Radical Change Processes

Structures evolve over years to be the best fit as the averaged-out understanding of how things are. Just as the meaning of words is the averaged-out understanding of that word (the mathematical mean-ing), so the meaning of structure is the averaged-out understanding of what works, as it is understood to be by the people. By further extension then, it doesn't matter what the vision or the policy is, or how senior management understand it, new structures and processes will only be enabled and put into action (or not) if the staff view it as relevant – and then only *in the way* that the staff understand it. For certain, it won't happen in the way the leadership understand it, regardless of however much middle managers might tell senior managers it is happening the way their bosses want it. And they will tell them all is well; it is a very brave middle manager who will tell his or her boss that it isn't working. Yet however excellent the vision is, if it doesn't work in the minds of the people then it won't work on the ground.

From all this, it becomes clear that good leaders make themselves redundant by creating positive circumstances in which people learn how to manage and lead themselves. Great leaders, on the other hand become irreplaceable by effecting systemic change that transcends their tenure; their positive influence remains 'in the very bricks' of the organisation long after they have left. Of course it follows that the worst leader's influence can also remain but it is a negative, not a positive. Senior managers often live in their own world, although the best of course do not. One problem is that a senior management narrative can be both alluring and self-deceiving. You then have to make a judgement call as to whether you are prepared to go with that narrative. This is a moral question: One may know what is expected and one may even know how to do it, but one may choose not to because it flatly contradicts one's own values, attitudes and beliefs. There are of course consequences for one's own career in this, but one must be able to sleep at night.

A colleague of mine once described an individual in a very senior leadership position at a university where we both worked some years ago as 'very, very good at being *thoroughly incompetent*'. These people become not irreplaceable but irremovable! Whatever the career implications, I would far rather be seen as 'very very bad at being *thoroughly competent.*' It takes an astute line manager to recognise the latter is infinitely better than the former, for they have to do the difficult thing which is to see through the immediately apparent and recognise the actual effect. And to recognise, too, that the latter is quite different from – and better again – than merely being 'a safe pair of hands'.

Formal systems of performance management have a tendency to make people feel bullied. Sometimes this is intentional, but I have found usually it isn't intentional. There is no room for bullying in the workplace although, having felt badly bullied on a number of occasions from both above and below, as well as having tried to deal with it on behalf of others, I understand there is a difference between intention and impact. Asking someone to change their behaviour rarely works and, on the other side of the equation, anyone who says you can just stop feeling bullied has never been bullied. Feeling bullied from below is very, very difficult to defend oneself against, much less stop as a manager. For the person who feels bullied can easily find themselves being accused of making the other person feel bullied through their attempts at self-defence, and as a manager one can end up on the receiving end of it as well! It takes very remarkably astute HR specialists to see all that and act positively (it's all too easy to act negatively), and thus in ways that limit the often unwitting harm caused to all the parties concerned.

In addition, performance management systems can stop people doing things; they become focused on meeting the metrics to save their jobs. This is not in my experience the purpose of performance management, but it seems to be almost invariably the unintended – if entirely foreseeable – consequence. Perhaps the very last group of people one should fit into metrics are people being employed for their self-starting creativity. That said, establishing 'narrow corridors of knowing' enables power to be built through the performance measurement systems by those in the organisation's 'leadership' cadre, and maintenance of a general 'ignorance' more widely. Knowledge truly creates power in universities.

VIII. Is There Another Way of Living on the Edge?

I do sense that most of the academic problems I have spoken of are perhaps a unique feature of English-speaking countries, and I have gone out of my way to emphasise this. English speaking countries by and large have electorates who mostly only see higher education as a private benefit. Any prospective government therein of any colour, blue, green, red or yellow, would not dare to go to the country with a manifesto that fully funded universities would lose.

United States universities are not as cash-strapped, by and large (although there are exceptions) simply because there is a culture of philanthropic giving by former students back to their universities that does not exist anywhere else to anything like the same degree.

Harvard University's history library has an annual endowment larger than the entire libraries' budgets in any of the universities I have worked at. There is an American university, at Claremont in California, I have been fortunate enough to have just quietly had a career-long connection with, in which one of the colleges has an annual endowment, i.e. money given by former students and other benefactors that is then invested, that amounts to one million dollars per student. I am given to understand that it is the wealthiest higher education institution per capita in the US, and being there on that campus gives one a completely different sense of what higher education can be. For the rest of us, it is but a pipe dream. To borrow the American model on the grounds that a private approach works is to miss this crucial philanthropic difference. In non-English speaking countries by contrast, where language learning is a must, the innate value of higher education to society seems to just be part of the culture. It is almost unthinkable in Scandinavia and Continental Europe for higher education not to be funded as a public good. As a colleague of mine from that part of the world remarked to me, it would be 'stupid' to do anything less.

The effect of not funding higher education as a public good is what I have witnessed and here described. Namely universities being forced by necessity to behave as if, if not indeed to become, quite ruthless businesses. Where money ends up dominating almost all decision making. Words and phrases can be created – and academics are excellent at creating all sorts of words and phrases – to effect the impression that money is not driving decisions, but it does. Where contribution margin is delivered *through* teaching, the teaching of students is by necessity secondary to the making of money. For 'contribution margin' of course read 'profit margin'. When I was starting out as an academic 30% or 40% was sufficient from the business school, and we academics working in it were emphatically not happy about that. Little did we know what was to come!

Today there are not many businesses, or even departments in businesses, making 50% and upwards of 60% or 70% profit these days, unless perhaps they are banks. Or business schools so it seems. Rest assured, these can easily be eight figure yearly amounts; they often have to be. That these sorts of figures are even possible is a tremendous signal of the incredible people that work tirelessly in university business schools (and other schools as well; again,

I am not suggesting it is just business schools but it is not unusually business schools). It is their dedication that stops them imploding under the weight of (increasingly unrealistic) expectation. I am sure any chief executive of any half billion-pound turnover organisation, which is what some universities are *and more*, would give their right arm for that sort of return from one of their departments. Nonetheless, the crucial question remains: how does one make the rest of a university sufficiently self-sufficient that it does not need 'cash cows' such as business schools? As things stand, it is not a 'sustainable business model' to be so 'point-dependent' for one's 'profit margins' as many universities are.

IX. Conclusions – of Sorts

So, how to conclude? My MS has forced a medical retirement and this is a good thing, and I should add that I am very fortunate. Like my father, it will be clear I have always been focused on enabling others. In my father's case, it was enabling wholesalers, for example, to build their businesses through their sales of NGK. Enabling others was central to his sales policy; in many ways his approach to developing his wholesalers' abilities to sell NGK with the confidence of technical product knowledge was similar to my approach to developing my cadre of PhD students. His reward came as a result of that enablement. My reward came from seeing people freed up to grow their careers as they wished, and this inevitably benefited the university. Like my maternal Grandfather Cyril Smith, my sense of loyalty to people was such that it engendered much affection (so I'm told), but I was easily taken advantage of.

All my academic life has, on reflection, been spent eluding the rising tide of managerialist corporatisation – what E.F. Schumacher forecast more generally of course – that has flooded the very special, supportive family culture out of academia and made universities lamentably little more than knowledge factories. Like my grandfather Cyril Smith too, then, I became quite disillusioned at what I saw and experienced, things that many would simply dismiss and even expect – 'that's academe'. The difference in my case was that my faith was restored to a very large extent by the people I worked with at the very top of the University of Tasmania in particular, who were without exception outstandingly *human* human beings; as long as you worked hard and did your best for the university, I found the loyalty and care was reciprocated.

But, you know, I sense most parents would conclude that getting their children into significant debt to achieve the sort of profit provided by business schools has a somewhat questionable moral standing. As Schumacher observed ([1973] 2011: 65), 'When people ask for education they normally mean something more than mere training, something more than mere knowledge of facts, and something more than mere diversion.' After twenty years in universities, I fear that part of the universities I was most closely involved with now rather actively shy away (with notable exceptions) from equipping people with the means to appreciate their own values, 'the clarification ... of our fundamental convictions' ([1973] 2011: 72). Unfortunately, the result it that on-the-job training, facts and focus are just precisely what is meant by 'employability.' Well, is that it?

In any event, what does become clear in applying E.F. Schumacher's principles to the question of universities, is that any attempt to keep small-scale values and ways of being is increasingly being overwhelmed by the pressure to corporatise for the sake of the economic wealth of the institutions themselves. Which is to say the 'good work' done in universities by academics focused on the needs of the students is being largely undone by 'the idolatory of giantism' (Schumacher, [1973] 2011: 49–50). That is, the ever-alluring temptation to reduce the number and increase size of 'business units' or 'departments' for the purpose of achieving economies of scale, at great cost to the human and societal values that underpin the purpose and practice of education. This is not to criticise anyone, *far from it*. I hope to have shown very few are in a position to correct what I observe has happened. I also hope that revealing the realities may bring more people to the discussion who may have new answers.

In short, the foregoing discussion has, we hope, alluded to the plain reality it is very difficult to create an environment that is conducive to the sort of meaning, satisfaction or indeed creative justification – the ability to grow and develop as human beings – that promotes human wellbeing (Schumacher, 1980), in the work contexts we witness in many universities today. As Schumacher noted, 'an entirely new system of thought is needed, a system based on attention to people, and not primarily attention to goods' ([1973] 2011: 57). This discussion has unfortunately revealed that the system that focused its attention on people was replaced by one whose primary attention was goods. We had it in universities, but we have lost it! Turning universities into businesses is a neat trick but it has to work. Just because there is a growing demand from international students to be educated in English speaking countries does not make it right that the universities therein should teach them. That is to say, the 'business-ification' of universities as money earners first and foremost (and there is absolutely no denying this is what has happened) seems to be doing more harm than good. It seems to me, through the lens of E.F. Schumacher, new answers to the questions here posed are desperately needed. Desperately needed. This is so for the sake of the students for certain, but also for the sake of the staff who invariably give their all for their students (see also Schumacher, 1980: 112–26).

I think, though, that the best place to end up is perhaps by making a return to the beginning. Of course I never knew my maternal Grandfather, but I was very fortunate that my Grandmother Irene married such a kind and caring man in Ron Barrett. He adopted me with all the love of his own and we were very close. It took me a long time to realise why it was my Grandmother would suffer from repeated nightmares and scream aloud 'No! Cyril! *Cyril – No!*' She would then hold her breath in her sleep until Ron managed to shake her awake. Such is pain on the one hand and understanding on the other. As I too have found, sometimes love is not enough. A colleague advised me only relatively recently, 'the serious decision before you now is the most important decision. Only then is there the next one. And so on.' How very true.

As part of the support for the MS I have been seeing a psychologist. People who say you can fight even secondary depression have never been depressed. Like chronic pain I find you almost have to 'go with it' to find a way through it, although with chronic pain it's more like 'leaning into it'. The week before I first saw him I had been speaking with a colleague at university, who said of themselves 'Of course I focus in on the detail because I'm Asperger's.' I thought to myself that was interesting and researched it. I took a test, and it was like a door opening. If the answer wasn't 'yes' it was 'no, but I know what you mean'. An 80% chance of being Asperger's.

Psychologists are excellent at helping us through complex issues: 'Having spent time with you now over the past few weeks, that result you got doesn't surprise me. But they didn't know it existed when you were a boy and anyway they don't call it Asperger's anymore. Besides which, defining you as an adult doesn't matter. It's all good, it's *all* good. So let's rather explore what it means for you now, to better understand who you are. You cannot change that, so we need to make the very most of *being* you.' What was meant to be a support for MS turned out to be support for that extra, let us say at least 'aspergic-like', part of my character as well. Many things that were unclear have become clear only in the past year. Why it is, for example, people often describe me as 'intense' (this chapter has been, in its own way I'm sure, *intense*), or why I see the world conceptually. It is very good to understand how one's successes (as well as one's failures) come about through one's character.

For one thing, the feelings of fear fell into place. As the psychologist said, it's all good. It's *all* to the good. *Keep at it.*

Mark considers the American Philosopher and Theologian Dr John B. Cobb Jr to be his 'academic father'. Source: https://upload.wikimedia.org/wikipedia/commons/5/5e/John_B._Cobb%2C_Jr.jpg

15

CONCLUSIONS: CONFESSIONS OF THINGS BELIEVED

The authors discussing the Model F prototype Norton racer at the Sammy Miller Museum, June 2015

1. First Reflections

Boarding school education was academically excellent, but was devoid of the ability to cater for the emotional needs of a fatherless boy and was too elitist. The single sex aspects of it left me totally unable to cope with girls. Apart from the few weeks in a year that I was in the company of my dear departed sister, I never spoke to one until I was nearly 15 years of age!

Service in the Royal Navy served me well and, looking back, I'm sure that my rejection by the RAF having volunteered was fortunate. In fact, at a race meeting a few years ago now, my old friend George Cohen introduced me to Miles McCallum the technical editor of a flight magazine. During a lengthy conversation, I told him about my teenage desire to fly Spitfires. A few days later, I had a phone call inviting me down to a nearby airfield. On arrival, an S2B Pitts Special was flying above performing some fantastic manoeuvres. When it landed, the pilot invited me for a flight. Well, I've never been one to say 'No'. It was quite an experience with banks, loops, stall turns and a few stomach-turning escapades. I wasn't sick, but I believe those involved in the invitation thought I would be. Having said that, it certainly made me wonder if I would have coped in a Spitfire, chasing German fighters and bombers during the war. My thanks to Miles and Paul Ambrose the superb pilot.

The Navy opened my eyes to the big wide world away from the parochial village life, and taught me much about personal endurance limits both physical and mental. The imposed discipline reinforced the already strong self-discipline learnt at school. There is no doubt, that without the nearly four years I served during World War Two, my life would have been entirely different. I remember when in Algiers, food got a bit short and we lived on dried egg and gherkins for a while. Clearly, fussy eaters have never been hungry!

Trumpet playing helped cure my considerable speech stutter, which was serious enough to make it difficult to even ask the bus conductor for a ticket to a destination, and was doubtless a residue of school days. By the time I was released from the Navy, the stutter had gone. My musical prowess earned me much needed cash, and had I received positive support from those around me at the time, coupled with proper extended tuition, should have been my vocation. Having said that, I am in no way critical of those people. They had no experience or interest in matters musical. Trumpet playing ceased for many reasons, among them, the lack of practice necessary during my racing career to maintain the required competency, coupled with the unsociable hours as a married man.

That is the one regret I'm sad about which is part of others. I wish I'd kept on with my trumpet playing. So, why did I stop? The dance music was all that I played because that's what earned me a few pounds. In playing to and watching lovers together, I found too much emotional trauma at a time in my life of so much disloyalty and hurt. On the odd occasion I even found a tear in my eye while playing. Many happy playing memories were outweighed by the sad emotional ones. Playing for dances, as on 1964 New Year's Eve, was hardly conducive to a contented partner either, and that was the last time that I played in any serious way, ever.

The concentration level necessary to play a musical instrument was no doubt instrumental in my success at motorcycling. Believe me, racing in World Championship events at the levels we attained demands extreme degrees of concentration, fitness, an acute sense of timing and above all, self-discipline. Never, before joining Eric Oliver, had I needed to match such positive focus, incredible determination and courage. The same was true too, of course, with Cyril Smith. I learnt much about myself. Reading biographies of recent and current racing stars, much of the poorly paid fun seems to have disappeared from their highly paid and sponsored ranks.

The years spent selling on a commission only basis were more rewarding than any employment. I very quickly discovered that loyalty to product and customer was the key to regular repeat business. Only twice in all the years that I was on the road did I engage in entertaining, once by taking a customer out to lunch, and once giving bottles of drink at Christmas. This form of bribery, so often the norm, leads to resentment when things go wrong. Too many top buyers of large organisations expect to be lavishly entertained out of a company expense account, and often will not do business without the 'bribe.' 'Hard luck to them' I say. Tax deductable entertainment in business is often nothing more than bribery and self-promotion at the company's expense; the bribers are just as guilty as the bribed, perhaps more so. Laws are in place to exercise some control over monopolies, perhaps similar steps should be taken to discipline the buying and selling activities of the supermarket 'quadopolies.' They have destroyed so many small businesses and their owners, and seriously diminished service and availability in rural areas and small towns. Convenience shopping?

We can only do our best with the cards life deals us. Rarely did I talk of my World Championship achievement or my involvement with the Donald Campbell land speed record. Too often, existing customers as well as prospective new ones would have seen this as 'bullshit', especially in the car parts trade. The bike trade of course was slightly different, but most of my customers were car parts people. In business it is better to be known and respected for what you're doing now, rather than run the risk of being seen as living on past 'glories'. I never did.

Thinking of the cards we are dealt, and the motor trade, leads me on to a bugbear of mine – cambelts. Many people buy second hand cars privately or from dealers who have not had the cambelts changed on their cars. It seems to be something that is forgotten; the cars are sold by their first owner just before they need doing, for example, and they aren't then renewed before being sold on to an unsuspecting new owner. He or she is then dealt a hand that will expire on them sooner or later. And when it does, assuming the engine (and the car) is not a write off, it will cost what amounts to a small fortune for most people, to have repaired. But it isn't the engine damage that frightens me most. It's the thought of the extreme case of a car travelling at motorway speeds suffering such a failure, the engine seizing, the wheels locking up, the car being out of control … imagine it happening in the fast lane during the rush hour. You most certainly would be on the edge of your seat, having to hold on very tight indeed! It would not be an experience one would be likely ever to forget.

Of course, it is experience that makes each and every one of us what we are. I have in my possession a Dr Johnson's Dictionary dated 1836, which is a reprint of his 1773 edition. He says, 'conceive as much as you can of the essentials of any subject before you consider its accidentals.' Perhaps he had been involved in a few horse-drawn carriage incidents and ensuing arguments over blame, and disagreed with those who called the incident an accident! In other words, before classifying a collision as an accident, the incident should be considered as well as its accidentals.

With this in mind, it could be argued that there really are very few true accidents on our roads; lots of collisions, yes, but are they really accidents? Collisions caused by bad driving, lack of experience, icy roads, aquaplaning, selfishness, lack of adequate concentration etc. These are not necessarily accidents. The word suggests an element of bad luck which unfortunately does nothing to encourage self-criticism, essential if one is to improve one's standard of driving – and that can always be improved with careful contemplation as opposed to careless complacency. Perhaps this is a reflection of modern society? Speed is rarely the major factor in collisions. Not understanding, or not driving according to the conditions obtaining is far more often the culprit; there isn't a car driver on the road who wouldn't be a better one with a couple of years riding a motorcycle.

2. Highlights of Later Years

I was invited to Buckingham Palace for the tea party celebrating '40 Glorious Years of Sport' during the reign of Her Majesty the Queen. It was fascinating to mingle shoulder to shoulder with the likes of Henry Cooper the boxer. I said a passing 'Hullo' and from the slight look of puzzlement in his eyes, I'm sure he went away wondering who that Lightweight boxer was that had just greeted him! I was invited to Buckingham Palace a second time as a member of the British Legion, in support of The Not Forgotten Association and I am always impressed by the work members of the Royal Family do in support of charities. It's always very good, and salutary, to meet people who have achieved more in life than you have yourself. This was true, too, of my visit to Malta as a part of the Malta Veterans reunion in 2005.

After many years of non-participation as a competitor, it was a joy for me to be invited in my 80s to attend one or two of the major classic events in Germany and Belgium. Attendance at the Nürburgring for their 70th Anniversary in 1997 was also a thrill. It brought back memories of wonderful successes and of a high-speed crash when leading a race there with Eric Oliver, not forgetting the win with Cyril Smith in May 1955 that was a real highlight of my racing career. In July 2003, I was delighted to be invited to the centenary celebrations at the Solitude race circuit near Stuttgart, and even more pleased to be presented with a special memorial plaque and commemorative specially bound book; a real treasure. Eric and I had a winning ride in 1953 and I also enjoyed podium finishes there with Cyril in 1954/55 if memory serves me well. My rides on the 500 cc Manx Norton were remembered by the organisers too, so I can't have done too badly on the solo there either I suppose.

The visit to Spa in 2005 was, to say the least, eventful. I was invited to ride with German and European Sidecar Champion driver Ralph Bonhorst for two race speed laps on a modern machine. There was not so much athleticism required, but very different acceleration and cornering g-forces. A thrill too to experience again the rush through Eau Rouge corner, although about 50% wider than in the 1950s. And how nice it was to be driven to that event by Eric Oliver's son Roger. In 1953, he was hoisted up onto my shoulders on the winner's rostrum. I visited there again with Mark some years later and we went around the old circuit, now no longer used. That brought back some fantastic memories, particularly of 1953 and 1955, and allowed him to get some sort of a feel for what it was like. He was amazed at the negative G you get going over the top of Eau Rouge even at sixty mph in a car. I'm very biased I admit but, having ridden both the old and the new circuits, I know which I prefer!

2007 found me at the Schottenring riding with Ralph Bonhorst again, this time on a beautifully prepared BMW with the, unfamiliar to me, right hand sidecar. A total of about 20 quick laps was a surprise for the 20,000 spectators. Their ovation even more of a surprise when I was re-introduced to the great Willi Noll, the 1954 and 1956 Sidecar World Champion who I had not seen for about 50 years. Thanks to the interviewer, my then 82 years of age was no longer a secret. I'm indebted to Ralph for his confidence in me. One lap at Donnington Park with World Champion Tim Reeves at the Ride for Health charity event at the Grand Prix weekend one year was really exciting. Shame it was only one lap on that 200 mph sidecar. I think those in charge were frightened I would have a heart attack. No chance! But it would have been embarrassing for them at a Ride for Health event.

I have always had a close connection with Australia as a result of the Bluebird Land Speed Record project and my friendship with Andrew Mustard, who had made his home in Townsville in the 1970s. I was introduced to the Townsville Motorcycle Restoration Club on one visit there and was dumfounded to be voted a Life Patron. The result is I have been entertained royally every time I have been there, and ridden pillion for many kilometres with their president Hedley Cooke on club runs. Of course spending time with Andrew again was very special, working on his outboard engines and witnessing his superb engineering abilities in his workshop, that had everything you could possibly need. I had forgotten until I saw him do it, that he always preferred to temper his own tools. It was great, too, to stay with Ian and Richenda Goldfinch, other Lake Eyre compatriots, on their incredible farm in Western Australia.

I enjoy writing and so I was honoured to have been named by the Association of Pioneer Motorcyclist their 'Writer of the Year' for a poem I wrote in 2009 entitled 'Passengers. Who Are They?' (see Appendix 3). It was inspired by reading a book by James Finn Garner, entitled *Politically Correct Bedtime Stories*, and so the poem was a politically correct description of the activity of sidecar riders. And of course to have a short film made about me by Cabel Hopkins that was picked up by the New York Times and National Geographic, entitled *No Ordinary Passenger* in 2013 was a bit special. Thanks to Cabel's work, and also Andrew Capone's support, it won a number of film festivals as I understand it. Andrew very recently retired from being Senior Vice President of Marketing and Business Development at NCC Media, the leading TV, Digital and Political Advertising Company in the United States. His hard work in 2016 resulted, too, in the tremendous honour of having an annual award in my name, the 'Stan Dibben No Ordinary Passenger Award.' It is given to the sidecar rider who has done the most for sidecar racing in American Historic Motorcycle Racing Association (AHMRA) events.

Perhaps the greatest enjoyment I have had recently has been my regular visits to the Isle of Man, for which I have Helen Gibson primarily to thank, and also Frances Thorpe and all the other wonderful people at the TT Riders Association (TTRA). Alongside Helen's tremendous and self-less hospitality putting me up at her home in Castletown, I seem to have made the 38th Milestone, the TTRA cabin at the back of the pits, a second living room during TT and Manx GP fortnights. An honour in itself.

3. Final Thoughts

I've been lucky, rarely bored really, even more rarely under the 'affluence of incahol'. My son Mark encouraged me to stop smoking some 30 years ago. We were on the ferry to Le Harvre when he challenged me, saying 'you couldn't stop if you wanted to, Dad'. At his request, I had not had a cigarette for two hours while driving to the ferry in a new car. My immediate reaction was to throw my cigarettes and lighter overboard! It was a challenge that worked, and I never smoked again. I am certainly better off without the nicotine. To stop was not easy, made more difficult by friends who smoked insisting that I hadn't stopped. 'Go on, have a fag for God's sake!'

State aid seems often to be given to the unhealthy, but little assistance seems to be available to help those who work at keeping fit. That said, the National Health Service has done me proud. Two hernia operations resulting from sidecar racing were entirely successful. An operation, a sub-mucous resection, to sort out a nose problem, resulting from a sidecar incident in the Isle of Man TT, proved equally effective. I remember this was done under a local anaesthetic. It sounded a bit like a pneumatic drill and I was staggered at the length of the two 12-inch-long cotton wool dressings when they were extracted from deep inside the nasal passages. In later years, the need for a prostate operation proved interesting when carried out, by personal choice, in an epidural-induced somnambulant state. Retaining the ability to watch the intrusion into one's appendage on a television screen, is not for the faint-hearted. Nor is listening to the commentary between a surgeon and his obviously first-time apprentice inserting a pace maker and attempting to connect the wires to my heart a couple of years ago! I managed to calm my own mid-surgery trepidations by asking the nurse where the electrician was. Again, like the gall bladder op I've also had, it was ultimately satisfactory in the end.

Now that advancing years have caught up with my eyesight, the NHS is doing me proud yet again – although I can no longer drive. This is a frustration, but thankfully I have a chauffeur in Mark. At least that's what he insists on calling himself! I have had over 50 injections in my left eye, and 8 in my right eye, to slow down age related macular degeneration. There is nothing so frustrating as not being able to see. Except not being able to hear! 'I'm so sorry, I missed that … Pardon? I'm having terrible trouble hearing you.' It's embarrassing, particularly when people are so unfailingly kind. I have also had two lots of radiotherapy to keep oesophageal cancer under control; without wanting to tempt fate, so far so good.

My lovely little old maternal grandmother said to me, 'Behave young man, if the Lord doesn't come he'll send.' In order to be financially responsible both at home and in business, it is necessary to be totally ruthless in differentiating between want and need. Advertising pundits wouldn't approve, neither would the supermarket shelf fillers like it, who continually move products around the store tempting the impulse buyers. Neither of course would anyone interested in growing the national spend.

In order to lead one must have learnt to be led, to have learnt the concept of discipline in order to accept its imposition. Having learnt and understood the concept, the imposition of self-discipline becomes automatic. Self-discipline doesn't have to destroy spontaneity. This is what learning to accept without rancour disciplines imposed by those in authority is all about. It's about learning to impose self-discipline. Some form of national service would benefit the majority, not necessarily learning to shoot guns, but learning one's physical and mental limits so necessary to lead a happy and fulfilled life, rather than a mere existence.

The major problem with advanced years is categorisation by age group, society's perception of infirmity and mental decline, assumed to be an unquestionable reality. Insurance companies are the major culprits in this area it seems, some doctors too along with others in the medical businesses, where perception of the age-related problems are expedient reasons for not only high motor insurance premiums and a refusal to insure for overseas travel, but also sometimes a refusal to perform surgeries. Insurance companies seem to look for minimal risk rather than acceptable risk, which sometimes creates injustice. Categorisation is the curse of the aged, in that it presumes everyone within an age group suffers, without exception, the same disabilities and infirmities as everyone else in that group. Human rights and compensation laws are gold mines ruthlessly 'dug' by the legal profession.

Shopping around for the best price does little for the majority of the population, most of whom either (like me) abhor bargaining, lack the ability to barter, or both. It was much better for them, the majority, when manufacturers' recommended resale prices were the norm. This allowed manufacturers to fight each other over price and quality, and retailers did the bargaining with their wholesalers over service and availability. End user buyers by and large don't like shopping around. The supermarkets would never have grown into the 'quadopolies', with all the monopolistic implications, if manufacturers' resale price maintenance had not been made illegal. I rather think society is much happier when people are able to shop in the local community, safe in the knowledge they know what the price is. They feel deceived to find it cheaper down the road. We are much happier as a society when we are connected to the businesses and thus, through them, the people around us.

The privatisation of the public utilities like gas, water and electricity seems to me to have resulted in uncontrollable pricing since their chief function as a business is not customer service but to give their owners, the shareholders, the maximum possible returns on their investments. When they were nationalised industries their inefficiency, due to the profligate spending of tax payers' money fought for by greedy unions and poor management, resulted in the privatisation. Now, as privatised industries, greedy capitalism and its demands on public money, warrants re-nationalisation. Too many don't appreciate the difference between honest enterprise and ingenious deceit, and see this deceit as clever business. People should be rewarded for loyalty not expediency.

I don't like unions but I loathe and detest the bad employers that make them necessary. I know, from personal experience the need for unions of course, having been told by Renold that I was living in a house above my station in life, and I should accept the move asked of me and live in the area like the rest of the factory staff. And to be told too when asking for a pay rise at Nortons (as a current World Champion no less), 'what do you need a rise for, you're not even married!' Unions serve a useful purpose in industry. Single trade unions are an asset, but multi trades unions are a liability it seems to me; they seem to be primarily political parties.

I was always impressed by Ralph Waldo Emmerson's 1841 'Self Reliance' essay. There is insanity in inexperienced reckless bravery, total fear in complete cowardice. Never walk in the fear of being fearful. Never walk in the shadow of past disappointments or experiences over which you or your family had no control. This shadow will shut out the sunlight of happiness. Love is not that which alters when alterations loom. How important it is to give encouragement to the young, teaching them to think and not rush into things;

'Hold on a minute, let's think about it' is, you may have guessed by now, a favourite saying of mine. How important, too, to give and receive similar levels of encouragement to each other in sexual relationships. The same is true of interests shared. Not forgetting, finally, the benefit of helping work mates and friends of every age.

For there is no caring in total indifference. There is no idleness in genuine effort. There is no subservience in a genuine 'thank you', nor dominance in genuine courtesy. There is no hypocrisy in genuine belief. You have to learn and understand the past to appreciate and accept the present. Problems then deemed worth fighting, prove their worth by fighting back, by retaliating. Who you know in life helps, but what who you know knows about you is more important. Without recognition there is no reward, without reward can there be recognition? Acceptable truths elicit comment, unacceptable ones engender silence. One would have thought it would be the other way around but it's rarely the case; a moment's reflection provides the explanation.

The one problem with democratic voting is that we mostly only seem to vote according to our own self-interest and parochial benefits, and not the community at large. Democracy suffers when idealism takes precedence over attainability. These two seem to me to be as bad as each other: First, left wing politics that encourage and actively promote the envy and jealousy of the disadvantaged, then satiate these by profligate unaffordable social benefits to gain and hold on to power regardless of the long term fiscal consequences. Second, right wing politics that promote the 'have it now' competitive markets, encouraged by ruthless business entrepreneurs unable or unwilling to differentiate between the aforementioned honest enterprise and ingenious deceit, satiated by unaffordable credit by banks and their credit cards, money suppliers and union greed, regardless of the long term fiscal consequences. I'm glad I didn't get involved in politics. It's so often full of expedient half-truths if not downright lies.

That said, I do have a rather special coffee mug that has Abraham Lincoln's fiscal policy on it, and I have tried to live by it. They're truisms but no less valid for that: 'You cannot help people permanently by doing more for them than they can do for themselves. You cannot build character and courage by taking away man's initiative and independence. You cannot strengthen the weak, [permanently] by weakening the strong. You cannot help the poor [permanently again] by destroying the rich. You cannot prosper by discouraging thrift.' And, most importantly I think: 'You cannot keep out of trouble by spending more than you earn.'

We seem as a society to have lost the ability to distinguish wants from needs.

I had a hard-working Mum who never really got over the death of her husband who died when her 3 children were very young, me of course only 15 months old. I learnt a lot about all things rural from one of my Uncles, the gamekeeper. I remember many happy hours with him in his workshop learning woodworking, sharpening saws etc, and in the woods with his birds. That connection to the countryside has never left me. So I feel able to say with some real conviction that the human race will destroy the planet unless it learns to live with everlasting true regard for it and its other creatures, with the self at the bottom of the list of priorities. Unfortunately, we now have the same 'necessary commodity' view of potatoes as we do of toilet rolls! Profit is now more important than customers and the environment. We have lost contact with food and the countryside. Wind farms financed by the tax-payer, yet run entirely by private /public companies are a good example, where profit has become that prime consideration, and much more important than megawatts or the windfarm environment. Capitalism is committing suicide, by overdoses of short termism in all things.

I haven't liked retirement. It's very difficult. The 'so what?' question … I have by and large managed to keep very active. I am fortunate to have been healthy and have enjoyed a fair degree of not-very-well-off contentment. My double bed has only one pillow. Not sure if there is a connection, but I'm told for my years the blood pressure and pulse rate are well below the norm. During the medical before the 1978 vintage races I did with Eric Oliver, the GP stood quietly with his finger on my wrist taking my pulse and then laughed, 'It's an effing clock!' I very recently got referred back to the cardiology department of my local hospital by another clinic because they didn't believe my pulse rate was 60, and convinced themselves there was something wrong with my pacemaker. There's nothing wrong with my bl-dy pacemaker, thank you very much!

Still my general good health has allowed me to enjoy great times with friends and support the great motorcycling events that enrich so many peoples' lives, particularly through the Norton Owner's Club and the TT Riders' Association. I have found it very humbling to be asked, and have been very lucky to be able to do it; it is through them that I have been able to *give something back*. This is very important to me, it has been a joy doing it, and I intend to keep doing it for a good while yet.

Throw the 'no's' away and be positive. Always say 'Yes!' Time for tea and cake.

***

I. Room for Thought

This has been a person-centred study spanning one hundred years of two families, and eight industries. As Kobrak and Schneider note in their discussion of the varieties of business history for the 21st century, 'good history not only needs rich sources but also poignant connections to contexts' (2011: 406). There can perhaps be no more poignant connection to context than to the prisoners of the First World War, or the experience of life as a prisoner of war in Changhi jail in the Second World War, or to the reasons for and impact of Cyril Smith's suicide. One of the hopes we have harboured in regards to this book is that, by presenting two entirely contrasting experiences of the Japanese, Andrew Mustard Sr's on the one hand and Stan Dibben's on the other, and by allowing Noboru Torii's own family story to be told spanning much the same period, then even in only a small way we might have at least provided room for thought as to what this means for our understanding and acceptance of those times. One of the other hopes we have is the discussion of Mark's psychological counselling and, most particularly, the detailed exploration of Cyril Smith's life and death might in some small way help to bring mental health and suicide yet farther out into the open. And so make it possible for people to discuss productively, and without a sense of shame. This is not without its importance: It's very easy for us to forget we live our lives through our minds; suicide prevention is infinitely better than cure, because cure is impossible.

The death of Stan's father Reginald from tubercular meningitis, secondary to urogenital tuberculosis, carries with it a double injustice. Not only was his widow Mabel wrongly denied a War Widow's Pension, but Reginald most likely contracted the disease from repeated exposure to bloodied bandages as a medical orderly in the Langensalza camp. That is, while volunteering to help his fellow British and no doubt other Allied PoWs and thereby putting himself, however unwittingly, in harm's way once more. The urge to do good work for his country even after he was a prisoner of war ultimately cost him his life. The determination of a government committee not to award a pension, despite clear anomalies in the medical reports that might have given pause for thought to anyone not pre-disposed to an outcome in the face of the post-war financial pressures of the day, cost Mabel and her young family decades of hardship. But for the kindness of Miss Wynn organising an intentionally unprofitable mortgage, they would have been on the streets. While the children each worked their way out of poverty in time, Mabel lived largely on the edge of subsistence; it was an existence she did not deserve, and that was through no fault of her own.

It is doubtful that Stan went to the right school, not that there was much choice in the matter given the financial strictures on the family. A Montessori school or other alternative type school founded in child-centred education would have been far better suited to his character – were it even available of course, and free of charge. For it is more likely to have found a way of meeting not just the learning needs but also the interlinked emotional needs of a fatherless child. True, his mother loved him, but she was understandably remarkably busy. All that traditional boarding school seems to have taught a bullied, lonely, overwhelmed boy was to add up three columns of old money, which admittedly got him his job at Hardings the grocers, and either to shrug his shoulders or otherwise say 'get stuffed'. Unfortunately, there were indubitably occasions in the boy's adulthood where neither response was the best reaction, even if it was satisfying at the time. Further, the stories (of both father and son) speak directly to the idea that boys who have a serious sense of responsibility can find girls intimidating, whereas by contrast those who don't can appear self-confident in their presence. Of course self-confidence is a great attraction.

Unlike Ron Barret, Stan has always seen the value of monarchy in that, in his view, except for the very few of us chosen to do so we don't serve them, they serve us. His unremitting determination in the later years of life to attend as many motorcycle events as he can get to and answer as many requests to support events as possible, in his role as a Vice-President of the Norton Owners Club (NOC) and as a World Champion sidecar rider, stems in no small part from that lesson. While 2013 was a landmark year as it coincided with the 60th anniversary of his World Championship and the NOC made it a focus of their year, he continues as far as advancing age allows to give as much service as he can in this respect. Service is a rendering too of the underpinning principles of his 'Teach, to Sell' approach to pioneering new products in the marketplace. Some of its elements can be found in Joe Pulizzi's Content Marketing Institute, in New York, first established in 2007. In 'Teach to Sell', however, the focus is emphatically on putting the needs of other people first – and it was the basis for its success.

The opposite tendency of serving one's own interests before other peoples', Stan argues from 70 years of business experience on the edge of industries, extends into management. His view is that management in corporations rarely give credit where credit is due for fear of self-denigration. Rarely is the focus on helping others rather than themselves (and Mark has witnessed it too in universities). The shining exception that proves this rule, in this particular tale, is Noboru Torii; with that in mind, we intentionally paid a good deal of careful attention to his business career. Further, Stan's rapid appreciation while at Perry Chain Company, perpetually strengthened in self-employment, that markets are often replete with 'bully buyers and weak sellers' was his own rendering, unbeknown to him, of much of Michael Porter's Five Forces analysis (1979) long before Porter thought of it.

The womens' role in the Help Committees and the connection to the Women's Institute is highly significant to the story. Without it, it is unlikely Reginald Dibben would have survived internment as a PoW and there would consequently have been no story whatsoever to tell. After all, his children were all conceived after his repatriation. There is no doubt that, just as occurred in World War Two, women were longing to do their bit for the war effort, and a philanthropic tradition already existed in society. Middle and upper-class women were used to working in voluntary capacities, and this expanded massively to meet the needs that existed, e.g. in support of not only prisoners of war but also of refugees, railway buffets on stations, and of course work in munitions factories. The Women's Institute was established in the First World War, and many of these women will have been working for more than one organisation. There was a wide variety of these organisations run solely or mainly by women during World War One.

The success of the PoW Help Committees – not to mention their support of even the prison guards in the closing stages of and immediately after the war – was undeniably a function, too, of a selfless moral code of behaviour that ensured parcels largely reached their intended recipients, a moral code that was not to be seen in World War Two. It has probably now largely disappeared even in civilian life; it is in hindsight therefore remarkable in itself, and a sign of what has perhaps been lost in society in the ensuing decades. There is no doubt that, were it not for the work of the women (and men, but mostly women) of the Help Committees, there would likely have been a very significant humanitarian disaster on the edge of World War One. The vast extent of their work is not really recognised, and sadly, has not been as explored as much as one might have thought in these World War One centenary years. In explicating the role of the Hampshire Regiment Help Committee and focusing on Mrs Barlow and Miss Bradbury as most apposite to the wider story of the book, therefore, we have sought to highlight one example as an illustration of the many others worthy of note, and of further study.

More broadly, and even beyond the example of 'Teach, to Sell', this has been the tale of a way of doing business that seems largely to have passed into history. It need not be so. Viewing the business activities of both Stan Dibben and Andrew Mustard with as dispassionate an eye as possible, however, and with some understatement, it becomes obvious that a great many of their ventures were not a resounding success. The reality of business for those trying to eke out a living on the edge of the main players is that they are almost invariably faced with tremendous opposition from those players. Or they otherwise find that their inventions and innovativeness leaves them 'swimming against the tide' of oligopolisitically oriented markets. We are left to draw the following observation, that things are not always better now, for the innovation arrow does not go in one direction. When an innovation is forgotten it is as if it never was. This is true of Fossdrive, Stanley Trailers, Andrew Mustard's Jet Unit, and of course, the Variguide castor; the best that can be hoped for is that it is re-invented again at some point later in time, but this does not always happen. We wonder how many inventions arising on the edge of industries that could have been revolutionary have been lost permanently to us, and at what cost to the end user? Not to mention, of course, at what cost to those (and their families) who quite possibly lost everything they owned, trying to get their inventions or new products off the ground? Only for a big player to – 'hey presto!' – come up with it at a time that suited them.

II. We Do Not Respond to Tables – Tables Respond to Us

On the inside front cover of one of Cyril Smith's notebooks from his time in the Eighth Army is a line 'We do not respond to Rommel, Rommel responds to us.' Montgomery refers to this approach, i.e. not having one's plans dictated to by the enemy, in his memoirs (1958/2012: 87). It also forms a key part of historical analysis of El Alamein (e.g. Hamilton, 1981, Barr 2004 and Royle 2010), and there is little doubt that the initial Battle of Alam Halfa, where the Eighth Army was not lured out of its defensive positons but instead, and contrary to previous practice, stood firm on its own ground thereby forcing the enemy to respond having *already* attacked it, exemplified this new mentality. It was a mentality that was conveyed in Montgomery's first address to his staff, described by the Chief of Staff as having an effect that 'was electric – it was terrific!' (Barr, 2004: 208). But while the line 'I do not respond to Rommel, Rommel responds to me!' would be just the sort of riposte Montgomery might have uttered in response to demoralised staff focused on the brilliance of the opposition's Commanding Officer, at the time of writing the quote itself simply eludes us.

There is no doubt such a clear repositioning of mindset would have had a very positive effect, right down to the level of individual men such as Cyril doing his job repairing tanks as the El Alamein battles wore on. It says something about Cyril, too, that he wrote it down. Further, it neatly sums up Eric Oliver's view of the opposition he was racing against and explains his ability to dictate races. No doubt Cyril was equally minded when it came to his racing also. It didn't always work on the race circuit, of course, but it is a powerful mentality to apply to any competitive scenario – so long as this is not in a conceited way.

It should by now come as no surprise that Stan's view of sales targets was very much the same, in that he simply didn't respond to targets when they were imposed on him, for example, by the post-Torii regime at NGK (UK). He never defended his sales figures to Jim Hughes and saw no need to do so; at most he might reply 'they speak for themselves', but most often he simply didn't respond to the invitation! In business, where possible, this approach rather removes a key performance management tool. Neither was Mark ever enamoured of or influenced by targets set in the university environment, for example in the name of league table positions. As Deputy Chair of the Senate at the University level and as a Head of School at the Faculty level within the University, he was clear, purposefully adapting Cyril's notebook line, 'we do not respond to tables, tables respond to us.' Performance determines position; a focus on position *always* leads to the tail wagging the dog. It is also the starting point for managerialism, i.e. managing to the numbers for the sake of the Management's position.

III. The Value of Smallness

The incessant pressure to corporatise, the lure of 'giantism', has been for better or worse a feature of all the businesses and organisations – with the understandable exception of the Ropley village grocers Hardings – we have studied. Like so many other village grocers, though, Hardings has long-since been replaced by the supermarket. Corporatisation, then, is not a new phenomenon and neither is resistance to it. Both appear to transcend industries and eras. That Stan Dibben and Andrew Mustard, and the great many others on the edges of countless other industries whose stories have never been told, but who no doubt suffered similar failures, actually made a living on the edge of industry at all is therefore a remarkable feat. The mindset of the small businessman is not a function of scale or aspiration, it is a function of attitude, of the focus of one's interest, of the beliefs you hold about how business should be conducted, and even of the moral values you apply to it.

To render the argument from the perspective of Stan's conclusion that he didn't like big ships in 1943, his experience both in the Royal Navy and in business was that while it is possible to run a 'big ship' on 'big ship' principles of managed departmentalisation and strict rules, highly corporatised, in fact with skill it is perfectly possible to run one on more informal 'small ship' principles. The very worst thing is when a 'small ship' is run as if it is a 'big ship'. This was Colonel Sleeman's undoing when he was the Commanding Officer of the 50th Royal Tank Regiment in Italy, and often it was Mark's experience in 20 years of university life. It was also very nearly the undoing of the Bluebird Land Speed Record Project. As the pressure to corporatise has only intensified in universities so, unfortunately, the values, attitudes and beliefs of 'big ship' seem to have become, through managerialism, the only accepted way of operating even small entities within universities.

M.G. Scott's conclusion 'small businesses are not little big businesses' (1989), applies also to the people who run them. Small business people are not little big business people. If the assumption that small firms operate as if they are little large firms falls into error, how much more so a similar assumption regarding the people themselves! A good number of the businesses we have 'looked into', Hardings, Cyril Smith's and Eric Oliver's (different) approaches to the business of sidecar racing, Donald Campbell's Bluebird project, NGK (GB) and particularly Stan's agency of it, the Wool and Sheepskin Country Shop and Variguide are perhaps better understood as being at the micro end of the small business category. Here, the 'the owner is the business' adage holds true to an even greater extent. Here too, therefore, what is meant by success is person-specific.

What then of MSUCo., surely a prime example of inter-war entrepreneurial success? By the time Stan joined MSUCo. as an apprentice in 1941, it was already a sizeable organisation that had transcended its entrepreneurial origins; the mindset of the directors of that time was instead one of the big business. After all, the original founders were long since deceased. A comprehensive study of the company from its very origins might be able to discern the moments this transition occurred and thereby gain another insight into the rural electrification of the UK, beyond what we have attempted here. All this being said, in the telling of the stories of Stan Dibben and Andrew Mustard and their families and associates, if we have brought the experience they share with all their peers – the small men and women of industry – more to the fore then this is all to the good.

IV. E.F. Schumacher – Food for Thought?

In the Introduction, we quoted E.F. Schumacher's argument regarding the need for enterprise to focus on people ([1973] 2011: 57), that is

> The economic calculus, as applied by present day economics, forces the industrialist to eliminate the human factor because machines do not make mistakes which people do … This means that those who have nothing to sell but their labour remain in the weakest possible bargaining position. The conventional wisdom of what is now taught as economics by-passes the poor, the very people for whom development is really needed. The economics of giantism and automation is a left-over of nineteenth century conditions and nineteenth century thinking and it is totally incapable of solving any of the real problems of today. An entirely new system of thought is needed, a system based on attention to people, and not primarily attention to goods – (the goods will look after themselves!).

It will be readily apparent that Schumacher too had thought of Michael Porter's Five Forces (1979) long before Porter. We have hoped to show that the 'system of thought' Schumacher calls for is perhaps inherent in people who develop their livelihoods with a focus on others. The economic calculus, by contrast, encourages ruthless big business practice. Again, Stan's 'Teach, to Sell' approach for pioneering new products in the marketplace is an expression of Schumacher's call for common decency. Mark's approach to 'creating and enabling opportunities for people to grow and develop as human beings' in universities, speaks to Schumacher's call also for it eschewed any 'primary attention to goods'. Both demonstrate that it is possible to operate in another way, if there is a sufficient courage to stand against the tide. We say courage, because unfortunately the personal costs can be great in a corporatised environment in which the economic calculus trumps all other concerns. From our study at least, the 'nineteenth century left-over', as Schumacher described it, seems still to be persistently hanging around. It may even be becoming more entrenched in some industries. We maintain however, per Schumacher's thesis, that the traditional economic argument fails at the level of the individual and the community, when the focus of the individual is on the community. One example we have discussed in detail is Andrew Mustard's approach to reconditioning Seagull and Volvo outboards in Northeast Queensland. As Andrew noted, making money from this activity 'misses the point entirely.'

As Schumacher again notes ([1973] 2011: 8),

> One of the most fateful errors of our age is the belief that the problem of production has been solved. Our inability to recognise that the modern industrial system, with all its intellectual sophistication, consumes the very basis on which it has been erected. To use the language of the economist, it lives on irreplaceable capital which it cheerfully treats as income. [There are] three categories of such capital: fossil fuels, the tolerance margins of nature, and the human substance.

Herein lies an explanation for why it is we have come to view potatoes in the same way as toilet rolls, i.e. as replaceable commodities entirely disconnected in our ongoing illusory state from Nature. Getting back to the land is possible, however, but is obviously far beyond the scope of this book (see e.g. Tudge, 2016 and HRH The Prince of Wales, 2011)

Schumacher further suggests the modern economy is being 'propelled by a frenzy of greed and indulges in an orgy of envy, and these are not accidental features but the very causes of its expansionist success' ([1973] 2011: 18). He continues ([1973] 2011: 20),

> Scientific or technological 'solutions' which poison the environment or degrade the social structure and Man himself are of no benefit ... Ever bigger machines, entailing ever bigger concentrations of economic power and exerting ever greater violence against the environment, do not represent progress: they are a denial of wisdom. Wisdom demands a new orientation of science and technology towards the organic, the gentle, the non-violent, the elegant and the beautiful ...

The problem of giantism, the insatiable urge to grow businesses and the mindset that arises in the culture of these organisations, be this MSUCo., Renold, NGK (UK) post Torii or indeed almost all of the universities that have formed the basis of Mark's experience of contemporary academe ironically enough, seems to us to stem from a loss of wisdom.

We wonder, too, whether the loss of wisdom extends farther still. Like Schumacher ([1973] 2011: 23–4), we ponder continuing economic progress may be

> obtainable only if we employ those powerful human drives of selfishness, which religion and traditional wisdom universally call upon us to resist. [When the] human vices such as greed or envy are systematically cultivated, the inevitable result is nothing less than the collapse of intelligence. [...] Economically, our wrong living consists primarily in systematically cultivating greed and envy and thus building up a vast array of unwarrantable wants [...] If greed were not the master of modern man – ably assisted by envy – how could it be that the frenzy of economism does not abate as 'higher standards of living' are attained, and that it is precisely the richest societies which pursue their economic advantage with the greatest ruthlessness?'

Which is to say envy and greed, and the ensuing jealousy, are the curses of modern society. In the light of the businesses we have explored, we would ask in addition – does the ruthlessness not extend also, inevitably, down to the level of the individual business or businessman? Schumacher suggest that, with exceptions, the answer may be yes:

> The strength of the idea of private enterprise lies in its terrifying simplicity. It suggests that the totality of life can be reduced to one aspect – profits. The businessman, as a private individual, may still be interested in other aspects of life – perhaps even in goodness, truth and beauty – but as a businessman he concerns himself only with profits. In this respect, the idea of private enterprise fits exactly into the idea of The Market, which ... [is] the institutionalisation of individualism and non-responsibility. Equally it fits perfectly into the modern trend towards total quantification at the expense of the appreciation of qualitative

differences; for private enterprise is not concerned with what it produces but only what it gains from production. [...]

Everything becomes crystal clear after you have reduced reality to one – only one – of its thousand aspects. You know what to do – whatever produces profits; you know what to avoid – whatever reduces them or makes a loss. And there is at the same time a perfect measuring rod for the degree of success or failure. Let no-one befog the issue by asking whether a particular action is conducive to the wealth and well-being of society, whether it leads to moral, aesthetic or cultural enrichment. Simply find out whether it pays; simply investigate whether there is an alternative that pays better. If there is, choose the alternative. ([1973] 2011: 215)

It is no accident that successful businessmen are often astonishingly primitive; they live in a world made primitive by this process of reduction. They fit into this simplified version of the world and are satisfied with it. And when the real-world attempts to make its existence known and attempts to force upon their attention a different one of its facets, one not provided for in their philosophy, they tend to become quite helpless and confused. They feel exposed to incalculable dangers and 'unsound' forces and freely predict general disaster. As a result, their judgements on actions dictated by a more comprehensive outlook on the meaning and purpose of life are generally quite worthless. ([1973] 2011: 215–6) [...] The real strength of the theory of enterprise lies in this ruthless simplification [...] ([1973] 2011: 216).

We have included this lengthy but thought-provoking quote because it seems to us so instructive. The story of 'Variguide and the supermarket oligopolies' exemplifies the problem it articulates for, although Variguide was a small business, its owners had a strong background in the motor industry, were themselves quite understandably steeped in its cooperate culture. They closed the business because they could no longer see substantial profits when the simple model of quickly fulfilling a contract came undone. Many of the business histories we have described suggest that the changes Schumacher proposed to correct the issues he observed – a refocusing on human scale, appropriate levels of technology for the circumstance, and decentralisation – have never been implemented or even agreed with by those running big business. The reason for this lies in their cast iron adherence, even perhaps in many universities these days, to the 'theory of enterprise' Schumacher critiques.

We hope to have shown, however, that Schumacher's solutions are practised, because all the businesses we have studied have demonstrated, each in their own way (and sometimes like for example Variguide, Renold and MSUCo. in the reverse), that small business people are just precisely not little-big business people. As Schumacher noted (1980: 66), 'I have come to the conclusion that where you have lots of small businesses fulfilling all sorts of [local] demands, they do not constitute a social problem.' While we have shown that there are occasions where the administrative disciplines of corporate operation are necessary, such as with the Government's centralisation of the Help Committees in World War One, nonetheless the circumstances of successful operation that led to the need for centralisation arose as a result of a different way of operating. That said, the scale effect was damped by the simple reality that the institutionalisation was focused in the delivery aspect from London to the PoW camps. The mechanisms and social processes of supply to London remained within the local help committees and so the 'initiative' that underpinned the good work being done (Schumacher, 1980: 70) was not lost; it was instead maintained and even enhanced.

As another example of the same phenomenon, Jim Hughes' big-business approach at NGK post-Torii could not have worked when the business was being built, the product pioneered, and nor would there have been any opportunity for him to change the business model at all had the pioneering not occurred in the first place. Further, Stan was able to continue operating as an agent even in the face of NGK (UK)'s corporatisation because of the tremendous good will built up through the 'good work' of the local scale initiative inherent in his 'Teach, to Sell' approach. It will be remembered that the only reason he retired was because he was forced to – not by any lack of business or at the request of his customers, but by NGK (UK) wanting to bring all the business inward, to paid employees.

Of course this turned the focus of NGK sales in his former territory away from support of the businesses buying NGK to a more self-centred approach to NGK's growth and even, perhaps, the advancement of employees within the company. Further, the MSUCo. directors' focus on profit for the select few preference stockholders demonstrates how far awry things can get when growth and market dominance take precedence over community service as the *raison d'etre*. The result – nationalisation and unionisation of the industry to protect customers and employees – was we suggest in the light of what we uncovered at MSUCo. inevitable. Yet it is possible to achieve 'smallness within large organisations' (Schumacher [1973] 2011: 202), as the BSA Gold Star shop demonstrated. That is, if the mindset required to achieve it is not snuffed out by managerialism, as was Mark's common – though not universal – experience in universities.

The advance of the managerialist corporation and, far more than this, the growth of corporatist ways of thinking and operating *regardless* of scale or scope, has thrown into doubt what were commonplace small business peoples' ways of thinking and doing. E.F. Schumacher's work, while at Oxford University during World War Two and later at the Coal Board, is credited as being one of the lynch pins of Britain's late-war and post-war economic revivals; his theories are particularly relevant therefore in a study focused primarily though not entirely on that period. What our study has shown, perhaps, is that it is highly likely a great many people other than Schumacher have held the very same views as he did and practiced them successfully. Indeed, he suggested this was the case himself ([1973] 2011: 48–50):

> With practical people in the actual world, there is a tremendous longing and striving to profit, if at all possible, from the convenience, humanity, and manageability of smallness. [...] When it comes to action, we need small units because action is a highly personal affair, and one cannot be in touch with more than a limited number of persons at any one time ... Today we suffer from an almost universal idolatry of giantism. It is therefore necessary to insist on the virtues of smallness ...

We can't but agree. However, *to practice smallness* requires a remarkably different mindset than seems to take hold of those willingly engulfed, lured, by giantism, the urge to grow ever larger, firm in their belief that the big business way is The Right Way. In applying Schumacher's 'people-focused economics' and principles of 'good work' as we have tried to do, we hope to have demonstrated that the *other way* is both more natural and a more humane way of being. Hardings of course, but also Serge Binn's Mobyke and Watsonian Sidecars are all cases in point. As 'Teach, to Sell' also emphasises, there is far more to be gained in business by focusing genuinely on the needs of others, rather than the needs of yourself. It does require a purposeful resistance not only to corporatisation and its inevitable internal emphasis but also to managerialism, its main architect. The phrase 'share the love' has become a mantra of managerialism, but in that setting that phrase means something quite different.

***

We live in the era of global warming. It is driven in no small part by the 'disconnection' of big business (and sometimes too big universities) from communities, and from Nature. Squirrels, rabbits, butterflies. This in turn is for the sole purpose of tremendous profit *regardless* of individuals or society at large – much less the environment. Of course the VW emissions scandal (and it was probably not solely VW) is but one example. Many ruthless and self-centred approaches to growth and profit are seen by their practitioners as really very clever business. Nothing could be farther from the truth: These approaches are not wise. They are fundamentally immoral.

It is important to end on a positive note. Our historical study of business practice in eight industries through a century's experience of two families, we venture to suggest, shows another way is still possible. Perhaps it is more necessary now than ever it was before.

Mark and I hope you've enjoyed the 'stories within stories' in *Enterprise on the Edge of Industry*. Definitely time for tea and cake! Source: Charlotte Brooks

APPENDICES

1. INTERNMENT AT CHANGI PRISON IN WORLD WAR TWO, BY ANDREW MUSTARD MC

Andrew Mustard Sr's account of his time in the run up to the British capitulation and his subsequent internment under the Japanese in Singapore continues directly on from where we left it in Chapter 11, as follows.

1. Over the Edge Towards the Darkness

A few days later the storm broke. From multiple reports and rumours which reached the estate from various quarters that day there was one of which there could be no doubt; the Japanese had landed on the Malay Peninsular. They were attacking at Kota Bahru on the East coast from the sea. What was the Navy doing? The answer to that when it eventually came through in detail was tragic. Powerful Naval forces sent north from Singapore had been totally destroyed off the east coast by dive bombers. Thousands of our men had died magnificently but all to NO purpose. As day followed day the news grew worse. The Japanese had established a firm foothold on the Kelantan coast despite enormous casualties. They were creeping across the north of the peninsular. Pahang fell. Penang was bombed and all civilians hastily evacuated. Ipoh, less than twenty miles away from the estate was bombed. From Pahang they drove, faster now, towards Penang and had soon established a starting line across the peninsular for an attack southwards. Penang, a first-class port on the west coast would soon be in their hands. The Japanese had entered Malaya by the back-door and we had been unable to atop them.

It wasn't much good attempting to carry on estate routine work with hell let loose only one hundred miles away, and I welcomed instructions to contact and assist a company of Royal Engineers [R.E.s] guarding a pontoon bridge over the Perak river. My job was to collect all motor boats and launches in the area, and hand them over to the Indian major who commanded the company. This fleet of launches which carried goods up the Perak river from the west coast port of Teluk Anson was owned by a number of Chinese shopkeepers. Most of the launches were condemned years ago, and 'decrepit', was a polite term for them. Their engines had once belonged to American cars which had gone off the roads long past. To start them was a work of art known only to the syces [a syce was an Indian butler] who tended them. To keep them going required constant coaxing, a great quantity of petrol – and nearly as much oil, were all necessary. My job turned out to be a more difficult one than might be expected. At first the owners of most of these hulks refused point-blank to co-operate. Promises and threats were equally futile. I had to refer the matter to the commanding officer of the R.E.s who on two occasions accompanied me to argue with the uncooperative owners. Eventually they had to be told that unless they obeyed orders their wretched launches would be sunk, even then it was with great reluctance that they surrendered their property.

One day the General Officer Commanding troops arrived at Parit with his staff. I accompanied him on his tour of inspection. The 'fleet' was anchored off the jetty when we walked down to the river. Pointing to one of the launches which for the past thirty years or more had struggled between Parit and Teluk Anson with excessive loads of rice, he asked whether I thought a gun could be mounted in its stern. My reply to the effect that the first round would undoubtedly capsize the wreck didn't seem to please him. 'Humph!' was his sole comment. It was the last I saw of him.

About mid-December a company of the Gurkha Regiment arrived at Parit. They had been fighting a rear-guard action from Pahang. As I was talking to one of their officers a car came through with police escorting a suspected spy. The Japanese were certainly getting closer. That evening a weary Gurkha officer arrived at my bungalow with a real thirst on him. I gave him the two or three remaining bottles of whisky I had, and added a hope that he would share them out. He was most grateful. Next day orders came for me to distribute ammunition to Malay 'kampongs' [villages] near the big rice growing areas down river, Bota and Lambong. The ammunition on arrival turned out to be three thousand sporting cartridges loaded with slug. I reckoned the job would be completed in twenty-four hours, and so took with me little food and no mosquito net. Had it not been for the kindness and assistance of Malays and Chinese, I should have been in a different position, for it was three days before I finally returned to Parit.

I chose one of the less dilapidated launches for the journey down river and made an early start. As we pushed off from the jetty and swung into the main stream, I was reminded of happier days in the past when parties of us used to set off on the same journey to shoot snipe in the Bota district. Dawn is the most beautiful and refreshing hour of the Malayan day. I remember that day well, the colours in the sky as the sun was rising were incredibly and indescribably beautiful. There was a mist over the sluggish water, which dissolved in minutes under the heat of the rising tropical sun. As we glided downstream at the speed of the stream, the syce not yet having succeeded in coaxing the engine into life, troops of Kra monkeys chattered at us from the thick jungle overhanging the river banks. The first village we came to had a rickety landing-stage consisting of a single plank, one end of which was sunk in the muddy water. Several Malay women, their sarongs tied above their breasts were bathing themselves on the edge of the river, their children, naked as they were born, splashed about in the shallows, protected from roving crocodiles by a semicircle of wooden palings. The women turned their backs, the young ones shyly and slyly looked over their shoulders at the white man.

My arrival appeared to be expected, for a deputation, headed by the Penghulu (Head Man), awaited me at the top of the bank. Not only did they seem to expect my arrival but they knew my mission and evinced little interest in the boxes of cartridges which were unloaded from the launch. The Penghulu was a fine looking old man, and with grave courtesy led me to the village school, built under the shade of a clump of cocoanut palms a few yards from the river bank. The school was an attap (leaf) roofed building with walls not more that three feet high, there being a large space between the eaves and the top of the wall so that what breeze there was could help to cool the interior. There was very little furniture: a table, one chair and a large blackboard. The school-children squatting on the floor during their lessons. A meal consisting of bananas, mangostene and jack fruit was laid on the table and I was invited to take the only chair. The fruit was welcome, and I tucked in whilst the Penghulu and his following squatted on the floor behind me.

Outside greatly interested in my every movement stood the younger generation of village. The meal over, I lit a pipe, passed round a packet of cigarettes, and got down to business. It was expected, I told them, that the enemy would drop from aeroplanes into the large open spaces of the paddy fields. This might happen any day now. The cartridges I was handing over to them should be used to fire at them before they landed. Wait, I said, until they were about twenty to thirty yards off, then let them have it up the back-side. This appealed to them enormously. 'Baik Tuan' (Alright Sir), they replied with broad grins. We walked to the main paddy fields, a large expanse of land divided up by two feet high banks into numerous plots, each some forty or fifty square yards in area. The plots were flooded with water a few inches deep. Here I pointed out the most suitable places to post the men with guns. I told the Penghulu that he would be well advised to have his plans ready by the next day. By the time the trek round this area and the distribution of cartridges were complete it was well on into the afternoon, and I realised how I had misjudged the length of time the job would take me. That night the police sergeant in charge of Bota police station very kindly gave me food and I bedded down as best I could in the launch.

Similar visits were made to all the other villages. In each I was supplied with food, usually at the local village shop. All the Penghulus were only too willing to co-operate. The idea of shooting Japanese floating down from the sky appealed to their sense of humour. It was probably very fortunate that a need for this action never arose as the village would undoubtedly have suffered horrible punishment when they were finally over-run. The return journey up-stream was painfully slow, the launch made poor headway against the current. However I was tired after walking around all day in the sweltering heat, and slept most of the journey.

I arrived back at the estate bungalow two days before Christmas. With the exception of the syce, cook, houseboy and their families there wasn't a soul on the place. The factory was deserted, and the machinery idle. The Chinese engineer, and all the labourers had disappeared into the blue. The lines where the tappers and their families lived were empty; they had cleared out with all their possessions, and had no doubt joined the stream of refugees cluttering up the few roads leading south. The clerks and dresser's bungalows were deserted, showing signs of hasty evacuation. It was a truly depressing sight. The office was intact and there had been no attempt to loot on any part of the estate. I spent an hour in the office clearing up what business I could, and then went down to the factory armed with a sledge hammer.

The Petter engine that was the source of all power in the factory was put thoroughly out of action and, by the time I had finished, it was of value only to a scrap iron merchant. It was a rotten business having to destroy everything which had been built up and maintained with such care, but rather that than leave it to be of use to the enemy. Next I cycled over to Manong to pay the labourers. Manong was a branch property of the company and was under my management. It was seventeen miles away. On the way I was stopped by a patrol of the Gurkha regiment. They would not allow me to continue farther. I told them I was a police officer, and was carrying pay for distribution. They had noticed the bag I was carrying, and after warning me that the enemy was expected any moment now, and some might have filtered through already, they let me pass. The Manong labours were there when I arrived, and I paid them. This was a particularly isolated spot and they did not appear to realise the full significance of their position.

I wondered whether or not to tell them and advise them what to do. After some deliberation I decided against it. What advice could I give them? I knew they would not attempt to join in any fighting which might come their way, and for that reason would stand a good chance of being left unmolested when their dwelling places were over-run. If I advised them to clear out quickly they would probably panic, jam the roads and get massacred wholesale by bombers strafing those roads. Finally I left them, realising I should probably never see them again. An officer of the Gurkha stopped me as I was returning, and advised me to clear out quickly. He said I could be of little assistance to them now, and would do better to make my way back to Kuala Lumpur. So I prepared for the journey, planning to start on the following morning.

Sleep that night was almost impossible. The magnitude of what was happening was overwhelming. My whole life and livelihood had been wrapped up in this country from the time I left school. I had left it once to fight in the First World War and I was being chased out of it during a war of even greater magnitude. Next morning I called in the cook and the houseboy, and advised them to clear out, while the going was good. I gave them everything they asked for, food, clothing, bedding, utensils and enough money to keep them for some time. The syce volunteered to come south with me, but I decided against it, and told him to join his wife in the kampong. I then packed the suitcase myself, chucked a few tins of food and bottles of beer into the car, and set off alone. My feelings as I drove away can be better imagined than described.

My orders included the job of visiting all rubber estates on my journey south and destroying any stocks of rubber found. The first factory I came to had a store in the smoke house, and on the drying racks. It made a fine blaze; cluds of acrid, black, oily smoke billowed above the trees as it burned. At another estate, I found thousands of pounds of rubber all packed up ready for transport. An Australian R.A.S.C. was billeted on the premises, and I told the sergeant in charge that I intended to burn the lot. He besought me not to do so as his men were sleeping on the bales, their only bedding. He promised that he would carry out the job himself as soon as he had orders to move. With that I had to be content, and I often wonder whether he carried out his promise. I told him that I had left at the bungalow a substantial supply of food to which he and his men were welcome if they cared to fetch it. He implored me to show him the way back. It was a return journey of some twenty miles but we collected one of the lorries and set off. The Australians half-filled this lorry with every description of goods which they thought might be of some use to them. Several planters had dumped their goods and chattels at my bungalow on their way south, so these Australian lads must have lived fairly well for several days. I picked up my car again and continued the journey south. I had Christmas dinner by the roadside and thoroughly enjoyed it. It consisted of a tin of cold sausages washed down with a bottle of beer.

2. First Experiences of the Enemy

On arrival at Kuala Lumpur, the capital city of the Federated Malay States, it was not long before I was given a taste of things to come. I stayed the night with a friend of mine, and on the following morning, which was Boxing Day, I looked up another friend J. Barron whose office was in the main Government buildings. Barron had just returned from a trip to New Zealand, and when I arrived at his office I found him sitting on his desk engrossed in a letter from a lady-friend. I insisted on being given the full details of this letter, and we were so engrossed in its intricacies that we failed to hear the approach of enemy planes. Their objective was evidently our very building, for two bombs fell slap upon it. As the first detonated I was amazed to see Barron lifted bodily into the air and hurled several feet across the room. I was standing behind a pillar which protected me from the blast and splinters. My turn came with the second bomb, and I felt myself swept off my feet and hurled on to the floor. Poor old Barron had a nasty gash on the leg and a wooden splinter two feet in length was quivering in the wall a few inches from his chest. I was fortunate to get away with a few bruises and scratches.

After three days in Kuala Lumpur I received orders to go down to Port Sweetenham, twenty-four miles away on the west coast. There was a landing ground for aircraft there which had been partly constructed from reclaimed swamp land. A gang of one thousand Indian and Chinese labourers had been collected to complete the work as urgently as possible. My job was to organize this labour force. Like the first job I was given, this turned out to be a farce. The enemy reconnaissance planes, which seemed to have nearly everything their own way, soon spotted the activity, and before long frequent visits were paid to us by bombers. With the result that as soon as any aircraft engine was heard, every labourer on the place beat a hasty retreat for the nearest cover. Who could blame them? I soon learned that the best policy was to dive for the deep drainage ditch that surrounded the landing-ground. Plans for effective work during the day had to be jettisoned and an attempt was made to work under the light of the moon, but it was almost impossible to control one thousand scared labourers under such conditions. One day when we were attempting to carry on the unequal task set us, the usual stampede of the labourers gave warning of approaching aircraft, and I hopped over the drain into a cocoanut grove and dropped into a ditch. The planes were evidently making for a battery of anti-aircraft guns on the far side of the field. They came straight towards my cocoanut grove flying fairly low, and proceeded to let go their first bomb before arriving overhead.

It felt as if that bomb was aimed straight at me. As it was, it fell about twenty feet away, splaying mud and earth over everything. After waiting for a few seconds I peered over the top of the drain and to my amazement saw a pile of earth a few yards away start to move. A moment later there appeared, covered with slime and filth, the head and shoulders of a British soldier. I hurried over to help him extricate himself, and when sufficient mud had been scraped from his features, I recognized a young nephew of mine. He had no time to chat however as he had his men to look after. It was the last I ever saw of the lad, for he was killed in action farther south near Seremban.

It was not long before the plans to complete the Port Sweetenham Landing Ground were jettisoned. It was decided to wreck the place so that it could be of no use to the enemy. This job was left to the R.E.s, and I returned to Kuala Lumpur. There wasn't much that I could do there. Most of the Europeans, with the exception of the Volunteers [The Volunteer Forces of the Federated and Unfederated States of Malaya and the Straits Settlements], had cleared out. All offices were run with a skeleton staff, and the Clubs and Hotels were almost empty. I could be of little use in the town so I decided to go down to Singapore. At Johore I was roped in to assist mapping roads in the area, but soon got fed up with this and continued the journey south. I thought it strange and rather significant that the roads in this area were exceptionally good, and all of them seemed to run north – south. A short time before the invasion of Malaya there was a large colony of Japanese in Johore State working on the rubber plantations, tin mines and iron ore mines, and I was told that parties of these Japanese used to come over for three years at a time, after that they were replaced by new men.

3. Singapore

I arrived at Singapore late in January, and joined a friend of mine D. Hampshire who had taken a flat in the Eu Court Buildings. The flat, No.14, was the end one at the top of the building. Next day I reported myself to the Central Police Station and was enrolled as a sergeant in the Straits Settlements Police. I was ordered to take up duty at Joo Chat Police Station some way out of Singapore. Except when on night duty, I returned to sleep at the flat. My duties at the police station were varied. Most of the time was spent on patrols, keeping a sharp look out for disorders and looting of bomb damaged buildings. Personally I never discovered any incidences of disorder or looting, but I think this was due mainly to the fact that the populace was too scared to worry about much beyond the preservation of their own skins.

One morning orders came through from the Central Police Station that all intoxicating liquor was to be destroyed immediately. Two large Chinese liquor shops were allotted to us for destruction of their stocks. A European Assistant Superintendent of Police, three European Inspectors, all armed, needlessly as it happened, and I raided these shops. The Chinese proprietors heard the reason of our visit with implacable features. 'Great trouble', was all they said, and watched the wreckage of their goods without a murmur. The stocks of liquor we found were large, and the value must have run into several thousands of dollars. The heaviest stock was Chinese 'samsu', a liquor distilled from rice in local, licensed distilleries. This liquor is also distilled illicitly in large quantities by Chinese squatters in the isolated districts up-country. The quality, needless to say, is considerably inferior and less wholesome than that distilled under licence. Excise officers find a great deal of their time taken up with tracking down the bootleggers and breaking up their illicit stills. This illicit samsu, sold at a few cents a bottle, finds a ready market amongst the Indian labourers. It is a potent drink and these labourers get fighting drunk on it in a very short time. Consequences are sometimes serious, and many a crime can be traced to over indulgence in this illicit brew.

We tackled the unpleasant job before us in the quickest possible manner. The bottles of liquor were handed out and smashed in the concrete drain running along side of the road. In one of the shops I discovered a stock of Dewars Black Label whisky. My feelings at having to destroy this can well be imagined. As I was throwing one of the bottles into the drain a large rat ran between my legs, and I hurled the bottle at him bowling him over into the drain. This amused the large crowd of Malays who had gathered to watch the breaking up of Mr Chinaman's shop. This order to destroy all intoxicating liquor was, to my mind, one of the most sensible yet issued. Had the victorious Japanese been given any opportunity of filling themselves with liquor when they finally came in, the massacre of the local population would probably have been worse than it actually was. We therefore took very good care that they should find nothing in these shops, and I only hope that the Chinese proprietors, who were resigned to the necessity for such drastic action, and did not attempt to interfere, will be adequately compensated for the total loss of their property and livelihood.

At this time the Japanese Air Force was fairly active over Singapore island; there were intermittent raids during the day. My journey by road from the flat to Joo Chat Police Station took me through the aerodrome, the main gates of which were heavily guarded by military personnel. Arriving at these gates one morning I was surprised to find them open and unguarded. The reason for this became evident when I had travelled a short way along the straight mile of road traversing the area; flames and smoke were rising from the main buildings and hangars. The whole place had been bombed to such effect that it must have been useless for many months.

I was driving along slowly, the only car, or for that matter the only human being within sight, pondering on the latest blow, and wondering about the future, when I heard a peculiar sound coming from somewhere outside the car. 'Br-Br-Br', a short pause and then again closer 'Br-Br-Br-Br-Br-Br'. I suddenly realised what it was; a Jap plane was machine-gunning the one and only object within its view which showed any signs of life – me and my car! I put my foot down on the accelerator, and the car, a Ford V8, leaped forward, soon touching sixty m.p.h. My troubles however were not over. I had forgotten a dip in the rood which had resulted from a badly filled in bomb crater. The car hit that at over sixty m.p.h., and my head came into contact with the roof of the car with such force that I was almost stunned. This was a very unpleasant experience, but I must have been born under a lucky star for on the following day another incident occurred which might have ended in disaster for both my friend Hampshire and myself:

That morning, before leaving the flat, I was prompted by some inexplicable premonition to warn Hampshire 'whatever you do,' I advised him, 'stay in No.14 and don't leave it today.' On my return from Joo Chat, Hampshire was still there looking a bit bored with life. He suggested a visit to friends in another flat but I was tired and said I did not feel like it. That evening Jap bomber came over and dropped a stick of bombs on the Bu Court flats, totally demolishing the centre ones and damaging others. No.14 came off lightly and neither Hampshire nor I were hurt. My car, which was standing out in the yard, was burnt to a twisted, useless tangle of metal.

One more job I had which, though extremely pathetic, is worth recording. A European Police Inspector and I were sent out to a place near Changi village to report on the number and condition of the British dogs which had been collected there. I am a great lover of dogs myself, and it had upset me considerably when I had to send my two spaniels and my retriever to the vet some time before I had finally left Parit. The sight which met our eyes on this occasion nearly made me weep with shame and pity. There were Alsations [German Shepherd Dogs], Bull Terriers, Spaniels, Retrievers, Great Danes, Scotch Terriers and many other breeds all herded together in kennels far too small for them. What little food there was consisted of foul smelling, dried and salted fish and tapioca roots. The stench was appalling and the perpetual whining and howling went to my heart. It was indeed a sorrowful sight. The kennels were in the charge of a Chinese woman and her small son who were obviously doing their best under almost impossible conditions. What became of all these fine animals I do not know, and I hate to think about it even now.

All this time the Japanese were steadily over-running the whole of the Peninsular. Attempts had been made by our troops to form defence lines across the Peninsular whenever and wherever possible. The enemy overcame this opposition by infiltration, by encircling tactics, and by landing parties of troops in the rear of the defence lines. They used all manner of craft which sailed down from Penang and crept into the innumerable creeks which lay along the west coast. The Japanese had been training for jungle warfare many years before the invasion of Malaya, and had devised all manners of effective strategies, whereas most of our own troops found themselves in tropical jungle for the first time in their lives. They were only partially trained for jungle warfare, and had difficulty even in recognizing the enemy from the local natives, particularly when that enemy very often dressed as Malays or Chinese. Many stories and rumours of sabotage and fifth columnism came back to Singapore at this time but I am fairly confident that most of them could be attributed to this deception practised by the enemy.

4. Witnessing the Japanese Military First-Hand

The second week in February was now approaching. The enemy had reached the shores opposite Singapore Island, and our troops had withdrawn to the island across the Johore Causeway. To my mind the position was virtually hopeless, and it could only be a matter of time before Singapore itself tell. It is not intended to discuss or comment in these pages upon military strategy or civilian administration and organization during this period. It is hoped that one day an impartial and detailed account will be published from data collected by people competent to piece together a puzzle complicated enough even to a man on the spot. Indeed my duties at that period did not permit me the time nor the opportunity to observe the picture as a whole, and it would have needed a highly trained observer to complete that picture in its true perspective.

When it was realised that the enemy might land at any moment on the island, Police H.Q. decided to close down and evacuate Joo Chat Police Station. Before finally leaving I was told to remove all bolts from rifles and all magazines and spring from revolvers in the station. This took some time and when I had finished the revolvers my fingers were extremely sore. From Joo Chat I was sent to Beach Road Police Station. By now, the bombing was more intense and concentrated, and orders were given that cover should be taken immediately aircraft were heard approaching. One morning an Inspector and I were holding a pay parade in the station, a number of senior police officers being also present, when the sound of aircraft engines was heard. Most of the officers showed remarkable, and rather surprising, agility by diving underneath tables, whilst most of the rank and file stood fast. It is of course possible that the that the rank and file were concentrating to such an extent on their pay that they forgot the order to take cover on such an occasion. However, at that time I did think it would have been more appropriate for the officers to see to the safety of their men before considering the preservation of their own skins.

Shortly after this it was decided to pay off all ranks in the police force below that of inspector, and promote any European Volunteers such as myself, as well as Inspectors, to the rank of Assistant Superintendent of Police. The other ranks were advised to return to their villages, and, so far as the Japanese were concerned, to forget they had ever been policemen. The officers forgathered in the Central Police Station which henceforth became their quarters for all purposes. So far as the police were concerned the stage was set for an inevitable capitulation. There was not a great deal of work to be done now except that all cooking and other domestic duties had to be carried out by Europeans, whose normal occupations had never included such activities. Food was now rationed fairly drastically with the result that meals were usually inadequate and unappetising, and more often that not I used to clear off to the flat and fry up some eggs to appease my hunger.

The city itself, except when under bombardment, was ominously quiet; the lull before the storm. I believe many of the native population had gone across to the mainland hoping to get through unmolested to the safety of up-country villages. My only duty at Central Police Station was an occasional spell as a sentry on the main gate, and it was at a time when I was taking over this duty from another sentry that an unpleasant incident occurred almost under my nose. The Inspector General of Police [I.G.P.] was standing in the veranda of the Police Station talking to a subordinate when some unknown assailant threw a grenade into the veranda. It detonated near the two men and both were fortunate to escape with their lives. As it was the I.G.P. received stomach injuries and a splinter through the lung, the subordinate also received stomach injuries and a severe cut across the forearm. Both were taken to hospital. Who the perpetrator of the outrage was we never discovered. The 'fly-off' lever of the grenade was found in the road and there was no doubt that it was a British hand grenade probably of the 36 H type.

It was on 13 February 1942 that the dreaded but expected news came through. Singapore, the gateway to the Far East, and one of the bastions of our Empire had capitulated to the Japanese enemy. Hopelessly outnumbered, out-manoeuvred, with inadequate armaments and without an air force, there was no other course open. It was indeed a day of bitter sadness, exasperation and dread at the thought of the future before us, lying as we did at the mercy of an Asiatic power of whose unscrupulous behaviour there were already examples. When the news came to us, we were instructed to remain in Central Police Station to await developments. Orders were expected next day; this time those orders would come from a Japanese officer. The following morning the officer arrived and expressed his intention of inspecting us. With two or three others I stayed in the background and did not put in an appearance. As we were waiting to hear the result of the visit, I saw a Japanese lorry in the yard; sitting at the wheel was a European, probably a German.

When the others returned from the inspection they told us that, after being warned to behave themselves, they had been split up into parties and were to assist in traffic control duties in various parts of the city. I was told to go to Kandong Kerbau Police Station for this purpose. The European population, other than the Military and Police, were instructed to parade on the cricket ground bringing with them sufficient clothes for ten days. They were then marched four miles to a temporary internment camp in the vicinity of Joo Chat Police Station. I arrived at Kandong Kerbau Police Station in time to see the first batch of enemy troops march into Singapore. They were equivalent to our Corps of Military Police. The rank and file were badly dressed and equipped, and marched in a slovenly manner, out of step with heads downcast, not at all like conquerors. The officers were better turned out, sporting leather jack boots and spurs, each of them carrying a sword. Even on this occasion they treated their men like dirt, and this no doubt partly accounted for the hangdog demeanour of the other ranks. The column was led by a man head and shoulders above his fellows, and looking at his face I saw he was a European, no doubt another German and probably a fairly senior officer.

During the past ten days or more the city had been constantly and heavily bombed and there had been no time or opportunity to deal with the hundreds of fatal casualties. Corpses lay in the open streets, a few covered with sheets but most of them just lying where they had been thrown in gruesome and fantastic attitudes. About twenty feet from the police station was a fairly wide canal filled with water held up by a dock gate. Against this gate many swollen corpses, victims of this bombing, had piled themselves up completely jamming the mechanism which operated the gates. The stench was awful, and it grew worse daily as the tropical heat did its work of decomposition. Finally to our intense relief the gate was forced allowing the water to carry away its gruesome cargo.

Stories of frightful atrocities being committed against the native population, particularly the Chinese reached us from time to time. I have little doubt that many of them were true for I saw an example myself: One morning I was standing at the entrance to the Police Station looking up the street when I saw a Tamil labourer elbowed off the pavement by a Japanese soldier. The Tamil was a large man and evidently resented such treatment to which he was not normally accustomed, for unwisely he elbowed his way back on to the pavement pushing the soldier into the wall. A tussle resulted and the soldier, finding himself getting the worst of it blew his whistle. In a moment about half a dozen Japanese appeared on the scene and soon overcame the unfortunate Tamil. They gave him such a hammering that at the end of it he could hardly stand, and then proceeded to lash him up to a lamp-post in a most brutal manner. Here he was left for six hours in the glare and heat of the sun, unable to move sufficiently even to rid himself of the flies and insects which settled on his wounds, tormenting him to distraction. Finally he was loosed and carried away I no doubt to be dispatched as a character hostile to the occupying forces. A friend of mine, who is not given to exaggeration, and whose word I am prepared to believe told me that he had seen a Chinese beheaded in the public street by a Japanese officer, the severed head rolling into the gutter. This ghastly sight had made him violently ill.

5. The Hell of Internment

We were not left long at Kandong Kerbau. Whenever we put in an appearance to assist in traffic control, we were completely ignored, and might just as well have stayed at the station. After ten days we were carted off in lorries to the temporary internment camp to join the remainder of the Europeans sent there at the start. Part of the internment camp was the same police station at which I had been working before the capitulation, except that it had suffered from bombing since we left it. Joo Chat temporary internment camp was almost luxurious compared with the conditions under which we were compelled to live at a later stage of our internment. In the police station and barracks, constructed originally to house fifty to sixty persons, there were herded eight hundred men. Living conditions were bad, there being no sanitary arrangements, no supplementary sleeping accommodation, insufficient cooking facilities, and a supply of water which would not cover washing. Food was inadequate and only temporarily appeased a gnawing hunger. In spite of all this everyone was feeling comparatively cheerful when we arrived, and this was due to a rumour which had been going round that we would soon find ourselves housed in bungalows throughout the island. How this rumour originated I cannot imagine unless it was that some people were already installed in bungalows in the area, it being impossible to cram any more into the police station barracks.

The rumour was rudely shattered three days later when news came through that we were to move on the following day, our destination – Changi Prison. On the morning allotted for the move some two thousand five hundred of us, men of all ages and walks in life, paraded outside the camp. We were marched eight miles in the heat of the day when the temperature approached one hundred degrees; the heat was that intolerable damp heat of the tropics, rather similar to the atmosphere of an overheated greenhouse. Armed Japanese sentries marched with us, a consoling feature as they had rifles and equipment to carry, and the only advantage over us was the fact they probably started with full bellies.

Mercifully an ambulance driven by one of our own men was permitted to follow in the rear. Some of the older men succumbed to the heat. All of us were tortured by thirst before the march was half competed, but were given no water until we finally arrived at Changi in an exhausted condition. The only source of water to satisfy out thirst on arrival was a Public Works Department water cart. Some receptacles however were hastily improvised, but it took a long time for two thousand five hundred people to get enough to drink under such conditions. It would have taken six times as much of something stronger than water to put me right after that ordeal. So we arrived for internment, exhausted and dispirited, prisoners of the Japanese after ten weary weeks of futile efforts to repel them from the country which we had guaranteed to protect, and which contained our homes and livelihood, destined to remain for three and a half long and agonizing years. Years in which we were completely at their mercy with nothing but supreme faith in the power and endurance of the British Empire to uphold us in our misery.

The first order on arrival was to dump all baggage in the prison courtyard. No sooner had this been done than we were overwhelmed by a tropical storm. A downpour in England would be considered a drizzle when compared with a tropical storm, for rain comes down in a solid sheet soaking everything; a human being caught in such a storm is soaked to the skin in a

412

few seconds. This storm was a wonderful refresher but we were all like drowned rats by the end of it; our baggage was soaked and now lay in pools of water. A sorry start which only increased our misery. The next order was to fall in. We were then split up into three blocks, A, B and C, a party of approximately eight hundred to each block. I found myself allotted to block C, cell 22, which I was to share with two other internees, W---- and H----, the former rather an eccentric individual, and the latter a cheerful, likeable, little cockney. Changi Prison was built after the style of the American Sing-Sing prison. The maximum accommodation was intended to be for six hundred criminals. The Japanese herded two thousand five hundred of us into its buildings.

There were three separate blocks of cells. Each block was rectangular in shape and four stories high, the cells being built in three stories above the ground floor against the longest side of the rectangle. Additional to the blocks were several other rooms, including a large, well equipped kitchen, an equally well-equipped laundry, a dining hall and other subsidiary rooms such as bathrooms, offices and staff rooms. The construction was of reinforced concrete. Each block had its own courtyard about the size of a tennis court, and there was an open recreation ground not larger than a football pitch. The whole place was enclosed by a high wall. The cells were seven feet by twelve feet; the roof, walls and floor were all cement. To reach my cell I had to climb seventy-four concrete steps: it was not long before I knew that number too well. The only furniture in the cell was a latrine in one corner, and a solid block of cement built up from the floor in the centre of the cell. This had to serve as a bed, a table, and a place to seat oneself; its size was six feet by two and a quarter feet raised two feet from the floor. Placed as it was, it left sleeping spaces two and a quarter feet in breadth on either side of it for the second and third inmates of the cell. The cell door was solid, and metal covered. Ventilation was through two narrow openings at the top of the back wall and over the door, each protected by iron bars let into cement.

Fortunately there was a good water supply and electric light. What we should have done without those amenities God only knows. It was found that the cell accommodation, even herding three into a cell, was quite insufficient to account for all the internees. Those left over were compelled to find corners in the various rooms and even in the corridors. There they had to sleep, eat, and store their meagre possessions. Sanitary arrangements were quite inadequate for such a number, and we supplemented latrines already available by digging pits on the recreation ground and in any other available place.

All this was to be our home. For how long we could not even guess. When I first went into the cell, and the full realization of the situation struck me, the feeling of depression which already gripped me sank to utter despair. How long were we to expect this existence to last? This was the first part of the first day and my morale was almost at its lowest ebb. What would it be like in six months time? What was the extent of human endurance? I thought of the peaceful, contented life I had led only a few months past. I thought of the seven stalwarts of Parit, of the Australians sleeping on the bales of rubber who at least had a few days of good food and comfort, of my house servants and labourers on the estate; where were they all now? I thought of my family in England.

6. First Days and Months in Changi

But what was the use of brooding? It didn't help anyone, least of all myself. The best antedote was some sort of action. I decided to take stock of my possessions, all contained in a small fibre suitcase which I had dropped on the floor as I entered. They didn't amount to much: three shirts, a pair of shoes, two sets of underclothes, a few pairs of socks, two pairs of drill trousers, two towels, a few handkerchiefs and an old raincoat. My brushes and razor had been stolen, and I had only a toothbrush and a packet of razor blades. Soma kind person had already given me a blanket. I had about twenty-five dollars and private papers in my wallet and the clothes I stood up in. This was the sum total, and this was all I had for the three and a half years of my internment. When I finally came home, I brought back me the fibre suit case and my best 'Sunday trousers", which by that time were reduced to shorts, and were so darned and patched that few threads of the original material remained.

One more small item I had which, as it turned out, was perhaps the most valuable; a bottle of purgative oils. That they turned out to be as precious as gold will be believed when I say that one poor devil went for a fortnight without opening his bowels, and could get no relief. Some of the other internees were considerably more fortunate than I, particularly those living in Singapore who had managed to bring in a large supply of clothes, some food, and large sums of money in cash, the last item being of immense help to them at a later date when conditions became desperately bad.

The first night in cell 22 will remain in my memory until I die; it was hell, absolute, unadulterated hell. I had chosen the cement block for my bed; between my body and the block was nothing but the blanket. It was impossible to remain in one position for any length of time. I did succeed in dozing off for a minute or two only to roll off the block onto the unfortunate Cockney lying below. I soon abandoned any hope of sleep that night; apart from severe physical discomfort my mind was sick with despair. I left the cell and wandered along the landing into the open air to get away from the heat, the snores, and the restiveness of all those unhappy fellow prisoners.

For the first few months of our internment conditions were tolerable physically. The Japanese appointed a Camp Commandant, a Major-General in the R.A.M.C., under him were three block commandants, one representing each block. These officials were responsible for the internal organization of the prison, and were of course under the supervision of the Japanese. They had no special privileges and to all intents and purposes were on an equal footing with everyone else. In fact each individual considered himself as good as his neighbour; age, rank and station of life all went by the board. Apart from Japanese sentries who patrolled both inside and outside the prison with swords, rifles and cudgels, we were left very much to ourselves and to our own organization. I had the misfortune to be appointed a block policeman, and found it a thankless task. I was supposed to see that everyone in the block behaved himself and obeyed the numerous rules and regulations in existence. More about these later. When food was being prepared a policeman was always on duty at the cookhouse door to prevent scroungers pestering the cooks. With food probably the most important item of our daily life and always uppermost in our minds, the cooks were considered fortunate as they naturally managed to get extra supplies of food. Whilst on duty at the door I was sometimes given a tit-bit by the cooks, but this was one of the few advantages of being a block policeman.

7. Food – the Mainstay of All Life and Much Activity in Changi

At the start the food, though unappetizing was fairly plentiful. As I have said the kitchens were good and the cooking facilities, although insufficient for such numbers were otherwise satisfactory. There were some professional cooks in the prison mostly from ships which had bean sunk in Singapore harbour, or so badly damaged by bombing that they had bean unable to make a bid for safety before the capitulation. Food was collected by the orderlies at eight a.m., one p.m. and six p.m. carried around to the cells and carefully distributed, the orderlies getting a little extra by scraping out the large wooden pails at the end of the round. Rice was the main dish at every meal; at that time the ration was plentiful. This was supplemented by four ounces of bread made from a mixture of wheat and maize flour, stodgy and unpalatable. Occasionally we were given a tin of sardines amongst seven people, but there were always six sardines to a tin making a fair division none too easy. A tin of pilchards was another occasional luxury; one tin to six persons with never more than five fish to a tin so once again division was difficult. Special luxuries included a teaspoonful of jam or native honey, or a miniature portion of cheese.

Many internees had brought in a quantity of tinned food amongst their possessions, and shared them with friends but that supply was soon exhausted. When these luxuries were dished out the division was always meticulous, even to the oil in the tins of fish; the recipients made sure of that. For a time internees driving ration lorries managed to obtain various goods such as eggs, local native sweets and biscuits, native cigars and locally made cigarettes from the natives. Malays succeeded in evading sentries and selling such goods to us. But for some reason the Japanese soon gave orders that there was to be no contact with the natives, and supplies from this source dwindled on account of the risks involved in getting them. At the beginning of our internment, the Japanese permitted us to send out fatigue parties to purchase coconuts and collect wood as fuel tor cooking purposes. There was never any lack of volunteers for this duty, and it was a practise to draw lots for those to go out.

These parties also managed, at some risk to themselves, to purchase a certain amount of tinned milk, cheese, jam and butter and smuggle it into the camp. Various methods were employed to get it past the sentries. The coconut fatigue parties took with them a number of hollowed out husks, one of which would hold two tins of milk or jam. These were concealed amongst the genuine nuts loaded on to the lorry. The wood fatigue party hollowed out a number of large logs which could contain quite a substantial number of goods, and when plugged at the open end easily passed into the camp with the genuine logs. Unfortunately this state of affairs did not last long, as one day an overzealous sentry spotted natives handing over goods to some members of the fatigue party, and reported the matter to higher authority. Consequently all fatigue parties were searched before going out and when they returned. Anyone caught smuggling was promptly placed in the guard room and went without any food for two or more days.

The prison also had a cash pool to which anyone and everyone contributed according to the quantity of cash he had managed to bring into the prison. With this money food was purchased from the local market and brought in by a Swiss neutral. Saturday was the red-letter day when the lorry carrying the goods purchased arrived at the prison. There was usually some fresh fish, enough for about four mouthfuls apiece; dried, salted fish, the smell of which made one shudder; eggs, usually of the Chinese variety which had been preserved and invariably included a percentage of rotten ones; curry powder, chillies, condiments and a certain amount of tinned foods. The eggs, when cooked were as tough as leather and their yolks were a bright orange colour. Poor in quality as most of these goods were, they were more than welcome to us as a supplement to unappetizing rations and what few luxuries could be smuggled into the prison.

Fruit and vegetables, for some reason, were very much in short supply from the very start, except for an occasional banana per man and an unripe pineapple cut into four or five portions depending on its size. A few internees managed to buy bunches of bananas from Malays. Vegetables we lacked acutely at the start, but two or three months after our internment an area of land about three acres in extent was set aside for growing vegetables. It was a hard, barren piece of land but there was no lack of volunteers to cultivate it. These volunteers did a magnificent job, worked like slaves and produced vegetables which undoubtedly saved the lives of many of us at a later stage of our internment when the food situation became so desperate. The gardeners worked with nothing on but a pair of shorts or a loin cloth, and by the time they had turned the soil and made it into condition to plant seed, everyone of them was tanned a mahogany colour by the scorching heat of the sun. The Japanese would not supply us with seeds of any sort, so we had before us at the end of all our preliminary labour the problem of what to plant. Fortunately before starting to turn the soil one plant of a local vegetable called 'Bium' was found seeding and the seeds were carefully preserved. 'Bium' was a species of spinach: it is a very leafy plant growing some five to six feet in height. The seeds so carefully preserved from this one plant paved the way to feeding the entire prison every day for nearly two and half years. A small quantity of Ceylon spinach seed was also smuggled into the prison, presumably by one of the lorry drivers.

There was another source of extra food supply and it was

perhaps a surprising one: the Japanese themselves. On one occasion when I was on duty at the prison gate, a sentry called up to me. He could speak a few words of English and said he was a Formosan and a farmer. He produced a sheet of paper on which was written a number of food items: cocoa one dollar one tin, milk one dollar fifty one tin, cheese two dollars one tin, etc., etc. He asked me in broken English and by making signs whether I wanted to buy anything on the list, if so I must write down how many tins of each I required. I had heard that this was being done fairly extensively, in fact on several occasions sentries would come up and produce a sheet of paper on which was written a word in Romanized Malay and asked me to write against it the corresponding English word; this made it simpler for them to understand orders given for tinned food. On this occasion I managed to obtain a few tins of cocoa, condensed milk and cheese which I shared with my friends. It was not long before the Japanese sentries began to pluck up more courage and were far bolder in their dealings; sackfuls of goods were brought in late at night to the cells of their retailer, prices soared and a miniature black market was created. Whether or not this will be condemned as 'trading and fraternizing with the enemy', I leave to the judgement of the reader. I will say this in its favour, it brought in extra supplies of food which ware badly needed even at that time, although there were numbers of us who were unfortunate in having insufficient funds with which to purchase this extra food.

A few South African and American Red Cross parcels came into the prison at that time, but they didn't go far amongst us; usually one parcel was shared by seven internees. A few internees managed by some means unknown to me to smuggle Dover Stoves into the prison. These stoves were a great asset as we were always able to obtain a certain amount of wood fuel. They were used for heating water and for cooking the odd luxuries smuggled in. I often saw as many as sixty internees gathered around one stove, each with his own little tin, brewing cocoa or coffee or some foul concoction which, when the owner was questioned, would jealousy and proudly describe as soup or curry. Curry was usually made from such ingredients as salted dried fish, a small type of onion similar to a shallot, and an occasional sweet potato, potato leaves, spinach, all soaked in coconut water and liberally sprinkled with curry powder. The wonderful mixture of aromas arising from about sixty tins cooking every sort of concoction can well be imagined. The very thought of those tins makes me shudder now, but they were a most welcome addition to the daily diet. Incidentally it was the duty of a block policeman to stop these activities. What a hope! Personally I should never have attempted to stop them even if it were possible.

It may be apparent from the description of the extra food finding its way into the prison that we obtained food which was of reasonable quality and ample in quantity. It should also be appreciated however that the amount of extra food obtained was insufficient for a substantial share to be issued to every one of the two thousand, five hundred internees. We were always hungry, but at the initial period of our internment we did not suffer severely from undernourishment.

8. Guards and Punishments

The first lot of sentries who acted as our guards were with us for about a year, some for a longer period. Most of them treated us reasonably well; a few behaved badly, and it was they who remained with us throughout our internment. Some of them committed foul crimes on defenceless internees. This however did not happen until a later period. I never came in contact with the Japanese officer commanding the camp but he was reputed to be a reasonable character. Later he was replaced by the notorious Yamado. I remember on one occasion when I was duty policeman on the prison gate a drunken sentry came up to me and jabbered something that I did not understand. He beckoned me to follow him. This I did, and was led outside the prison to the bungalows which formerly were the quarters of the prison warders and were now occupied by Japanese sentries. On arrival at the bungalow which this sentry evidently occupied he told me to wait behind the building. I was left standing there about five minutes, wondering what it was all about and what would happen next. I judged by his behaviour that his intentions were not evil. When he appeared again he was carrying three bottles of locally brewed beer: I was wearing a shirt and shorts at the time; I tucked one bottle under each arm beneath my shirt, the other bottle down my shirt front, and hurried back to my cell where I shared the spoils with my two cell mates. One of them only drank half the bottle and said he did not want anymore, so I polished it off for him.

There were also a number of Sikh guards amongst the sentries; they were ex-prison warders and police who had been instructed prior to the capitulation to put themselves at the disposal of the Japanese and obey the orders given to them. Some of these Sikhs behaved badly: one degrading fatigue imposed on us consisted of cleaning out the barracks of both the Japanese and Sikh sentries; some of the Sikhs used to stand over their captives with sticks whilst they were doing this work. On one occasion a prisoner was so unwise as to lose his temper and called the Sikh guard by a name which is considered by them extremely insulting: perhaps he was full justified, but he received a severe beating from the Sikh for his rashness. It was rumoured that some of these Sikh guards had beaten women in the female internment camp. Such behaviour was however by no means universal; many of them did everything they could to alleviate the suffering of the Europeans they were compelled to guard; some of them went still farther, co-operating with Europeans who had previously been their senior officers. Unfortunately the Japanese discovered some of these activities and executed the Sikh sentries involved. Those who behaved badly met a fate which will be described in a later chapter.

Rules and regulations in the prison were numberless. Notices were displayed in cells, corridors and rooms. During the whole time I was there I never read the damn things. Some of the regulations however were evident enough for the reasons that they applied regularly in our everyday life. One rule is worth mentioning: For some peculiar reason the authorities were very particular about cigarette ends and ash, and every smoker had to carry about with him a small tin into which the ash had to be dropped. I suppose it was sensible enough, as to my mind it is particularly disgusting to see cigarette and tobacco ash, and stumps of burnt out cigarettes littering the interior of the building. One odious and degrading rule which was enforced more rigorously at a later stage of our internment was that every internee was forced to stand up and bow to a Japanese whoever he might be and whenever he passed him. Punishments for disobeying this were a slap in the face, a beating or, as happened to me later, a blow from a rifle butt or cudgel. There were the usual regulations about lights out; this was enforced at 10 p.m. At the start, but was later cut down to 9 p.m. No one was of course permitted outside the prison except on fatigue duties.

I remember one individual who broke camp on two occasions; he succeeded in getting back in safely on the first occasion, climbing a rope let down by his friends inside. On the second occasion however he indulged too heavily; although he succeeded in reaching the wall of the prison he had insufficient control of his limbs to climb a rope, and was found next morning by a sentry snoring heavily with the rope dangling from the wall above his head. As a punishment he was severely beaten and suffered a few days in solitary confinement with little or no food. Punishments at that time were not so severe as later. They usually took the form of a solitary confinement or beating for more serious offences.

There were few attempts to escape. If anyone had succeeded they could have only spent a precarious and hunted existence in some native village. Sumatra, Java and all the islands of the Archipelago were in the hands of the Japanese and it would have been impossible to reach the safety under such conditions. A few Europeans did succeed in getting away but we strongly suspected they had originally been placed in the camp as spies and stool-pigeons [informers]. Before the fall of Singapore, the British authorities had interned a Dutch subject married to a German woman; he was suspected of anti-British activities. When the Japanese came in he was released by them. For some reason however he was interned again, and whilst in prison was foolish enough to announce his pro-German sympathies. Needless to say he was given a thin time of it. We could never really understand why he was re-interned unless he too was a stool-pigeon. As against this he was put in solitary confinement by the Japanese when he complained to them of ill-treatment in the prison.

Two members of the British Intelligence Service, S---- and M---- were imprisoned some time after the rest of us. They were put in solitary confinement for six months poor devils. Their food, a heap of rice, was taken to them three times a day by an internee orderly and we usually managed to slip a few cigarettes or tit-bits under the rice for them. When they came out they had grown beards; no doubt they had not been permitted to have razors with them. The Governor of the Straits Settlements, Sir Shenton Thomas, was also confined to a cell for six weeks; for what reason I do not know.

It is unpleasant to have to record that there was a considerable amount of petty theft and pilfering in the prison throughout the whole period of our internment; food, clothes, cash and personal treasures disappeared mysteriously from time to time. Occasionally a culprit was caught and dealt with by our own court. The court consisted of a judge and jury, the judge being a Civil Servant, and the jury consisted of a judge and jury, the judge being a Civil Servant, and the jury consisting of three or four of the accused's fellow internees. Court discipline was enforced by the police and the trial was conducted strictly in accordance with British justice. Apart from the sentences administered, the Criminal Procedure Code, the Penal Code and the Evidence Ordinance were strictly applied and the accused could be defended by a chosen lawyer. Sentences varied according to the seriousness of the crime committed, but were necessarily restricted to terms of solitary confinement, or to forfeitures of issues of such luxuries as native cigarettes, cheroots, or food which took place every Saturday after arrival of the lorry already mentioned. Solitary confinement was served in a wooden hut especially set aside for the purpose, and the block policeman on duty was responsible both for the culprit's safe detention and for his food.

The conditions under which we were living were a true test of character and endurance. It is not intended in these pages to describe particular personalities but rather to give the reader a true description of the condition under which his fellow human beings were compelled to exist whilst at the mercy of a savage and unscrupulous enemy. I will say however that there were certain individuals whose behaviour was an unpleasant surprise to me, particular when compared to others who had been less fortunate in their upbringing and education. The principle trait which showed up against them was meanness, meanness of such a nature as to be blatant, uncontrolled and unashamed. On the other hand there were men who would share with their friend or those in need everything they had and anything they managed to acquire however great their own need or craving. This behaviour was a direct contrast to those who were mean; it was the very essence of generosity. At a later stage of our internment there were cases of greed and selfishness which were so outstanding that I intend to describe them in the clearest of terms. It is possible that the strain imposed on the equilibrium of some individuals was too great for them to consider how they would be seen in the eyes of others, but as I have said there were examples of complete selflessness and generosity which stood out as achievements of endurance under these exceptional conditions of privation and need.

Here the account ends. Andrew Mustard's daughter Denise explained that he stopped writing for two reasons. First, the cathartic process of 'getting it out of himself' and onto the page had largely done the trick of improving his wellbeing. Second, the remainder of the book, for it was intended to be such, was inevitably going to take a much darker turn, particularly as it would have required an account of the infamous 'Double Tenth', 10/10/43, when civilian prisoners were interrogated at length over an explosion in the port, with over a dozen dying as a result of their torture and of the conditions they were held in. It would also have required the telling of the latter stages where food became scarce and the 'meanness' of some of his fellow internees, to which he refers, would no doubt have risen prominently to the surface. This caused him to question humanity just as much as the war itself, as he so clearly alludes to in the introduction quoted in Chapter 11. Understandably, writing this up was a task he could not face; it would have added to his pain not relieved it (pers. comm. Denise Bompas, 30 Aug. 1991).

Mustard's account adds more detail to Turnbull's suggestion that 'the main hardship was shortage of food' (2009: 292). Food, 'though unappetizing, was fairly plentiful.' It seems that, even towards the end of the time at the camp when externally sourced food was extremely scarce, the 'Bium' spinach grown in the camp fed 'the entire prison every day for nearly two and half years.' Only later was the lack of food a source of hardship; it seems from Mustard's account that food was rather more perhaps a source of inventiveness, and an outlet for a determination (and towards the end an absolute need) to be self-sufficient. Indeed the self-sufficiency evidently extended to vegetables, which were scarce from the beginning. Growing them in the camp 'undoubtedly saved the lives of many of [the prisoners] at a later stage of [their] internment when the food situation became so desperate.' Perhaps it is possible now to suggest that food was the main preoccupation of the prisoners, not least because they had little else to do and because it provided them with ways of focusing their energies in a productive way. Further, it seems from Mustard's account that the main hardship was in fact the serious over-crowding and lack of sanitation.

The effect of Andrew Mustard's internship was to so weaken him physically that, after the British re-established the colony following VJ (Victory over Japan) day, and a period helping to re-establish Amalgamated Malay Rubber's affairs, Andrew returned to England in September 1946. By this time, he was 60 years old, and was not well enough to fully resume his business life in the rubber industry on the Malayan peninsula. It was a life that had lost much of the colonial luxuries and would have been far more difficult than ever it had been pre-war, for the societal circumstances had been permanently altered by the Japanese occupation (Turnbull, 2009). That said, Amalgamated Malay was clearly a thriving business, benefiting from the boom in the rubber industry and the insatiable demand for the product for motor-cars, a demand that only increased in the first years of the war when Malaya was still at peace, and continuing after the war when rubber and tin hastened the colony's economic recovery (ibid.). The Russel estates – of which Amalgamated Malay Estates were a subsidiary – adopted the practice of putting the plantations in the hands of non-Europeans to be administered during the war and they were paid retrospectively in 1945, with the estates largely reverting back to pre-war ownership after the reestablishment of British rule (pers. comm. Claire Grey, 10 Jan. 2017). Andrew was thus able to return to a retirement in the UK reasonably secure financially. He died at home in Pewsey, Wiltshire on 26 June 1963.

2. VICTORIAN RECIPES FROM HOME

There is at home a little recipe booklet that cost the princely sum of 6 pennies. It was written by a Mrs Robinson who lived in Bath. It's fascinating, since its title *Guide to the Housewife, Useful Family Recipes*, gives an idea of what it was like to cook without our modern cooking devices. The quantities for 'family' recipes are mind boggling. It covers Wine making, Pickles, Meat and Fish, Pastries, Cakes, Puddings. To say the least, very comprehensive in such a very small soft paper booklet.

All cooking was done in the living room on a wood and coal fired black iron stove, with an area on top for the Kettle and saucepans, and an oven on either or both sides of the fire place. We had one of these in our living room when I was a child in the 1930s and I remember it well, since one of my weekly chores was to polish it with a product called 'black lead.'

Raspberry Wine

To every quart of well-picked raspberries, put a quart of water, bruise and let them stand for two days; strain off the liquor, and to every gallon, put 3 pounds of lump or powdered sugar: when dissolved, put the liquor in a barrel, and when fine, which will be in about two months, bottle it, and to each bottle, put a teaspoon of brandy.

Pickled Red Cabbage

Slice into a colander, and sprinkle each layer with salt, let it drain for two days: then put it into a jar, pour over boiling vinegar, enough to cover; put in and boil with the vinegar, ginger, cochineal, or red beetroot sliced, to give a beautiful colour. Cauliflower, when thrown in, will look of a very fine colour.

A Cheap and Good Gravy

Fry three onions in butter a nice brown: toast a slice of bread a long time till quite hard and brown but not burnt, set these and any bits of meat or bone of a leg of mutton etc, and some herbs, water as proportion, and stew till the gravy is rich and thick: add salt and pepper, strain off and boil up with a piece of butter and flour.

To Cure Tongue

After having cleaned them, for two tongues allow an ounce of saltpetre, with which rub them daily; the third day, cover them with common salt, turn them every day for three weeks, then dry them, then rub them over with bran, and smoke them; in ten days they will be fit to eat. [Ha! That's a total of 34 days!]

3. A SIDECARIST'S POEM – OF SORTS

Sidecarists. Politically Correct of Course

Why am I still talking about the passenger misnomer? I am doing it not really for me, I am doing it for all sidecar 'riders', to hopefully help reveal the very real skill involved, and at whatever level of the sport one is competing in. Here is a piece of poetic-prose that I hope provides some explanation. It is difficult to overcome the English language but it's important; in their word 'Beifahrer' the Germans for example don't have the problem!

Sidecar Passengers (?). Who Are They?

Homo sapiens categorised by the morally righteous, health and safety impaired, unable to accept the observed risks taken by those perceived to be intellectually disadvantaged, and displaying testosterone overloaded extreme athleticism.

Engaged in an ultra high-speed activity, totally unsuitable for weight impaired 'poulet' brained car TV petrol heads to experience.

Near outcasts by a few sports writers hampered by ancient traditional ideas and perceptions.

Considered by some activity co dependants, as replaceable by a sack of vegetables commonly consumed as chips.

Some, serious, dressed in very tight fitting multi coloured animal skin, sylph-like and bodily enhanced. A few, almost similarly dressed, but hampered by a mass of alcohol induced, non health immobility flab, in the activity for fun or brief experience.

Combatants, blessed with camaraderie on one hand, resolute and reliable in their macho muscular gyrations of possible destruction on the other.

Loved by thrilled spectators, both age advantaged and disadvantaged, with visibly anxious demeanour, waiting for anticipated disaster.

Misnomered as those not fully involved in the non-gendered activity.

REFERENCES

Atkinson, C.T. (1952) *The Royal Hampshire Regiment, 1914–18*. Uckfield: N&M Press.

Barker, D. (2018) 'Trevor Bayliss Obituary: Prolific Inventor Famous for His Wind-up Radio', *Guardian*, 6 Mar. Accessed 6/3/18: https://www.theguardian.com/technology/2018/mar/05/trevor-baylis-obituary.

Barlow, D.H. (1917a) 'Report of Proceedings of Hampshire Regt. Prisoners of War Fund', *Hampshire Regimental Journal*, Apr: pp. 76–7.

Barlow, D.H. (1917b) 'Report of the Hampshire Regiment P.O.W. Help Fund', *Hampshire Regimental Journal*, Nov.: pp. 239–40.

Barr, N. (2004) *Pendulum of War: The Three Battles of El Alamein*. London: Jonathan Cape.

Bonython, C.W. (1955) *Lake Eyre, South Australia: The great flooding of 1949–50*. Royal Geographical Society of South Australia, South Australia Branch

Bonython, C.W. (1956) *The Salt of Lake Eyre – its occurrence in Madigan Gulf and its possible origin*. Transactions of the Royal Society of South Australia 9: 66–92

Brassley, P. et al. (eds.)(2017) *Transforming the Countryside: The Electrification of Rural Britain*. Abingdon, Oxon: Routledge e-book 9781315550060 downloaded 1/5/17.

Brassley, P., Burchardt, J. and Sayer, K. (2017a) Conclusion to Brassley, P. et al. (eds.) *Transforming the Countryside: The Electrification of Rural Britain*. Abingdon, Oxon: Routledge e-book 9781315550060 downloaded 1/5/17.

Brassley, P., Burchardt, J. and Sayer, K. (2017b) Introduction to Brassley, P. et al. (eds.) *Transforming the Countryside: The Electrification of Rural Britain*. Abingdon, Oxon: Routledge e-book 9781315550060 downloaded 1/5/17.

Bula, M. (2001) *Continental Circus 1949–2000*. Torino: Chrono Sports SA.

Burbury, A.D. (1918a) 'General Report of the Hampshire Regiment Prisoners of War Fund', *Hampshire Regimental Journal*, Feb.: p. 53.

Burbury, A.D. (1918b) 'General Report of the Hampshire Regiment Prisoners of War Fund', *Hampshire Regimental Journal*, Mar: p. 68.

Burbury, A.D. (1918c) 'Prisoners of War', *Hampshire Regimental Journal*, Aug: pp. 180–2.

Campbell, D. (1956) *To Conceive, Design, Construct an Automobile Intended to Carry the World's Land Speed Record to Beyond 400 M.P.H., The Estimated Cost Is as Follows*. Document held by the 'Bluebird (World Record Breaking Car and Boat) Archives.' Beaulieu, Hants: National Motor Museum.

Campbell, D. (1960a) *Steering Committee Meeting Held at the Embassy Club, Berkley Street, London W.1. on 7 Dec. At 6 p.m.* Meeting Minutes held by the 'Bluebird (World Record Breaking Car and Boat) Archives'. Beaulieu, Hants: National Motor Museum.

Campbell, D. (1960b) *Private and Confidential: Estimated Overhead Expenditure, Land Speed Record Project – 1961.* Date sent 10 Dec. 1960. Document held by the 'Bluebird (World Record Breaking Car and Boat) Archives'. Beaulieu, Hants: National Motor Museum.

Campbell, D. (1961) *Minutes of the Steering Committee Meeting Held at the Dorchester Hotel on Thursday 23 Nov. 1961.* Meeting Minutes held by the 'Bluebird (World Record Breaking Car and Boat) Archives'. Beaulieu, Hants: National Motor Museum.

Campbell, D. (1963) *Operational Estimate for the World Land Speed Record Attempt at Lake Eyre Based on Six Months Period from Time of Departure from U.K. To Return.* Itemised Ledger held by the 'Bluebird (World Record Breaking Car and Boat) Archives'. Beaulieu, Hants: National Motor Museum.

CAMS (1979) *CAMS Manual of Motorsport.* Melbourne: Confederation of Australian Motorsport.

Chamberlain, P. (1953) *Motor Cycling Year Book 1953.* London: Temple Press.

Coombes, D. (2011) *Crossing the Wire: The Untold Stories of Australian PoWs in Battle and Captivity During World War I.* Newport. NSW: Big Sky Publishing.

Crozier, S. ([1951] 2014) *The History of the Corps of Royal Military Police.* Uckfield. The Navy & Military Press.

de Lara, D. (2016) *Donald Campbell: 300+ A Speed Odyssey.* Stroud, Glos: The History Press.

Dibben, M. and Dolles, H. (2013) Participant observation in sport management research: collecting and interpreting data from a successful world land speed record attempt. In: S Soderman & H Dolles (eds.) *Handbook of Research on Sport and Business.* UK: Edward Elgar Publishing. pp. 477–94.

Dibben, M.R. and Garrett, P. (2006) Flying Kiwi Promotions Ltd: The story of a world land speed record breaker. In: C.L. Hill et al. (eds.) *Strategic Management: An integrated approach,* 6th edition. Milton, Queensland: John Wiley & Sons ISBN 0-470-80929-9. pp. 513–19.

Dibben, R. (1917) *Letter to Mrs J. Murphy,* 20 Dec. http://www.eurpeana1914-1918.eu/de/contributions/3529. Accessed 27/02/17.

Dibben, R. (1918) Letter to Miss Burbury. Published in *The Hampshire Regimental Journal,* Apr.: pp. 92–3.

Dibben, S. (1964) Personal Diary – entry *Big Row. Andrew sacked and reinstated!!.* 1 June.

Dibben, S. (2012) *Hold ON!* (e-print edn.). High Wycombe: Panther Publishing.

Doitsch, E. (1917) *The First Springbok Prisoner in Germany.* London: McBride,

Nast & Co.

Feldman, J. (1964) Drama at Lake Eyre. *Modern Motor* 11(3): pp. 27–9, 78–9.

Fox, A. (1985) *History and Heritage: The Social Origins of the British Industrial Relations System.* Boston: Allen and Unwin.

Ganapathi, R. (1982) *The White Belts: History of the [Indian] Corps of Military Police.* New Delhi: Lancers Publishers [https://babel.hathitrust.org/cgi/pt?id=ucl.b4244561;view=1up;seq=7]

Grace's Guide, Perry and Co, http://www.gracesguide.co.uk/Perry_and_Co. Accessed 04/10/18.

Grace's Guide, Perry and Co (Holdings), http://www.gracesguide.co.uk/Perry_and_Co_(Holdings). Accessed 04/10/18.

Grant, P (2014) *Philanthropy and Voluntary Action in the First World War: Mobilizing Charity.* Abingdon, Oxon: Routledge.

Grey, C. (2009a) 'No Medals, The Saga of Thiel Marstrand during the Malayan Campaign' – the memoirs of Thiel Marstrand. *Dearie: Russell Family History.* Accessed 23/3/18. http://www.clairegrey.co.uk/rd_grandchildren/archie/thiel_marst.html.

Grey, C. (2009b) The Straits Times, and [Articles] *The Singapore Free Press and Mercantile Advertiser,* 21 September 1935, Page 10 AMALGAMATED MALAY. 'PERFECT CONDITION' OF THE ESTATES. DIVIDEND MAKING 11 PER CENT. In *'J. A. Russell and Co. Ltd. News and other Sources 1935; Amalgamated Malay Estates, Ltd'.* Dearie: Russell Family History. http://www.clairegrey.co.uk/rd_grandchildren/archie/aa_jar/jar_ltd_sources/1935.html. Accessed 23/3/18.

Hamilton, N. (1981) *Monty: The Making of a General, 1887–1942.* London: Sceptre Books.

Hamilton, S.D. (1996) *50th Royal Tank Regiment: The Complete History.* Cambridge: The Lutterworth Press.

Hammond, J.L. and Hammond, B. ([1911] 1995) *The Labourer 1760–1832.* London: Alan Sutton.

Hannah, L. (1979) *Electricity Before Nationalisation: A Study of the Development of the Electricity Supply Industry in Britain to 1948.* London: Macmillan.

Harnet, P. (2014) NGK pays unique global accolade to Jim Hughes. *NGK (UK)* webpage. http://www.ngkntk.co.uk/index.php/2014/06/19/ngk-pays-unique-global-accolade-to-jim-hughes/, 19 June 2014. Accessed 7/8/18.

Harrison, C. (1918) Letter to Mr Dibben. Published in *The Hampshire Regimental Journal,* Feb.: p. 46.

Hawtin, D. (1993) The Les Nutt Story: Only the Brave. *Classic Legends* 24(Spring), pp. 28–31.

Historic inflation calculator, http://www.thisismoney.co.uk/money/bills/article-1633409/Historic-inflation-calculator-value-money-changed-1900.html. Accessed 04/10/18.

Historical UK inflation, http://inflation.iamkate.com/. Accessed 04/10/18.

HRH The Prince of Wales (2011) *The Future of Food*. Emmaus, PA: Rodale Books.

Hopwood, B. (2007) *Whatever Happened to the British Motorcycle Industry? The Classic Inside Story of Its Rise and Fall*. Yeovil: Haynes Publishing.

Horn, P. (1976) *Labouring Life in the Victorian Countryside*. London: MacMillan.

Howkins, A. (1992) *Reshaping Rural England: A Social History*. Abingdon, Oxon: Routledge

Jackson, R. (1989) *The Prisoners, 1914–1918*. London: Routledge Kegan & Paul.

Jones, H. (2011) *Violence Against Prisoners of War in the First World War*. Cambridge: Cambridge University Press.

Kelly's Directory of Wiltshire 1867 http://specialcollections.le.ac.uk/cdm/compoundobject/collection/p16445coll4/id/339947/rec/5.

Kennett, B.B. and Tatman, J.A. ([1970] 2003) *Craftsmen of the Army: The Story of the Royal Electrical and Mechanical Engineers*. Lyneham, Wilts: Corps of Royal Electrical and Mechanical Engineers.

Khaneman, D. (2011) *Thinking Fast and Slow*. London: Penguin.

Kobrak, C. and Schneide, A. (2011) Varieties of Business History: Subject and methods for the twenty-first century. *Business History* 53(3), pp. 401–24.

Kulchavenya, E. et al., (2016): Urogenital Tuberculosis: Classification, Diagnosis, and Treatment. *European Urology Supplements* 15(4), pp. 112–21.

Lewis-Stempel, J. (2014) *The War Behind The Wire: The Life, Death and Glory of British Prisoners of War 1914–18*. London: Phoenix.

Louth, L. (1983) *Racing Around Europe in an Austin Van. Louth Leader*, 28 Dec.: p. 5.

Luckin, B. (1991) Questions of Power: Electricity and Environment in Inter-War Britain. Manchester: Manchester University Press.

Mallpress, M. and Mallpress, P. (1999) *8th Tank Battalion History*. Bovington: Tank Museum.

Miles. M. et al. (2017) Exploring Public Universities as Social Enterprises. *International Journal of Educational Management* 31(3), pp. 404–14.

Mingay, G.E. (1990) *Rural Life in Victorian England 1800–1900*. Stroud: Sutton Publishing.

Mitchell, M. (2012) *Sultan of Slide: A Privateer's Story*. Ormeau, QLD: SuperCool Franchising.

Montgomery, B.L. (1958/2012) *The Memoirs of Field Marshal Montgomery*. Barnsley: Pen & Sword Books.

Montgomery, B.L. (1960) *El Alamein to the River Sangro*. London: Hutchinson & Co.

Moynihan, M. (1978) *Black Bread and Barbed Wire: Prisoners in the First World War*. London: Leo Cooper.

Mulford, G.A. (1919) *My Two Years Amongst the Huns*. Unpublished talk, 12 Oct.

IWM Access Asset A00043045, Box N 84/41/1.

Munro, J. Forbes (2003) *Maritime Enterprise and Empire: Sir William McKinnon and His Business Network.* Glasgow: The Boydell Press

Mustard, A.H. (1983) Haymust Goldmines Development Report, South Palmer Operation. Unpublished Report, 28 June.

Mustard, A.H. (1963a) *Letter to Stan Dibben from Andrew Mustard,* 29 Nov.

Mustard, A.H. (1963b) *Letter to Stan Dibben from Andrew Mustard,* 26 Dec.

Mustard, A.H. (1968) *Letter to Stan Dibben from Andrew Mustard,* 30 July.

Mustard, A.H. (1991) *Interview – at the National Motor Museum,* Beaulieu, 30 Aug.

Mustard, V. (1968a) *Letter to Stan Dibben from Via Mustard,* 4 Aug.

Mustard, V. (1968b) *Letter to Stan Dibben from Via Mustard,* 22 Sep.

Nitobe, I. (1969) *Bushido – The Soul of Japan.* Tokyo: Tuttle Publishing.

NGK (2017) *NGK UK Sales Revenue History 1976–2017.* Unpublished sales graph (see photo essay on 'Self Employment' accompanying this book). Nagoya: NGK Spark Plug Co. Ltd

Noble, R. (2012) *Thrust: The Remarkable Story of One Man's Quest For Speed.* London: Bantam.

O'Brien, P.K. (1977) Agriculture and the Industrial Revolution. *The Economic History Review* 30(1), pp. 166–81.

Paterson, S. (2012) *Tracing Your Prisoner of War Ancestors – The First World War.* London: Imperial War Museum.

Paterson, S. (2012a) *Tracing Your Prisoner of War Ancestors.* London: Pen and Sword.

Pearson, J. ([1965] 2002) *Bluebird and the Dead Lake.* Melbourne: Text Publishing.

Pope-Hennessy, C.H.R. (1919) *Papers Relating to Ruhleben PoW Camp, 1916–1919.* Imperial War Museum Archive, Box Copy 03/35/1–2.

Porter, M. (1979) How Competitive Forces Shape Strategy. *Harvard Business Review* 59(2), pp. 137–45.

Post Office Directory of Wiltshire 1859 http://specialcollections.le.ac.uk/cdm/compoundobject/collection/p16445coll4/id/339944/rec/6.

Pratten, G. (2009) *Australian Battalion Commanders in the Second World War.* Cambridge: Cambridge University Press.

Preston, R. (1980) *The First World War Memoirs of R. Preston.* London: Jet Stationery Co. Ltd. IWM Access Asset 11307, Box P438.

Probert, S. and Probert, J. (2001) *Prisoner of Two Wars: An Australian Soldier's Story.* Kent Town, SA: Wakefield Press.

Renold, http://www.renold.com/company/history/. Accessed 04/10/18.

Rightmove, http://www.rightmove.co.uk/house-prices/SO24/GASCOIGNE-LANE.html?country=england&locationIdentifier=STREET%5E2185858&searchLocation=Gascoigne+Lane. Accessed 04/10/18.

Richardson, M. (2013) *This Terrible Ordeal: Manx Letters, Diaries and Memories of the Great War*. Douglas: Manx National Heritage.

Robert Millward, R. (1991) The Market Behaviour of Local Utilities in Pre-World War I Britain: The Case of Gas. *The Economic History Review* 44(1), pp. 102–27.

Rockstuhl, Harald (2013) Gefangenenlager *Langensalza 20 November 1914 bis 18. März 1919 [The Langensalza Prison Camp, 20 November 1914 to 18 March 1919]*. Bad Langensalza: Verlag Rockstuhl.

Ropley, http://www.myropley.org.uk/about/. Accessed 04/10/18.

Royle, T. (2010) *Montgomery: Lessons in Leadership from the Soldier's General*. New York: Palgrave Macmillan.

Schumacher, D (2011) *Small Is Beautiful in the 21st Century: The Legacy of E.F. Schumacher*. Totnes: Green Books.

Schumacher, E.F. ([1973] 2011) *Small is Beautiful: A Study of Economics as if People Mattered*. London: Vintage.

Schumacher, E.F. ([1997] 2004) *This I Believe – and other essays*. Totnes: Green Books.

Schumcher, E.F. (1980) *Good Work*. London: Abacus.

Scott, E. (1936) *Australia During the War*. Sydney: Angus & Robertson.

Scott, M.G. (1989) The Dangers of Assuming Homogeneity in Small Firms. In: Rosa, P.J. et al. (eds.) *The Role and Contribution of Small Business Research*. Aldershot: Avebury.

Sheffield, G.D. (1994) *The Redcaps: A History of the Military Police and Its Antecedents from the Middle Ages to the Gulf War*. London: Brassey's (UK)

Sprayson, K. (1988/2012) *The Frame Man*. High Wycombe, Bucks: Panther Publishing.

Stevens, D. (2010) *Bluebird CN7: The Inside Story of Donald Campbell's Last Land Speed Record Car*. Poundbury, UK: Veloce Publishing.

Strait Times (1930) Personal and Social Column. *The Strait Times*. 10 Nov, p. 10. Webpage: http://eresources.nlb.gov.sg/newspapers/Digitised/Article/straitstimes19301105-1.2.29. Accessed 23rd March 2017.

Summer, N.L. (1999) *War Diary for 8th Battalion, Tank Corps, August 1917 to December 1918*. Bovington: Tank Museum.

Tank Corps (1917) *8th Battalion Honours and Awards*. Bovington: Tank Museum.

Texas State University's Virtual Tour of Pharmacy Artefects, http://pharmacy.wp.txstate.edu/2016/07/04/angiers-emulsion./ Accessed 04/10/18.

The Women's Institute, https://www.thewi.org.uk/about-the-wi. Accessed 04/10/18.

The Women's Institute, Alice Williams, https://www.thewi.org.uk/about-the-wi/history-of-the-wi/the-origins/alice-williams. Accessed 04/10/18.

Thompson, P. (2005) *The Battle for Singapore*. London: Piatkus.

Todd, G. (2012) *Shoestring Racer: The Todd–BSA story and other projects*. San Francisco, CA: Blurb Publishing Inc.

Torii, N. (1994) *Welcome Speech to the NGK–Indy Car Press Meeting.* Hotel Hyatt Newporter Hotel, Newport Beach, California, 21 Jan.

Torii, N. (1995) *Welcome Speech to the Honorable Mr J.D. Rockefeller IV, U.S. Senator, and His Project Harvest Trade Mission.* Komaki, Japan, 11 Jan.

Tremayne, D. (2004) *Donald Campbell: The Man Behind the Mask.* London: Bantam Books.

Tudge, C. (2016) *Six Steps Back to the Land.* Cambridge: Green Books.

Turnbull, C.M. (2009) *A History of Modern Singapore.* Singapore: NUS Press.

Warren, A. (2002) *Britain's Greatest Defeat.* London: Hambledon Continuum.

Watson, G., T. & R. (1913–61) *Directors Minute Books.* Blockley, Moreton-in-Marsh: Watsonian Archive.

Wheeler, M. (2014) Archive Shot: The Next Stage – from 'The Motor Cycle, 2 July 1953'. *Classic Racer,* January/February, pp. 6–7.

White, H.E. (1944) *The Organisation and Activities of 23rd Armoured Brigade R.E.M.E. Workshops.* Army Forms A3091, Bovington: Tank Museum.

Whitehead, A.N. (1941) Immortality. In: P.A. Schilpp (ed.), *The Philosophy of Alfred North Whitehead. The Library of Living Philosophers Volume III.* La Sale, Illinois: Open Court.

Wilson, P. (1999) *The War Diary of the 50th Battalion Royal Tank Regiment.* Full transcript. Bovington: The Tank Museum.

Yarnall, J. (2011) *Barbed Wire Disease: British & German Prisoners of War, 1914–1918.* Stround, Glos: The History Press.

Ropley, June 1914. 'There she is Dad, there's my Mabel!'

INDEX

ABOUT THE AUTHORS

Stan Dibben is the 1953 World Champion sidecar rider. Growing up in rural Hampshire, he served as an apprentice with the Mid-Southern Utility Company and as such played a part in the rural electrification of the South of England in the early 1940s. After serving in the Royal Navy in the latter half of World War Two, he joined BSA where he hand-built Gold Star motorcycles before joining Norton as Chief Experimental Tester, where he did the development work on the Norton 'Dominator 88' twin. After a successful racing career, he developed race chain with the Perry Chain Company. During the successful Donald Campbell 'Bluebird' World Land Speed Record Project on Lake Eyre in Australia, in 1964, he was Deputy Project Manager responsible primarily for the track. He was also a pioneer of full-face helmets, and of NGK Spark Plugs in the UK. He is a Vice-President of the Norton Owners Club.

Mark Dibben is a retired academic, a Distinguished Fellow of the Schumacher Institute. He is a former Head of School and Deputy Chair of the Senate in the University of Tasmania.

Lightning Source UK Ltd.
Milton Keynes UK
UKHW04f1300241018
331115UK00001B/356/P